GREAT PUEBLO ARCHITECTURE
of CHACO CANYON

# GREAT PUEBLO ARCHITECTURE
## of CHACO CANYON,
## NEW MEXICO

Stephen H. Lekson

With contributions by William B. Gillespie
and Thomas C. Windes

University of New Mexico Press
Albuquerque

Originally published 1984 by the National Park Service, U.S. Department of
the Interior, Albuquerque, New Mexico, as Publications in Archeology 18B,
Chaco Canyon Studies. Reprinted 1986 by the University of New Mexico
Press by arrangement with the authors and the National Park Service.


Library of Congress Cataloging-in-Publication Data

Lekson, Stephen H.
   Great Pueblo Architecture of Chaco Canyon, New
Mexico.

   Reprint. Originally published: Albuquerque, N.M.:
National Park Service, U.S. Dept. of the Interior, 1984.
   Bibliography: p.
   Includes index.
   1. Pueblo Indians—Architecture.   2. Pueblos—
New Mexico—Chaco Canyon.   3. Indians of North America—
New Mexico—Chaco Canyon—Architecture.   4. Pueblo
Indians—Antiquities.   5. Indians of North America—
New Mexico—Chaco Canyon—Antiquities.   6. Chaco
Canyon (N.M.)—Antiquities.   7. New Mexico—Antiquities.

I. Gillespie, William B.   II. Windes, Thomas C.
III. Title.
E99.P9L45    1986    722'.91'0978983    85-8613
ISBN 0-8263-0843-0 (pbk.)

# Foreword

Since 1971, the National Park Service, in cooperation with the University of New Mexico, has supported a major archaeological study of Chaco Canyon, New Mexico. One of the most intriguing results of this program was the discovery of the remarkable extent of the Chacoan cultural region. Research revealed the existence of over 75 "outliers" -- Chacoan sites built at considerable distances from Chaco Canyon, which functioned as the center of the system. To preserve this extensive system, legislation was sought in 1980 that resulted in the expansion and redesignation of the Monument as Chaco Culture National Historical Park.

Preservation management of the widely scattered Park units is nearly as unique as the resources themselves. Chacoan outliers have been found on lands of quite varied ownership. Some are on private lands, while others are on Navajo Tribal lands, State of New Mexico lands, or lands administered by the Bureau of Land Management, the Forest Service, and the National Park Service. To accommodate this unique situation, the National Park Service initiated the development of a Joint Management Plan, a cooperative effort among all land owners designed to carry out the long-range preservation of the archaeological remains of the Chacoan phenomenon.

The central Park area preserves the spectacular ruins of a dozen large pueblos--which this report describes--as well as literally thousands of smaller, but no less important, sites. This report is unusual in that the conclusions presented here are based mainly on data acquired nondestructively. Information from earlier field work by the National Park Service and others (including the University of New Mexico) are incorporated, but the author emphasizes the use of observations obtained without damaging excavations. Preserving the fragile standing walls of the Chacoan ruins is a constant challenge, and one fully in keeping with the National Park Service's conservation mission. This study should assist the Service in the continued wise management of these important cultural resources.

Heightened interest in Chaco Canyon is evident in the number of articles and books recently appearing about the Park, in recent museum exhibits, and in steadily increasing visitation. This report should be of use to both the Park visitor and the professional archaeologist, as a timely synthesis of our current knowledge. I am pleased to introduce the latest presentation of the results of National Park Service research in Chaco Canyon.

RUSSELL E. DICKENSON
Director
National Park Service

# Preface

In the summer of 1976, the Chaco Center, six years into a planned ten-year run, hired some new people for the excavation and subsequent analyses of Pueblo Alto. Most of the analytical responsibilities had been assigned to members of the original staff: someone had the ceramics, someone else had chipped stone and so forth. As one of the Pueblo Alto newcomers, I needed to find something to do.

No one was studying the architecture of the big sites at Chaco. This was a little surprising, since we were digging one; but still, it looked like a job that needed doing. Of course, the big sites had been recorded by Al Hayes' survey, but there was a lot more to be done, and architecture was certainly more intriguing than life behind a binocular microscope.

After preparing an outline of the proposed research, the first actual task was a synthesis of the published data. Putting this together occupied the fall of 1977; the result, completed in January 1978, was a manuscript titled "Working Notes" -- a distant ancestor of the present work. The years of 1979 and the first half of 1980 were devoted to field and archival work, leading to the first version of Chapter 4, early in 1981. During the latter part of that year and the first part of the next, early versions of Chapters 2 and 3 emerged through many drafts and several blind alleys.

Several months, late in 1980 and early in 1981, were devoted to architectural theory, particularly theories of form. I assembled a collection of concepts and ideas (Lekson 1981b), lifted from other disciplines and other contexts but tantalizingly applicable to archaeology. The more I struggled with this body of disparate theories, the more it became

clear that while individual ideas or theories might answer a specific question, none seemed likely to answer the big questions archaeologists routinely, though naively, ask. Basic issues, like house form, were not going to be "solved" by theoretical eclecticism. I gave it up as an interesting dead end. But hope burns eternal, as evidenced by a recent spate of archaeological shopping trips into the architectural literature.

By 1982, most of the present text existed in various stages of completion. In the fall of 1981, in a moment of weakness, I enrolled in the University of New Mexico graduate program and reduced my National Park Service job to half time. With other publication responsibilities, my own research in southern New Mexico and back-to-schooldays, the pace of production was more than halved. Thus the final stages in finishing the manuscript dragged on at a maddeningly slow pace -- maddening both to your author and his admirably patient boss, Jim Judge. Final revision of the manuscript was not completed until very late in 1983.

Many sections of this text were sent up as trial balloons in short articles (in the New Mexico Archaeological Council Newsletter, Southwestern Lore, the New Mexico Journal of Science, and the Papers of the Archaeological Society of New Mexico) and papers (at annual meetings of the American Anthropological Society, the Society for American Archaeology, the first Anasazi Symposium and various Pecos Conferences). I thank the editors of those journals and organizers of those meetings for the opportunity to express my opinions, and I thank many correspondents, fellow conferees, and bar-room debaters for their responses.

Some of the conclusions in Chapter 5 were to be summarized in a Chacoan volume of a regional journal with a different and wider distribution than the Chaco Center Report series and the NPS Publications in Archeology series. For reasons beyond anyone's control, the Chaco volume was not produced, so its contents are to be published in a Report of the Chaco Center. Parts of the section on Chetro Ketl appeared first in the detailed study of that ruin (Reports of the Chaco Center 6). The architectural analyses in The Outlier Survey (Reports of the Chaco Center 3) -- which cover some of the same territory -- were entirely the work of that study's senior author, Bob Powers.

The reader should know a bit more about the place of this report in the Chaco Center's research. Between 1971 and 1978, the Center investigated about 45 sites, including Pueblo Alto. Most were simply tested, but about ten were extensively excavated. Reports on most of these excavations, as well as analyses of the artifacts, faunal, and burial remains recovered are on file as manuscripts at the Chaco Center. The present report is only icing; the unpublished excavation manuscripts are the cake, and the actual work of the Chaco Center.

I owe much to my colleagues at the Chaco Center; many of the ideas in this study are actually theirs. I acquired them by osmosis and am presenting them here as my own; nevertheless, it would be wrong to assume that my colleagues agree with my conclusions. Innumerable arguments in defense of my odd notions have contributed to both the refinement of my ideas and increasing slipperiness of my prose. In particular, Marcia Newren (Truell), Tom Windes, Wolky Toll, and Bill Gillespie suffered through my harangues. If I did not always follow their advice, it is not their fault; they tried. Other National Park Service personnel read and commented on parts of the text, including Alden C. Hayes, Tom Mathews, Steve Adams, Randall Morrison, and Larry Nordby. At the University of New Mexico, John Fritz and Bainbridge Bunting encouraged my work; at the University of Arizona, David Saile, Gwinn Vivian, and Jeff Dean offered insight and assistance. Other Chaco scholars -- John Stein, Mike Marshall, Rich Loose, and John Roney -- freely shared their data and thoughts. I must particularly recognize William Gillespie and David Stuart, whose careful, critical reading of the nearly complete text resulted in a number of important changes in organization and content -- mainly, the thing got a lot shorter.

The metamorphosis from smudged typescript to finished book required the hard work of a number of people. Angie Bratcher, Judy Stern, and Rosemary Ames typed. Lea Hott typed, corrected, retyped, organized, and formatted the manuscript. Her hard work, cheerfully performed, is greatly appreciated. Jerry Livingston and I did the drafting. Final drafting, layout, and design were admirably handled by Livingston. Barbara Daniels edited and re-edited the text. Daniels was not given a complete text, with everything in one place, until about the fifteenth (or was it fiftieth?) editorial cycle. She did a remarkable job, pulling a pretty disorganized endeavor out of the fire.

I hope I am not presumptuous in acknowledging the examples set by Alden Hayes and Bainbridge Bunting. At the beginning of this research, I was not sure that the study was worthwhile. Surely Chacoan architecture was the proverbial "sucked orange"? Both Hayes and Bunting were enthusiastic and encouraging. Their enthusiasm was tempered by a wisdom and common sense I hope someday to bring to my own work. When I found myself bogged down in trivia, or sidetracked on intellectual dead ends, I tried to decide what Hayes or Bunting would do. I am not suggesting that the following pages are what either would have done; however, I hope that if I keep using that test, someday I will get it right.

This study was originally issued in 1984 as number 18B of the NPS's Publications in Archeology. Through a series of bureaucratic mishaps, only 400 copies were printed. Almost all of that ill-fated first printing were donated to various libraries. I am very grateful to the University of New Mexico Press for reprinting this work.

This book is dedicated to my colleagues in the old Chaco Project. They were a group of talented, remarkably hard-working people. The National Park Service did not realize what a resource it had assembled, and let them go, their studies largely written but unpublished. Their excavation reports and artifact analyses have languished for years in the Chaco Center archives, while the office pursued other goals. The dearth of published results from the Chaco Project has been a disappointment, but my old colleagues are not at fault. They gave the Chaco Project their hearts and all their energies.

Stephen H. Lekson
March 23, 1985

# Contents

# Illustrations

# Tables

Those who have filled books of unusually large size, Emperor, in setting forth their intellectual ideas and doctrines, have thus made a very great and remarkable addition to the authority of their writings. I could wish that circumstances made this as permissible in the case of our subject, so that the authority of the present treatise might be increased by amplifications; but this is not so easy as it may be thought. Writing on architecture is not like history or poetry.

Marcus Vitruvius Pollio, De Architectura

# Chapter One

# Introduction

The ruins in Chaco Canyon (Figures 1.1, 1.2) are among the most impressive north of Mexico. The largest cover several acres, with sections of wall standing three and even four stories. Roomblocks massed around enclosed courts create a sharply circumscribed area of architectural complexity that excited the imagination of nineteenth century explorers and continues to impress twentieth century visitors. Viewed from the cliffs, the ruins are tremendously impressive. Their placement, just below the platform of the canyon rim, seems designed to show the ruins to their best advantage. Viewed from ground level, the texture of the rubble masonry, especially on a long exterior wall, suggests immense and carefully detailed labor. Ruins this massive and complex seem incongruous in a desolate desert canyon, a sense of incongruity that has been carefully nurtured by a century of travel writers and tour guides. It is now nearly impossible to read popular works about Chaco without confronting "mysteries."

In recent years, Chaco has become something of a media event. Foreign and domestic documentaries feature vistas of Chaco and its ruins (invariably accompanied by exotic flute music). The canyon has inspired sculpture, painting, chamber music, opera, poetry and photo essays beyond number, but -- if we exclude archaeological reports -- surprisingly little prose fiction.

For evocative ruins, there are few rivals to Chaco in the Southwest. Enjoyment of Chaco as a stimulus to the imagination is a legitimate use of the park. Unfortunately, the romantic view of Chaco tends to obscure the archaeology. It is sometimes difficult to explain why Chaco, the archaeological phenomenon, is important without seeming to detract from Chaco, the national inspirational re-source, for the value of Chaco for the average visitor is often not the same as for the archaeologist.

Chaco is important to archaeologists because it figures very prominently in the evolution of archaeological knowledge of the Southwest. The impressive and very conspicuous ruins attracted archaeological attention as early as the late 1800s. Along with the pioneering work of Bandelier and the Mindeleffs for the Smithsonian, and the privately funded Hemenway Expedition, the American Museum of Natural History's excavations at Pueblo Bonito (Wetherill and Pepper's work, discussed below) were among the first major archaeological investigations in the Southwest. By historical precedent, research questions and technical problems arising from excavations at Chaco have had a disproportionate influence on the development of Southwestern archaeology. From this perspective, Chaco is important because archaeologists have made it so, investing a tremendous amount of capital, both monetary and intellectual, in its ruins.

From a broader perspective, the ruins at Chaco are important because of their place in Southwestern prehistory, and for their ability to answer some particularly interesting questions. Chaco figures prominently in most discussions of later Southwestern prehistory. One archaeologist, vexed at buck-passing explanatory references to Chaco, admonished: "Chaco must cease being both the deus ex machina and bête noire of Southwestern archaeology." To date, it remains both. Chaco is central, geographically and conceptually, to our understanding of Southwestern prehistory.

The archaeology of the Canyon can address interests less provincial than the prehistory of one small section of

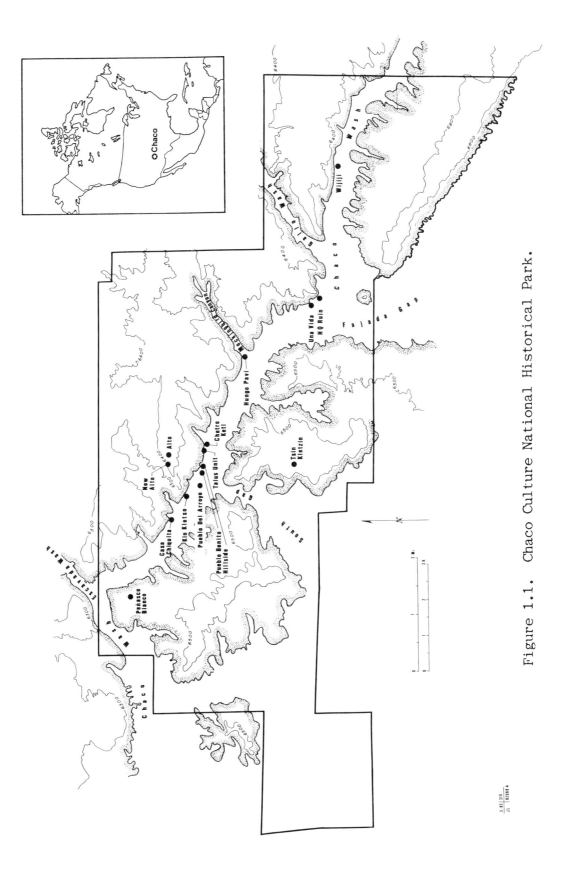

Figure 1.1.   Chaco Culture National Historical Park.

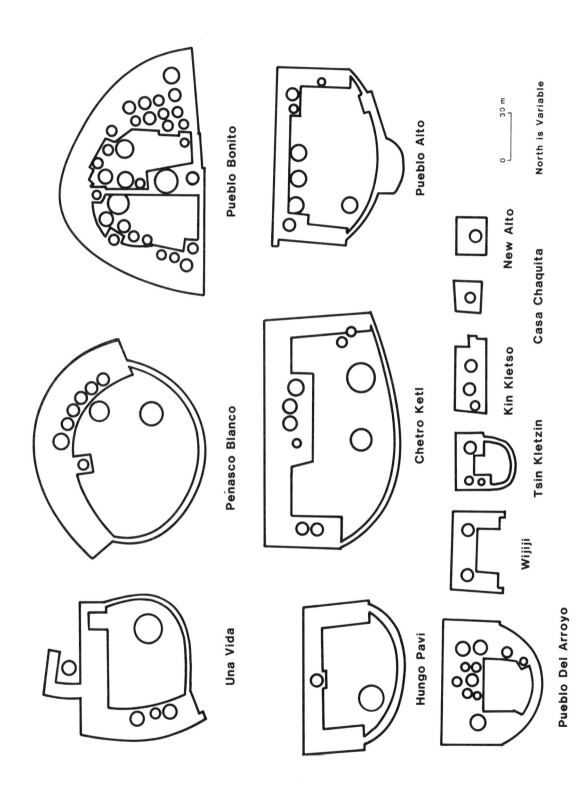

Figure 1.2. Major ruins of Chaco Canyon.

North America.   Between A.D. 900 and about 1140, there is evidence for the evolution of significant complexity at Chaco, of something smaller in scale and less elaborate than the high civilizations of antiquity, but still more complex than the Pueblos at the time of historic contact.   Because of the aridity and remoteness of the San Juan Basin, Chaco's record of evolving complexity is almost unrivaled in its preservation. Questions about the earlier steps of the evolution of this complexity can be asked of the Chacoan archaeological record that would be all but impossible elsewhere.

## ARCHAEOLOGY AT CHACO CANYON

The ruins at Chaco Canyon were first described by Lt. James H. Simpson, who visited Chaco in 1849 with a military expedition.   He relied on Carravahal, a guide from San Juan Pueblo, for the names of many of the ruins.   Lt. Simpson's published account (Simpson 1850) was the first thorough description of the large ruins in Chaco Canyon.

William H. Jackson, photographer with the Hayden Expedition, arrived at Chaco in 1877.   He revisited Simpson's ruins, expanded the Lieutenant's descriptions, and discovered several other ruins that Simpson had missed.   His findings were published with the report of the Geological and Geographic Survey (Jackson 1878).

In 1896, Richard Wetherill, the famous rancher-archaeologist of Mesa Verde, moved to Chaco (McNitt 1957). With the financial support of the Hyde Exploring Expedition, and in cooperation with George Pepper from the American Museum of Natural History, Wetherill began extensive excavations of Pueblo Bonito from 1896 to 1899.   Questions about the Hyde Expedition's intentions sparked a government investigation by Special Agent S.J. Holsinger.   Holsinger's report (1901) included a comprehensive description of all the ruins in the canyon.   Concern for the protection of these ruins led to the creation of Chaco Canyon National Monument in 1907.

The establishment of the monument resulted in large part from the efforts of Edgar L. Hewett, later head of the Museum of New Mexico and chairman of the Department of Anthropology at the University of New Mexico.   Hewett began his own investigations at Chaco in 1920, but pulled out when Neil M. Judd arrived, leading a large expedition jointly sponsored by the National Geographic Society and Smithsonian Institution.   Judd excavated the remaining portion of Pueblo Bonito and half of Pueblo del Arroyo, from 1921 to 1927.

After Judd left, Hewett returned with the University of New Mexico Field School, which continued to work in Chaco (with brief interruptions) until 1947. The field school's efforts centered first on Chetro Ketl, but later included the excavation of numerous smaller sites.

The field school trained several archaeologists who did further research at Chaco.   Most notable was R. Gordon Vivian, who began with the field school and went on to become a National Park Service archaeologist.   He excavated Kin Kletso in 1950-1951 (Vivian and Mathews 1965), and excavated other small sites and portions of larger ones incidental to stabilization.   In the 1950s and 1960s, most of the archaeology done in the park was related to stabilization or salvage.

The National Park Service, Division of Cultural Research, was organized in the late 1960s and conducted field studies in the canyon from 1971 to 1979 (Maruca 1982), culminating with the partial excavation of Pueblo Alto.   Limited fieldwork continues, concentrating on management needs of the park.

In the late 1970s, field studies documenting large sites in the San Juan Basin (Marshall et al. 1979; Powers et al. 1983) illustrated the surprising extent of the Chacoan regional system. In recognition of the extensive nature of Chacoan remains, and in response to heavy development in the surrounding area, Chaco Canyon National Monument was increased in size and became Chaco Culture National Historical Park in 1980.

For more detailed histories of archaeological research at Chaco, consult Brand et al. (1937), Hayes (1981), Lister and Lister (1981), Pierson (1956), and Vivian and Mathews (1965).

## THE NEED FOR
## AN ARCHITECTURAL STUDY

After a century of excavation and survey in Chaco Canyon, a new study of Chacoan architecture should be redundant. Oddly enough, this is not true.   The most extensive field studies of Chacoan building were the earliest (Holsinger 1901; Jackson 1878), undertaken before the development of tree-ring dating; while the most important dendrochronological studies (Bannister 1965; Robinson et al.

1974) were accomplished without the benefit of concurrent fieldwork.

Chaco's archaeological literature, though immense, is marked by curious lacunae. There is no recent reliable, ruin-by-ruin field study. The "old Chaco hands" were so steeped in the canyon and its lore that these baseline data were simply understood; a guidebook was unnecessary for an intelligent exchange of views among the small circle of Chaco scholars. They all knew each other, and they all knew the canyon.

For a number of reasons, Chaco is no longer the special province of a local group. Recent media coverage alone should ensure that scholars in New York, or old York, can address the archaeology of Chaco Canyon without fear of breaching academic etiquette. In my opinion, this is the best development in Chacoan archaeology since tree-ring dates. The National Park Service still tends to be a trifle proprietary of its ruins.

Anyone can now write about Chaco without making Edgar Hewett growl, but it is still perfectly possible to write about Chaco and make serious gaffs. At the Chaco Center we see a seemingly endless series of papers, articles and books about Chaco, and we see lots of gaffs. In this study, I have tried to approximate the "common knowledge" (updated) of the earlier Chaco scholars, and this has meant occasionally offering impressions and opinions to supplement the "facts." I am acutely aware that I will never know the canyon as Edgar Hewett, Neil Judd, Paul Reiter, Florence Hawley, or Gordon Vivian did, but I fear that kind of personal knowledge is no longer possible in a national park.

## METES, BOUNDS, AND CONTENTIOUS TERMINOLOGY

The large ruins at Chaco Canyon are the most spectacular evidence of what formerly has been termed the "Bonito Phase," and more recently the "Chaco Phenomenon." Harold S. Gladwin (1945; Gladwin and Gladwin 1934) originated the name "Bonito Phase." He argued that the large buildings at Chaco were preceded by an earlier phase with less imposing architecture, and called the smaller, earlier sites the "Hosta Butte Phase." Vivian and Mathews (1965), among many others, took exception to this scheme. They countered that instead of being sequent, Hosta Butte phase and Bonito phase sites were actually contemporaneous. At the same time they proposed a

third contemporaneous phase, the "McElmo Phase," which included a number of large sites previously assigned to the Bonito phase. The architecture and artifacts at the "McElmo" sites suggested to Vivian and Mathews that they were the remains of an intrusive group, transplanted lock, stock, and barrel from the San Juan area.

This was the archaeological picture at the inception of the Chaco Center's work; sites of three contemporaneous phases occupied the canyon during the later eleventh and early twelfth centuries. The Bonito and Hosta Butte phases (frequently called "towns" and "villages," respectively) were so different that they were considered either the product of different cultures sharing the canyon, or the result of Mesoamerican architectural influences on the towns but not the villages. To add to the confusion of an already complicated picture, "McElmo" phase sites, sharing the canyon with Pueblo Bonito and Hosta Butte sites, were supposedly built and inhabited by a "foreign" people from the north. Recent publications of the Chaco Center have perpetuated this three-phase system (Lister and Lister 1981; and -- with reservations about the "McElmo Phase" -- Hayes [1981]).

This study is limited to only those sites traditionally included in the old Bonito and McElmo phases: Peñasco Blanco, Casa Chiquita, Kin Kletso, Pueblo del Arroyo, Pueblo Bonito, New Alto, Pueblo Alto, Tsin Kletzin, Chetro Ketl, Hungo Pavi, and Una Vida. These ruins form an easily defined group; all have extensive standing walls. The standing walls attracted the first explorers' attention and assured the ruin a name, a spot on the map, and a place in this study.

There are a few other large buildings at Chaco that might also belong with this group, but which usually escape notice because they have no standing walls. These heavily reduced or buried structures include Hillside Ruin (Judd 1964: 146-147), Headquarters Ruin (Vivian and Mathews 1965:81), an unnamed structure below Shabik'eshchee (Roberts n.d.), and perhaps the structure behind Kin Nahasbas (Windes and Mathien 1984). Talus Unit (Lekson 1984a), another candidate, is a casualty of the Chaco taxonomic wars. Lister and Lister (1981) called Talus Unit a "Hosta Butte" site, but it is arguably as "Bonito phase" as Pueblo Bonito. With more fortunate preservation, these structures would probably have trails and guidebooks, "Keep off the walls" signs, and a place among the elect. Rightly or wrongly, they are not considered here.

With the exception of brief references to Aztec Ruin, Salmon Ruin, Pueblo Pintado, and Kin Bineola, this study is confined to Chaco Canyon. For the geography of Chaco-like architecture outside the canyon, the reader is referred to the two standard studies of outliers, buildings with Chaco-like architectural characteristics (Marshall et al. 1979; Powers et al. 1983). The problem of Chacoan building in the broader Anasazi context is well beyond the scope of this work. It would be another (and much longer) study.

The problem of Chaco-like building outside the canyon underscores a usage of the term "Chacoan" peculiar to this study. For the purposes of this study, "Chacoan" is meant to identify the architecture of the eleven buildings listed above, and their close environs. My use of the adjective excludes the many smaller buildings that shared the canyon with the eleven large structures. The problem of large and small sites -- "towns" and "villages" -- continues to vex Chacoan studies. The two sizes of buildings, clearly elements of a single settlement at Chaco, will be discussed at some length in the following chapters. The Chaco Center's analysis of canyon architecture was structured by the old divisions, and small sites are treated in a separate monograph (Truell 1983). This suggests a separation that neither Truell nor I support.

Finally, the reader familiar with Anasazi architecture should be warned of my substitution of the inelegant term "round room" for the more familiar "kiva." In my opinion, almost all of the "kivas" at Chaco Canyon were simply elements of domestic building, one room of several (together with rectangular living rooms and storage rooms) making up a "house" or the basic unit of domestic building.

GOALS AND SUMMARY

The original Chaco Center research design (the "Prospectus" [Bradley and Logan 1969]) called for architectural studies. Reflecting the multi-ethnic, three-phase framework current at that time, the research design stated that architectural studies would be of use primarily in answering questions about "external cultural contacts" (Bradley and Logan 1969:14), either San Juan (the "McElmo" phase) or Mesoamerican (Mexican influence in the Bonito phase). "Cultural contacts" are not a major focus of this research. The McElmo question is

discussed (and dismissed) in Chapter 5; I have addressed the Mesoamerican problem at length elsewhere (Lekson 1983a).

The question asked of the large Chacoan ruins in the research design was "Who built them?" The next two most frequently asked questions are surely "How were they built?" and "What were they?"

How were the Chacoan buildings constructed? We can never expect to know, precisely. By refining our temporal control over their construction histories, by analyzing the building technology, and by translating that technology into labor requirements, we can attempt to define the social parameters within which our arguments and reconstructions will be realistic. In the long-standing tradition of academic obfuscation, I have restated the simple question "How were they built?": What are the social ramifications of construction?

What were the Chacoan buildings? The answer to this second question is infinitely more elusive than the first. One common archaeological approach to the determination of building function involves the analysis of the artifacts found within each structure. The present study includes some fixed features, such as mealing bins and firepits, but generally does not consider portable artifacts. Since half of the buildings considered are essentially unexcavated, it was impossible to frame general approaches to their study relying on portable artifacts. Given a choice between excavated detail or surface generality, I have consistently chosen the latter.

I have restated this question as: What are the social correlates of form? Again, like the social ramifications of construction, we will never know precisely how the form of the buildings reflects the society that designed and used them; however, within certain limits, we can use the formal-functional conventions current in Southwestern archaeology to discuss the Chacoan sites. In some instances, I will extrapolate from these conventions and in other instances I will argue against them for the interpretation of Chacoan architecture. The weakness of this approach lies in the use of conventions, agreed-upon archaeological fictions, to impute meaning to the buildings. The interpretations are only as sound as the conventions upon which they are based; unfortunately, very few archaeological conventions are well founded. I believe that most of these formal-functional "truisms" are widely accepted, but the test of that belief would require a poll of Southwestern archaeologists.

Why were they built? How can we "explain" the large ruins at Chaco? The central problem of Chacoan archaeology is not directly addressed here, although a few ideas will be offered in the conclusions. It would be foolish to think that the question could be answered by the architecture of the buildings alone. The answer requires the synthesis of a wide variety of data, ranging in scope and scale far beyond the buildings themselves. The general conclusions of the research of the Chaco Center, yet to be written, may resolve the problem of why they were built.

Chapter 2, Construction, describes Chacoan building technology, providing the data necessary to address the social ramifications of construction. Chapter 3, Form, traces formal change in Chacoan building, presenting a framework for the interpretation of social correlates of form. Chapter 4, The Sites, describes the history of research, dating, and unusual or unique features, and construction history of each site. And Chapter 5, Conclusions, is an interpretive essay, or series of arguments, addressing questions of construction and form.

The first requirement for this research was a detailed analysis (or reanalysis) of the architecture and especially the construction history of each site. Individual construction histories are the framework for all that follows.

Construction histories are divided into "stages," each of which includes all construction during a given interval at a particular site. Thus, the stage "Pueblo Bonito I" is all the earliest construction at Pueblo Bonito (dating about 920-935). (Note: all dates hereafter are anno Domini.) When possible, stages are subdivided into substages, as when two wings of a building were added at the same time. An example would be "Pueblo del Arroyo IIA" and "Pueblo del Arroyo IIB," two entirely separate wings (added to the existing structure, Pueblo del Arroyo I), both built about the same time (1095-1105). Reference to the figures illustrating the construction histories of each site in Chapter 4 may be useful when references are made to specific building stages in Chapters 2 and 3.

Construction histories appear late in the text (Chapter 4) because this study also is a description of Chacoan building technology (Chapter 2) and Chacoan building form (Chapter 3). Technological details and formal characteristics that would be endlessly redundant in the individual site descriptions in Chapter 4 are thus summarized in Chapters 2 and 3. At the same time, Chapters 2 and 3 use the temporal framework developed in the construction histories. As (I hope) the reader will see, all this is far less confusing than it sounds.

# Chapter Two

# Construction

Chaco has been lauded as the acme of Anasazi architecture, something extraordinary, far better than what came before and all that followed. Even Chaco's few detractors (which, in the course of this text, occasionally includes your author) have difficulty finding anything adverse to say about its finely detailed masonry, its elegantly battered walls, or its imposing massiveness.

In a passage that now seems quaint (even embarrassing), Neil Judd recounted the reaction of some modern Pueblo Indians to Chaco:

> ...the four Zuni accompanying me returned from their first tour of Pueblo Bonito and voiced their joint conclusion: "White men built these walls; Indians could not" (Judd 1964:22).

Judd's Zunis, of course, were mistaken; nevertheless, early explorers and even the first anthropologists who visited Chaco thought sites like Pueblo Bonito were the work not of the predecessors of the Pueblos but of Toltecs or other Mexican high civilizations. Aztec Ruin (a Chacoan site about 80 km north of the canyon) was named in error, but not in jest.

Even today, this attitude persists. A number of archaeologists consider Chaco to be either the handiwork or the inspiration of the advanced civilizations of Mexico. In newspaper accounts, magazine articles, and popular books, Chacoan building is often discussed as something nearly marvelous, something beyond reasonable expectation for its desert setting. After all, historically this same desert supported only the Pueblos and their hunter-gatherer neighbors. The impression is that Chacoan building technology was somehow beyond the capabili-

ties of these groups. Our "amazement" at Chacoan architectural genius, or environmentally sensitive design, or preternaturally complex solstice markers, is (no doubt unconsciously) oddly condescending, a carry-over from a long-standing paternalism toward Native Americans.

Is it amazing that Chacoan building conformed to the canyon's micro-climates? People had been living and building in Chaco for four centuries before the first stone was laid at Pueblo Bonito. It would be amazing if Chacoan builders had not incorporated the accumulated folk wisdom in the design of their structures. Agriculture in the desert is a tricky business at best; it would be staggering if Chaco had developed without some form of celestial observations and calendrics to mark the seasons. Were Chacoan walls the work of a guild of master masons? Sober reflection suggests that they were more likely built by people with a supply of good stone, fair craftsmanship, and a lot of patience.

In the broad view, there is little that is extraordinary about Chacoan construction technology except its remarkable preservation. By any reasonable scale, Chaco is not the eighth, eightieth, or even the eight-hundredth wonder of the world. Chacoan construction technology answered the formal requirements of buildings designed and built by a moderately complicated society (see Chapters 3 and 4). This chapter discusses Chacoan construction technology with particular reference to the question, "What were the social ramifications of construction?" A brief description of Chacoan architecture will suggest that it was chiefly a matter of labor, not technical expertise, that was responsible for the construction.

An illuminating parallel can be found in central Mexico; monumental architecture which required engineering and technical expertise has been contrasted to other building, impressive in size but less impressive in technique. This latter group was not constructed of huge ashlars or structurally complex masonry but of hundreds of thousands of small stones laid up in simple walls. "As such, these would indicate an expenditure of energy rather than a disciplined display of technique" (Outwater 1957: 258). At Chaco, we are looking at a comparable expenditure of energy but not technique.

Chacoan buildings consisted of rectangular rooms, built in contiguous room-blocks, and round rooms. Some of the round rooms were semisubterranean, located in the plaza area in front of the roomblock; others were elevated into roomblocks, and built into rectangular rooms, usually enclosures specifically built for this purpose.

After the site had been leveled or otherwise prepared, and foundations laid, a roomblock typically began as a series of continuous, parallel long walls. Cross walls were a structural afterthought, although they probably were laid at the same time as the long walls. Chacoan building proceeded one story at a time. One story of long and cross walls would be completed, the rooms roofed individually, and those roofs used as a building platform for construction of the next story. In the following section, the elements of Chacoan construction are discussed in approximately the order they entered the building process, i.e., site preparation, materials, wall construction and details, roofing, and so forth.

## SITE PREPARATION

The placement of Chacoan buildings undoubtedly answered multiple requirements, many of which we will never know. One of the factors was undoubtedly solar efficiency; studies at Pueblo Bonito show that the original plan, and subsequent additions to it, was sensitive to solar considerations. Another important aspect of site placement may have been the direction of the wind; mesa top buildings particularly, may have been sited to protect the nearby plazas from prevailing winds. The view -- particularly field of view to other large Chacoan buildings -- was important. Less easy to define, but probably more significant, were the visual qualities of the site for the building itself. Perhaps some structures were sited to offer a dramatic view to people entering the canyon. In particular, the Pueblo Alto complex must have been a very impressive sight for the travelers coming into Chaco through South Gap.

The design of some Chacoan buildings incorporated the existing terrain and natural features. Kin Kletso was built around a huge boulder, which served as a platform for a Tower Kiva on the second story. At many outliers (and less often within the canyon) buildings were situated on elevations and promontories; the added height raised the Chacoan structure to visual dominance over its surrounding community.

More often, the existing terrain was altered or prepared prior to construction, e.g., in the continuation of a great earth terrace to support the extension of the building level out over a hill slope (as at Peñasco Blanco), or the excavation into slopes to allow the construction of a line of rooms on a given level (as at Una Vida). Artificial features were similarly altered in building projects; occasionally whole rows of earlier rooms were filled with sand to provide stable foundations for later building.

## MATERIALS

### Walls

Three materials were required in bulk for Chacoan walls: stone, clay-sand, and water. A cubic meter of wall contained about 1440 kg stone, 463 kg clay-sand, and 130 liters of water.

### Stone

Stone was procured from the sandstone cliffs that form the canyon. The Cliff House sandstones, in the Chaco area, consist of two very thick layers of massive, buff-colored stone separated by a layer of shales, siltstone, and a harder, dark brown laminated stone. The harder stone forms the surface of a bench about 50 m above the canyon floor. Sandstone from this layer and the buff-colored stone that forms the lower walls of the canyon were the sources of the stone used in Bonito phase walls. (Vivian and Mathews refer to the massive stone as "Chacra sandstone" [1965:34].) The differential use of these two types of sandstone, remarked upon since the earliest published reports (e.g., Holsinger 1901:60), has been variously explained as an increasing mastery of masonry techniques, the use of various types for ornamentation, or differing cultural affinities.

The harder stone requires more effort in quarrying than the massive buff-colored stone, which is available as talus along the entire north slope of the canyon; however, the harder tabular stone is more easily reduced into usable fragments with one or more flat faces. It weathers less rapidly than the softer stone. More importantly, the harder stone could be fractured at right angles to the bedding planes, requiring less work in shaping than a "freestone" like the softer buff-colored sandstone. This type of fracture would be easier to produce on a thin tabular stone than on a thick stone.

Compressive strength of the stone was probably not a significant consideration in Chacoan walls. Strength in compression might be important in a few limited functions, such as pillars or piers. Stone pillars were seldom used in Chacoan building, although wood for vertical posts must have been much more difficult to obtain than the omnipresent mud and stone. Pillars were used successfully under exceptionally heavy loads in Great Kivas (see "Piers").

The low tensile strength of stone undoubtedly was the reason for the preference for wooden lintels over longer spans (i.e., doors). In some parts of the Southwest, lintels are often stone, but this was not common practice at Chaco. Stone lintels for shorter spans (i.e., vents) are infrequently encountered.

Holsinger (1901) noted that open quarries for the darker hard stone could be seen at distances from up to 5 km from the sites where the stone was used. Hayes (1981) recorded numerous quarries of the darker stone; he noted that the dark stone seems to have been almost completely stripped from some areas of the bench on the north side of the canyon. The quarrying of this stone probably involved extensive, although shallow, excavation since much of the observable stone is coated with caliche.

Procurement of the softer buff-colored stone was less difficult as it is available in chunks of various sizes all along the base of the cliffs. Most of the smaller-sized fragments of this stone are too weathered for use. Once procured, the production of usable fragments of the softer stone was more work than the initial shaping of the harder stone: "...it cannot be split along bedding planes as can the other, and it had to be worked down from fortuitous chunks by pecking and rubbing" (Vivian and Mathews 1965:35).

The vertical dimension (or thickness) was probably most important in the initial shaping, either at the quarry or at the site. Since each stone was laid on its bedding plane, the layering of the stone generally determined its thickness. Masonry laid on its bedding planes is much stronger than masonry laid at angles to these planes (Winkler 1973:40); however, earlier masonry in the Chaco area frequently used upright slabs of sandstone as the base course for masonry. While this practice may have been acceptable for single story walls, it probably would have been a problem in multistoried walls. Upright slabs may have been used in earlier masonry to provide a plumb lower wall surface that could resist transverse forces more effectively than could thin walls of poorly laid masonry.

Given a stone of the required vertical dimension, several techniques were used to shape the face. These include (1) simple fracture, (2) grooving and snapping, (3) spalling, (4) pecking, and (5) grinding (Figure 2.1). Simple fracture consists of breaking a stone of suitable width to create a face perpendicular to the bedding planes, or upper and lower surfaces of the stone. This can be accomplished by striking the stone with a large stone or maul or by dropping the stone on a pointed or ridged anvil. Much of the harder dark stone seems to have been shaped in this way. The technique is not particularly successful when used on the softer buff-colored stone.

Grooving and snapping is similar to simple fracture, except the stone has been prepared with a groove around the margins of the intended face to guide the fracture. This groove can be produced by sawing with a flake (Wheeler 1965) or by pecking with a pointed hammerstone. Stones prepared in this way usually exhibit a slight bevel around the exposed face, the remnant of the groove. This technique is effective with both the hard tabular stone and the massive stone.

Spalling, also referred to as scabbling (Hayes 1964:37), involves the removal of mass through direct percussion. Two forms of spalling can be distinguished. In the first, spalls are struck from the margin of a face prepared through fracture. An example of this technique would be the squaring up of a fracture, one that had proceeded through the stone at a slight angle, by striking a series of spalls from the overhung edge of the face. This type of spalling leaves a slight arris along the midline of the face. The second type of spalling proceeds from the edge of a lenticular stone, or from a fracture at a high angle to the perpendicular of the bedding planes, and removes material bidirectionally, producing a sinuous edge

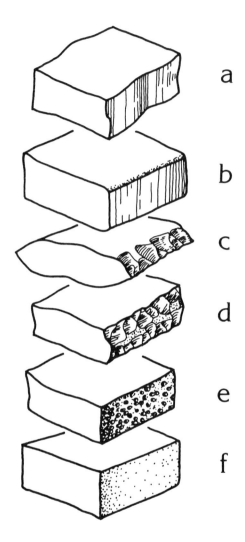

Figure 2.1.  Stone facing treatments:  (a) simple fracture;
(b) groove and fracture; (c) chipped, bi-directional;
(d) chipped, from edge; (e) pecked; and (f) ground.

similar to that of a chopper. Swannack (1969:28) names this type "chipped-edge," while Judd refers to it as "spalled" (1964:Figure 10).

Generally, only the exposed face of the stone was carefully shaped. The upper and lower surfaces seem to have been -- as much as possible -- unmodified while the sides and back of the stone were shaped by simple fracture only and were not squared.

Mud Mortar

Mud mortar was made from clay or clay-sand and water. Mortars were usually made from alluvial deposits, although some of the clays may have been obtained from rock-clay exposures at the base of the cliffs.

Clay and clay-sand in soils or stream deposits were undoubtedly procured simply by digging pits. The acquisition of sufficient water for construction must have been as much of a problem then as now. Rain water would have been available during the rainy seasons of late summer and early fall. Other sources of water were small reservoirs in holes and pools in the slick rock, and wells in the bed of Chaco Wash.

Specific clays or clay-sand mixes were selected for particular structural purposes at Chetro Ketl (Reiter 1933:13), a practice also seen at Pueblo Bonito and Pueblo Alto. At Chetro Ketl and Pueblo Alto, one type of clay was used for mortar and the "scratch coat" wall plaster. A second, sandier mix was used for the finish plaster.

Roofs

Upper story floors and -- presumably -- exterior roofs typically consisted of primary beams (vigas), secondary beams (latillas), one or more layers of split shakes, probably of juniper or piñon (called closing material [Ferguson 1959]), a layer of clay mortar, and a covering of sand (Figure 2.2).

Morris (1919:43) noted that there is no evidence that trees were felled by burning. The ends of beams in Old Bonito are usually conical, showing the marks of ax cutting (Judd 1964:26). It seems that most trees were felled with stone axes (Morris 1939:137; Sarayader and Shimada 1971); however, there are remarkably few stone axes at Chaco (Breternitz 1976; Judd 1954:239).

Many later Chacoan beams were squared off at both ends. The technique used to square these beams is not fully known. The beams were grooved with a flint chip or knife; flint and obsidian flakes and knives were found wedged into grooves around beams (Holsinger 1901:22). Morris thought that such grooves were gradually enlarged and deepened until the conical end of the timber could be snapped off (Morris 1919:45 and Figure 26). Judd argued that the groove was merely a guide for the ax and the final squaring with abrasives such as sandstone (Judd 1959:15). In almost all cases, the bark was peeled and knots were rubbed down.

Outwater (1957) discusses the use of flake saws in prehistoric Mexico. If his interpretation of these tools is correct, the grooving observed on Bonito phase beams might have been produced by this type of saw. The results of recent experiments by Shelley (1980) suggest that thin sandstone slabs, used as saws, could have felled the trees used at Chaco. This is an intriguing idea, and might explain both the lack of axes and the squared ends of Chacoan beams, but to date no conclusions on the efficacy of sandstone saws have been reached.

Judd notes that most beams had been cut in winter or late autumn (Judd 1964:17), and data from Room 57 at Chetro Ketl tend to support this (Bannister 1965:151). However, the secondary beams of Room 93 at Chetro Ketl were all cut around the beginning of June (Bannister and Robinson 1978), and analysis of the entire Chetro Ketl beam collection supports the suggestion that Chacoan wood cutting was primarily a spring activity (Dean and Warren 1983:230).

Most of the primary and secondary beams were of ponderosa pine. While small stands of ponderosa might have been found in the heads of side canyons at Chaco, there were no local forests. The nearest extensive ponderosa forests were either upstream, beyond Pueblo Pintado, or to the south, on the mesas behind Kin Ya'a, 40 km or more from Chaco. One use of the Chacoan roads was surely for the transport of construction timber (Betancourt et al. 1984).

Dendrochronological data support the possibility of timber stockpiling "either for convenience or for seasoning" (Bannister 1965:123 and 151). However, analysis of the large sample of beams from Chetro Ketl indicates that stockpiling "seems to have been a relatively minor practice" (Dean and Warren 1983: 227).

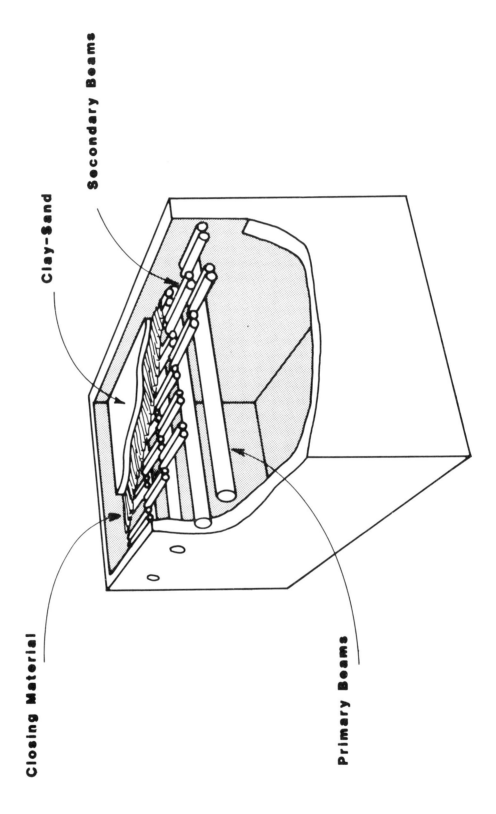

Figure 2.2.   Flat roof.

In addition to bulk materials, construction required other items in smaller quantitites. Cordage was used for lashing roof elements together. Baskets and wood frames were needed for transporting mortar and rock. Hammerstones, digging sticks, and other tools must have been used in quantity; many discarded hammerstones have been found built into the wall interiors.

## SITE LAYOUT AND FOUNDATIONS

Construction began with the laying out of the structure. This may have meant placing poles or posts at corners, or tracing walls on the ground surface with a stick, or even laying out rough stone lines. There is only the most scanty evidence for the initial layout.

When the final design was agreed upon, the outline was permanently marked by the first step of actual construction -- the foundations. All the foundations for a building project would be laid before wall construction began. During construction, additions to the original plan required added foundations, while deletions left unused foundations. Walls "as built" do not always correspond to foundation lines; frequently, walls are off-center and sometimes even overhang their foundations.

Foundations were fairly substantial, consisting of a trench about 50 cm wide by 50 cm deep, filled with rubble and clay mortar. Foundations kept walls from settling unevenly. Even low retaining walls, with no effective vertical load, were begun with foundations.

Identical foundations were used for the four-story walls and for retaining walls with no vertical load. This suggests both that the structural functions of foundations were not fully understood and that foundations served at least partly as a design device.

## WALL CONSTRUCTION

The two most important considerations in Chacoan wall building were stability and craftsmanship. Strength was not an major problem, because the more immediate problem of wall stability was solved by building very wide walls, which coincidentally were very strong (Figure 2.3).

Great width not only ensured that the walls stood, but also (with the excellent local materials and careful Chacoan workmanship) that the walls were more than adequate for any conceivable Anasazi load. Other solutions to instability were attempted in the Anasazi Southwest. At many post-Chaco sites, thinner multistoried walls were buttressed at very short intervals by cross walls. Chacoan building, with large rooms (and consequently widely spaced cross walls), relied on wall width rather than buttressing for stability.

The main load on Bonito phase walls was the weight of upper story walls; the next largest load was that of roofs/floors. One of the most celebrated characteristics of Chacoan walls is the reduction of wall width with each succeeding story. The width of walls decreases with each story, providing a greater area for the distribution of weight from upper stories and lowering the load per unit area. Decreasing wall width was probably less a conscious effort to increase strength than it was a self-evident technique to ensure stability.

One of the most critical factors in the performance of masonry walls is workmanship (Caravaty and Plummer 1960:22). Two workmen, beginning with identical materials and designs, can produce two very different masonry walls. Although craftmanship is a difficult quality to measure, it is a canon of Southwestern archaeology that Chacoan masonry workmanship was outstanding. "The later walls are of excellent workmanship and certainly mark an achievement of great technical skill" (Martin and Plog 1973: 110). Certainly, the time-consuming construction of Chacoan walls evidenced more care than, say, the "judicious piling" of the "wretched masonry" at four-story tall Pecos Pueblo (Kidder 1958:68). If Chacoan walls were more artfully stacked than other Anasazi or Puebloan building, they still were not technically outstanding as examples of masonry. The economy of materials and skill in stone cutting and laying were secondary to massiveness and labor investment; nevertheless, Chacoan masonry worked, and many walls still stand.

### Wall Types

#### Facing Styles

Because archaeologists are disinclined to disect standing walls, the surface patternings or "veneers" have historically been more important than cross sections and structural properties in Chacoan building studies. Typologies

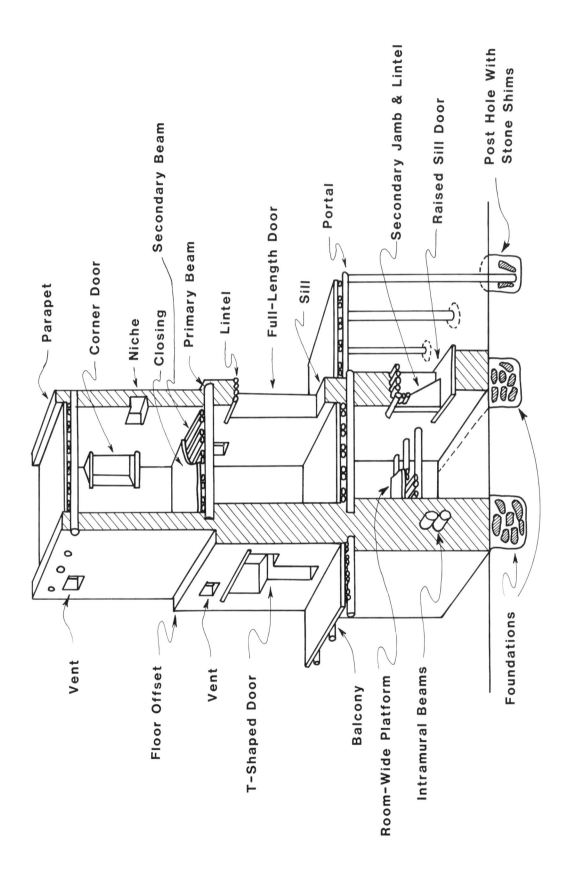

Figure 2.3.   Construction features.

of Chaco masonry were devised by Jackson (1878), Judd (1927, 1964), Hawley (1934, 1938), and Roberts (1938). Most of these acknowleged the importance of the wall structure, but in practice the schemes are applied to the wall facings or veneers. The most elaborate scheme is Hawley's (1938); I use the Judd (1964) typology, with the addition of the "McElmo" type of Vivian and Mathews (1965) (Figure 2.4). A correspondence is given in Table 2.1.

Type I: Long thin slabs of hard tabular sandstone, with edged (scabbled) exposed faces, with wide mortar joints. Uncoursed. Rarely, covered with a thick mud veneer set with small horizontal spalls.

Type II: Long thin slabs of hard tabular sandstone, either edged (scabbled) or flush (snapped) exposed faces, with side mortar joints filled with small gallets or spalls. Gallets placed horizontally in both vertical and horizontal joints. Uncoursed.

Types III and IV: Rectangular stones, flush (snapped or scabbled, frequently ground) exposed faces, with very thin mortar joints and few, if any, gallets or spalls. Coursed or poorly coursed. Type III: Alternating bands of a one or two courses of large brick-shaped stones (of both the thin hard and massive softer sandstone), and three or more courses of smaller, thinner tabular stones. Type IV: Thin, hard tabular stones alone. Types III and IV represent ends of a continuum of stone selection and coursing characterizing post-Type II, Pre-"McElmo" masonry.

"McElmo": Rectangular brick like stones (exclusively of the massive hard sandstone), ground flush faces. Thin mortar joints, usually with one and never more than three rows of gallet spalls, placed horizontally in the horizontal joints, and vertically in the vertical joints. Well coursed.

The veneers (or, more accurately, facings) of some Chacoan walls show considerably more attention to coursing and detail than other Anasazi building, and veneers of various styles have become synonymous with Chacoan building. However, many walls are much less patterned than the classic Chacoan styles described above.

The earliest Chacoan walls had large mortar joints between stones, and evidently required extensive maintenance and

buttressing. A good facing minimized the amount of mortar exposed in the wall face, and at the same time maximized stone contact. Less exposed mortar reduced the maintenance required for keeping the stone and mud wall standing in an area of unpredictable thunderstorms. More stone-to-stone contact in the face increased the strength of the wall and reduced the possibility of structural failure.

Aside from these structural considerations, some facings are obviously the result of highly skilled masons working within well developed craft traditions. These masons need not have been full-time craftsmen builders. Repeated facing patterns may indicate a widespread style used during a particular period, or they may suggest the work of a single social group, or they may identify a specific line of builders. We do not know the true implications of these patterns.

Sectional Types

Load-bearing Chacoan masonry walls were of four general types, based on sectional characteristics: simple, double-simple, compound, and core-and-veneer.

1. Simple wall (Figure 2.5a). A simple wall is a single stone in width; the walls of the earliest part of Pueblo Bonito are of this type, "...wall-wide sandstone slabs spalled around the edge with hammerstones and laid one upon another in generous quantities of mud..." (Judd 1964:57).

The earliest (Type I) walls at Pueblo Bonito were laid with very wide joints. The thick beds of mortar were occasionally exposed on the interior wall faces, but the exterior wall faces were often protected by a veneer of very small spalls or fragments of sandstone pushed into a thick mud coating over the load-bearing masonry in the wall. "This surface covering of close-lying chips occurred so frequently on exterior [Type I] stonework exposed to our explorations, we came to regard it as a standard Old Bonitian treatment" (Judd 1964:57). The spall veneer is not load-bearing; it is a true veneer.

2. Double-simple wall (Figure 2.5b). When more width was required in early wall building, the simple wall was occasionally repeated, in parallel, with minimal structural bonding between the two walls. This type of wall is reported by Judd at Pueblo Bonito (1964:58) and occurs at Mesa Verde (Swannack 1969:28), but the type is not currently observable in Chaco.

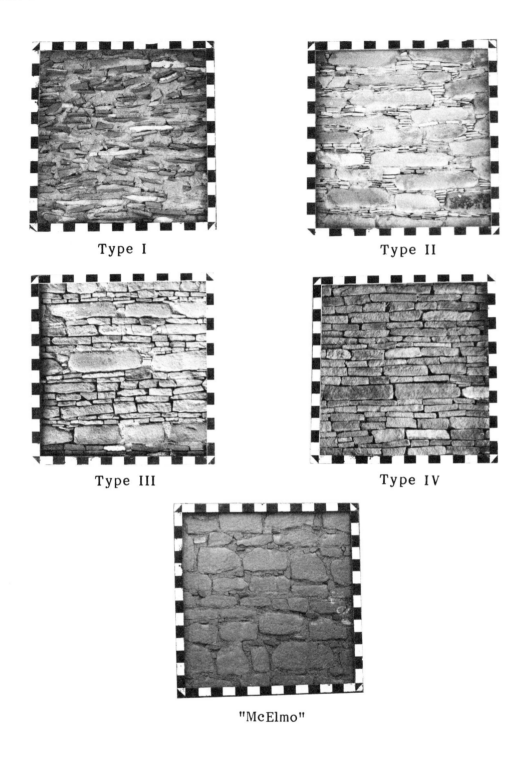

Type I                    Type II

Type III                  Type IV

"McElmo"

Figure 2.4.   Masonry types.

Table 2.1.  Correlation of masonry types.

| Judd | Hawley | Suggested Dates |
|:---:|:---:|:---|
| I | 4 | 900–950(?) |
| II | 5 | 1020–1060 |
| III | 6 & 7 | 1050–1115 |
| IV | 9 | 1050–1115 |
| McElmo* | 8 | 1114–1140(?) |

*Vivian and Mathews 1965.

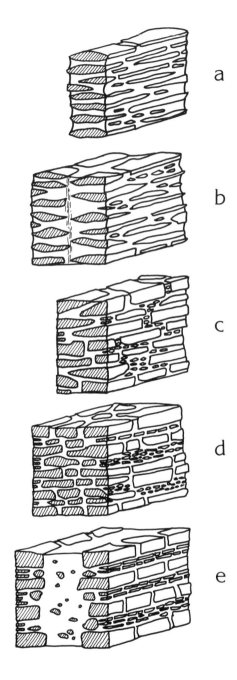

Figure 2.5.   Wall section types:  (a) simple; (b) double simple;
           (c) compound; (d) core and veneer, solid core; and
           (e) core and veneer, fill core.

3. Compound wall (Figure 2.5c). The compound wall, is essentially an internally bonded double-simple wall. Compound walls are two, or occasionally more, stones in width. Consequently, most stones are visible only on one face of the wall. Generally, the stones interdigitate in the interior of the wall.

Compound walls, at Chaco, seem to be a function of desired wall width. When used in conjunction with simple walls the compound wall was wider; it was first observed in the three-story rear wall of Pueblo Bonito. When used with core and veneer walls, the compound wall was thinner, for example, in upper story walls above wider core and veneer lower walls.

4. Core-and-veneer walls (Figures 2.5d, 2.5e). Core-and-veneer walls are a hallmark of Chacoan building. These consist of two facings, similar to the compound wall, but separated by a core of varying width.

Core-and-veneer walls are not all alike. Distinctions can be drawn, first, in terms of the core material. In some core-and-veneer walls, the space between the two facings is filled with rubble laid up on the same course as the facings (Roys 1936:120). In others, the core had been filled with a variety of materials (mud, earth, household trash, rubble, etc.) after several courses of the facings were completed. This second type of core is known from excavation (e.g., Vivian 1959:Figure 50), but is now seldom observable due to stabilization requirements. This latter type of construction is most evident in very wide walls, though only a few of these are load-bearing.

A second variable in core-and-veneer walls is the relative width of the core (the facings are usually about equal in width). A hypothetical continuum of core widths runs from the compound wall (i.e., two facings with no core) to the widest core-and-veneer wall.

It is possible that wall types defined by the relative width or presence/absence of the core may be associated with facing types and may not reflect required wall widths. Morenon's (1977) data from Salmon Ruin tend to suggest that facing widths vary with wall widths; however, Morenon was dealing almost exclusively with the uppermost portions of walls.

Another factor affecting the relative widths of facings and cores is the general size of the stones employed. A wall built entirely of large stones will naturally have a higher facing-to-core width ratio than a wall of identical width built entirely of small stones. Through time, there appears to be a trend from large to small. For example, the large "wall-wide" stones of Old Bonito walls are many times larger than the visible stones of the same type sandstone in later Bonito Type IV walls (Judd 1964). It is likely that convenient sources of the harder, tabular sandstone became exhausted over time, making the use of smaller fragments more economical in later work, that is, by the time Type IV masonry was being built, the choice may have been between small fragments of hard sandstone or massive soft sandstone.

Finally, stone size (and core/facing ratios) will depend in part on the morphology of the wall. In particular, curved walls (as in round rooms) will require smaller stones than straight walls. The use of large stones in a round room bench, for example, would transform the outline of that bench from a circle to a polygon, thus it is little wonder that round rooms consistently use Type IV masonry -- a fact often cited as evidence of the additional labor expended on their construction.

In most walls with relatively wide facings and narrow cores, the core appears to have been built up along with the facing stones. The core functions mainly as a spacer or filler in the small interstices between some facing stones. Walls with massive cores and relatively narrow facings are often considered typical of Bonito phase building; however, they are mainly limited to the lower stories of Chacoan multistoried buildings. This type of wall consists of a core four or even more stones in width, with relatively narrow facings; the core and facing seem to have been laid up together.

A Speculative History of Chacoan Walls

Table 2.2 correlates facing styles with wall sections. Tree-ring dates allow fairly tight control of the sequence of wall and facing types at some structures.

Unfortunately, the conclusions reached from one building may not be applicable to others. For example, Judd thought that Type III and Type IV were sequential at Pueblo Bonito. The ground

Table 2.2.  Facing styles and wall sections.

| | | Double | | WALL SECTIONS | Core-and-Veneer | |
| | Simple | Simple | Compound | C < V | C = V | C > V |
|---|---|---|---|---|---|---|
| FACING STYLES | | | | | | |
| I | C | R | R | | | R* |
| II | | | C | C | R | |
| III | | | C | C | C | R |
| IV | | | C | C | C | R |
| McElmo | | | R | R | C | R |

C = common; R = rare.
*Massive Type I walls at Una Vida, Stage II.

plan and architectural sequence at that structure argue against this (see Chapter 4, Pueblo Bonito); perhaps more importantly, the two types are visible in reverse sequential order in abutted walls at Peñasco Blanco. Types III and IV, probably contemporary, were two extremes of a continuum of coursing with the two types of sandstone. However, most of Judd's Pueblo Bonito sequence (and Hawley's Chetro Ketl sequence) still obtains today.

The Type I style, dating to the early 900s, is the predecessor of later wall types. There is a structural sequence at Pueblo Bonito that illuminates the development of those later types, but my reconstruction of that history is somewhat speculative.

The earliest portion of Pueblo Bonito (Stage I in Chapter 4) was a multistoried arc of Type I masonry. Although part of the rear wall of this structure was double-simple, most of it was simple masonry, with lenticular spalled stones set with thick mortar joints. Some joints received gallet or non-bearing spalls. There was little stone-to-stone contact, and because of the lenticular shape of the stones, most contact was in the center of the wall, not at its edges. Pueblo Bonito I was built in the early 900s; its rear wall stood until sometime shortly before 1020. Erosion of exterior mortar joints, settling, and the consequent rocking of the stones on each other caused the rear wall to bulge alarmingly (Judd 1964:80, and Figure 10), as the Type I wall began to fail.

Rather than raze the building and start anew, the occupants surrounded the century-old structure with a new outer wall -- actually two parallel walls with numerous cross walls abutting the bulging Type I wall. This addition, in the 1020s, buttressed the old Type I wall, and improved its masonry. In much of the addition, a stone similar to the old Type I large, lenticular slab was used but in a compound and, in some places, a core-and-veneer section; most importantly the mortar joints were decreased, and the joints filled with gallets or spalls. These changes in construction (1) increased greatly the stone-to-stone contact along the wall face, making a stronger and much more stable wall, and (2) decreased the amount of exposed mortar.

This was the first distinctively "Chacoan" wall: a compound and occasionally core-and-veneer wall with a Type II facing. The Type II wall solved many of the structural problems of the Type I wall by transferring the load from the core to the facings, and coincidentally decreasing maintenance of the mud mortar exposed in the wall face. Reiter (1933: 67) cited the use of spalls to transfer the excess weight from the center of the stone to the outer edge of the facing as one of the most important technical achievements of the Bonito phase builders. The new wall type appeared almost immediately at Chetro Ketl and Pueblo Alto, and set the stage for subsequent refinements, Types III and IV. The development of those embellishments is beyond discovery, but I suspect that the shift from Type II to Types III and IV was gradual, and both a function of decreasing availability of the preferred tabular stone and the increasing formalization of the masonry craft.

The "McElmo" style is a problem. There is "McElmo" masonry at almost every site, and at almost every site it is among the last major building that can be defined. There are several sites, built late in the sequence at Chaco, which are exclusively of "McElmo" masonry. Vivian and Mathews (1965:110) saw "McElmo" masonry as evidence of "site intrusions into the area" from the San Juan. It resembles the pecked masonry of Mesa Verde, and is named for the main drainage (McElmo Creek) northwest of Mesa Verde National Park. There are problems with this interpretation, some trivial and some fundamental. Among the trivial is the fact that banding (a Chacoan "diagnostic") is far more common in "McElmo" masonry than is generally known. Every "McElmo" site includes walls of banded masonry, usually in walls facing the terraces on the roofs of elevated round rooms. At Kin Kletso, Vivian and Mathews dismissed one banded wall as "a very evident prehistoric patch" (Vivian and Mathews 1965:36), but it is in fact a consistent part of "McElmo" style building. Vivian and Mathews raised another issue by suggesting that "McElmo" masonry at Chaco might be considerably earlier than the supposed prototype at Mesa Verde; as I date these sites (see Table 2.1 and Chapter 5), this is not the contradiction it might seem to be. The "McElmo" style is probably later at Chaco than at Mesa Verde; nevertheless, it is probably a solution to a local problem.

"McElmo" masonry is generally limited to the central canyon area. At Wijiji, built at about the same time, there is practically no use of the massive sandstone and of course no "McElmo" masonry, while in the central canyon it is ubiquitous. "McElmo" masonry may have begun as a response to the exhaustion of the supply of easily accessible tabular sandstone. With the substitution of the massive sandstone in wide Chacoan walls, new stone shaping techniques were required to ensure stone-to-stone contact, and gallet spalls returned from a century's disuse. The use of massive sandstone in walls quickly replaced the older Type III and IV facings, and I suspect that "McElmo" did in fact become a popular "style" rather than just a strictly practical response to the problem of stone procurement.

## Wall Bonding

There seems to be a rather general belief that there are very few if any bonded wall junctures in the larger Chaco sites; that the practice was merely to abut one wall against the other with no provision for tying the corners together. This is not correct. The bonding of wall junctures is far more prevalent than is generally supposed, or that a casual glance would indicate. This is true at Chetro Ketl, Pueblo Bonito, Pueblo del Arroyo, and other classic towns with which we are familiar,...(Vivian and Mathews 1964:36).

Chacoan wall bonding displays a bewildering variety. Cores and facings do not follow the same pattern; bonding and abutment change within a single story and between two stories. The relationship of bonding to building stages is anything but straightforward. Commonly, two walls are bonded in the core while their facings abut. This was facilitated by laying stones to project outward from the through wall along the axis of the not-yet-built abutting wall. The cross wall was built up incorporating these projecting stones with the unbonded facings oriented around the shared core. This type of bonding is very common and may be the most frequent treatment of wall corners. Many other, more complex patterns are known.

The apparent ubiquity of bonding makes truly abutted walls all the more significant. Most of these appear to be partition walls, probably much later than original construction. Abutted walls that appear to be a part of the overall pattern in the structure are rare indeed, and almost certainly indicate major building stages. Rebuilding resulting in tied or bonded walls sometimes occurred; bonds of this type -- post-facto bonding -- are known from Kin Kletso, Pueblo del Arroyo, and Pueblo Bonito.

Walls may abut or bond at very acute angles, sometimes "feathering" into one another, as in the rear wall of Pueblo Bonito. There, the barely sub-parallel walls were tied with poles running through the exterior wall into the inner wall:

>...where the newer stonework veneers the older, tie poles were employed to prevent separation. The architects...inserted neatly trimmed pine poles, 2 to 3 inches in diameter, into holes purposely made in the concealed wall and brought them forward horizontally through the added stonework to be cut off flush with its exterior. Both the diameter of these tie poles and the intervals between them increase as the veneering continued eastward until it was able to stand without anchoring (Judd 1964:156).

## Intramural Beams

From the point of view of modern ruins stabilization, one of the major shortcomings of Bonito phase building was the frequent inclusion in wall cores of horizontal timbers or intramural beams that rot and leave serious cavities in the walls. Of course, it is not likely that the rotting of intramural beams was any problem while the buildings were occupied.

It is difficult to say how often beams were built into walls, but the results of the 1947 Chetro Ketl flood (see Chapter 4) are enlightening. The flood destroyed the standing walls of about a half dozen rooms, and over 200 beams were exposed in the wreckage. Almost all of these timbers were intramural beams.

The beams range from about 15 to 20 cm in diameter and in length up to 2.25 m. Intramural beams were generally built into the core of the wall, occasionally in pairs; though rarely done, the beams were occasionally coursed into one facing of a wall, as at Pueblo Bonito and Chetro Ketl. Martin (1936) suggests that similar beams in two rooms at Lowry Ruin were used as wall plates to distribute the load of the roof beams; however, this use of intramural beams is very limited at Chaco (specifically, in portions of Chetro Ketl II, Chapter 4).

Vertical intramural beams are very

rare. These appear to extend from the base of the wall, perhaps to the top of the wall, are generally located at short intervals (much like the vertical posts in jacal walls), and are exposed in one face of the wall, or as single posts in the core of room corners.

## Nonload-bearing Walls

Thin, nonload-bearing masonry walls were used in Chacoan building, but their use was infrequent. Jacal (or post-and-mud) walls are better represented. These walls consisted of closely spaced uprights, with a series of horizontal wooden rods lashed to one or both faces. This post and rod grid was coated with a thick layer of mud.

Judd describes two of these walls at Pueblo Bonito. One (in Room 257) consisted of "13 posts, 2-3 inches in diameter with imprints of willows bound to the south face" (1964:162); the second (Room 256), "...was supported by nine posts to which willows had been bound horizontally at intervals of about 15 inches and held in place by other willows lashed vertically to the posts" (1964:256).

Judd's two to three inch posts seem too thin for roof support, but more massive jacal structures may have served as the load-bearing posts for a post-and-beam framework.

## Openings

### Doors

Lintels almost always consist of wooden poles, 8 to 10 cm in diameter (longer spans are larger), placed horizontally side-by-side, and often lashed together, across the entire width of the opening. Above these lintels there may be large sandstone slabs; however, more often, the normal wall core and facing construction begins directly on the lintel. Stone lintels over doors or large vents/windows are practically unknown. Stone lintels over shorter spans -- such as vents -- are common at Chetro Ketl, but less so at Pueblo Bonito and other Chacoan sites. The length of the lintel poles built into the wall on either side of the door varies, but rarely is the exposed lintel more than half of the total pole length. Occasionally, a lintel pole will extend up to 1.5 m into the wall.

Doorways did not have framed jambs, nor did they routinely have masonry quoins (larger rocks, cut square at the corners). Quoins occur only in the "McElmo" style in later building. Larger stones were used, and ground down to a true corner after being laid up (Vivian and Mathews 1965:40). On the corners of most doors, smaller stones, more carefully fractured and finished, were used. At Pueblo Alto, and at some other buildings, corners were built up of very small stones, as small as the spalls used in chinking of Type II masonry. The "typical" construction, however, probably involved the continuation of the wall facing with no exceptional shaping.

Sills almost always consist of a flat sandstone slab with shaped edges. The sill frequently projects beyond one wall face defining a direction of door construction that is normally repeated by lowered sills and secondary jambs (these features will be described below). The sills of windows did not have slabs, suggesting that people were not walking or crawling through them.

There are at least four types of Chacoan doors (Figure 2.6): (1) small doors with sills high above floor level; (2) large doors with the sill just above the floor level; (3) T-shaped doors; and (4) corner doorways. It is possible to group these four types under two headings: doors one walked through (large doors, T-shaped doors) and doors one crawled through (small doors, corner doors), depending on sill height above the floor. The variability of sill height is sometimes considerable in multiple doors of older rooms (e.g., Rooms 323 and 325 at Pueblo Bonito, Room 103 at Pueblo Alto). In the majority of exposed walls, sill height seemed to be fairly consistent from wall to wall within, and between, rooms.

Small doors with sills high above floor level are the most common type at Chacoan structures. Dimensions range from 60 to 70 cm in width and from 75 to 110 cm in height, with sills located 30 to 60 cm or more above the floor. As noted above, sills often project over one wall face. The reverse face of the sill is frequently less well shaped than the projecting edge and irregularities may be finished with smaller fragments of tabular rock.

Small doors are frequently equipped with lowered lintels and secondary jambs (Figure 2.6d) forming a collar to support a stone or wood slab used to close the door. A lowered lintel consists of one

Figure 2.6. Wall features: (a) partially blocked T-shaped door, south wall of Room 38, Chetro Ketl; scale is 30 cm; (b) full length door, south wall of Room 243, Pueblo Bonito; door is 70 cm wide; (c) raised-sill door, east wall of Room 139, Pueblo Alto; shoring prevents collapse of rotted lintels; scale is 30 cm; (d) detail of door shown in c; note secondary jamb and lintel; scale is 25 cm; (e) corner door, northeast corner of Room 225, Pueblo Bonito; door is 55 cm wide; (f) vent, south wall of Room 139, Pueblo Alto; scale is 30 cm; (g) niche, north wall of Room 147, Pueblo Alto; scale is 30 cm.

or two lintel poles set a few inches below the real lintel on the "reverse" side of the door (opposite the projection of the sill slab). Secondary jambs slope down from the lowered lintel to the center of the sill slab. Since the slab-and-collar arrangement can only be operated from one side of the door, and since the sill projection pointed toward the same side of the door, the direction of the door can be defined as opening into the room on the reverse side of the projecting sill. Almost always, these doors open into small interior rooms (storerooms?). Often, low post steps or toeholds in walls are provided to allow easier access. Judd describes this type of door in earlier rooms at Pueblo Bonito as being basically rectangular, but plastered to a more-or-less oval shape (1964: 27,59). The shape of these small doors may have changed over time: earlier doors seem to have sides that slant inwards at the top (i.e., the lintel span is less than the sill width), while later doors seem to have parallel sides (lintel span equals sill width) (Judd 1964:164). Whatever their function, it seems likely that smaller doors were used when secure, temporary closure was required.

Larger doors with the sill at or just above floor level are less common than small doors. More are found in later construction (e.g., the east end of Pueblo Bonito and in Pueblo del Arroyo) than in the older parts of Pueblo Bonito and other earlier buildings. These doors are identical to small doors, except in height. While the height of the lintel above the floor is similar between the two types of doors, the sill height of the larger door is much lower, usually only a few centimeters above the floor. These doors in the east end of Pueblo Bonito began on the wall foundation, but were later modified by raising the sill slightly (Judd 1964:163). Large doors at Pueblo del Arroyo are in excess of 1.7 m in height.

T-shaped doorways, familiar features in the Southwest, have been the subject of a considerable literature (see Love 1974) which will not be summarized here. T-shaped doorways at Pueblo Bonito (Judd 1964:28) and most other Chacoan buildings open into the plaza or onto terraces formed on the roofs of elevated round rooms. These doors are large enough to walk through easily. Sills are generally at or just above floor level.

Corner doorways, a very rare but very famous type of wall opening, con-nect two rooms on the same story through the intersection of two walls. This is a fairly unlikely construction that could not have done much for the structural stability of the walls. Only seven such doors are known from Pueblo Bonito, all late and in the eastern part of the site. There are three at Chetro Ketl in the earlier portion of that structure. One more survives at Pueblo Pintado and three in the northeast portion of Aztec.

Most of these doors connect one interior room with another. In two second-story interior rooms at Pueblo Bonito, there are regular doors in nearly every wall, but these are supplemented by multiple corner doors. This excessive connectedness defies easy explanation. In the east wing of Pueblo Bonito, it is almost impossible not to get there from here.

Closing doors. Slab closure of small raised-sill doorways has been described. An alternate method for closing doors was to secure a reed mat at the top of the door (Reiter 1933). Presumably, blankets or hides could have been hung in the same way or from poles set across the door opening for this purpose. The unrolled mat closed the door.

Dry wall masonry was a long-term, but not permanent, closure. Doors temporarily closed with dry masonry were common at Hopi and Zuni (Mindeleff (1891:190). Mindeleff indicates that some of these temporary doors were laid up in mortar and plastered and then dis-manteled when the owner desired to reopen the door. This is significant since many of the doors and windows of Chacoan buildings were closed with finished masonry laid up in mortar. It seems likely that most of these were intended to be closed permanently, a situation discussed in the sections on Chetro Ketl and Pueblo Bonito in Chapter 4.

In some early historic pueblos

...a doorway on the ground is always provided in building a house; it was left merely for convenience of passing in and out during construction and was built up before the walls were com-pleted (Mindeleff 1891:182).

This may not explain the blocked doorways at Pueblo Bonito and Chetro Ketl, how-ever, since these doors had been com-pleted to the lintels prior to closure.

## Vents

Small, nearly square openings set high in walls near room corners are usually called vents, since these openings are too high (usually 1.8 m or more above floor level) and too small (usually 30 to 50 cm square) to be doors (Figure 2.6f). Vents usually lack sill slabs and have either wood or stone lintels. In most Chacoan buildings, vents are paired (i.e., two in each wall) in the long walls of the room (opening from the plaza or plaza-facing wall to the exterior). Most vent systems thus run across the short axis of the building.

Vents pierce exterior walls which are otherwise unbroken. At Kin Kletso, vents appear only in exterior (or originally exterior) walls (Vivian and Mathews 1965:42). Judd (1964:29) noted that vents in second-story walls were larger than vents in first-story walls; however, this does not seem to be the rule at other structures.

Two unusual (and unique) vent forms should be mentioned. The first is an "oblique" vent running from an upper story to a lower story at Pueblo del Arroyo (Judd 1959:40). This appears to be similar to a common type of vent at Zuni (Mindeleff 1891:207) which is rare or absent at other Chacoan sites. The second, a corner vent, much like a corner doorway, was found at Chetro Ketl.

Air flow depends on the location and type of inlets and outlets, but the location of the inlet and the relative size of the outlet are the two most important factors. The greatest volume of air is moved when inlet and outlet size are equal. Of course, the greater this size is, the greater the volume of air circulated, but, given an inlet size, the optimum outlet size is the same. Maximum air speed (an important aspect of cooling for human occupation) is achieved when the inlet is smaller than the outlet, or when the inlets and outlets are aligned (a characteristic of Chacoan vents).

While investigating the ventilation system at Chetro Ketl, Reiter attempted an experiment. He built a pine fire in a roofed room at (Reiter 1933). There were no openings in the roof, but a door was located in each wall. Doors were alternately blocked with no effect on the smoke's progress. "The smoke rose to the ceiling and completely filled the room to just below the tops of the doorways, then went out through them" (Reiter 1933:20-21). Vents, placed higher in the wall than any door lintels, might have functioned to remove smoke before it filled the room to the door level. The unusually high Chacoan ceilings might thus be a design feature for the removal of smoke trapped above the "living" level in rooms without openings in the ceiling (specifically interior rooms).

Arguing against ventilation systems is the rigid pattern of vent placement in Chacoan building. Particularly in later building (after 1050) every room has nearly identical vents in the upper corners of each long wall. This pattern is repeated regardless of story (vent systems will give different flow patterns on different stories) or orientation (vents run perpendicularly from the plaza regardless of the orientation of the building). Nor are the systems designed to accommodate siting: the typical pattern is repeated in structures located on top of the mesa and those built a few meters in front of the high canyon wall. It is evident that vent systems were not designed for specific placements, and probably not for specific room functions.

## Finishing

After the masonry structure was built and roofed, the exterior was plastered with mud. Plaster covered the fine stonework of the facing, but it also preserved it from its greatest enemy, rain. Mud plaster could be easily reapplied after a rain, while rain damage to the mortar of the wall was less easily repaired.

Room interiors were finished as befit their functions. Plaza-facing (living?) rooms were plastered and often whitened; most rear and interior (storage?) rooms were not. Some rooms were probably decorated with murals or simple bichrome dados. Only a few decorated rooms have survived, and these are often considered ceremonial. The practice was probably common in the domestic rooms as well.

## FLOORS AND ROOFS

### Ground Floors

The construction of ground floors varies considerably. Some floors were bare soil, tamped down through use. Others were leveled (with building debris or sand) then covered with a layer of sand or with mud plaster. Very rarely, sandstone slabs were used as flagstone flooring (e.g., Room 83 at Pueblo Bonito).

Sand and mud floors are the most frequent ground floor types. They may reflect different room functions: sand floors (usually found in rooms with unplastered walls) suggesting storage functions, and mud-plastered floors (usually in exterior rooms with plastered walls) suggesting a living room. Floor features such as firepits and mealing bins (see Chapter 3) are much more frequently found on plastered floors.

Construction of a plastered floor probably consisted of spreading mud plaster over the sand fill and, after partial drying, buffing with a stone to compact the surface. The mud seems to have been more like the wall plaster than the mortar. A slightly wetter, more plastic consistency was undoubtedly required for flooring than for wall plastering, since a stiff mud would not spread well on a sand or fill base.

### Roofs on Rectangular Rooms

The earth-covered, viga and latilla roof is a hallmark of Pueblo architecture (Figure 2.2). Prehistoric examples of this type of roof are limited to sheltered sites -- cliff dwellings -- or the massively walled and timbered open Chacoan sites. Flat roofs seem to have been employed with all rectangular, load-bearing wall construction in the Anasazi area, but any conclusions concerning their ubiquity should be tempered by the almost insurmountable problem of differential preservation.

Chacoan roofing is remarkable for its massiveness and workmanship. Prodigal timbering is in part a function of the relatively large size of Chacoan rooms, the longer spans and heavier dead loads to support. Workmanship is certainly impressive in Chaco roofs, but it is evidenced mainly in details which have not been preserved in other open sites. We cannot compare the workmanship of Chaco roofs to the vast majority of non-Chaco roofs, because in almost all cases, the latter have not survived.

When the highest course of masonry below the primaries was finished (rarely including an intramural beam or wall plate to distribute the load of the roof), either of two techniques was used for seating the beams: most often, the primaries were simply placed across the open room, and the masonry continued up around their ends; less frequently, walls were built up leaving rectangular openings, into which the primaries would later be set. After the round primaries were placed into the square holes, the surrounding voids were filled with heavily chinked masonry. Beams were

occasionally surrounded by a thin layer of juniper bark, perhaps, to prevent the ponderosa from rotting through contact with the moist wall interior. In rare instances, one free end of a beam was supported by a post or a masonry pier (Judd 1964:96).

Primaries which ran through walls were generally left untrimmed in early Pueblo Bonito (Judd 1964:26), projecting outward from the wall (Stage I, Chapter 4). Most beams in the later portions of Pueblo Bonito and other Chaco sites are cut flush with the wall face which Judd and others interpret as an indication that the beams were measured and cut prior to installation.

Primary beams, which averaged about 22 m in diameter, are the main load-bearing members of roofs. In almost all cases, these beams run across the short axis of the room, with an average span of about 2.6 m. A typical beam pattern divides the room into thirds. The average Chacoan room was twice as long as it was wide, and a single primary running the length of the room would be about as long as the combined length of two primaries across the width. Given a constant beam width, the two shorter beams would be stronger than a single long beam. The span of the secondaries would be less with the beam running lengthwise, but only slightly less.

While a two-primary pattern is common in many later Chacoan rooms, early rooms at Pueblo Bonito (Stage I, Chapter 4) frequently have more, closer spaced primaries. A few of the intact ceilings at later parts of Pueblo Bonito and Chetro Ketl have far more primaries than the typical two -- perhaps this is way they survived intact.

Multiple units of two or three primaries placed side-by-side are not uncommon, possibly structurally equivalent to thicker single beams. At Pueblo del Arroyo, where paired primaries are relatively common, the beams seem to be somewhat thinner (about 15 cm diameter) than average.

At right angles to the primaries were the thinner secondary beams. These beams were finished with much the same care as the larger primaries, but their ends were less frequently cut square. The secondaries were often set in alternate pairs, with the beams lashed together.

Secondaries, in length corresponding to primary spacing, were about 1.7 m long and generally about 5 to 10 cm in diameter (Dean and Warren 1983:Table V:12; Judd 1959:13, 1964:163; Morris 1928:306; Reiter 1933:15). Wood of this small diameter has a more pronounced taper than larger beams. To equalize this taper, secondaries were often paired with the butt ends in opposite directions. These paired units (or in some roofs, individual secondaries) generally spanned a single pair of primaries, interdigitating with secondaries spanning adjacent primaries. In very small rooms, secondaries occasionally spanned the entire length of the room.

Secondary beams were usually lashed to each other and presumably to the primaries (Holsinger 1901:22). This prevented jarring the secondaries while laying the closing materials above them. In very small rooms, closely spaced secondary-sized beams directly supported the flooring materials. In effect, primaries were eliminated.

Secondaries spanning the distance from the wall to the first primary were socketed in the wall. Two methods of secondary socketing were observed: one, the wall was built up around the secondaries, which were seated only as deep as the facing (i.e., secondaries did not continue into the core or through the wall); and two, and probably more frequent in occurrence, a shallow inset band was built into the wall providing a ledge for seating the secondary beams. After the beams were placed, the ledge was brought flush to the wall face by building around the beam sockets with fairly small stones.

Not all roofs had secondary beams. Several materials were used in place of secondaries. In early construction at Pueblo Bonito, secondaries were replaced by brush, reeds, grass, cornstalks, etc., laid directly upon closely spaced primaries (Judd 1964:16, 59). In some roofs at Chetro Ketl, Kin Kletso, and Pueblo Bonito, carefully finished willow rod mats were placed directly on the primaries. Boards or planks of shaped and smoothed wood, 10 - 20 cm wide and 3 cm thick, were used between primaries and floor materials at Pueblo Bonito (Judd 1964:82), Peñasco Blanco (Mindeleff 1891-150), and Chetro Ketl. Planks were not wooden floors; the planks supported the standard earthen floor and were not visible from the room above.

Above the secondaries the closing material was laid, usually several layers of ca. 1 m x 5 cm splints or shakes (thin strips of wood), each layer at right angles to the next. Rush mats occasionally replaced the juniper splints. Laid on the secondaries, the mats were visible from the room below. The layers were often separated by thin layers of mud, which, when dry, sealed the roof. Above the last of these layers were several centimeters of loose soil.

Since the roof was frequently the floor of a room above, its timbers had to support considerable loads of stored goods and occupants in addition to the weight of the closing material, mud, and loose clayey sand. Several roofs are known that supported masses of fallen rubble and wind blown fill for many years -- probably for centuries -- and remain intact.

Roof construction was not a difficult or time-consuming task. The major effort was expended in procuring and processing the materials involved: cutting and transporting the beams, and then smoothing and cutting them to the required length. Splitting shakes with stone or wood wedges was a difficult task; the production of rush mats, willow rods, and boards was more laborious still.

Roof support posts, while common in Old Bonito (Judd 1964:58) and the early parts of Pueblo Alto and Una Vida, do not appear with any frequency in the later building. Presumably, the few later roof supports are repairs, but the earlier use of roof supports is surprisingly consistent and seems to be a standard practice.

Sullivan (1974) proposed that Pueblo roof type should reflect the original function of the room that roof shelters. Insofar as room function is reflected in room size, this may be true; however, in a planned multistoried structure the roof type will probably reflect the function of the room above, which uses that roof as a floor. It seems likely that a principle cause of variation in size and spacing of primaries and secondaries might be the builder's estimate of live load. Live load reflects the activities, fixtures, and stored materials the builder envisioned for the room above the roof.

We have no intact, prehistoric exterior roofs, and it is unlikely that any of the intact interior ceiling/floors originally functioned as exterior roofs. Exterior roofs probably were very similar to existing interior roofs (with the addition of facilities for drainage) and probably functioned as activity surfaces, as they do in historic pueblos.

Openings through interior roofs/floors were usually rectangular hatchways, often located in the southeast corner of the room (Judd 1964:83). Very few of these features have been preserved in tact. Examples at Chaco are limited to Pueblo Bonito, Chetro Ketl, and Pueblo del Arroyo:

> The hatchway in the southeast corner measured 25" x 27"; its western end was formed by the eastern main beam, 37" from the wall, and its northern margin by one of the ceiling poles [secondaries]. On the east, the opening was bordered by two pine poles about 4 feet long (Judd 1959: 17).

Apparently, no framework surrounded this opening. Neither framework nor coping is known from other hatchways at Chetro Ketl.

## Roofs on Round Rooms

The round room and its square enclosure had a flat roof, which often served as a terrace for the second-story rooms behind. While all authorities agree that the exterior roof was flat, the structure and substructure of this flat roof was and is a matter of great disagreement. Judd (1964) and Morris (1921) both contend that the normal method of supporting the roof was a corbelled framework of beams, usually referred to as cribbing (Figure 2.7); Reiter (1946) is equally emphatic that the roof was supported only by horizontal beams running across the room at the top of the walls.

Round rooms are discussed in some detail in Chapter 3, but a brief summary of some of these features is necessary here to understand the roofing options. Almost all round rooms had a raised masonry platform running around the base of the wall; this platform is traditionally called a bench. On the bench were two features of significance to the question of roofing: pilasters and wainscotting. Pilasters are low masonry or masonry-and-timber piers, at equal intervals on the bench surface. There were usually six or eight pilasters. Bench backing is jacal or wickerwork rising from the rear of the bench (for more detail, see Chapter 3).

In a preserved example of a corbelled roof (Kiva L at Pueblo Bonito), the first series of beams in the corbelled framework rests directly upon the low pilasters. These form a hexagon, upon which rests a slightly smaller hexagonal framework running from mid-point to mid-point of the lower beams. Upon the second layer rests a slightly smaller third, and upon the third a slightly smaller fourth and so on until the roof

level is reached. A level roof covers the corbelled dome. The Kiva L roof required at least 190 timbers.

Judd considered the corbelled or cribbed roof standard in Chacoan round rooms. Holsinger (1901) described what is probably another fully corbelled roof at Pueblo Bonito. Miller (1937) noted round rooms at Chetro Ketl (Kiva G-1) and Kin Kletso (Kiva B) that had only the first series of beams resting horizontally on the horizontal log pilasters when excavated. Shiner (1961) tested a very large subterranean round room at the Talus Unit, which had five tiers of beams in place. There is certainly evidence for corbelled roofs at Chaco. Reiter, however, believed that corbelling was the exception rather than the rule (1946). The main evidence against the corbelled roof involves the bench, the pilasters, and the bench backing.

First, a corbelled roof rising directly from the low pilasters on the bench would completely obscure the bench surface, the bench backing (whatever its purpose), and the wall of the round room itself. Both the bench surface and the room wall were often found to be plastered (and replastered), suggesting that they were both visible and accessible. Further, Reiter (1946:85) noted that few of the horizontal beams in masonry-and-timber pilasters showed the indentations that would have been inevitable if they had supported a heavy corbelled framework. These are telling arguments, since bench backing, plastered benches, and beam pilasters are almost standard in Chacoan round rooms.

Arguing against the flat, free-span roof that Reiter proposes is the length of the span itself. Chaco round rooms ranged from about 4.7 to 9.3 m in diameter, with a mean value of about 7 m. Reiter suggested a flat roof supported on two primary beams, each running alongside the probable hatch entry and therefore only slightly shorter than the maximum diameter, or about 7 m. This is more than twice the usual span of beams in rectangular rooms. Could this span have been routinely roofed by the Chaco Anasazi?

Evidence from Great Kiva construction suggests that it could. Seven meters is slightly less than the span between the four posts or piers of a Great Kiva, which averages about 8 m; therefore, this span was quite possible for Chacoan building technology.

A flat roof would require four to six primary beams of about 30 cm in diameter, and 50 to 60 secondary beams of 10-15 cm in diameter. This is less than

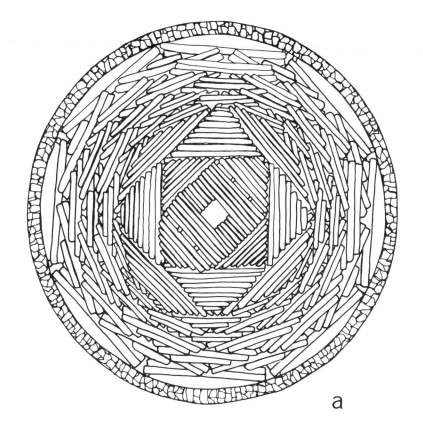

a

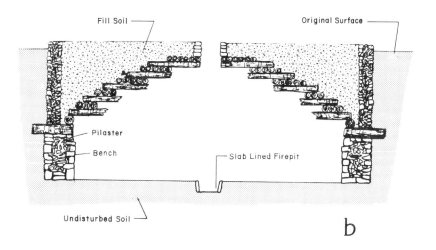

b

Figure 2.7.   Dome roof.   (a) plan; (b) cross section.

half the timber required for a corbelled roof of comparable diameter. In treeless Chaco, a substantial savings in timber was doubtlessly important.

Corbelling was a very expensive way to achieve a domed interior ceiling. I suggest that wainscotting was another, less expensive way to achieve the same form. There is little evidence to suggest that it continued more than three quarters of a meter above the bench (see Figure 3.7), with the exception of one intriguing photo in Judd (1964:Plate 56). This backing was clearly over 2 m in height. It is possible that the backing around the circumference of the bench continued upward, in a sort of upside-down basket arrangement, meeting at an apex just below the flat roof. Plaster over the wickerwork or jacal would create a domed ceiling. While plausible, there is no direct evidence to support this reconstruction.

If the wainscotting in fact formed a dome roof, what then was the function of the pilasters? I suspect that they, indeed, supported horizontal beams or poles, but not a corbelled roof. In several round rooms only two or three layers of corbelling were found in place. It is possible that the remainder of the roof was prehistorically salvaged, but it seems odd that if a corbelled roof was being removed, these long beams would be left in place. I suggest that these beams, and beams like them in other Chacoan round rooms, were not the lower remnants of a corbelled roof, but were rather of a shelf-like structure (perhaps no more a shelf than the "bench" is a bench) similar to the "inter-pilaster shelves" at Kiva D, Lowry Ruin in south-western Colorado (Martin 1936).

The evidence is ambiguous; at best we can say that while some Chacoan round rooms definitely had corbelled roofs, some probably had free-span flat roofs. In my opinion, the flat roof was standard and the corbelled roof the exception, particularly in later building, with the dome form of the corbelled roof duplicated by the wainscotting.

## ARCHITECTURAL DETAILS

Several details of Chacoan construction, unusual or otherwise noteworthy, will be described here; some of the reasons for past interest in them will be discussed in the next section.

## Masonry Piers

Masonry piers or pillars were used only in a few, specialized contexts, the most famous being the colonnades at Chetro Ketl and at Bc 51 (Ferdon 1955). While these colonnades were probably roofed, it does not appear that they supported any second-story walls. The second major use of masonry piers is in the four roof supports of several Great Kivas (Vivian and Reiter 1960:90). Great Kiva roofs were incredibly massive, e.g., Earl Morris estimated the weight of the Great Kiva roof at Aztec at 95 tons (1921:127). Piers are also found rarely as free-standing supports for vigas. Examples would include Room 117 and 120 at Aztec (Morris 1928:333) and Room 308 at Pueblo Bonito (Judd 1964:96).

Earlier Great Kiva roofs (early 1000s) were supported on a beam-and-post framework with four pine posts, each up to 55 cm in diameter. These posts were seated on elaborate and massive footings in a masonry-lined pit, upon a buried stack of massive sandstone discs, each disc weighing up to 700 kgs.

The masonry pier was a later development, perhaps a response to the difficulty in obtaining 55 cm diameter, 6 m long pine posts. Perhaps an increasing familiarity with the properties of well coursed masonry allowed Chacoan builders to replace the log posts with more easily acquired stone. Great Kiva piers are unlike the solid masonry piers of the colonnades. Most Great Kiva pillars were a little over 75 cm square, with alternating courses of masonry and 7 to 10 cm diameter beams laid parallel to the roof or the load-bearing surface of the pier.

## Buttressing

There were at least two forms of structural buttressing at Chacoan sites. The first braced long exterior walls. Along the south wall of Pueblo del Arroyo, a series of masonry buttresses about 1.15 m long, 0.40 m wide, and 1.50 m tall supports the sagging wall (Judd 1959:96). Similar arrangements, but with the addition of a wall paralleling the wall being supported (creating a series of tiny "rooms"), can be seen along the south wall of Kin Kletso (Vivian and Mathews 1965:44, "Area 60"), along the south wall of Casa Chiquita, and along the west wall at Kin Bineola. This type of buttressing does not appear to have been over one story in height, although the buttressed walls were two and even three stories tall.

The second type of buttressing was limited to elevated round rooms enclosed in rectangular rooms (Figure 2.8). Frequently, beams were inserted or masonry buttress walls built between the rectangular enclosures and the cylindrical round room walls. In many instances (e.g., Kin Kletso, Pueblo Bonito, Chetro Ketl, Kin Bineola), the interior facing of the enclosure and the exterior facing of the cylinder are inferior in stone and workmanship to the exposed, exterior faces. At fairly close intervals, stones project to a height of 30 cm from both wall faces. Hewett suggests that these projecting stones were used to brace scaffolding (1936:102). Alternatively, these projecting stones may have been left for the bonding of masonry buttress walls built after the completion of the enclosure and the cylinder. Far more projections were provided than were used in tying buttress walls. Neither suggestion is compelling; the intended function of projecting stones is still unknown.

Typically, masonry buttress walls run perpendicularly from the center of one side of the enclosing room toward the center of the cylinder, paralleled by a second wall midway between the first wall and the corner of the enclosing room. This second wall would not, of course, run toward the center of the cylinder; furthermore, the second wall of the pair was not a particularly efficient buttress. A few examples (Kiva C, Pueblo del Arroyo) of buttress walls running from the corner of the enclosing room toward the center of the cylinder are known. Buttress walls are often better finished than the backs of the walls they abut.

Buttress beams were socketed in both walls. Beam buttresses at Chetro Ketl Kiva G run from one enclosure wall toward the center of the cylinder and perpendicularly from the enclosure wall to a near-tangent point on the circumference of the cylinder. The beams are at several heights.

## Filled Rooms

Frequently, lower floors of multi-storied rooms were filled with tamped earth, sand, or -- a possibly unrelated phenomenon -- trash. Earth-filled rooms are known, e.g., Kin Kletso (Vivian and Mathews 1965:Figure 15), Chetro Ketl Lekson 1983b; Reiter 1933:56), Pueblo

Bonito (Judd 1964), and other Chacoan sites.

Rubble or earth fill was often placed in the spaces between square enclosing rooms and elevated round rooms (Holsinger 1901:35, among others). Although Morris suggested that this type of fill was intended to save failing walls (1928:327), fill around rooms was probably part of the original design.

There are two practical reasons for filling the area between the enclosure and the round room. The first is structural: a cylindrical wall can be seen as a continuous "arch" in the horizontal plane. The fabric of the wall will resist inward force, but is less successful against outward forces. Domed and flat roofs created a substantial outward force on the round room walls; unless supported on the exterior, round room walls would probably fold outward like the petals of a flower, only louder.

A second possible reason for earth fill was insulation. Many elements of round room design (round shape, dome roof, etc.) suggest an effort to maintain a warm and comfortable environment in the room. Earth fill between the round room and its enclosure would aid materially in its insulation.

The deposition of trash in rooms may have little to do with the type of room filling discussed above. This type of room fill probably pertained less to the structural considerations than to a change in the function of the buildings themselves, a topic we will return to in Chapter 5.

## Use of Natural Features

Many Chacoan buildings are located at the base of sandstone cliffs. The cliff provided a sturdy rear wall for several smaller sites built on the talus, and supported more delicate walls than those in a completely free-standing structure. In most instances, the "talus pueblos" have collapsed completely, leaving beam sockets in the cliff face and surprisingly small rubble mounds. The small size of the mounds may reflect the amount of stone in the walls; talus pueblos needed substantially less stone than did the larger Chacoan structures. The few standing walls that were built against the cliffs evidence a great deal more mortar and considerably less stone than walls at open sites.

Pueblo Bonito, Kin Kletso, and Una Vida all have rooms or roomblocks built over large boulders, detached fragments of the cliff lying on the canyon bottom

a

b

c

Figure 2.8.   Round room buttressing: (a) beams, Kiva G, Chetro Ketl; (b) radial walls, Kiva D, Pueblo Bonito; (c) projecting stones, exterior wall of Kiva B, Kin Kletso.

prior to construction. The inclusion of these boulders in the ground plans of sites suggests that the location of sites and their orientation were, to some degree, inflexible. Alternately, Chacoan builders occasionally incorporated huge boulders as ground floor fill for upper story construction (see the Tower Kiva at Kin Kletso, Chapter 4).

Parts of two sites, Una Vida and Casa Chiquita, are built over sizable knolls. These portions of the two sites tower over lower areas, a situation suggesting that in some construction height was perhaps more important then the actual volume of enclosed space. Lower stories may have functioned more as a structural device to elevate the upper stories, i.e., to achieve a terraced section, than as designed interior space. While no more than speculation, this notion may account for the massed empty interior rooms (an infamous characteristic of Chacoan building addressed in Chapter 3).

## Ramadas and Portals

Light roofs supported on a timber frame, either free-standing ramadas or portals attached to buildings, occurred at Chaco (Figure 2.3). These types of structures were prominent in earlier sites at Chaco, and the presence or absence of ramadas and portals has some significance in the interpretation of the development of Chacoan building.

Free-standing ramadas would be indicated archaeologically by postholes, presumably in plazas or on roof terraces. Very few of these have been reported, but this may be a function of a lack of careful excavation in plazas.

A portal may be indicated by a series of four 20 cm diameter beams projecting 2.4 m into the plaza from the first-story floor of Room 3 at Pueblo Bonito (Judd 1974:95; Pepper 1920:7). Since beams at Pueblo Bonito rarely projected beyond the walls, these beams might be the roof of a portal or a balcony. A second possible portal on the terrace formed by the roofs of first-story round rooms is described at Pueblo Bonito, Chapter 4.

## Balconies

Archaeologically, the distinction between a second-story balcony and a portal is fine indeed. At Chaco, balconies are suggested by the evidence of cantilever beams and floor offsets along the second and third stories of the rear wall of Chetro Ketl (Lekson 1983b), parts of the rear wall at Pueblo Bonito (Hewett 1936:33, but see Judd 1964:34), and the north wall of Pueblo del Arroyo (Judd 1959:53). Jackson (1878) and Holsinger (1901) noted other possible balconies at Hungo Pavi and Peñasco Blanco.

Though our knowledge of Chacoan balconies is slim, it is interesting that all known examples are on north-facing walls. Perhaps this is not surprising; large Chacoan buildings are typically south-facing (Hayes 1981:Figure 39), and evidence of balconies would be found on the multistoried rear walls of these buildings, and not on the more reduced or single-story south face. However, the placement of balconies on the north walls obtains even at Pueblo del Arroyo, which faces east. While the function(s) of balconies was doubtless manifold, perhaps one function was to increase the usable space in the shadow of these tall north walls. At high noon on a summer day at Chaco, shade is scarce.

Balconies would also have served as building platforms for the upper stories of the tall exterior walls. This is self-evident. What is not so apparent is how the tall rear walls without balconies were constructed. Some sort of lashed scaffolding would have been required.

## Stairs

Stairs are of two types: steps into doorways and staircases. Many raised-sill doors were provided with rudimentary steps, e.g., the tops of low posts set in the floor a step away from the door, small toehold niches in the wall just below the sill, etc. Actual masonry steps were more rare and are usually only a modification of normal doorways in which steps are built up across the sill, and the lintel of the door is correspondingly raised above each step. Steps of this type occur in a corner doorway at Aztec (Morris 1928), and in large doorways at Pueblo del Arroyo (Rooms 41 and 52, Judd [1959]) and Pueblo Bonito (Judd 1964).

Staircases are stairs built on masonry ramps leading to a doorway or other opening (or, in exterior features, to pecked "stairways" on the cliff). These are very rare indeed. One of the best examples is in Room 44 at Pueblo del Arroyo (Judd 1959); another is in Room 112 at Pueblo Alto.

## Room-wide Platforms

At Pueblo Bonito, Pueblo del Arroyo, and Chetro Ketl, and in several of the exposed rooms at Pueblo Alto and Peñasco Blanco, there are series of secondary-sized beam sockets in the long walls of rooms. These sockets are oddly positioned, halfway between the primary beam sockets of the floor below and the ceiling above. In a few cases, the beams socketed into these wall features remain in place. They appear almost like half-story roof/floors extending across the width of the room. Judd called them "shelves"; I call them "room-wide platforms." Although they are wall features, room-wide platforms are more properly room fixtures (see Chapter 3), that is, not really part of the building structure.

# Chapter Three
# Form

Much has been written on the subject of planning in Chacoan building. Compared to most other Anasazi building, the units of Chacoan building are much larger, the scale of construction more massive. It seems intuitively obvious that more thought, more preparation, more administrative coordination -- in short, more planning -- were required to build Pueblo Bonito than to construct the ubiquitous five-room, rubble masonry house.

Although we may all agree there must have been qualitative as well as quantitative differences in the planning processes at large and small sites, there is a very real and in some respects fairly important disagreement as to how to conceptualize this difference. As a result, we have odd terms like "pre-planning" to describe Chacoan building. The five-room house was surely also the product of planning, for to suggest otherwise is to imply that the Anasazi built by reflex or instinct (Lekson 1981a).

It is useful to consider architectural form as the product of three roles: designer, builder, and user. The designer determines the form with a plan, verbal or graphic. The builder translates this plan into a physical structure; the user has to live with the results. In our society, it is common for these three roles to be filled by three individuals: an architect, a contractor, and a client; in simpler societies, these roles are often synonymous. If the three roles are united, the fit of form and function over time should be close. If they are separate, the fit will be less close (Alexander 1964).

In the five-room small house, the designer, the builder, and the user could easily have been the same person. Although other residents may have influenced the design of the structure, for most small site construction the three roles of designer, builder, and user were at least confined to the household, if not to one individual.

For the larger structures, this cannot have been the case. Typically, units of construction consisted of 20 or more rooms. Since complete sets of foundations were laid out and wall widths (and thus, the number of stories) were fixed prior to construction, we can be sure that the form of the structure did not somehow "evolve" during building. Someone had a plan rather firmly in mind before the first stone was laid. Since the scale of construction obviously exceeds the needs of the household, that someone assumed the role of designer for a group of users. It is in this way that the planning of Chacoan building differs most significantly from that at small sites. The larger the building, the more differentiation probably existed between the role of designer and of builder and user.

Let us add the element of permanence. At a small site, with a relatively plastic and mutable building technology, any change in perceived needs could be met almost immediately by modifications of form. The result is the repeated rebuildings and alterations that are a hallmark of the archaeology of small sites. In the massive Chacoan buildings, any but the most minor modification was a formidable task. Since several of these buildings were in use for perhaps 250 years, the original designs were almost literally imposed on several generations of users.

To discuss form and design in Chacoan building, we recognize a series of forms:

Room: four walls and a roof
Suite/module: patterned,
    interconnected rooms
Roomblock: a series of suites or
    rooms, built as a unit
Building: free-standing structure
    composed of one or more
    conjoined roomblocks
Settlement: the community of
    buildings

## ROOMS

The smallest formal unit in Chacoan building is the room, usually defined as a small roofed area in a building separated from other areas by walls or partitions. A room has walls and a roof. In most Chacoan building, walls and evidence of roofing are readily apparent. In smaller or less well preserved Anasazi building this is seldom true. Walls are often difficult to define, and a roof is frequently a matter for demonstration rather than observation. Even in Chacoan building, however, the subject is less simple than it might be. Balconies, ramadas, and terraces are included in this section, even though they are not rooms by the above definition. (After reading the descriptions that follow, the reader, if dissatisfied, can amend the Table of Contents.)

Another point of possible confusion -- particularly for those familiar with Southwestern archaeology -- is the use of the term "round room" for the structure traditionally referred to as a "kiva." I have abandoned the use of the term "kiva" except for highly specialized forms (Tower Kivas, Great Kivas) -- where new terminology would be tedious (e.g., Great Round Room) -- and in the case of specific named or numbered units, for example, Kiva G or the Court Kiva, both at Chetro Ketl. The argument for this usage is given below, in the section on round rooms.

### Rectangular Rooms

The majority of rooms in Chacoan buildings are above ground and have four corners. Not all these rooms are truly rectangular; for example, in buildings with curved plans, long walls in many rooms may be parallel arcs. In other cases, where construction meets at odd angles, corners are more or less than 90°. The three aspects of rectangular rooms -- size, proportion, and function -- will be discussed in this section.

### Size

The mean size of 1133 rooms at Chacoan buildings is 11.97 $m^2$ (sd= 8.03). This statistic really means very little, for it masks a great deal of temporal variation, and presents in one figure the several distinct size classes included in individual construction programs. Rooms vary in size with their distance from the plaza, thus room size will be discussed in terms of front, intermediate, and rear rows of ground floor rooms in single construction programs. Ground floor lengths and widths, measureable when upper stories have vanished, were usually repeated in upper stories; that is, upper story rooms were not appreciably different in size and shape from those below. Floor offsets/setbacks cause room size to increase slightly from lower to upper floor, but this increase is insignificant. Using ground floor data, Figure 3.1 shows the average floor areas of front, intermediate, and rear row rooms through time.

The area of rear row rooms is much less variable than that of front row rooms. In fact, the former varies little from an average area of about 12 $m^2$ through the entire two centuries of Chacoan building.

Intermediate rows of rooms seem to repeat either front or rear row room areas up to about 1075; after 1075 the intermediate row rooms seem nearer in size to the rear than the front rooms.

Front row room areas vary greatly, from 45 $m^2$ in the early 900s to only 10 $m^2$ in the early 1100s. There is a strong suggestion of a steady decrease in front row room size through time, particularly when the data noted as questionable or unique on Figure 3.1 are eliminated. It is also possible that beginning about 1060, there are two size classes of front row rooms: first, those tending toward floor areas identical to intermediate and rear row rooms, and second, those continuing the earlier distinction in size between front and rear rows.

Room area involves only length and width; the third dimension of room size is height, the distance from floor to ceiling. The average room height is about 2.40 m (sd=0.53, N=804, with 90% of the sample from Pueblo Bonito and Pueblo del Arroyo), but heights up to 4.28 m are known (at Pueblo Alto) and 3.0 m heights are common.

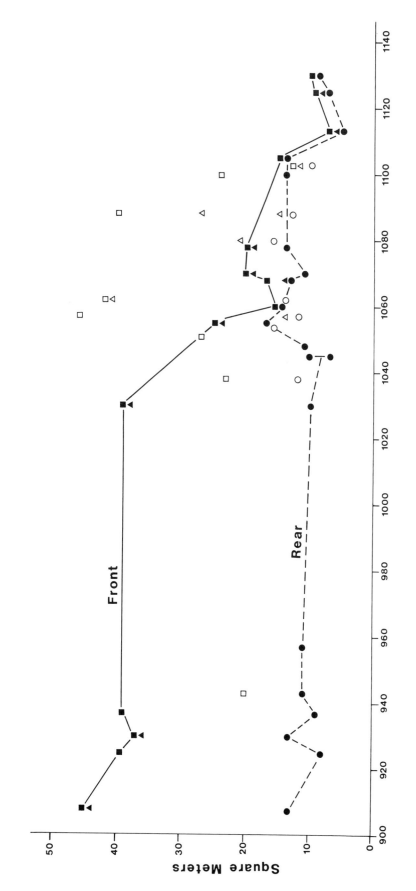

Figure 3.1.   Rectangular room mean floor areas.

Variation in room height was examined along three dimensions: first, with respect to distance from the plaza, perhaps reflecting room function; second, between stories, perhaps in response to structural requirements; and third, through time. There is a suggestion of slightly lower room height in rear row rooms in some construction programs at Pueblo Bonito when compared to front row rooms; however, this difference is not statistically significant. There is no evidence elsewhere (Chetro Ketl, Pueblo del Arroyo, Pueblo Alto, Kin Kletso) for significant variation from front to rear rooms in individual construction programs. The variation in room height does not seem to correspond to room function, insofar as room function is reflected by distance from the plaza.

Average room heights by story at eight buildings are given in Table 3.1. Room height decreases from the second to the fourth story, but first-story heights are less than those of the second. It is important to note that the range, and particularly the maximum heights, of first-story rooms is larger than that of any upper story. Lower average first-story heights may be the result of multiple, superimposed ground floors.

Analysis of room heights through time is limited to samples from Pueblo Bonito and Pueblo del Arroyo. Mean values for room heights for Pueblo Bonito I, II, and III-VI, and Pueblo del Arroyo IIA, which approximate a temporal sequence, are given in Table 3.2. This table shows no clear trends through time, although the earliest (Pueblo Bonito I) figures are generally lower than later ones given for the heights of each story. Since most of the Pueblo Bonito I rooms are one story, the ground floor bias may affect these figures.

Room height does not appear to vary with distance from the plaza, nor does it appear to vary through time. Height does seem to vary in the upper stories, decreasing from the second (and perhaps the first) story up.

## Proportions

In Chacoan building the long axis (length) of a room was almost always parallel to the plaza-facing wall of the roomblock. An index of proportion was calculated by dividing the width by the length. An index of 1.0 means the width equals the length, 0.50 means the width is one-half the length, etc. The mean index is 0.53 (sd=0.25, N=1133). Table 3.3 shows this index for a series of selected plaza-to-rear room suites.

While rear row rooms average about 0.50, with little variation, front row rooms range from indexes of 0.30 to 0.40 in early building to almost 1.00 in later building. There is clearly a trend towards squareness in front row rooms through time, although the small front row rooms at Pueblo Bonito I complicate this picture, as they are almost square. One or two long, narrow rooms (with very low indexes of proportion) are found at almost every excavated Chacoan site. These are discussed below as a separate class of rooms.

## Room Types

The function of a room refers to those activities which the room was designed to house. Defining functions of rooms in prehistoric buildings is an immensely difficult task. In Chacoan building the problem is complicated by the long life of the structures. Built over a period of two centuries, and occupied for at least a century after construction, the original (designed) functions of the rooms may be entirely obscured by architectural modifications required for later functions.

Archaeological approaches to room function usually involve the congruence of several lines of evidence, including artifacts, plant and animal remains, and the manner in which these were deposited in the rooms. This wide variety of information cannot be considered here. In the absence of these data, my discussion of rectangular room functions is limited to rather obvious classes of rooms with conspicuous fixed features: mealing bins, firepits, bins, etc., rooms with combinations of these features, and rooms with no fixed features (Figure 3.2).

Featureless rooms (storage rooms). A room with no fixed features or furniture is often called a storage room, that is, a room designed for housing goods, rather than activities. Featureless space in a room does not, of course, automatically indicate absence of activities in that space, but the equation of featureless space with storage is probably correct when applied to rooms at least one room removed from exterior access (i.e., interior rooms). With limited artificial lighting, interior rooms would probably not have been useful for many domestic activities. Interior rooms were no doubt used for sleeping, staying warm in the winter, and retreats (either from domestic routines or for religious seclusion or both); nonetheless, they probably generally functioned as storage facilities.

Table 3.1.  Mean room height by story.

| Story | Mean Height | SD | N |
|-------|-------------|------|-----|
| 1 | 2.33 m | 0.67 m | 345 |
| 2 | 2.53 | 0.67 | 277 |
| 3 | 2.33 | 0.21 | 130 |
| 4 | 2.17 | 0.26 | 23 |

Table 3.2.  Mean room height by story in a sequence of sites.

| Story | Pueblo Bonito I | Pueblo Bonito II | Pueblo Bonito Late | Pueblo del Arroyo |
|-------|-----------------|------------------|--------------------|-------------------|
| 1 | 2.18 m | 2.68 m | 2.61 m | 2.16 m |
| 2 | 2.25 | 2.38 | 2.86 | 2.48 |
| 3 | 2.23 | 2.86 | 2.43 | 2.43 |

Note:  N and sd are omitted for clarity.

Table 3.3.   Indexes (width/length) of proportion for selected suites.

| | Rear | Intermediate | | Front |
|---|------|--------------|------|-------|
| Pueblo Bonito I (920–935) | 0.53 | 0.38 | | 0.91 |
| Pueblo Alto IA, IB (1020–1040) | 0.29 | 0.30 | | 0.31 |
| Pueblo Alto III (1040–1060) | 0.50 | 0.47 | | 0.44 |
| Pueblo Bonito IIIA (1050–1060) | 0.56 | | | 0.51 |
| Pueblo Bonito IVA (1060–1075) | 0.45 | 0.48 | 0.52 | 0.75 |
| Pueblo del Arroyo I (1065–1075) | 0.66 | 0.77 | | 0.78 |
| Pueblo Bonito VIA (1075–1080) | 0.50 | 0.69 | 0.75 | 0.87 |
| Pueblo del Arroyo IIA (1095–1105) | 0.60 | 0.57 | 0.68 | 0.96 |

Note:  For all suites, Mean = 0.76, sd = 0.14, N = 52.

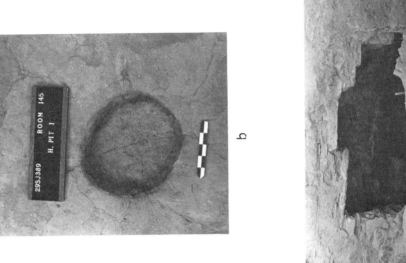

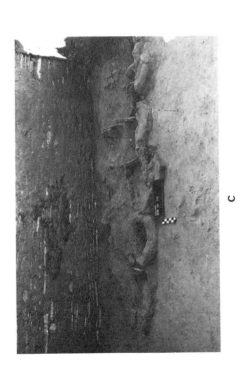

Figure 3.2. Rectangular room floor features (Pueblo Alto): (a) firepit, scale 30 cm; (b) heating pit, scale 25 cm; (c) mealing bins, scale 30 cm. (d) storage bin, scale 30 cm.

Storage is the shelter of goods, a definition that may include many potentially distinct functions. Domestic storage of food, either short or long term, is a function different from the storage of religious paraphernalia, or the storage of craft/goods, or building materials: all these can be documented in Chacoan storage rooms (e.g., at Pueblo Bonito) (Judd 1959, 1964). It is likely that a given room might be used for different storage functions at various times, yet the only positive architectural evidence for a storage function of any kind might be room-wide platforms (see "Rooms with room-wide platforms").

Rear row rooms in Chacoan building have usually been considered storage rooms. In buildings of the tenth and early eleventh centuries, paired small rear row rooms probably continued the formal storage function of earlier "tub" rooms of the ninth century (Truell 1983). These rooms connect directly to the large rooms in front of them, This pattern of front-to-back connection continues even after the paired rear rooms give way to single or even irregularly spaced rear row rooms in the middle and later 1000s. In the early 1000s, some rear rooms are added to existing structures (e.g., Chetro Ketl II, Pueblo Bonito II) and designed to connect laterally, but not frontally; that is, rear row rooms open into other rear row rooms, not into the front row of rooms. These rows of rear rooms continue the cross-wall spacing of the older rear rooms they adjoin, and are almost identical in size. Are they similar in function to the earlier rear row rooms?

Size and placement suggest that they are; however, at Pueblo Bonito and Chetro Ketl, the evidence informing our interpretation goes beyond size and location. At Pueblo Bonito, several (probably most) of the added rear row rooms in the north central part of the arc had single-pole racks or room-wide platform supports. The absence of this feature in the earlier rear row rooms suggests different functions.

At Chetro Ketl, at least two of the added rear row rooms have room-wide platforms as do at least two of the original rear row. More indicative of other functions is the presence of an unusual feature in the Chetro Ketl row. Each of the rooms in the added row at Chetro Ketl has a very large niche centrally located in the south wall; these niches are unique to this row of rooms. There is nothing comparable known from the earlier rear row rooms at Chetro Ketl, or any other Chacoan building. Again, the presence of a unique feature suggests different functions.

Connections differ radically between the old and new rear rows. If domestic activities were oriented toward the plaza (centered in large front row rectangular rooms), patterns of access suggest that the old rear row rooms were intended for shorter term storage (more frequent introduction or extraction) and the newer rear row rooms for longer term storage (less frequent introduction or extraction). While the repetition of older cross-wall patterns in the newer rear rooms suggests an extension of the existing suite associations into this row, the lateral connection of those rooms also suggests a community wide (supra-suite) function for the newer rooms. Room-wide platforms and niches suggest differing or added functions in newer rear rooms. I believe that these rooms continue the storage function of the earlier rear rooms, but with suprasuite, long-term dimensions.

These additions of multistoried rows of storage rooms underscores a prominent Chacoan design characteristic from the 1020s on, i.e., the addition of massed interior rooms with decreasing proportions of rooms adjacent to the exterior. The ratio of interior or rear row "storage" rooms to exterior, adjacent rooms in the 1020s-1050s building approaches 1:1, while from 1075 to 1105 that ratio is closer to 4:1.

After 1105, the ratio of rear and interior rooms to rooms with exterior adjacency was about 2:1, a decrease from the 1075-1105 ratio. It is unlikely that the rooms with exterior access after 1105 were functionally similar to their counterparts in earlier periods -- most importantly, the later rooms were considerably smaller (see the discussion of rectangular room size above).

The general pattern from 1075 on is one of greatly increased proportions of interior room space, presumably for storage. Unfortunately, we have almost no knowledge of what was stored in this added space. Pepper (1920) and Judd (1954) found perhaps half a dozen rooms at Pueblo Bonito which contained bulk materials, but probably 90% of the excavated "storage" rooms at Chaco were empty. A few interior and rear rooms are equipped with room-wide platforms, but the majority were simply large empty rooms. The generalized space created suggests that the goods stored varied from room to room and perhaps through time within individual rooms.

Long narrow featureless rooms. A number of rooms have very low indexes of proportion. Many of these are the result of partitioning a large square room for construction of a round room within it, and as such belong to the broad category of "incidental" rooms (discussed below).

Some long narrow rooms were clearly designed as such. These include two rear row rooms (Pueblo del Arroyo Room 9-10-11, and Chetro Ketl Room 1-4); one intermediate row room (Pueblo Alto Room 105); and two plaza-facing rooms (Chetro Ketl Room 81-105-76-32 and Pueblo Alto Room 131-135-141-143-160). The two rear row rooms were both long on the ground floor, but were subdivided on the upper story with cross walls supported on beams. The ground floors of both were originally featureless; both apparently had direct access to the exterior. The only clue to the function of these rooms is from Room 1-4 at Chetro Ketl which contained three or more extremely large timbers.

Timber storage could hardly have been the function of Room 105 at Pueblo Alto, an intermediate row room with no direct access to the exterior except through the roof. The room is unexcavated, and little more can be said about it.

The two remaining long narrow rooms (the "Gallery" or Room 131-135-141-143-160 at Pueblo Alto and the "Colonnade" or Room 81-105-176-32 at Chetro Ketl) are both plaza-facing units but of greatly different age and detail. The Pueblo Alto room, which consists of an extremely narrow, long passage along the front of a row of very large rooms, dates to 1020-1040. The Chetro Ketl Colonnade fronts a complex of elevated round rooms and a Tower Kiva, and postdates 1110. While the Gallery at Pueblo Alto had only a few doors, aligned with the doors of the larger rooms behind it, the Colonnade at Chetro Ketl consisted of a series of square piers or columns. The columns did not rise from the floor or plaza level; rather they were set upon a low wall. The Colonnade, did not exactly facilitate traffic, for a step over the base wall was required for movement from the plaza to the area behind the columns.

Rooms with room-wide platforms. In many rooms, several small beams (10-15 cm diameter) ran across the short axis of the room about 1.40 m (sd=0.27 m, N=19) above the floor, midway between floor and ceiling. The line of beams extended, on the average, about 1.40 m (sd=1.39; N=20) from the side wall toward the center of the room (see Figure 3.3). Smaller, secondary beams were laid at right angles to the larger beams; over these were all the closing materials, clay, etc., normally found in a regular roof or ceiling. Some rooms had these constructions in both ends, extending from the side walls into the center of the rooms and narrowing the standing area to a walkway from the front to the rear door (e.g., Room 62, Pueblo Bonito; Room 92, Chetro Ketl; Room 145, Pueblo Alto).

Judd identified these features as shelves (1954:45, 1964:29); DiPeso (1974:238) suggested that they were sleeping platforms. Depending upon which of these interpretations you wish to believe, rooms with platforms would have had either storage (shelves) or domestic (sleeping) functions. The only direct evidence came from Room 249 at Pueblo Bonito, where Judd (1964:107) found the remains of five macaws which had apparently occupied a platform in one end of that room. It would be wrong, of course, to infer that all platforms were parrot perches.

While room-wide platforms are not particularly common (fewer than 25 rooms in the canyon are known to have had them, although many more were undoubtedly present in both the unexcavated and excavated buildings), their interpretation is fairly important. If they are in fact storage shelves, then "...such shelves would measurably increase the storage capacity of a given room" (Judd 1964:29), particularly for items which could not be stacked above about 1 m. In rooms with two very deep shelves, the storage area (not volume) of a room would be almost doubled. If, on the other hand, the platforms are for sleeping (and it must be noted that the reasons for this interpretation were never made clear by DiPeso), the design of both fixed furniture and specific rooms for this function is unique in the Anasazi record. Whatever their function, room-wide platforms seem to be a peculiarly Chacoan item in the Anasazi area.

Room-wide platforms are particularly evident at the Chacoan outlier at Aztec (Morris 1928). In the east and north wings at Aztec, platforms are found in several plaza-facing rooms (e.g., Rooms 50, 51). Room 66 at Aztec, the plaza-facing room in a five-room suite, had a pair of room-wide platforms and no other features; passing through Room 66, one reached two rooms with large firepits and mealing bins -- features usually associated with domestic rooms; behind these were two more rooms totally devoid of furniture, both of which would usually be interpreted as storage rooms. Ceramics date these features to the Chacoan occupation of Aztec, rather than the Mesa Verde reoccupation. The room-wide platforms in Room 66, the plaza-facing room, seem oddly positioned for storage.

Figure 3.3.   Primary beams of a room-wide platform, Room 48, Chetro Ketl
(Reiter No. 1115.599, Chaco Center Archive No. 2176H).

At Chaco, most platforms are in rear rooms. Room-wide platforms first appear at Chaco about 1040 in the rear rooms of three- or four-room deep room suites (e.g., Chetro Ketl I and II). In later construction (Chetro Ketl IV, Pueblo Bonito IVA and VIB, Peñasco Blanco IIA, about 1050-1085), room-wide platforms are generally found only in rear row rooms. In the canyon, at least, room-wide platforms do not occur in post-1085 building.

The most notable exception to the rear row rule was Pueblo Bonito IIIA, a block of uniformly sized rooms, two rows deep and six rooms wide (built about 1050-1060 but subsequently heavily modified). In the rooms of Pueblo Bonito IIIA, room-wide platforms occur in at least three (and probably more) rooms of both the front and rear row. A few platforms in plaza-facing rooms were also found in Pueblo Bonito VIA and Pueblo Alto I.

There is one important similarity between the Aztec plaza-facing and Chaco Canyon rear-row room-wide platforms: in both cases, the platforms were in rooms which originally had direct exterior access. Even in the rear row rooms, platforms were usually in upper story rooms. More than three-quarters of the room-wide platforms at Chaco were in rooms with direct access to the exterior, either through a door or through the roof.

It would be difficult to use exterior access to argue for exclusivity in either sleeping or storage functions, although an argument might be made against long-term storage. Exterior access at least implies frequent introduction and retrieval of whatever had been left on the platform (sleepers or goods). Evidence is either absent or ambiguous. The function of room-wide platforms is moot, but very important.

Rooms with firepits. Firepits, presumably used for cooking, heating, and lighting, are often cited as evidence of domestic activities. Firepits have often been equated with a minimal domestic unit or family, a relationship which may overlook the considerable variability in these features (they range from relatively small, shallow hemispherical unlined pits to very large cylindrical or rectangular deep masonry-lined pits) and in their architectural contexts (firepits in large versus small rectangular rooms, firepits in round rooms). However, since firepits have been considered indicative

of a very broad class of domestic functions in the past, and since a detailed analysis of firepit form is beyond this study, all rectangular rooms with one or more firepits of any form or size are considered to be of a single class.

About 20% of the ground floor rooms at Pueblo del Arroyo and Pueblo Bonito had firepits, but less than 10% of the ground floor rooms at Kin Kletso and the excavated portion of Chetro Ketl were so equipped. In many of these rooms, firepits were not the only floor features; for example, all but one of the half dozen storage bins reported from Pueblo Bonito are located in rooms with firepits, and four of eight rooms with mealing bins (described below) also had a firepit. In several cases, rooms had more than one firepit or heating pit.

Ground floor firepits were located in rooms with direct access to the exterior -- specifically, in plaza-facing rooms. At Pueblo Bonito, rooms with firepits are found mainly in two areas: first, in an almost continuous arc of plaza-facing (or originally plaza-facing) rooms around the front of the older sections of the building (Pueblo Bonito I and IVA); and second, in the rooms immediately surrounding Kiva B (Pueblo Bonito VIIE). Of the dozen firepits not included in these two areas about half were located in exterior spaces (plazas, terraces, etc.); several others were in the lines of rooms enclosing and subdividing the plaza. Only three firepits were found in interior rooms.

Judd and many others have suggested that firepits were also located in upper story rooms with direct access to the exterior. Some second-story floors survived intact, and a few of these (two at Pueblo Bonito, two at Pueblo del Arroyo, and three at Aztec) had firepits (Judd 1959:9,51, 1964:93; Morris 1928:361, 367). The vast majority of upper story floors are gone. This is cause for archaeological grief, since the presence or absence of firepits in upper story rooms would drastically affect the number of inferred domestic units, and hence, the population estimates for each building (Judd 1964:93; Morris 1928:361,367; Windes 1981).

The implications of this problem are profound, at least for students of prehistoric architecture in remote desert canyons. Because of the importance of this problem, I will digress briefly and discuss various inconclusive attempts to determine if, in fact, upper story rooms had firepits.

It is not impossible to detect fragmented firepits in the debris of a fallen upper story. Very few are reported from Chacoan sites. We might assume that earlier excavators, treating room fill as overburden, simply failed to observe the evidence. Some earlier workers, clearly aware of the possibility of upper story firepits, carefully monitored the room fill (Reiter 1933; Vivian and Mathews 1965). Recent, more tightly controlled work at multistoried Chacoan buildings has failed to define upper story firepits (Cynthia Irwin-Williams, personal communication, 1978). There remain justifiable doubts concerning their recognition by earlier workers, and their absence in the published literature is probably not sufficient evidence to conclude that upper story firepits were not present.

A second line of evidence involves extrapolating from ground floor rooms with firepits to upper story rooms. Room size is recoverable in both ground story and upper story rooms. As noted above, intermediate and rear row rooms of all stories are, on the average, smaller than front row rooms in which most known firepits are located. It might be reasonable to conclude that features in the larger front row rooms were not repeated in the smaller rooms to the rear, regardless of story. However, not all front row rooms have firepits, and some of those that do (at Pueblo Bonito and elsewhere) are rather unusual in size and shape. The mean size for all ground floor rooms with firepits at Pueblo Bonito is 11.89 m$^2$ (sd=8.05 m$^2$; N=72), which is very close to the mean size for rear row rooms of all periods at Chaco (see Figure 3.1). This suggests, of course, that there is no reason on the basis of size alone to exclude any upper story rooms from those potentially having firepits.

Many of the rooms with firepits at Pueblo Bonito are "incidental" rooms (i.e., rooms built into the corners of the square enclosures around the elevated round rooms described below) and do not represent designed front row rooms. If "incidental" rooms are excluded, the average size of a room with a firepit at Pueblo Bonito increases to almost 17.66 m$^2$ (sd=8.73 m$^2$, N=22), a figure in general agreement with mean front-row room area from 1070 or 1075 on. Even with the elimination of "incidental" rooms with firepits, however, the picture is still unclear. Arguments could be made from the 17.66 m$^2$ figure both to support and deny the presence of upper story intermediate and rear row firepits, since after 1070 rooms of all rows are very similar in floor area.

A third approach involves wall niches, which remain visible in standing walls regardless of floor preservation. Niches, like firepits, are clustered in plaza-facing ground story rooms at Pueblo Bonito. Twenty-nine plaza-facing rooms with niches lack firepits; forty-three rooms with firepits lack niches. In fifteen rooms they co-occur. Fifteen rooms are about twice the number of rooms that would be expected to have both features if firepits and niches were randomly distributed with respect to each other in plaza-facing rooms. If the relationship observed in ground floor rooms holds for upper story rooms, there should be about four rooms with firepits for every three rooms with niches. At Pueblo Bonito, there are six upper story rooms with niches, and by extension, eight upper story rooms with firepits.

In summary, the evidence from published reports and that of the association of firepits with niches both suggest few upper story firepits, while the evidence of room size is ambiguous at best. I believe that some upper story rooms -- particularly second story rooms opening onto plaza-facing terraces -- might have had firepits, but that the majority of upper story rooms did not.

Rooms with mealing bins. Only eight rooms with mealing bins are known from excavations at Chaco (Pueblo del Arroyo, Rooms 41 and 55; Pueblo Bonito, Rooms 90, 222, and 291; Chetro Ketl, Room 35; Pueblo Alto, Rooms 103 and 110). The usual complement of bins in these rooms ranged from three to six, with Pueblo Bonito Room 90 being an exception with ten bins. Four of these rooms also had one or more fire or heating pits; four had none. One room, Room 35 at Chetro Ketl, may have had a room-wide platform at one end of the room, opposite four mealing bins. All but one of these rooms had evidence of direct access to the exterior, either through the wall or the roof, a fact which suggests that more mealing bins might have been located in upper story rooms of the middle and rear tiers of multistoried buildings. All these rooms probably postdate 1050, and several (at Chetro Ketl, Pueblo del Arroyo, and Pueblo Bonito) date as late as the 1100s.

Rooms with firepits, ventilators, and deflectors. These rooms are a subset of rectangular rooms with firepits, but some authors (notably Judd 1964) consider them entirely distinct, and probably ceremonial. Several rooms in this group are exceptional (e.g., Rooms 350 and 351 at Pueblo Bonito -- a pair of odd rectangular pit structures with corner ventilator shafts). In general, ventilators in other rooms are obviously later modifications of partially buried earlier rooms, allowing their continued use (e.g., Rooms 71, 315, 316, and 328 at Pueblo Bonito). The rooms are remnants of earlier building, which continued in use even though the plaza level rose well above the original roof level. At least two other rooms at Pueblo Bonito (Rooms 3a and 309), three rooms at Una Vida (Rooms 23, 60, 63) and perhaps two at Chetro Ketl (Rooms 38, 87) were equipped with less explicable ventilators and occasionally deflectors in front of their firepits. Are these rooms ceremonial chambers? This is possible, but I do not think it is a necessary explanation for the construction in later aboveground rooms of what, in earlier pithouses, was part of the essential furniture of domestic structures.

For example, Judd records Room 309 at Pueblo Bonito as an aboveground ceremonial chamber, with firepit, deflector, and ventilator, but a map of its features (Judd 1964:Figure 12) shows the floor littered with pits and bins, the very features most archaeologists believe are evidence of domestic use. Other rooms at Chetro Ketl and Una Vida also have the general appearance of domestic rooms with ventilators, perhaps without the plethora of bins and pits that characterized Room 309. If we ignore the ceremonial connotations of the ventilator and consider it as a functional construction, these rooms seem similar to other rooms with firepits, although the former have a more complex pattern of air flow. The system of ventilation serves much the same purpose in pithouse, kiva, or rectangular room. Rooms with firepits, ventilators, and deflectors fall in the same size range and are located in the same situations as other rectangular rooms with firepits only. In the absence of compelling evidence to the contrary, I consider these rooms architecturally the same as other rectangular rooms with firepits.

## Round Rooms

Round rooms at Chaco are usually called "kivas" -- a term that refers to any of a wide variety of round or rectangular rooms used by male ceremonial associations in the modern Pueblos. Kivas at modern Pueblos continue an architectural form dating back to the earliest Anasazi pithouses. When did the pithouse become a kiva? The usual answer is sometime in the 800s or 900s.

A great many pages have been filled with discussions of this problem, usually in terms of architectural form and detail, or through the analysis of activities taking place within the struc-

ture (absence of female activities, presence of male craft and ceremonial activities). A third approach, not often taken, concentrates less on architectural details and activities, and more on the architectural context of the room.

The pithouse was domestic, and presumably functioned on the domestic group level; that is, it was associated with one or more households. A modern kiva is supra-domestic, in that it is used by members of numerous households and, in fact, integrates a village. A simple index of the pithouse-to-kiva transition (if such a transition is definable as a boundary rather than a continuum) should then be found in the number of domestic groups per pithouse/kiva. Archaeologically, we can substitute the number of aboveground rooms for the number of domestic groups in this ratio.

In the past, archaeologists have divided Chacoan kivas into three groups: Great Kivas, Tower Kivas, and "clan kivas" (with some subdivision of this last, to be discussed below). My disagreement is with the usage of the designation "clan kivas," the term most often used to identify round rooms.

"Clan kivas" are smaller subterranean and aboveground single-story round rooms. At Pueblo Bonito, with a total of about 530 rooms, there were about 30 of the smaller round rooms built as part of the original structure (5-10 more were later built into existing square rooms). The ratio of "clan kivas" to rectangular rooms was about 1 to 18. However, not all rectangular rooms were habitations. As a general rule, we can assume that habitation was limited to the exterior rooms. Fewer than half of the rooms at Pueblo Bonito had direct access to the exterior. The ratio of "clan kivas" to those rooms is only 1 to 7.

In fact, only a small fraction of exterior rooms actually contained firepits, so the ratio of "clan kivas" to actual habitations was probably considerably less than 1 to 7, possibly about 1 to 3. With so few potential domestic units per "kiva," it is difficult to see what is being integrated at the village level. Is a "clan kiva" a kiva, or is it simply a pithouse built in stone? I suggest that the latter is correct, and "clan kivas" are in fact domestic rooms. The absence of some pithouse floor features should be not alarm us; obviously there were reorganizations of domestic architecture during the 900s and 1000s. Many archaeologists, I think, are aware of the unlikely implications of a pithouse-kiva transition in the 900s, but their use of the term "kiva" leads to some amazing interpretations of the archaeology of that period. One National Park Service sign suggests that the inhabitants of Chetro Ketl were unusually religious, because they had so many kivas. I offer only this example, but the nonsense pervades much of the archaeological and especially the ethnohistorical literature.

Smaller, round rooms more likely represent units of domestic architecture organizationally similar to other functionally specific domestic spaces. For this reason, I do not refer to the small circular rooms as "kivas," although I retain the terms Great Kiva and Tower Kiva. Hereafter, the more diminutive round rooms will be termed simply "round rooms" -- an unfortunate loss in color, perhaps, but an overdue recovery of precision in the use of the the term "kiva."

Great Kivas and Tower Kivas will be described below followed by more extensive discussion of two subdivisions of the former "clan kiva" group: Chacoan round rooms and small round rooms.

## Great Kivas

Great Kivas are clearly multihousehold in association. For example, Great Kivas A and Q, the last in use at Pueblo Bonito, had a total room count: Great Kiva ratio of about 265 to 1. Correcting for probable habitation rooms, this ratio is more like 50-100 to 1. This suggests that Great Kivas may be more relevant to the historical development of the village-integrating kiva than are the more numerous, small round rooms at Chacoan sites.

At their peak (about 1120) Chacoan Great Kivas were very large, round, semi-subterranean structures, containing a set of highly formalized interior features and furniture: a low masonry bench around the base of the wall, four wooden posts or masonry piers to support a square room frame, raised floor vaults running north-south between the posts or piers, a raised fire box and deflector, an antechamber on the plaza level north of the subterranean structure, and, frequently, peripheral rooms on the plaza surface surrounding the Great Kiva (Marshall et al. 1979; Vivian and Reiter 1960). In the tenth to twelfth centuries, there were at least 12 of these structures at Chaco:

Pueblo Bonito -- at least four, though probably no more than two were in use at one time.
Peñasco Blanco -- two in the plaza, and two outside the building.
Hungo Pavi -- one.
Una Vida -- one and probably two in the plaza.
Chetro Ketl -- one, plus the remodeled Court Kiva.

In addition there were at least three Great Kivas that were not associated with large buildings: Casa Rinconada, Kin Nahasbas, 29 SJ 1253 (in Fajada Gap, opposite Fajada Butte), and 29 SJ 1642 (below Shabik'eshchee). Others may exist in the plazas of Pueblo Bonito and Chetro Ketl, although additional Great Kivas elsewhere in the canyon are unlikely.

Great Kivas in Chaco Canyon represent a local form of a building type with a very long history and a very broad distribution. All Great Kivas share an organizational definition. All are substantially larger than the individual pithouses and surface rooms of the villages with which they are associated, and all are architecturally central to a settlement. Great Kivas at Chaco are best viewed in relation to their architectural centrality within the surrounding settlement. The "isolated" Great Kivas at Chaco are a terminological fiction; they cannot seriously be considered as isolated from the dense settlement in the canyon.

Reiter (1946) and DiPeso (1974) saw early Great Kivas as "community houses, i.e., public structures, communally built, for village-wide activities, gatherings, ceremonials, etc. In a Chacoan building, the Great Kiva was still the largest of numerous round structures. Presumably, much of the "community house" function of earlier Great Kivas remained in the Chacoan structures, but it is possible that more formally defined integrative functions were also housed. This is suggested by the number of rooms per Great Kiva at several structures.

It is difficult to determine the association of a Great Kiva with specific building programs; however, from an analysis of building events and Great Kivas at Pueblo Bonito, Chetro Ketl, Una Vida, Peñasco Blanco, and Hungo Pavi, it appears that a Great Kiva was constructed with each increment of about 150 rooms (mean=147, sd=27, N=8). This suggests an integrative function geared to increments of population (or, at least, structure) rather than a simple "community house" not necessarily tied to village population levels. It is interesting that

Pueblo Alto, with only 100 rooms in the original west, central, and east wings, did not have a Great Kiva.

Formalization of integrative functions in the Great Kiva may also be reflected in the impressive labor investments in their construction. Several details attest to heavy labor investment in these large structures: (1) up to 1,104 m$^3$ (Judd 1964:141, 216) of fill were removed for a single Great Kiva at Pueblo Bonito; (2) the circular masonry walls built in the excavated pits were apparently faced on both sides when only the interior actually required facing (Reiter 1946); (3) in several Great Kivas, the huge posts supporting the roofs were seated in faced masonry cylinders, upon a stack of several sandstone discs, each over 1 m in diameter and 15 cm thick, and weighing over 680 kgs (Hewett 1936; Vivian and Reiter 1960); (4) the roofing of the relatively small Great Kiva at Aztec, when reconstructed by Morris (1921), required fifty 20-30 cm x 3.7 m and eight hundred 1.8 m x 8 cm timbers. Similar material requirements were projected for a never-completed roof at Casa Rinconada (Vivian 1936).

Beyond these costs in materials and labor, additional wealth was expended on Great Kivas in the form of impressive deposits of beads, sealed in "wall crypts" or niches (Hewett 1936); the addition of presumably high value goods to the building fabric suggests a transfer of that high value to the Great Kiva structure itself, creating a value beyond that of a simple enclosure for community activities. The organization required for the prodigious labor investments in construction further implies that at least part of the structure's value reflected formalized integrative functions. In a limited sense Great Kivas can be considered public monumental building.

## Tower Kivas

The Tower Kivas are two- or three-story tall, round rooms in rectangular enclosures. The two best known Tower Kivas are outside Chaco Canyon: Kin Ya'a and Kin Klizhin (Marshall et al. 1979; Powers et al. 1983). Both of these structures consist of small roomblocks (10-30 ground floor rooms) with several elevated circular rooms toward the front of the building, and near the center of the rear wall, a three-story Tower Kiva.

In the canyon, similar towers at Kin Kletso (Kiva A) and Chetro Ketl (Kiva N)

stood at least two stories tall. Each had a T-shaped door on its lowest floor. (The tower at Kin Kletso was built over a large boulder, which raised the tower's lower story to the building's second-story level.) No floor features were found on the lower story of either tower. Neither had a bench on the first story, but a bench was evident on the second story of the Chetro Ketl tower. The heavily modified cylinder in and below Rooms 29-31 at Chetro Ketl may be the lower part of a third tower. Its interior diameter falls within the restricted span of 5.0 to 5.6 m of the Kin Ya'a, Kin Klizhin, Kin Kletso, and Chetro Ketl towers. All Tower Kivas appear to have been built after about 1110.

The function of Tower Kivas is a mystery. Simple explanations, which make Tower Kivas raised platforms for signaling or for observation in a basin-wide communication network are not convincing, since a similar height could have been obtained without the Tower Kiva. Marshall favors Fewkes' interpretation:

"...the kiva, in modern mythology, represents the underworld out of which the early races of men emerged. The tower kiva at Kin Ya'a may have been four kivas, one above another, to represent the underworlds in which the ancestors of the human race lived in succession before emerging into that in which we now dwell" (Marshall et al. 1979: 204).

## Chacoan Round Rooms

Thirty-five of 53 excavated small round rooms "clan kivas"), neither Tower nor Great Kivas, form a group long recognized as distinctively Chacoan:

The majority are equipped with a central fireplace, an underfloor ventilating system, a subfloor vault to the west of the fireplace, and an enclosing bench having 6 to 10 low pilasters and a shallow recess at the south. These several features unite to distinguish what I have termed the "Chaco-type" kiva (Judd 1964:177).

Judd described an assemblage of features (see Figures 3.4 and 3.6) that characterize the highly formalized Chacoan round rooms of the 1075-1130 period. To his list could also be added the elevation of the round room in a square, aboveground enclosure, and a wattlework or board wainscotting (or bench backing).

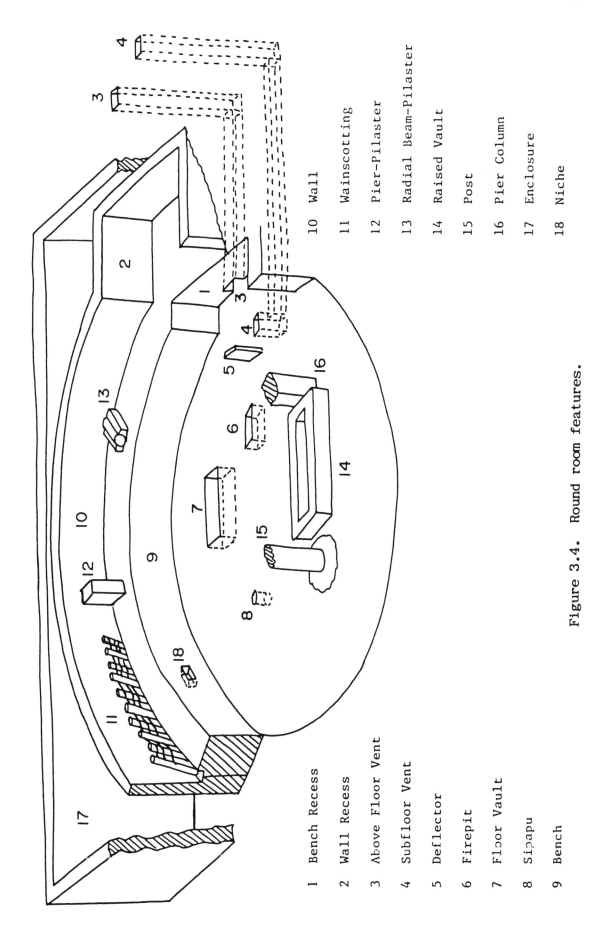

Figure 3.4. Round room features.

1  Bench Recess
2  Wall Recess
3  Above Floor Vent
4  Subfloor Vent
5  Deflector
6  Firepit
7  Floor Vault
8  Sipapu
9  Bench

10  Wall
11  Wainscotting
12  Pier-Pilaster
13  Radial Beam-Pilaster
14  Raised Vault
15  Post
16  Pier Column
17  Enclosure
18  Niche

The Archetype. Chacoan round rooms of the 1075-1130 period are so distinctive that the term "type" is entirely appropriate. As a type, however, they are not limited to Chaco. They form one of the few definable groups in Pueblo II and Pueblo III round rooms at Mesa Verde (McClellan 1969:131); they are documented as far south as Zuni (Hodge 1923); and various elements, such as the subfloor vault, range farther still. Rightly or wrongly, this type of round room is referred to Chaco wherever it or elements of it are found. Perhaps this is justified, since the Chacoan circular room is definitely associated with large-scale construction in the canyon. Small round rooms of various other forms (discussed below) are also found in the large buildings, but most and probably all of these are later additions to existing structures.

The later Chacoan round room was an aboveground structure, built in a square enclosure on the first- or (occasionally) second-story level of the building. The interior diameters of excavated examples appear tri-modal at 6.0-6.5 m, 7.5-8.0 m, and 8.5-9.0 m (see Figure 3.5). The inclusion of unexcavated, elevated (almost certainly Chacoan) round rooms suggests tri-modality is the product of sampling error (Figure 3.5). For combined excavated and unexcavated round rooms, the mean (7.08 m, sd=1.37 m, N=65) diameter is nearly coincident with the mode (about 7.25 m).

The insertion of a circle into a square created four empty corners; these were often crossed by masonry or beam buttresses supporting the rear of the exposed arc of the circular room. These corners were sometimes filled with trash, rubble, shale, or soil. Occasionally, they were left unobstructed and were used as incidental rooms (see below).

A consistent set of features, aligned north-south, occupied the south half of the floor. Off-set slightly to the south in the Chacoan round room was a deep circular or square firepit. This pit was usually masonry-lined. In front of the firepit was the opening of a subfloor ventilator shaft (see Figure 3.6). In a few rooms, between the ventilator opening and the firepit stood an upright slab, or a short, low and thin wall, called a deflector (Figure 3.4). It deflected the flow of air from the ventilator and reflected the heat and light of the firepit.

About three-quarters of Chacoan round rooms had floor vaults, or subfloor rectangular boxes west of the firepit. Because these vaults were frequently filled and plastered (occasionally over board covers), it is likely that the real proportion of round rooms with this feature is considerably higher than the three-quarters reported in the literature and notes. The function of these features is obscure. The board-covered cavity has suggested to some researchers that the vaults were "foot drums" or resonators for dancing, but since many were filled with sand, this seems unlikely.

Relatively few Chacoan round rooms had niches in the bench or wall, although for some reason Judd (1964) considered a large niche at the northern point of the bench standard. No elevated Chacoan round room had a "sipapu," the symbolic hole in the floor seen in many prehistoric pit structures and historic kivas.

A low masonry bench, ran around the entire circumference of the room, with a short recess (Figures 3.4 and 3.6) usually to the south. There is some evidence (at Pueblo Bonito) that there was a shelf over the recess, continuing the level of the bench and creating a very large niche. The width of the bench (mean=0.62 m, sd=21 m, N=37) varied with the diameter of the room; the larger the room diameter, the wider the bench (r=+0.7451, N=37), while the height, about 0.66 m tall (sd=0.18 m, N=37), did not vary with room size.

Built upon the bench were six or eight evenly spaced pilasters (Figures 3.4, 3.6, and 3.7). In Chacoan round rooms, these usually consisted of a short section of beam seated in the wall and laid horizontally on the bench, extending radially to the center-point of the room. The beam segment was often encased in a masonry box, and less frequently, a round cavity was carved out of the top of the beam to receive small caches of beads, etc. Three variations on this basic pattern are notable: in four rooms, the beams were of squared wood of about the same size as the beam-and-box unit; in two other rooms, pilasters consisted of three or four smaller beams placed side by side, again with a masonry box built around them; and in one other room (which Judd considered "foreign") two beam and box units were built one upon the other, to form a double height pilaster.

Rising from the back of the bench (in round rooms over 6.75 m in diameter, as discussed below), was wainscotting (also called bench backing or bench padding). This is one of the most peculiar features of the Chacoan round room, and one of the most mysterious. It consisted of wooden boards or upright posts supporting wattlework, running around the back of the bench between pilasters, and

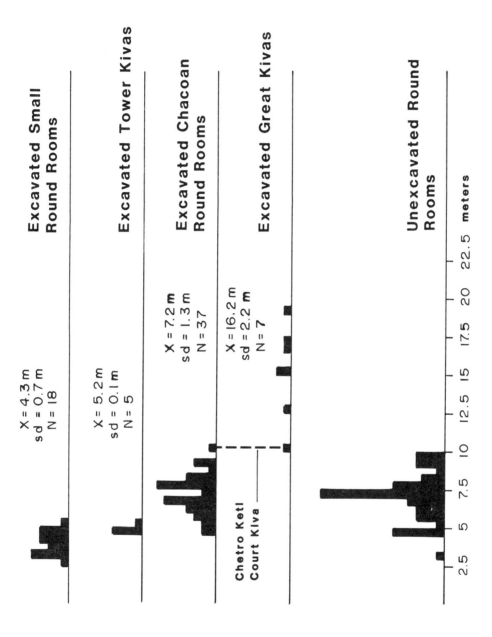

Figure 3.5.  Interior, above-bench diameters of round rooms.

Figure 3.6.  Round room floor and bench features: Upper:  Kiva B, Kin
Kletso (Vivian and Mathews 1965:Figure 26).  Kiva G-1,
Chetro Ketl (Courtesy Museum of New Mexico, Neg. No. 67126).

(a) ventilator opening (subfloor is partially collapsed in
Kiva B); (b) firepit; (c) floor vault; (d) bench recess;
(e) horizontal-log type pilaster; (f) wainscotting or bench
backing (Kiva G-1); (g) stub of masonry deflector-rubble
removed (Kiva G-1).

A.  Kiva 16, Pueblo Bonito (George Pepper, American
Museum of Natural History Neg. No. 176.)

B.  Kiya G-1, Chetro Ketl (Courtesy Museum of New
Mexico, Neg. No. 67049.)

Figure 3.7.  Pilaster and wainscotting details.

leaning outward from the wall slightly, perhaps 10° from the vertical (Figure 3.7). The space behind the boards or wattlework was packed with vegetal material, possibly with trash, while the front was plastered with mud. Although Reiter (1946:85) states that no backing taller than about 0.70 m was preserved, Judd (1964:181, Plate 56 lower) shows a post-and-wattle backing which was slightly over 2 m. Reiter also states that the top of the backing was finished, the mud plaster continuing across the vegetal packing and onto the vertical masonry wall behind it (Miller 1937; Reiter 1946). (See the discussion of wainscoting in "Roofs on round rooms" in Chapter 2.)

The development of the type. The best evidence of the development of the Chacoan round room of the 1075-1130 period is found in the northern plaza of Pueblo Bonito. The Pueblo Bonito series will be supplemented by examples from Chetro Ketl.

Early 900s round rooms are known only from Pueblo Bonito I. The earliest round rooms at Pueblo Bonito (the unnumbered structures below Rooms 83 and 324) were fully subterranean, and slightly under 5 m interior diameter. No details of floor features, roofing, etc., are known.

The next step in the development is not much better documented than the first. It is represented by the round pit structures fronting Pueblo Bonito I; round rooms that were, again, subterranean, but considerably larger (7.0 to 7.3 m in diameter) than their predecessors. Few construction details are known from these rooms, but Judd notes that they were "bowl-shaped," that is, the walls sloped outward above the bench, which was between 0.6 to 1.0 m high and close to 1.0 m wide. A larger pit structure, in the middle of the Pueblo Bonito I and II plaza, was about 9.75 m in diameter at the top of its walls, and about 3.7 m deep. This may have been a Great Kiva. Only the north half of this unit was exposed, but Judd noted:

An encircling bench, 25 inches high and averaging 34 inches wide was surfaced with sandstone slabs and plastered. In it, in the portion we exposed, were the remains of two pilasters, each consisting of small sandstone chips set in adobe mud and enclosing a 6-inch log that lay flat upon the slab surface, its butt end inserted into the masonry and packed about with shale...Here again, as with that under room 83, a 4-pilaster kiva is indicated (1964: 67).

There are no tree-ring dates from this room, but it certainly dates to the early 900s. In this second group of round rooms, we see two details foreshadowing later developments: first, the use of radial beam pilaster; and second, a diameter of slightly over 7 m.

Several of the 7 m diameter pit structures fronting Pueblo Bonito I were later modified or rebuilt. Modifications of these earlier rooms may represent the next step in the development of the Chacoan round room, intermediate between the pit structure and elevated round room. There are only nine excavated subterranean Chaco-type round rooms (Pueblo Bonito Kivas L, M, N, R and probably Kivas S and 67; Kivas F and G-5 at Chetro Ketl; and Kiva 10 at Pueblo Alto). They were built sometime between the early 900s and the late 1080s or 1090s; I suspect they date between 1030-1070. Of all nine, only Kiva G-5 at Chetro Ketl remains exposed.

Kiva G-5 dates to about 1035-1040. Because it largely escaped later rebuilding, it will be considered at some length. Kiva G-5's interior diameter of 7.9 m is only slightly larger than the Pueblo Bonito I pit structures; its depth of 3.7 m is close to that of the possible Great Kiva at Pueblo Bonito I. "The main wall was constructed with the inner face sloping slightly outward" (Miller 1937: 82), like the "bowl-shaped" pit structures of the early 900s at Pueblo Bonito.

The bench of Kiva G-5 had been razed; originally it measured about 0.8 m wide and 0.6 m in height. No pilasters survived intact on the bench, but a series of "three complete niches and part of a fourth," indicating six evenly spaced niches around the back of the bench (Miller 1937:83), undoubtedly represents mortises left for the insertion of the butt of the radial pilaster beams. An offset at the top of the wall indicated the beam seating of a flat roof. A deep circular masonry-lined firepit was the only floor feature found.

One of the features of subterranean Kiva G-5 may have presaged later elevated forms. This was a straight wall tangent to the exterior wall of the round room, exposed only for a short length. This wall appears to have been built into the Kiva G-5 excavation (Miller 1937:99). Does this represent an early subterranean form of the later elevated Chacoan round room enclosure? The depth of the wall was not determined, and it may not have continued to the floor level of the Kiva G-5. (Similar walls were noted for subterranean Kivas L and 2-C at Pueblo Bonito.)

Kiva G-5 and the other eight subterranean round rooms form a group that appears to be transitional between earlier (900s) and later (post-1070) round rooms. All these units were subterranean. Eight of these had six pilasters (the number of pilasters at Kiva 10, Pueblo Alto, is unknown), a transition between the rooms of the early 900s with four pilasters each and those postdating 1075 that had eight or ten. The walls of at least three (Kiva G-5 at Chetro Ketl, Kiva R at Pueblo Bonito, and Kiva 10 at Pueblo Alto) and probably all of these transitional units slope outwards, like earlier pit structure walls.

Interior diameters ranged from 6.7 to 8.0 m (except Kiva R, Pueblo Bonito, 9.3 m in diameter). Wainscotting would be expected in almost all later postdating (1075) round rooms of this diameter, but it was present in only half of this group. Only one floor vault was present, while at least three quarters of all later round rooms had floor vaults. All rooms (where data were available) had subfloor ventilators except Kiva G-5 at Chetro Ketl. In Kiva G-5, there was no evidence of an above-floor ventilator, which suggests that a subfloor unit in fact was present, but was not found.

The elevation of these rooms into rectangular enclosures and the more standardized use of floor vaults and wainscotting, produced the "classic" archetypical Chacoan round rooms.

## Large Chacoan Round Rooms, and the Court Kiva at Chetro Ketl

The very largest Chacoan round rooms (9.0 to 10.5 m diameter) represent an important subset of the group. The 9-10.5 m group (note secondary mode in Figure 3.5) includes both elevated and subterranean rooms. The two excavated examples (Kiva C at Pueblo del Arroyo and Kiva D at Pueblo Bonito) are identical to smaller Chacoan units in floor features, bench characteristics, etc. The other round rooms of this size are all subterranean, and -- with three exceptions -- unexcavated (five, all in the plaza of Pueblo Bonito: Kivas 67, P, O, an unnumbered earlier version of Kiva O, and the large unnumbered unit in the southeast plaza). The three excavated examples are Kiva R (Pueblo Bonito), and the Court Kiva (Chetro Ketl); a third, Kiva J at Talus Unit, was only partially excavated. Little is known about the interior features of Kiva J; Kiva R appears to have been a fairly typical Chaco-type structure, lacking the usual floor vault.

The Court Kiva at Chetro Ketl was originally built as a typically equipped Chacoan unit (Woods 1934). At 10.25 m in diameter, it was the largest of all Chacoan round rooms. It was subsequently converted to a Great Kiva by the addition of the characteristic Great Kiva features: masonry piers, fire box, raised vaults, etc. The largest Chaco-type round room thus became the smallest Great Kiva. Chacoan round rooms and Great Kivas are fairly distinct, but in the Court Kiva (and perhaps other very large Chacoan units) there is a suggestion of a continuum of size.

## Small Round Rooms

About 22 excavated round rooms from Pueblo Bonito, Pueblo del Arroyo, Chetro Ketl, Kin Kletso, and Pueblo Alto are neither Great, nor Tower, nor "Chaco-type." As shown in Figure 3.5, the average interior diameter of small round rooms (mean=4.3, sd=0.7 m, N=20) is considerably smaller than that of the Chacoan round rooms. There is little overlap between the two, hence the term "small round rooms." This category was defined originally by the absence of architectural details characteristic of Great-, Tower- and Chaco-type, and the presence of some features not found in the previously defined three types. The "key-hole" plan of many of these smaller rooms has been singled out as particularly suspicious. Judd (and many others) have interpreted these differences as indicating that many of the smaller units are "foreign" architectural intrusions into Chacoan buildings. While this interpretation may be correct, many of the small kivas have subfloor ventilators, bench recesses, and even floor vaults, features associated with Chacoan round rooms, although none of the smaller units has the full complement of features and details. It is also worthwhile to consider the wide variability in round rooms at smaller sites at Chaco Canyon (Truell 1983) when pronouncing on "foreign" intrusions.

Over half of the small round rooms are in fact round, and not "key-hole" in shape. Most are still rather different from Chacoan round rooms; only three have a bench recess, and only two of those three have subfloor ventilators. Neither of these two most-nearly-"Chaco-type" (Kiva J at Pueblo del Arroyo, Kiva U at Pueblo Bonito) has radial beam pilasters or floor vaults (but then no Chacoan round room of less than about 5.5 m in diameter has a floor vault). Both of these rooms are elevated in square enclosures which appear to have been built specifically for the purpose. They may actually represent the smallest Chacoan round rooms. (Because the analysis centers on the interpretation of unexcavated sites, diameter rather than architectural detail is the criterion for inclusion in the Chaco-type or small round room groups.)

Other small round rooms show a variety of forms including "keyhole" shapes with no pilasters (4), or with tall pier pilasters (2). All but two very late units (at Pueblo Alto) have subfloor ventilators: one has a south bench recess, and one has a floor vault.

All the excavated, elevated, small round rooms are later additions or modifications of existing buildings. There are no tree-ring dates from any of these small round rooms; however, all probably date to the early to mid-1100s.

Unexcavated round rooms of 5.0 m diameter or less are probably similar "small" rooms. Most of these unexcavated rooms also appear to be later additions to or modifications of existing buildings.

At least two, and probably more, of the few subterranean small round rooms are equally late. Units 2-E and sub-286 at Pueblo Bonito, despite tree-ring dates of 1058 and 1088, are probably quite late. The subterranean rooms at Chetro Ketl (Kivas A, B, D, and E) are associated with a very late plaza surface.

These subterranean rooms are less elaborate than their elevated counterparts, with the exception of Kiva 2-D and sub-162 at Pueblo Bonito. Kiva 2-D is an odd oval room with a subfloor vent, located next to two equally odd subterranean rectangular rooms with corner vent-fireplaces (Rooms 350, 351). Sub-162, an unnumbered round room beneath the later Chacoan round room (Kiva 162), is "keyhole" in shape, with a bench recess and four pier pilasters.

Some of these small round rooms may, in fact, be "foreign" architectural intrusions into Chacoan buildings, but the continued use of earlier Chacoan details such as bench recesses, and subfloor ventilators suggests that many, perhaps most, of the smaller round rooms represent a late expression of the Chacoan building tradition.

## Incidental Rooms

Rooms created more-or-less incidentally to more formal construction pro-

jects are often oddly shaped rooms at the conjunction of building programs built on different axes, or (more frequently) the subrectangular voids between round rooms and their square enclosures. These corners, often crossed by masonry or timber buttresses or packed with fill, occasionally accommodated oddly shaped rooms and passages (e.g., stairways from surrounding rectangular rooms to the terrace level atop the circular room), or even fully rectangular rooms. Several of these rooms at Pueblo Bonito (especially those around Kiva B) contained firepits, heating pits, bins, and -- perhaps -- mealing bins. Domestic furniture in incidental rooms may have been late introductions; Kiva B is a late addition to a roomblock, which probably postdates 1105.

Holsinger (1901) had great fun with incidental rooms; he described shapes ranging from diamonds to crescents, to very bizarre compound forms with partial incurving arcs, multiple corners, and reentrants. These were incidental rooms around much remodeled round rooms. As a product of formal design, this range of rooms shapes is misleading, as well as incidental to the basic formal vocabulary of round and rectangular rooms.

## Terraces

Terraces in front of rooms were on the roofs of lower story rooms. While terraced building is considered typical of Chacoan (and all Puebloan) building, very few buildings were consistently stepped up a story at each row's remove from the plaza. More frequently, the plaza-facing row of rooms was one story, and the rooms behind it were two stories from front to rear. Only the rear row of rooms along the back walls of buildings like Peñasco Blanco, Pueblo Bonito, Chetro Ketl, Hungo Pavi, and Wijiji stood one story higher than the intermediate two-story rooms; wings were not generally terraced beyond the first row of rooms. Large sections of Chetro Ketl, Pueblo del Arroyo, and the later (1110-1140) buildings were not terraced at all, in this sense. Although ramada or portal structures are likely, on first-story terraces, there is not much evidence beyond a hint of a line of ramadas on the first-story terrace of the east wing of Pueblo Bonito.

## ROOM SUITES

By tracing doorway connections, archaeologists can delimit sets of rooms that have been called suites (e.g., Rohn 1971). Suites are supposed to reflect the social units that occupied them: families, households, etc.

The extant walls of Chacoan ruins are an apparent advantage for the archaeologist; many walls stand high enough to show doors. Most Southwestern sites are not so well preserved. Unfortunately, there are two problems that more than offset the advantage of studying the standing walls.

First, in spite of all the standing walls, the record is actually rather fragmentary. Chacoan building was multi-storied. The reason that many first stories are standing is that the first-story walls were unusually wide, being designed to support second stories. We can see the first-story doorway connections, but the upper story connections and the very important hatchways through floors into those stories are usually absent. This discussion will be limited to ground floor plans.

Second, Chacoan buildings were not simply residences. Consider two of the earlier construction programs, Pueblo Bonito II and Chetro Ketl III. Both were additions to existing buildings, which had long rear walls unbroken by doors. At both buildings, a row of rooms was added to the blank rear wall. The new rooms were connected by doorways up and down the row; however, no doors were cut through the older rear wall into the original building. Both Pueblo Bonito II and Chetro Ketl III had 20 to 30 rooms, interconnected in line. Were these residential suites? I think not.

At Pueblo Bonito and Chetro Ketl, the older buildings comprised a series of gratifyingly well defined suites, each of about four or five rooms. The additions along the rear of these buildings cross-cut the older suites, but at the same time continued, almost exactly, the cross-wall spacing of the older building; the additions repeated exactly the size and arrangement of the older rear row of rooms. Surely, this alignment has implications for functions and use. The additions were community-wide construction projects, but the rooms themselves may have been allotted to the particular suites they backed.

These two construction programs, and others like them, discourage the simple equation of room suites with social units, e.g., households. The problem is one of detecting the less obvious non-suites, or conversely, discovering the interconnected rooms that might mean

something in terms of the social units occupying them.

Several construction programs of the early 900s were designed as series of suites, each consisting of two large rooms backed by a pair of smaller rooms (Figure 3.8). This pattern is identical to the suites of contemporaneous small sites (Truell 1983); the formal similarity suggests a functional parallel as well.

At small sites, the units comprised of one large room and two small rooms are almost certainly suites, and probably represent some form of household (Truell 1983). If these units were significant at small sites, then we may presume that large-room with paired small-room units were in fact units of some meaning in Chacoan building. This gives us a referent for the development of Chacoan room suites.

The paired-room unit remained in Chacoan building from the early 900s until the early 1000s (Figure 3.8). This is not say that it was the exclusive arrangement of interconnected rooms; simply that among the possibilities, the paired-room unit remained patterned and definable. After about 1030 (certainly by 1050), paired-room suites were no longer built.

During the middle 1000s, paired rear rooms were deleted from some suite arrangements (e.g., Pueblo Bonito III), while at other structures (e.g., Chetro Ketl IV and Pueblo del Arroyo I) the two small rooms of the rear row were replaced by a single room. This marks an important point of transition, from the paired room unit to the final Chacoan suite arrangement -- the linear suite (Figure 3.8). From about 1060 on, all patterned suites are linear in arrangement, with the cross walls aligned from the front row to the rear. In linear suites, rooms decrease in size from front to back. Since the rooms are all of equal length, changes in size obviously are the result of variations in width. In most cases, the front room was square, and rooms to the rear rectangular.

The importance and clarity of suites in building design seem to decrease through time. Pueblo Bonito of the 900s consisted almost entirely of a row of identical paired-room suites; later building might include only one or two linear suites in a building program of 35 ground floor rooms (e.g., Pueblo del Arroyo IIA). Either the formal concept of suites was changing and becoming less patterned, or many of the later

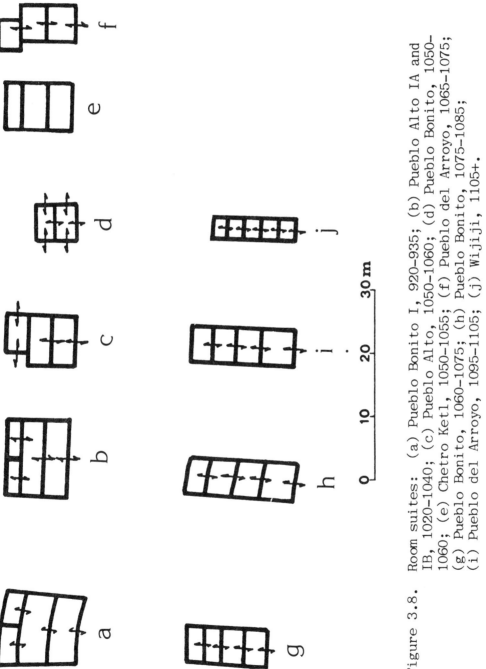

Figure 3.8.    Room suites:    (a) Pueblo Bonito I, 920–935;   (b)  Pueblo Alto IA and
IB, 1020–1040;   (c) Pueblo Alto, 1050–1060;   (d) Pueblo Bonito, 1050–
1060;  (e) Chetro Ketl, 1050–1055;   (f) Pueblo del Arroyo, 1065–1075;
(g) Pueblo Bonito, 1060–1075;   (h) Pueblo Bonito, 1075–1085;
(i) Pueblo del Arroyo, 1095–1105;   (j) Wijiji, 1105+.

structures were not designed for the
functions which were housed in the pair-
room suites and probably continued in the
linear suites. For a number of reasons,
discussed more fully below, I favor the
latter interpretation.

## UNITS OF DESIGN/
## UNITS OF CONSTRUCTION

The room may have been the smallest
formal unit, but the suite was almost
certainly the basic unit of design in
earlier building (900-1050). Early
Chacoan design was thus the product of
determining first the number of suites
required, and then -- using the suite
width as a module -- designing a building
containing the appropriate number of mod-
ules. Construction programs ordinarily
consisted of four or more suites. The
unit of design (the suite) did not equal
the unit of construction (the roomblock).
The process of design, based on suites
but producing roomblocks, could not correspond to the individual domestic groups
occupying the finished structure.

This situation is more confusing in
later Chacoan building, where suite patterns are poorly defined or absent. In
the latest Chacoan structures, such as
Kin Kletso, there are no evident suite
patterns, yet, the entire building of
interconnected rooms was clearly planned
as a unit. What then was the unit of
design? Presumably, the building itself
had replaced the suite as the unit of
design. The implications of this shift
will be discussed in Chapter 5.

## PLAZAS

Archaeologists speak of "plazas" or
"plaza areas" at Anasazi sites of the
700s and 800s. Like the term "kiva,"
this is a projection from later Pueblo
architecture that is probably unwarran-
ted. The earliest formal plazas at Chaco
appear in the early 1000s.

What was so different about the
areas in front of Chaco buildings?
Chacoan plazas were bounded by roomblocks, leveled and sometimes (perhaps
usually) surfaced. More importantly,
where earlier plazas were simply the
heavily used areas between roomblock and
pit structure, the Chacoan plaza is
essentially a bounded area beyond the pit
structure or round room. At some Chacoan
buildings, the area between the roomblock
and pit structure shows many of the same
kinds of use as the analogous space in

smaller, earlier sites. At Pueblo
Bonito, for example, there are large
firepits and other features along the
front of earlier roomblocks, between the
rooms and the subterranean round rooms
that continue in a line along its front.
The formal plaza, a Chacoan development
that may survive into the modern Pueblos,
is the bounded area beyond this zone of
domestic use. This kind of architectural
space may have been present at a few
earlier sites, particularly the large
pithouse aggregations of southeastern
Utah and southwestern Colorado of the
800s. In many ways, the formal plaza is
a correlate of large-scale masonry architecture and the massing of roomblocks.
Not all Chacoan buildings had plazas, of
course, but it is difficult to conceive
of a formal plaza without something very
like Chacoan building.

The use made of these plazas is
unknown. Although we noted that excavations have revealed zones of use along
the edges of these spaces, presumably
continuing the earlier function of use
areas between rooms and pit structures,
the area beyond these zones is a closed
book. The very few test excavations conducted in formal plazas have produced few
clues to their use.

## BUILDINGS

By the early 1100s there was a
bewildering variety of building types in
use at Chaco. The many buildings were
the product of over two and a half centuries of formal change and innovation.
In this section, formal change is described in four temporal segments: tenth
century buildings, a "hiatus" from 960 to
1020, eleventh century building, and
early twelfth century forms.

### Tenth Century Building (900 to 960)

Early tenth century building was
first noted at Pueblo Bonito: "...the
crescentic house cluster that identifies
the original settlement stands out conspicuously" (Judd 1964:57). Building in
the first half of the tenth century was
not confined to Pueblo Bonito. Peñasco
Blanco and Una Vida also have initial
sections that date to this period (Figure
3.9). Three aspects of tenth century
building at these sites stand out in con-
trast to earlier and contemporary smaller
sites: first, multiple stories; second,
the very large size of rooms and pit
structures; and third, the scale of
design and construction units.

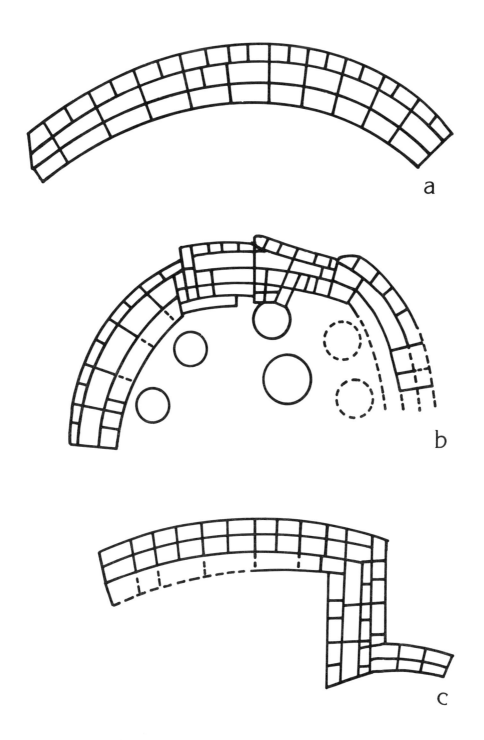

Figure 3.9.   Early 900s building:  (a) Penasco Blanco,
(b) Pueblo Bonito; (c) Una Vida.

Early 900s building at all these sites appears to have included sections of multiple stories. As described above, Type I masonry may have been unstable under loads developed in multistoried building. At the large sites, the tenth century sections were later surrounded by more massively built eleventh century additions, and this buttressing and enclosure preserved Type I multiple stories that may not have otherwise survived. Any other Type I building that was not incorporated into later structures, and instead fell into inconspicuous ruin, might not be recognized today as anything unusual.

The arrangement of rooms in suites parallels exactly that seen at many earlier and contemporaneous small sites (Truell 1983). As noted above suites consist of large rooms backed by paired smaller rooms. As in small sites, subterranean round rooms were located in front of the rows of rooms. Floor areas in plaza-facing rooms are generally about 40 m$^2$, about four times the size of their counterparts in small sites. Similarly, rear row rooms and subterranean round rooms are two to three times the size of their small site counterparts.

The number of suites in a single construction program varies from building to building, and between programs at each building. The eastern and central part of Pueblo Bonito I (Figure 3.9b) consists of small segments of one or two suites, with a notable irregularity in the size of front rooms and the number of rear rooms associated with each front room. The west arc, however, consists of five very regular suites, and is clearly a single construction program. The situation at Una Vida is more obscure, but Una Vida IIB (Figure 3.9c) consisted of no more than three suites. Peñasco Blanco, unexcavated, is even more difficult to interpret, but it is possible that the initial building at that site may have included up to 11 units.

With the possible exception of Una Vida IIA (which may have consisted of an 11-room wide, 2-room deep curved, multistoried block), tenth century building at these sites was remarkably uniform. At Pueblo Bonito, Peñasco Blanco, and Una Vida IIB, initial building was an arc of multiple large-room paired with two small-rooms suites. Along the front of the arc of rooms was a line of subterranean round rooms, one for every two or three suites.

## The "Hiatus" (960-1020)

For sixty years, from about 960 to 1020, there seems to have been a hiatus in building. Two construction stages probably date to this period. Both are very incompletely known and not very well dated: Hungo Pavi I, dating somewhere between 945 and 1010, and Chetro Ketl I, beginning about 1010.

The actual scale of building at Hungo Pavi is unknown; the length of the projected rear wall suggests that it approached the size of the three earlier buildings. However, there is a significant difference in form. The rear wall of Hungo Pavi was straight, while the three early 900s buildings were arcs with markedly curved rear walls. The earliest building at Chetro Ketl was also rectangular rather than curved. These two sites may represent a transition between the early tenth century plans and the earliest well documented eleventh century plans (Figure 3.10, discussed in the next section).

Was there a major reduction in building during this period? The early tenth century buildings continued to be occupied; there is a clear continuity in form, as we shall see, between them and the first well documented eleventh century building. Considered with the limited but suggestive evidence of formal transition at Hungo Pavi and Chetro Ketl, this suggests that building continued at a higher level than is evident from tree-rings or exposed building.

Earlier large-scale building seems to have progressed in a series: Peñasco Blanco (900-915), Pueblo Bonito (920-935), Una Vida (930-950). Perhaps this series continued, first at Hungo Pavi (954-1010) and then Chetro Ketl (1010+). I suspect the apparent "hiatus" is less a true reduction in building than a function of the vagaries of preservation and the conduct of archaeology in the canyon. In addition to Hungo Pavi and Chetro Ketl, it is likely that sections of Pueblo Bonito, Una Vida, and Peñasco Blanco (dated to either side of the hiatus) were actually constructed during this span.

## Eleventh Century Building (1020-1115)

Eleventh century Chacoan architecture has long been considered a radical departure from earlier Chacoan building. Judd (1964:24) thought that the occupants of the early 900s arcs were ethnically distinct from the eleventh century builders at Pueblo Bonito. However, as we shall see, this is probably not the case; early eleventh century building clearly continues the 900s forms. Through a series of stages, the tenth century plan was gradually transformed during the

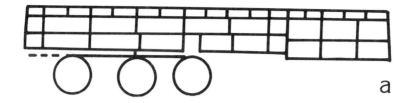

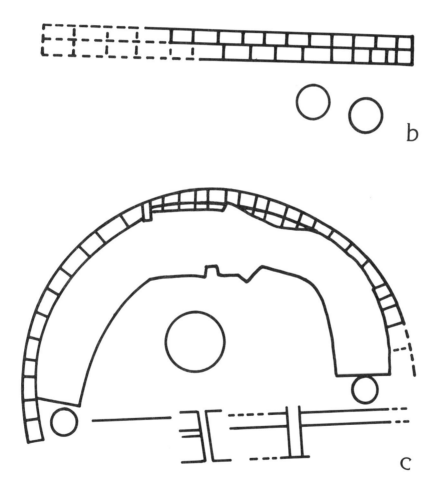

Figure 3.10.  A.D. 1020–1050 building:  (a) Pueblo Alto;
(b) Chetro Ketl; (c) Pueblo Bonito.

eleventh century into compact, rectangular units of the twelfth century.

## A.D. 1020-1050

The first eleventh century construction (Figure 3.10) includes the creation of two new buildings (Pueblo Alto and the currently visible version of Chetro Ketl) in the central canyon area. Early eleventh century Pueblo Alto (Stages I, II, and III) and Chetro Ketl (Stage II), both show an unmistakable continuity of form with tenth century building. This is most obvious at Pueblo Alto.

Pueblo Alto I-III consisted of two rows of large rectangular rooms, each about 40 m$^2$ in area, backed by a row of paired smaller rooms, each about 8-10 m$^2$ in area. Along the front of the rectangular rooms are two or three large subterranean round rooms (8-9 m in diameter). The arrangement and sizes of rooms are identical to parts of Pueblo Bonito I, built a century before (Figure 3.9b). Pueblo Alto I-III is simply Pueblo Bonito I, with Old Bonito's curved plan straightened out into a long rectangle.

Early construction at Chetro Ketl (Figure 3.10b) was greatly obscured by later building, but again, continuity with tenth century building is evident. A row of subterranean round rooms runs along the front of two rows of rectangular rooms. While front row rooms are larger than the rear row rooms, there is no clear association of paired rear row and large front row rooms. Subsequent (almost immediate?) additions of rows of rooms to the front and rear of the initial roomblock created a plan with a large front room, a slightly smaller room behind it, and two smaller rooms behind that. While the arrangement of rectangular and round rooms recalls the tenth century, the connections and layout of individual suites perhaps anticipates the later eleventh century linear suite.

The third notable instance of early eleventh century construction was at Pueblo Bonito. It too demonstrates continuity with tenth century building, but in an entirely different way. Pueblo Bonito II (Figure 3.10c) was a row of small, multistoried rectangular rooms added to the rear wall of the existing early 900s structure. Pueblo Bonito II preserved the earlier building by enclosing it in a shell of more massive construction.

In addition to the rear row of rooms, walls (perhaps representing rows of rooms) were built across the open plaza of Pueblo Bonito II. This is the earliest direct evidence for enclosed plazas at Chaco. (See Windes [1980] for an argument for on earlier enclosed plaza at Peñasco Blanco.)

Even with the addition of rear row rooms, the enclosed plaza, and a few minor alterations of plaza-facing rooms and walls, the earlier (tenth century) Pueblo Bonito was maintained essentially unchanged. Pueblo Bonito I remained useful through the eleventh century (and even into the twelfth). The form of Old Bonito remained an acceptable solution to Chacoan design problems into the early 1000s.

## A.D. 1050-1060

During the next decade, wings of one or two stories were added to the existing structures at Pueblo Alto, Chetro Ketl, Pueblo Bonito, and perhaps Hungo Pavi (Figure 3.11). There is little direct tree-ring dating of this construction; bracketed by earlier and later building, it postdates 1040 and precedes 1075. The decade from 1050 to 1060 seems most likely. Wings created the three-sided plan so characteristic of Chacoan building, and so vexingly difficult to name: "C", "E", "staple," or "bracket."

Wings are not added at right angles to the older buildings, but are generally about 5° off. Oddly enough, the wings added to Pueblo Bonito and Hungo Pavi are almost parallel (that is, they are off 5° in the same direction), while those added to Pueblo Alto and Chetro Ketl diverge (at a combined angle of about 10°). In the latter cases, the angle of the wings may simply continue the slightly diverging end walls of the older stuctures that they abut.

Each wing is about half the size of the building to which it was added, thus the addition of two wings doubled the size of the building. At Chetro Ketl, Pueblo Bonito, and perhaps Pueblo Alto, there is evidence of long parallel walls (or perhaps a row of very narrow rooms) connecting the two wings and enclosing the plaza. Enclosed plazas are certainly possible at the other two buildings, but direct evidence is lacking.

The tenth century suite lost definition in the building of 1050-1060. The association of subterranean round rooms with any of the wings added during this period is also doubtful. The only exceptions are the round room perhaps associated with the west wing of Pueblo Alto (Pueblo Alto IV) and another round

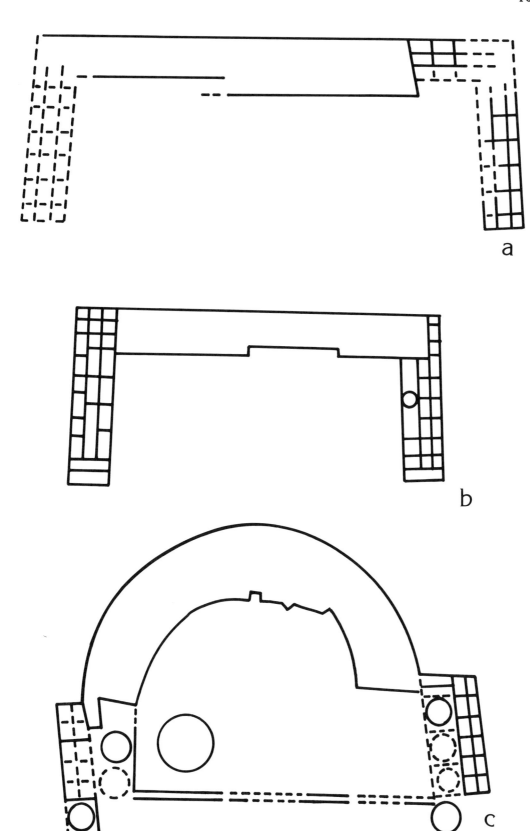

Figure 3.11.  A.D. 1050–1075 building:  (a) Chetro Ketl;
(b) Pueblo Alto;  (c) Pueblo Bonito.

room which may be associated with the east wing at Chetro Ketl (Chetro Ketl IVC). At both sites, however, extensive trenching indicates that these pit structures are the only ones possibly dating to this period. A few elevated round rooms may have been present, as I have indicated for Pueblo Bonito IIIA and IIIB, although these are very problematic assignments. They were inferred from fragmentary remains of an early version of Kiva G at Pueblo Bonito. (The currently visible round rooms fronting Pueblo Bonito IIIA and IIIB almost certainly postdate 1075.)

Whatever the status of round rooms, rectangular rooms certainly do not continue the tenth century pattern. The last vestige of the earlier large-room two small-rooms suite may be the east wing of Pueblo Alto (Pueblo Alto V); however, even here the pattern is confused by an odd, very small round room that divides the two large rooms. In almost all building programs, paired rear row rooms are absent.

With the possible exception of Pueblo Alto V, size differences between most front and rear row rooms are minor or non-existent; that is, rear row rooms are about the same size as front row rooms. The decreasing sizes evident in the later linear suite pattern are not evident in the wings built during 1050-1060.

A.D. 1060-1075

Major construction programs during this period (in which I include Peñasco Blanco IIA, 1050-1065) were additions to and asymmetric extensions of existing buildings. A single new building, Pueblo del Arroyo, was begun.

New stories were added over existing rooms at Chetro Ketl, and in some of the building at Pueblo Bonito. Rooms were built over rear and middle rows of these buildings. As we noted above, the interpretation of upper story additions is fraught with difficulties and ambiguities. The newer rooms naturally repeat the size and shape of the older rooms below them. Did the additions also repeat the functions of the older rooms? Since the upper story additions deprived the lower story rooms of exterior access, the function of those lower story rooms apparently did not require it. The older rooms continued to be serviceable, since they were not filled with trash, sealed off, or otherwise abandoned. The duplication of the lower story forms on the new upper story may represent an increase in the area devoted to that same func-

tion(s). Rear-row rooms were probably designed for storage; thus the upper stories added to Chetro Ketl and Pueblo Bonito during the 1060-1075 period may represent signfican additions of storage space, without proportionate additions of habitation space.

Upper story additions are only one part of 1060-1075 building, which also included asymetric extensions of existing buildings (Peñasco Blanco IIA, Pueblo Bonito IVA, Una Vida IVA). These extensions were two stories tall, at least in their rear rows, and were about the same size as the wings added in the previous period (1050-1060).

The single new building, Pueblo del Arroyo, is similar in scale to the other 1060-1075 programs. For example, the asymmetric extension of Peñasco Blanco (IIA) and initial building at Pueblo del Arroyo both have two rows of generally larger rooms backed by a row of much smaller rooms -- the smaller size being in part determined by closer spacing of cross walls. In number of rows and relative room sizes, these units recall the building of 1020-50.

On the other hand, the 1060-1075 additions to Pueblo Bonito (IVA) and Una Vida (IVA) consisted of up to four rows of rooms. Room size decreased from front to rear solely as a function of decreasing room depth, not cross-wall spacing, creating the linear suites described above. Pueblo Bonito IVA is the earliest clear example of a linear suite; this pattern of rooms may also be present at Una Vida IVA.

The earliest of these four programs, Peñasco Blanco IIA (1050-1065) shows formal continuities with earlier building forms; while the latest program, Una Vida IVA (1070-1075) anticipates the massed rooms and the linear suites of 1075-1115 building.

A.D. 1075-1115

The most massive Chacoan construction went up between 1075 and 1115 (Figure 3.12). Six programs were exceptionally large: the east and west wings of Pueblo Bonito (VIA and VIB), the rear row of rooms (along with two end roomblocks) at Peñasco Blanco (IIIA, B, and C), the north and south wings of Pueblo del Arroyo (IIA and IIB), and Wijiji (built in a single program). These six units were much larger than any preceding construction stage: four to five rooms deep (the rear row of rooms at Peñasco Blanco, although only one room wide, made that unit five rooms deep) and

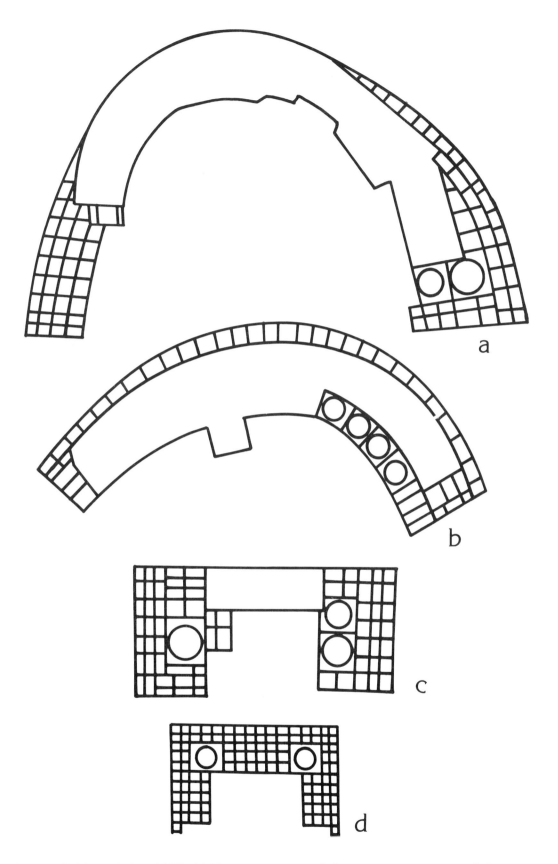

Figure 3.12.    A.D. 1075–1115 building:   (a) Pueblo Bonito;    (b) Penasco
Blanco; (c) Pueblo del Arroyo;   (d) Wijiji.

-- where evidence exists -- a mimimum of three stories tall.

The earliest of these programs (Pueblo Bonito VIB and Peñasco Blanco III) added rooms to the rear of existing buildings. At Peñasco Blanco, this was very similar to the first eleventh century addition to Old Bonito (Pueblo Bonito II); Peñasco Blanco III enclosed the exposed rear wall of an early tenth century arc. Rear rooms added to existing buildings recall the rows of upper story rooms added to Pueblo Bonito and Chetro Ketl during the preceding period but on a much more massive scale. Building at Pueblo del Arroyo (IIA and IIB) created two wings, almost independent of the older central roomblock. The last major building of this period was Wijiji, an entirely new building. Between 1075 and 1115, there is a progression from the addition of rows of (functionally specific?) rooms to existing buildings, to the construction of largely independent wings and roomblocks, to the creation of massive new buildings like Wijiji, presaging twelfth century construction of structures like Kin Kletso and New Alto.

Linear suites are evident at Pueblo Bonito (VIA), at both ends of the Peñasco Blanco addition (IIIB and IIIC), and in the south wing of Pueblo del Arroyo (IIA); however, most of the building during the 1075-1115 span consists of a tremendous number of interconnected interior rooms, or -- in the case of Peñasco Blanco -- rear rooms. In the east wing at Pueblo Bonito (added to the rear of an existing structure), and in both wings at Pueblo del Arroyo and at Wijiji, rooms are remarkably uniform in size.

In Chapter 4, the great majority of elevated round rooms have been assigned to this period; however, while many of the round rooms dated to this period are probably no earlier than 1075, many may be later, perhaps much later. The uncertainty of dating precludes any extensive discussion of round rooms here.

Twelfth Century Building (1115-1140?)

Building of the twelfth century generally corresponds to the so-called "McElmo" phase (Vivian and Mathews 1965). The reality of this phase will be examined in some detail in a later section; the sites are characterized by a particular ground plan (Figure 3.13), the use of "McElmo" style masonry (see Chapter 2), and a well dated assemblage of carbon-painted ceramics. The dendrochronology of these sites is below:

Casa Chiquita: two dates at 1063
New Alto: no dates
Tsin Kletzin: one date at 1112
Kin Kletso: dates from 1076 to 1124; most likely 1124+

The extremely close formal similarity of Casa Chiquita to Kin Kletso suggests that the 1060s dates come from a reused beam, and the building probably dates to about the same span as Kin Kletso. New Alto, Casa Chiquita, and each of the two major building phases at Kin Kletso (Kin Kletso IA and IB) are almost identical in ground plan (Figure 3.13): square, multistoried blocks with two or three rows of small, square rooms surrounding a central elevated circular room on three sides, with a single row of rooms on the fourth side. Sites with this plan probably all date to this period.

Pueblo del Arroyo (discussed above) is one of Vivian and Mathews' Bonito phase towns; however, its wings (Figure 3.12c) mark a clear transition into the later Chacoan building forms of the "McElmo" phase. Pueblo del Arroyo IIA and IIB each consists of large Chacoan round rooms surrounded on three sides by two or three rows of rooms. The rooms are remarkably uniform in size. Judd noted (1959:6) that much of this building, and particularly these wings, made use of recycled stone. Some construction is of the massive sandstone employed in the later "McElmo" style masonry. Reuse suggests a decreasing availability of tabular sandstone in the central canyon area; thus the wings of Pueblo del Arroyo may show the beginnings of both the ground plan and the stone selection which characterize subsequent twelfth century "McElmo" construction.

The first major twelfth century building in the central canyon was the Kiva G complex at Chetro Ketl (Chetro Ketl XIIA, 1110-1115). This unit is constructed almost entirely of pecked massive sandstone, in a "McElmo" style that would easily be lost at Kin Kletso, the "McElmo" phase type site.

Tsin Kletzin is built of massive sandstone in the "McElmo" style, but this is an asymmetric building with an enclosed plaza, resembling earlier ground plans more than Kin Kletso. Tsin Kletzin is located on the crest of South Mesa, well away from the most accessible tabular sandstone.

Small-scale repairs and additions undoubtedly continued throughout the twelfth century at the existing buildings. Two of the mega-outliers, Kin Bineola and Aztec Ruin, were largely or entirely built in the early 1100s.

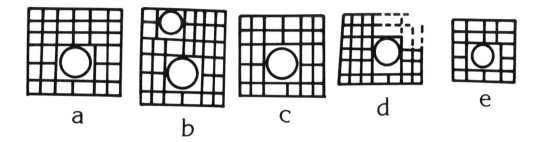

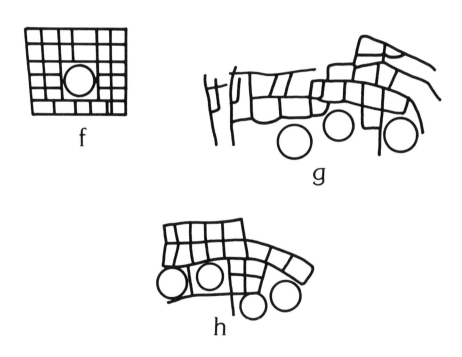

Figure 3.13.   A.D. 1115+ building:   (a) New Alto; (b) Kin Kletso, west;
(c) Kin Kletso, east; (d) Casa Chiquita; (e) Rabbit Ruin, west;
(f) Escalante Ruin; (g) Big Juniper House; (h) Bc 50.

## OTHER CONSTRUCTION

### Mounds or Platforms

Several extraordinary features at Chaco have been called trash mounds: one at Peñasco Blanco, one at Pueblo Alto, two at Pueblo Bonito, and one at Chetro Ketl (Figure 3.14). Mounds stood up to 6 m above the surrounding ground surface, and were about 60 m by 40 m in plan. Archaeologists, familiar with the hillside trash deposits of Pecos Pueblo and the trash-filled rooms of Aztec Ruin, were impressed by the size of the Chacoan mounds, but saw them only as expanded versions of the tiny middens of unit pueblos.

Most of the Chacoan mounds were composed mainly of trash. In addition to trash, the mounds typically include a great deal of sterile sand and construction debris (Judd 1964; Roberts 1927; Windes 1980). The mounds are clearly bigger and more impressive than most Southwestern trash deposits. They may be more than simple middens; these features are probably earthen architecture.

If the mounds were simply tidy Chacoan middens, they should be present at other Chacoan sites occupied at the same time as Pueblo Bonito, Pueblo Alto, Chetro Ketl, and Peñasco Blanco. The absence of trash mounds at several structures (e.g., Una Vida and Hungo Pavi) with construction histories paralleling the structures with mounds strongly suggests that the mounds are, in fact, architectural.

Our knowledge of mound structure comes from trenches and small pits designed to test midden stratigraphy. We know less about their construction than we might wish, but differences in construction (stratigraphy) from mound to mound are suggestive (Hawley 1934; Judd 1964; Roberts 1927; Windes 1980). Some mounds were constructed initially of masonry debris overlain by layers of trash and sand (Pueblo Alto, Peñasco Blanco). Others were largely constructed of razed building debris (Pueblo Bonito, Chetro Ketl). Mounds with nearly identical final forms were made up of very different strata, and similar strata were deposited in very different sequences. Form seems to have been more important, or at least more consistent, than content.

The most spectacular and convincing examples of mound architecture at Chaco are the paired earthen structures in front of Pueblo Bonito. These two rectangular, masonry-faced features had flat surfaces 3-4 m above the surrounding ground level. (These surfaces were later buried under other deposits.) When they were excavated, no one recognized the possibility of architectural mounds in the Anasazi area. As a result, the Pueblo Bonito mounds were repeatedly trenched by archaeologists who studied their stratigraphy, but who failed to see their architecture (Figure 3.15). Even though Judd realized that the mounds were "not a normal trash pile" (Judd 1964: 212), he continued to trench them as if they were. He did not excavate horizontally. Thus, we have no idea what sort of structures, if any, occupied the tops of the mounds.

On the basis of ceramics and the few available tree-ring dates, Windes (1980) concluded that the mounds at Pueblo Bonito, Pueblo Alto, and Chetro Ketl were constructed in the later eleventh or early twelfth centuries. The Peñasco Blanco mound contains earlier, tenth century ceramics. Either the Peñasco Blanco mound is the earliest Chacoan mound, or the mound was constructed with redeposited earlier trash. The position of the mound, outside a late (post-1090) plaza-enclosing arc of rooms, supports this interpretation.

### Tri-Wall Structures

Tri- and bi-walled structures are circular rooms surrounded by one or two concentric rows of rooms (see Figure 4.70). They are an unusual form, and since most of the known examples are located north of the San Juan River, archaeologists were excited when one was uncovered behind Pueblo del Arroyo. Most tri- and bi-walls were found at sites with Mesa Verde components, so it had been assumed that they were a thirteenth century Mesa Verde form.

The Pueblo del Arroyo Tri-wall was excavated in two separate projects, first by Karl Ruppert (Judd 1959), and later by Gordon Vivian (Vivian 1959). Ruppert cleared most of the tri-wall structure. The ceramics recovered, according to Judd included "a preponderance of Chaco-San Juan [Chaco McElmo Black-on-white] sherds...and a high proportion of Mesa Verde Black-on-white" (1959:118). The latter statement is contradicted by Roberts' (1927) analysis of the Pueblo del Arroyo ceramics. He recorded fewer than 60 sherds of Mesa Verde Black-on-white from all the excavations at Pueblo del Arroyo, and of these over 40 were in the fill of Kiva G, part of the main building to which the tri-wall was appended. Roberts' summarized the tri-wall sherds as follows: "The potsherds from

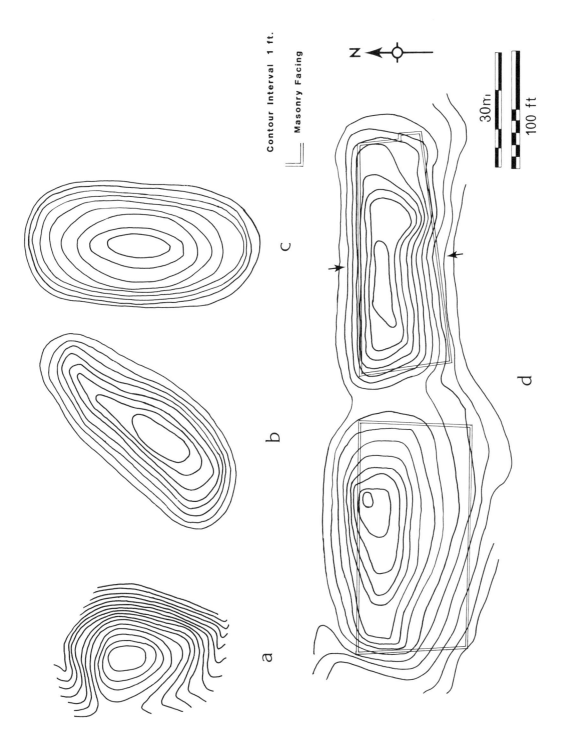

Contour Interval   1 ft.

Masonry Facing

N

30 m

100 ft

Figure 3.14.   Mounds:   (a) Penasco Blanco; (b) Pueblo Alto; (c) Chetro Ketl, reconstructed; (d) Pueblo Bonito.

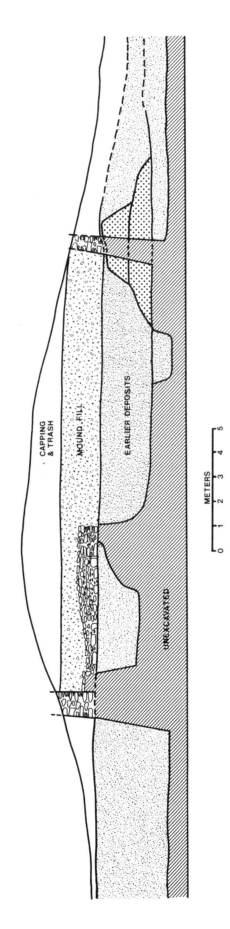

Figure 3.15. Stratigraphy of the East Mound, Pueblo Bonito (simplified; after Judd 1964: Fig. 24).

the [tri-wall] were practically all of the Chaco-San Juan Group. The few exceptions were typical proto-Mesa Verde [McElmo] pieces" (1927:240).

The decorated ceramics recovered by Vivian (1959:68) included only about one percent Mesa Verde Black-on-white. Vivian interpreted the presence of this small amount of Mesa Verde as coming "from a time of reoccupation of the canyon when the tri-wall was being razed for building stone" (1959:68). The northern distribution of tri-walls influenced Vivian's assignment of the Pueblo del Arroyo Tri-wall to his McElmo phase, which he thought was intrusive from the San Juan area; however, he noted that the Pueblo del Arroyo Tri-wall was the earliest of the building type.

The major pottery types in the Pueblo del Arroyo assemblage were McElmo, Chaco/Gallup, and Escavada Black-on-whites (probably including Red Mesa and Mancos; Vivian [1959: Figures 18 and 19]). The decorated redwares were limited to Wingate and Puerco Black-on-red. This assemblage agrees with the early 1100s ceramics found at almost every major Chacoan building. A single tree-ring date of 1109 from the Pueblo del Arroyo Tri-wall confirms early 1100s construction.

Tri-walls are a late architectural type in the Chacoan regional system, coincident with the shift of the regional focus from Chaco to the San Juan River and the north (Lekson 1984b). As a class of building, they are of only limited interest to the great pueblo architecture of Chaco Canyon. The single example, at Pueblo del Arroyo, had been prehistorically razed; little is known of the internal features of the central circular room and the concentric rows of rooms.

## Roads

Prehistoric roads radiate from Chaco to the edges of the San Juan Basin (for the most recent review, see Kincaid [1982]). These roads are perhaps the most spectacular, and, from an archaeological view, the most satisfactory demonstration of the regional extent of the Chacoan system. In addition to roads running out from the canyon, there were roads and roadway features (ramps, stairs, berms, etc.) within the canyon.

Holsinger (1901) was the first to report roads within the canyon. Many subsequent workers have investigated these roads, particularly in the Pueblo Bonito-Chetro Ketl-Pueblo Alto area (Vivian in Kincaid 1983; Windes 1982). Unfortunately, historic ranching, commer-

cial activities, a century of archaeology, and National Park Service improvements have cluttered the canyon floor with a maze of linear features; no definitive map of the prehistoric road network within the canyon exists. Many linear, road-like features have not been examined on the ground, and may not be prehistoric roads.

Despite our difficulty in producing an "accurate" map, roads were obviously an important part of Chacoan building. The evidence of stairs cut into the sandstone cliffs, massive masonry ramps, and several sections of prehistoric cut-and-fill attest to the extent of the roads, and hint at their integration into the overall community plan. At the Talus Unit (Lekson 1984a) and probably at a few other buildings, the road passed through the Chacoan building itself.

The precise arrangement of roads within the canyon is not critical. Numerous roads crisscrossed the canyon, running from wall to wall and from building to building. Their impact on the landscape should not be underestimated. The roads were undoubtedly one of the major land modifications in the Chacoan architectural repertoire.

## Long, Low Walls

Long, low masonry walls are visible in several areas of Chaco Canyon; most were less than 1 m in height but up to 1 m or more in width. Some of these walls run along the edges of roads, and are probably roadway features, while several seem to delineate large enclosed areas around major buildings. In particular, there are several long, low walls around Pueblo Alto, and another extends from Pueblo Bonito toward Chetro Ketl.

There is insufficient rubble at their bases to indicate the original height of these walls, nor do they appear to have been robbed of stone. Physically, they would not have prevented access to the areas they define; however, even their low height may have been an architectural convention sufficient to channel or exclude traffic. The low walls formalize areas and areal relationships.

The extent and arrangement of these walls is no better known than the intracanyon road system. The walls around Pueblo Alto are most visible, because they are not alluviated as are the walls on the canyon floor. The low walls at Pueblo Bonito were discovered only by excavation, and further excavation would doubtlessly disclose many more walls in the central canyon area.

# Chapter Four
# The Sites

The large Chacoan sites have been described by numerous authors, beginning with Simpson (1850), Jackson (1878), and Holsinger (1901), continuing with Hewett (1936) and Bannister (1965), and most recently including Hayes (1981) and Lister and Lister (1981). The present study is based on new tree-ring dates (Dean and Warren 1983; Robinson et al. 1974), new and more accurate maps (Drager and Lyons 1984), recently acquired wall elevations (Lekson and McKenna 1979), and on recently produced or previously unpublished excavation data. Despite all this new information, the descriptions that follow may not supercede earlier studies.

My versions of the buildings' architectural histories are often at odds with earlier schemes. I have assigned every major wall at each site to a series of dated construction stages. Not every wall at Chaco is tree-ring dated, nor indeed is every wall visible; therefore, I have occasionally strayed from observable structures and tree-ring dates to projected construction and guess dates. In these cases, other interpretations are clearly possible.

Two sites are described by individuals who know them better than I: Tom Windes, who directed the excavation of Pueblo Alto, and William Gillespie, who (with Nancy Akins) excavated portions of Una Vida. Although they probably winced at my request that all visible construction be assigned a date, both graciously wrote their accounts to conform to my requirements.

Some sites are completely excavated, some are untouched. Several have dozens, even hundreds, of tree-ring dates; a few have none. Because of these disparities, the organization of the descriptions varies from site to site. At a site with a few poorly provenienced dates, tree-ring data may be discussed in a separate section. At a site with numerous dates, the tree-ring chronology is included in the sections on construction stages. The organization chosen for each description best fits the kinds and quality of data.

## UNA VIDA

### William B. Gillespie

#### History

Like many of the other large ruins in the canyon, Una Vida (Figures 4.1-4.7) was first described and mapped by Simpson in 1850 and named by his guide Carravahal. As with other names supplied by Carravahal, the historical derivation of the name Una Vida ("one life") is now unknown. Franstead and Werner (1974:11) note the local Navajo name as "witchcraft woman's home," similar to Tietjen's "house of a woman who makes you thin by starving you" recorded in 1929 (n.d.:6). This name relates to a common local legend of a witch renowned for her practice of holding human hostages atop nearby Fajada Butte without food or drink.

In 1878 Jackson provided a more detailed map and more thorough description of Una Vida and ten years later, Victor Mindeleff took the first known photographs of the site. Comparison of these photographs with walls presently standing shows that relatively little deterioration has taken place over the past century.

Excavation during the first half of the twentieth century was limited to the undocumented clearing of three rooms and

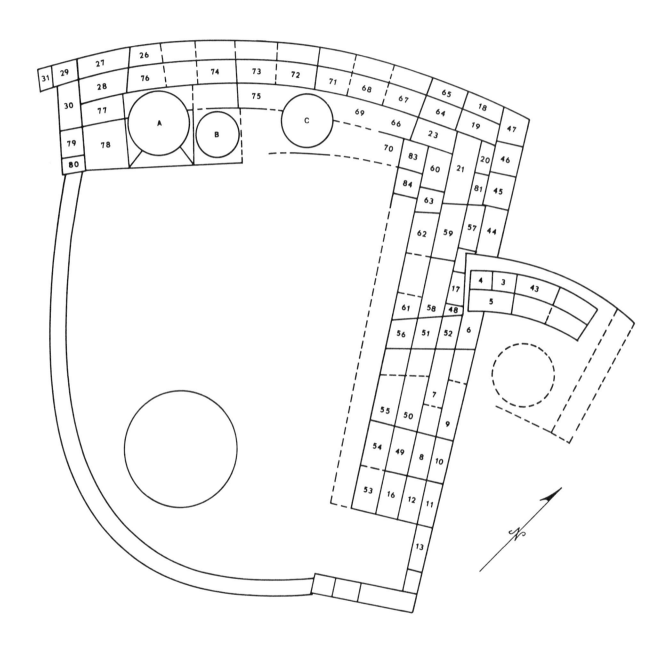

Figure 4.1. Una Vida.

Figure 4.2.   Una Vida, looking east.

Figure 4.3. Una Vida, looking north.

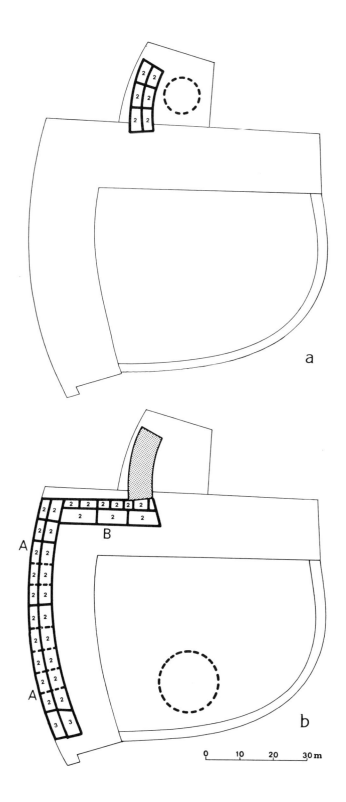

Figure 4.4.  Una Vida, construction stages:  (a) Stage I; (b) Stage II.
All new construction is one story, unless otherwise noted.

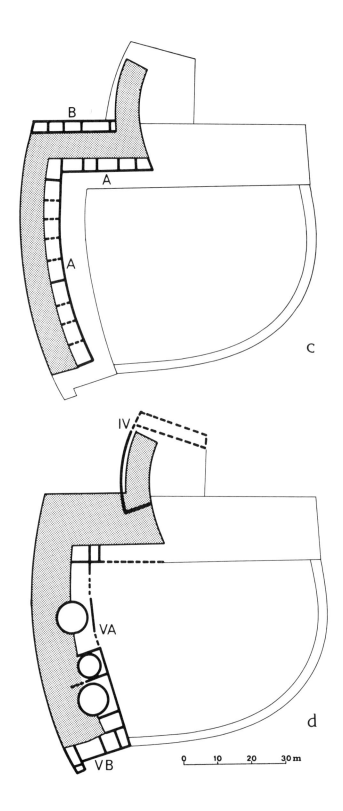

Figure 4.4    Una Vida construction stages con't: (c) Stage III; (d)
             Stages IV and V;

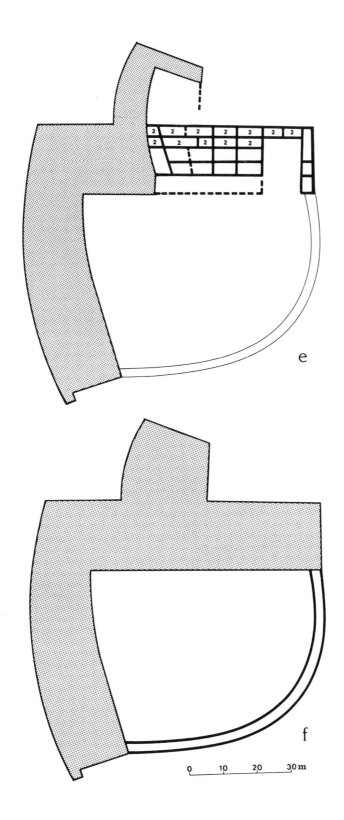

Figure 4.4    Una Vida construction stages con't.: (e) Stage VI; (f) Stage
VII.

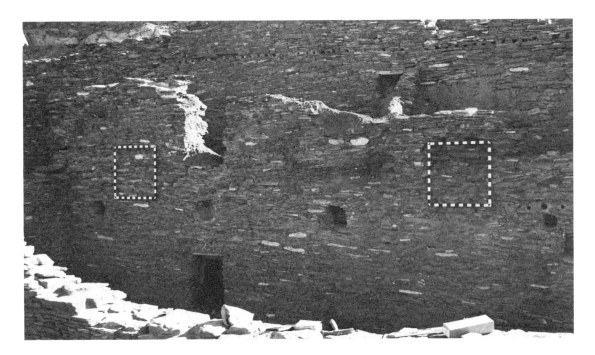

Figure 4.5.   Una Vida, Room 21, looking north (frames are 70 cm x 70 cm.)

Figure 4.6.   Una Vida, Room 23, looking west (frame is 70 cm x  70 cm).

Figure 4.7   Una Vida, examples of masonry (frames are 70 cm x 70 cm).
Room 4, NW wall; Room 20, E wall; Room 21, N wall.  Middle
row, left to right:  Room 19, W wall; Room 19, N wall; Room
29, NE wall; Room 45, N wall.  Bottom row, left to right:
Room 60, W wall; Room 84, W wall; Kiva A, SE exterior wall;
rear exterior wall, outside Room 10.

shallow digging in various parts of the ruin. This activity most likely took place during the early 1930s, when the University of New Mexico-School of American Research project became interested in many of the previously unexplored Chaco ruins (nearby Kin Nahasbas was excavated at this time). A sketch map by William Chauvenet in 1934 suggests that the rooms at Una Vida had been excavated by that date. Gordon Vivian did a small amount of digging in 1956 and 1957 in conjunction with mapping and stabilization efforts. At this time he dug near bench level in Kiva C removing tree-ring specimens and an intact jar resting on the bench, excavated an ca. 10 m long test trench across the east wing between Room 6 and Room 56, and excavated all five of the small Navajo hogans located on the site.

The most extensive work at Una Vida was the excavation of 15 rooms in the north corner of the site by Gordon Vivian in 1960. Vivian had originally planned to excavate the entire site, but halted after this block of rooms. No report was prepared and field notes are incomplete. Stabilization of walls exposed by the excavation was directed by Joel Shiner during the same summer.

During the winter and spring of 1979, the Chaco Center staff reexamined the floors of many of these rooms prior to the backfilling of the rooms in 1979 (Akins and Gillespie 1979). Previously excavated and unexposed features were cleared, mapped, and photographed, earlier floor surfaces were exposed, rooms were mapped, and walls were photographed.

## Chronology

Some 29 tree-ring dates (Table 4.1) have been derived from Una Vida with a range from 847v (first cutting date, 861r) to 1093+vv, one of the longest spans of any of the Chacoan buildings. Of these specimens, nine were collected by Hawley and Lassetter in 1932 and 1933 (Robinson et al. [1974] list seven of these); three are from Vivian's 1950s stabilization and testing; fifteen are from Vivian's 1960 excavations; and four were recovered during Chaco Center investigations in 1979.

The distribution of dates suggests five clusters which are presumed to represent times of construction activity. Two dates from the mid-800s (847v, 861r) provide tentative dates for the small upper arc of Judd's Type I masonry rooms on the northeast side of the site (Stage I, below). Clusters of dates at about

930 (four from 925+v to 932r) and about 950 (eight from 945+v to 950r) date the bulk of construction of the west wing of the site, i.e., the lower Type I arc which forms the core of the site (Stage II). The fourth cluster is in the 1050s with twelve dates between 1047v and 1056r while the fifth includes four dates in the late 1000s (1068+vv to 1093+vv). These eleventh century dates mark the construction of most of the east wing and modifications of existing structures (Stage IV). A single date of 987r is the only one between 950 and 1047, but does not appear to directly date any major construction episode. Two dates, which should be considered with doubt since they are not listed in the recent revision of Chaco tree-ring dates (Robinson et al. 1974), are the single 987 date (specimen lost) and a 950r specimen of unknown provenience (reason for exclusion unknown).

The basic chronology is similar to those of Pueblo Bonito and Peñasco Blanco with a few 900s dates indicating the main Type I construction in the first half of the 900s and the bulk of subsequent construction in the mid- to late 1000s. However, there are differences: Una Vida is the only site for which dates in the 800s can be related to a recognizable, standing structure, the small upper arc of about six rooms. Comparable early structures at any of the other sites were either razed, unrecognizable, or never existed. In addition, the main Type I roomblock at Una Vida is later than Type I construction at the other two sites. Pueblo Bonito and Peñasco Blanco arcs date before 920 while the Una Vida arc has dates at ca. 930 and 950.

## Architecture

Although the ruined condition of the walls makes the determination of room numbers and sizes difficult, there appear to be approximately 100 ground floor rooms, exclusive of the plaza-enclosing arc (Figure 4.1). About half of these are thought to be two stories high, suggesting a total of ca. 150 rooms. The front arc is now a very low mound, but if it is accepted as representing a single row of rooms, then as many as 40-45 additional rooms are suggested.

The number of stories at Una Vida has been greatly exaggerated in the past, reaching such giddy heights as six stories (see Robinson et al. 1974). Part of this overestimation is a result of parts of the site being built on prominent mounds of talus and colluvium such that the highest extant walls stand over 10 m above the ground surface of the plaza.

Table 4.1.  Tree-ring dates from Una Vida.

| Room 3, 4, or 5 | | | Room 64 | |
|---|---|---|---|---|
| UV–20 | 847v | | UV–89 | 949+vv |
| UV–18–1 | 861rl | | UV–95 | 949v |

| Room 17/48 (intramural beams) | | | Room 81 | |
|---|---|---|---|---|
| CNM–676 | 1047v | | | |
| CNM–679 | 1049vv | | UV–73 | 925+v |
| CNM–678 | 1053vv | | UV–72 | 948r |
| CNM–677 | 1053v | | | |

| Room 19 | | | North Wing | |
|---|---|---|---|---|
| UV–68 | 932r | | UV–53 | 1072v |
| UV–62 | 9484r | | | |

| Room 21 | | | West Wing | |
|---|---|---|---|---|
| | | | ? UV–12 | 945+v |
| UV–69 | 931vv | | UV–7 | 950r |
| UV–71–7 | 1053vv | | UV–8 | 950cL |
| UV–70–20 | 1055r | | | |
| UV–71–15 | 1055r | | Kiva C | |
| UV–71–2 | 1055r | | | |
| UV–70–9 | 1055r | | ? UV–24 | 1051vv |
| UV–71–16 | 1056r | | ? UV–26 | 1084vv |
| UV–70–19 | 1056r | | UV–51 | 1093+vv |

| Room 48 | | | No provenience | |
|---|---|---|---|---|
| CNM–355 | 1068vv | | UV–88 | 928v |

Note:  All dates from roof elements unless otherwise noted.
       Key to symbols, see Appendix C.

Vivian's excavated rooms and tests show that evidence of more than two stories is minimal; only near the southwest end of the west wing are there definitely three stories and here only in one or two rooms.

In layout, Una Vida is in the form of an L with the juncture of the two arms to the north.   Because of this unusual orientation, none of the rooms in the main roomblocks is oriented with the cardinal directions, even though the final form of the site is roughly symmetrical on a north-south axis.   For convenience, the roomblock forming the northwest side of the site is referred to as the "west wing," while that on the northeast is the "east wing."

An arc of rooms in the west wing of Una Vida, built in the early 900s, apparently continued in use throughout the span of occupation of the site.   In Vivian's excavated rooms McElmo-Mesa Verde Black-on-white pottery was found near the floors of rooms built before 950.   Later additions built after 1050 changed the overall plan, orientation, and symmetry, but did not significantly alter the original arc of rooms.

Stage I (860-865)

This refers to a small building of early Type I masonry which is apparent at the highest part of the site, on top of a prominence northeast of the east wing (Figure 4.4a).   This is a confusing area, one which has been interpreted variously in the past, though it has seldom been recognized as a small arc of early rooms. Part of the confusion stems from the presence of late, blocky masonry, most of which appears to be a refacing (perhaps for cosmetic as well as structural purposes) of earlier, more crude masonry. Type I masonry is undeniably present; slab rubble extends some 20 m to the east suggesting a small block of rooms. Hawley's brief written (1934:22) and photographic (1934:Plate 9) record of the provenience of the two 800s dates suggests them to be from the first-story ceiling of Room 5 at the west end of the arc.

Inasmuch as only the walls supported by later refacings are well preserved, it is difficult to delineate room outlines or estimate number of rooms for this small, early roomblock. A guess is about six rooms (12 assuming two stories throughout), three facing the small plaza to the southeast backed by three rooms of equal or slightly smaller area.   One of these back rooms has been partitioned, but the dividing wall is apparently a late addition.   The size of each of the original rooms is about 18 m$^2$.   Overall, the small upper arc is estimated to be 21 m long and about 9 m wide.   Standing walls at the west end show that the arc is definitely two stories, but it is unknown whether the second story is part of the original mid-800s construction or a later (900s) addition.   Second-story masonry is Type I and not noticeably different from the small amount of exposed first-story masonry.   The dated wood specimens are probably small secondary stubs from the first-story ceiling. If both stories are from a single construction episode and the 860s dates are accurate, then these would be the earliest multistoried structures known in the Chaco area.

The arc faces a small plaza area located to the southeast and somewhat lower than the presumed ground floor level of the rooms.   Although conclusive evidence is lacking, this plaza has a flattened space which may represent a round pit structure.

Stage II (930-950)

This is the bulk of the Type I masonry construction and includes two parts (Figure 4.4b): a two-tier curving arc of rooms that forms the basis of the west wing (Stage IIA) and early rooms in the north corner that abut the longer arc at a right angle (Stage IIB).   The larger Stage IIA arc is logically the earlier construction, but tree-ring dates from excavated rooms in Stage IIB indicate that it is contemporary or only slightly later.   The peculiar arrangement of the Stage IIB rooms, situated at an unlikely and unexpected angle, is apparently caused by the topography at the north end of the site.   Not evident on a simple plan of the site is a rather steep drop in the underlying terrain running from roughly the east end of Room 18 to the west end of Room 5 and averaging about 3 to 4 m in height.   This abrupt change in elevation greatly influenced the layout of the rooms.   Evidently, the builders considered it too much of a hill to be traversed by rooms oriented perpendicular to the slope, and so did not expand the small upper arc farther west than Room 5 nor the lower arc farther east.   Although this topographic limitation may be the main reason for establishing a separate lower arc rather than expanding the pre-existing Stage I upper arc, the builders apparently found that with some cutting and filling they could construct rooms parallel to the slope, and eventually used the slope to help in creating the characteristic pattern of stepped tiers. As a result not only Stage IIB, but in time the whole east wing, was aligned at unexpected angles to the southeast facing arc. Stage IIB may have been an attempt to physically join the arcs of Stages I and IIA. It appears, then, that the overall layout of Una Vida is to some extent a result of the natural topography. This seemingly simple factor may be an important reason for the failure of Una Vida to continue to develop along curvilinear lines as did Pueblo Bonito and Peñasco Blanco.

The two tiers of the Stage IIA arc each include about 11 rooms of roughly equal length but with the plaza-facing row somewhat wider. Vivian excavated two rooms in each of the two tiers (Rooms 19 and 64 of the front row; Rooms 18 and 65 of the back). These excavated rooms suggest floor areas of about 18-21 m$^2$ for the front rooms and 12-13 m$^2$ for the back rooms. Both tiers were evidently two stories high, but it is unknown whether the second story of the front tier is part of the original construction or was added along with a new plaza-facing tier (Stage IIIA). Overall, the arc is about 70 m long and about 8 m wide with an estimated 22 ground floor and 46 total rooms. Associated round rooms are presumably present in front of the arc, but later building has obscured any traces. There is also a possibility of an associated Great Kiva to the northwest of the conspicuous later Great Kiva, but surface evidence is inconclusive.

All four excavated rooms are relatively free of major floor features except the larger front row rooms that contain prominent roof supports, with postholes dug deep into underlying sandstone. The door pattern in the excavated rooms is consistent, with openings through the long walls connecting to the plaza (but not through the exterior wall at the rear) and through the cross walls of the front but not the back row. Preserved second-story walls show a door connecting Rooms 18 and 19 and a small blocked door in the east wall of Room 18 which, because of the steep terrain noted above, presumably led to the outdoor ground surface. Vents are missing in the cross walls and only one or two crudely stabilized cavities in the longer walls may have been vents.

At the southwest end of the arc are the prominent Type I walls of Rooms 27 and 28. These are clearly three stories high, the only indisputable evidence of a height of more than two stories anywhere at Una Vida. Rather than indicating a remnant of a more extensive third story, these high walls may represent a unique tower.

Tree-ring dates have been obtained from both ends of the arc. At the southwest end, Hawley removed two second-story intramural beams from Room 27, both with cutting dates of 950. At the excavated northeast end, Vivian recovered a first-story primary beam in Room 19 dating 932r and two major roof supports in Room 64 dating 949+vv and 949v. Two other specimens dating 945+v and 950r may have come from the Stage IIA arc. It is possible that the large posts from Room 64 represent supports required for a second story. If so, it can be noted that the 950 dates are all associated with the second story of front row of rooms while the only definite first-story wood dates at 932. This might be construed as an indication of initial construction at about 930 with the second story added to the front row of rooms in 950. This interpretation is supported by the occurrence of three dates at about 930 from first-story proveniences in Stage IIB rooms and the observation that the postholes dating to 949 in Room 64 are not original features, but instead they are superimposed over earlier room features (including another large posthole).

Stage IIB is represented by excavated Rooms 20, 21, and 81. This is the only known case at Una Vida of a large plaza-facing room backed by two small probable storerooms. It is unknown whether or not the pattern persists to the southeast throughout the rest of the posited roomblock, but it is possible that there are two more large rooms (58 and 59) backed by small paired rooms for an estimated total of nine ground floor rooms. All three of the excavated rooms are two stories high, though again, it is possible that the second story of the front room was not built until the fronting rooms were added. Room 81 has a small section of wall which suggested a third story, but Vivian's excavation notes indicate that the first story had been intentionally filled during occupation following the collapse of its ceiling. The addition of what appears to be a third story may have occurred after this infilling and thus, functionally, would have been a second story. Accordingly, while a third story for the small back rooms is a possibility, it is not definite.

Room 21 (Figure 4.5) with a length of over 10 m and floor area of about 39 m$^2$ is the largest exposed room at Una Vida. The back rooms are about 4.7 m x 1.9 m, with areas of about 9 m$^2$. The doors of Room 21 include a single opening in the long plaza-facing wall, a first-story connection with Room 19, both first- and second-story doors to the two back rooms, and a probable second-story door to the adjoining unexcavated Room 59 to the southeast. Rooms 20 and 81 had no connections other than to Room 21. As expected with two-story structures, floor features are sparse with the most conspicuous one being a row of large deep postholes in Room 21 cut into substrata for major roof supports.

Four tree-ring dates from Stage IIB suggest contemporaneity with Stage IIA. A large beam on the floor of Room 21, interpreted as a primary beam by Vivian, dates 931vv; a piece of wood apparently from the plaza-facing wall of Room 21 (UV-87/88; removed by Vivian from the Room 63 side) dates 928v; and two sealed-over secondary beam stubs from the collapsed first-story ceiling of Room 81 date 925+ and 948r. As noted above, these lend credence to the interpretation of initial construction of Type I architecture in the west wing and north roomblock at about 930 with extensive modifications at about 950.

Stage III (950-960)

This stage can be considered as Type I masonry additions to the Stage II rooms. Two substages are discussed (Figure 4.4c): Stage IIIA, plaza-facing rooms added to existing plaza-facing rows, and Stage IIIB, a row of small rear rooms added to the north corner of the building.

Stage IIIA. Stage IIIA structures were apparently added to the fronts of both Stages IIA and IIB. Excavated examples include Rooms 23 (Figure 4.6), 60, and 63 in the north corner. Bonded corners and door locations indicate that these rooms were built together, even though the layout suggests that Room 23, fronting Stage IIA, had priority. Other data also indicate approximate contemporaneity. Occasional low standing sections of Type I masonry suggest that rooms were added along the entire length of the Stage IIA arc, even though Kivas A and C later cut through this suggested row. On the other hand, completely fallen walls make it impossible to confirm the presence of added Type I rooms to the southeast of Room 63. Altogether, approximately 15 rooms are suggested for Stage IIIA, though this number far exceeds the confirmed total. All are thought to be single-story structures.

Shapes and floor areas appear to be less consistent than those of the previously built rectangular rooms. Of the three excavated examples, floor areas are 11, 17.5, and 19.5 m$^2$ though the smallest may be the result of later modification. Widths of rooms are fairly consistent at 3.3-3.6 m, about the same as the earlier Stage II front rooms, but lengths show more variability. The excavated rooms also display a suite of features noticeably different from earlier front rooms; for example, very large central firepits cut into bedrock, masonry subfloor ventilators, multiple floor surfaces, thick wall plaster with multiple replasterings, large wall niches, and above-floor masonry bins (2 of 3 examples). It is, of course, impossible to know whether or not these characteristics apply to other suggested Stage IIIA rooms. Door patterns seen in the excavated rooms are not consistent. The rooms initially had lateral doors connecting each other, but not other adjacent rooms; two of three had openings to the plaza; and two of three utilized existing openings to earlier rooms. Most of the doors, including all of those in Rooms 60 and 63, were sealed during occupation.

Stage IIIB. Stage IIIB involves only about five single-story, small rectangular rooms added on top of the prominent topographic rise on the northeast side of the Stage II structures. Three of these (Rooms 45-47) were excavated by Vivian and reveal fairly uniform shapes and sizes. Floor areas are 12.5-13.5 m$^2$ with the average length about 4.6 m and width 2.85 m. Doors are present only in cross walls so that there are no evident connections to the exterior or to the established roomblock (where floor levels are significantly different).

No tree-ring specimens directly date the construction of either Stage IIIA or IIIB, but masonry suggests a tenth century construction. As noted above, it is feasible that the addition of the Stage IIIA plaza-facing rooms is contemporary with the building of a second story over the front row of the Stage II structures. If so, then the Stage IIIA addition probably dates at about 950. A single tree-ring date was removed from a niche in the northeast wall of Room 63 (Stage III), but as noted above, this 928v date is thought more likely to pertain to the wall of Room 21 than Room 63. If this interpretation is incorrect, then the dated wood is probably a reused specimen. Stage IIIB may be somewhat later, but the predominance of Red Mesa Black-on-white pottery in the fill of the rooms indicates relatively early use and abandonment (Windham 1976).

Stage IV (1050-1055?)

The constructions included in Stage IV (Figure 4.4d) may not be the product of a single building episode. The associations are formal, i.e., they all modify the Stage I arc of rooms, but masonry styles are apparently different. The standing examples of this stage are two prominent walls which were built directly against the early Stage I walls near the southwest end of the arc. Most impressive is a section of wall added to the southwest ends of Rooms 4 and 5 which still looms above the excavated Room 17 and the plaza below. Although it has in the past been interpreted as a third-story wall of Room 17, it is far more likely that it was instead an exterior refacing of the earlier Stage I wall, which stood above the second story of Room 17. The masonry of this wall is Judd's Type III, and is nearly the only example of this style at the site. The wall is firmly dated to the 1050s by four short logs inserted to tie the added facing to the existing Type I wall; these logs date to 1047v, 1049vv, 1053vv, and 1053v.

The other extant case of the refacing of cruder Type I walls occurs on the northwest exterior face of Rooms 3 and 43. Here again, the intent appears to have been cosmetic as well as structural, but the refacing is more similar to "McElmo" style masonry. Rubble from fallen walls suggests that this facing continued to the northeast to cover most of the back wall of the Stage I arc.

The third and final part of the Stage IV construction is what appears to be a single row of small rooms which descend a low ridge forming the northeast side of the small plaza associated with the Stage I rooms. No walls are standing, but the small amount of rubble is predominantly large shaped blocks similar to the northwest refacing. Approximately five to eight small single-story rooms may be represented.

## Stage V (1050-1095)

Stage VA. Stage VA construction (Figure 4.4e) along the front of the west wing is dominated by three conspicuous round rooms (Kivas A, B, and C). One of these (Kiva B) is largely subterranean while Kiva C is above ground with a standing wall to the southeast possibly representing a raised rectangular enclosure. Kiva A, the largest (9 m diameter), is elevated above the plaza level to about the second-story level in a rectangular enclosure with buttresses and projecting stones on the outside of the circular drum. There is a hint of a fourth, subterranean round room farther to the northeast (Kiva D).

At least two and probably three tree-ring dates have been collected by Hawley and Vivian from these circular rooms. These specimens are all probably from Kiva C, but this is impossible to determine precisely. The dates, including the two latest dates from the site, are 1051vv, 1084vv, and 1093vv.

In the north roomblock, Vivian cleared two nearly square rooms (Rooms 83 and 84) which may also belong to Stage VA. Both are single story and have features which suggest that they were special use rather than habitation rooms. These features include the square shape, lack of any preserved door openings, thick colored wall plaster, large central firepits, a masonry deflector (Room 84), a recess in one wall (Room 83), and large niches (Room 83). Floor areas are about 10 and 11 m$^2$. There may be other, similar rooms in adjacent areas, but they are not readily apparent.

In addition to the dates from Kiva C mentioned above, there is a tight cluster of seven dates (1053vv, four specimens at 1055r, and two specimens at 1056r) from burned debris found in the lower fill of the earlier Stage II Room 21. It is unclear whether this represents debris dumped from some other structure or part of the roof section of Room 21 which burned in place. Nevertheless, these dates can be assigned to some Stage VA construction in the north part of the site.

Stage VB. At the far southwest corner of the site are five or six rooms of late masonry which are here labeled Stage VB (Figure 4.4e). These are butted against the high three-story Stage II Room 27 and other adjacent rooms. Not all room partitions are evident, but walls at the west side of the complex define a very small compartment (attached to Room 29). Another very small enclosure appears to be present at the southeast end of Stage VB. A single tree-ring date was recovered by Hawley from (probably) Room 29 and dates 987r; however, Hawley and subsequently Bannister (1965) consider this to be a reused beam and not indicative of the date of construction.

## Stage VI (1070-1075)

The ground plan of the Stage VI roomblock, uncertain because of the preponderance of fallen walls, appears to involve four or even possibly five tiers of rooms (Figure 4.4f). The southeast end of the structure, disturbed and reduced, in part through the construction

of a Navajo corral, apparently involves a
rather unusual L-shaped projection ending
in a small square room under the south
edge of the later corral. As with the
northwestern part of the east wing, the
structure has to cope with higher terrain
on the northeast side, as the back wall
is located along a ridgeline. The uncertainty of the underlying terrain makes
estimation of the number of stories difficult, but it appears that probably no
more than the back two tiers are two-
story rooms and that none exceeds that
height. There are an estimated 26 ground
floor rooms and a total of 36 rooms of
all stories.

Door and vent patterns are essentially unknown. However, the two-story
standing backwall of the only excavated
(but undocumented) room in Stage VI (Room
10) shows not only a ground floor door,
but a second-story blocked door leading
to the outside. This second-story door
may have provided access to a balcony.
The first-story ceiling is marked by two
primary beam sockets and an inset roof
ledge. No vents were present in standing
wall sections. Rooms appear to be
predominantly rectangular with sizes
about 15 to 35 m$^2$. In the better
preserved south end, rooms are about 6.5
m long but of varying widths with the
back rows somewhat narrower. Masonry,
conspicuously different from that of
previously described sections of the
site, is faced with small, flat-faced
laminar blocks of uniform material
(Judd's Type IV). Two dates from burned
roof material recovered by Vivian from
near the northwest end of the roomblock
are 1068+vv and 1072v.

Stage VII (1095+)

This is the designation for the
front arc which serves to enclose the
plaza (Figure 4.4g). There are no dates
from the arc, but it clearly postdates
the construction of both Stages V and VI.
The arc is presently obscure with very
little rubble showing, let alone definable room outlines. Vivian in 1956 estimated there to be approximately 44 rooms,
but this is no more than a guess. The
arc has been assumed to represent a single row of rooms, but it is possible that
in places only one or two closely parallel walls are present, without forming
rooms. Rubble is blocky, suggestive of
"McElmo" style masonry.

Jackson, who examined Una Vida at a
time when the arc was evidently better
preserved than now, suggested a gate, or
break in the arc at its east end. Surface evidence is now too obscure to ver-
ify such a feature, but it is a definite
possibility.

PEÑASCO BLANCO

History

Peñasco Blanco ("white cliff point"
or "white rock point") was probably named
for a prominent light-colored sandstone
bluff 0.3 km south of the ruin. The name
was originally given by Carravahal, Lt.
Simpson's guide. The Navajo name for the
ruin has been translated as "house around
which the wash bends" (Teitjen n.d.:8) or
"table-land-tapering-to-a-point house"
(Franstead and Werner 1974). These names
refer to the site's location on a mesa
100 m above the confluence of the Chaco
and the Escavada. The name was also
translated by an anonymous annotator of
Holsinger's manuscript (probably Edgar
Hewett) as "walled house."

Peñasco Blanco (Figures 4.8-4.16) is
a 180 m long arc of rooms, five deep and
up to three stories high, with a one-
room-wide arc enclosing an oval plaza.
There are two Great Kivas in the plaza,
and two more just outside the building to
the northwest and south. East and northeast of the building are a large trash
mound and a small "McElmo Ruin" built on
a massive artificial terrace. There are
many other features around the site,
including prehistoric roads, retaining
walls, and an upright slab that Mindeleff
thought might be a calendrical device
(Mindeleff 1891:148).

Simpson and Jackson visited the
ruin; Jackson described several (perhaps
ten) intact rooms in the northeast end of
the main arc (probably including Rooms
1-3) and behind Kivas F and G (Jackson
1878). Mindeleff (1891:150) described
intact plank roofs, which he saw in 1888.
When Holsinger visited Peñasco Blanco, 15
years later, no intact roofs remained.

Judd reports a conversation about
Peñasco Blanco with Hosteen Beyal, a
local Navajo who was born about 1830.

The old man describes Penasco Blanco
as having been in very good condition when he first saw it. The ruin
was then three stories high and most
of its rooms were still roofed.
Many of the rooms were in excellent
shape, with hair brushes hanging
from the walls and squash blossoms
(not squash stems), strung on yucca
cord, suspended like chilis from the
walls. Sticks used for stirring
mush had been stuck in wall joints;
pots and bowls still stood on the
floors. The general appearance was
that the inhabitants had but recently disappeared. Old Wello and

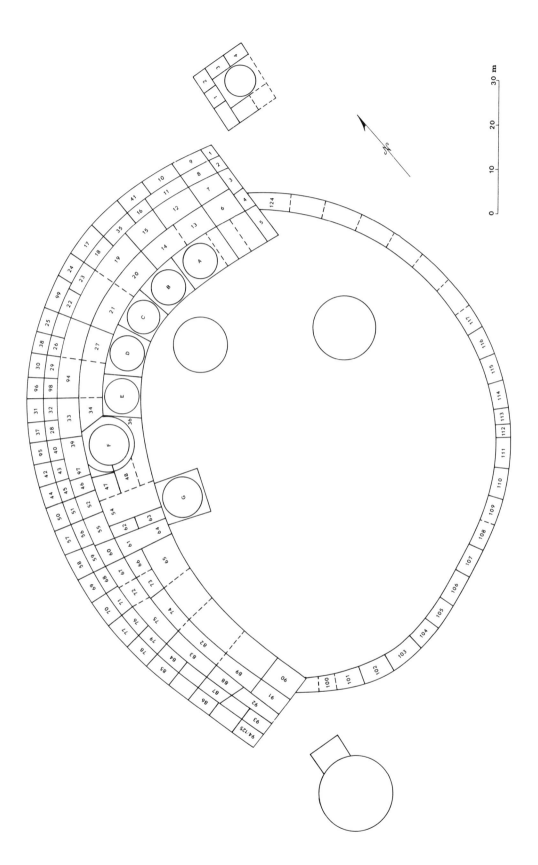

Figure 4.8. Peñasco Blanco.

Figure 4.9.  Penasco Blanco, looking east; Chaco Wash in background.

Figure 4.10.  Penasco Blanco, looking west.

Figure 4.11. Penasco Blanco, looking south; "McElmo Ruin" and retaining wall to left.

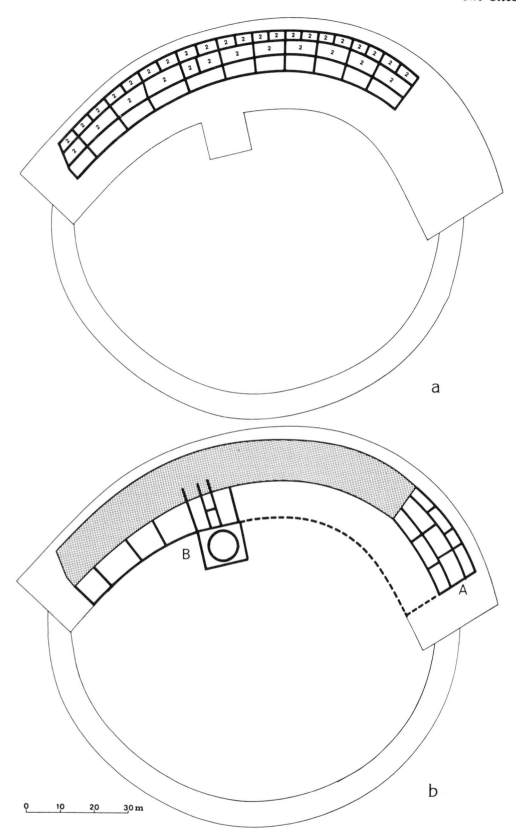

Figure 4.12. Peñasco Blanco, construction stages: (a) Stage I; (b) Stage II. All new construction is one story unless otherwise noted.

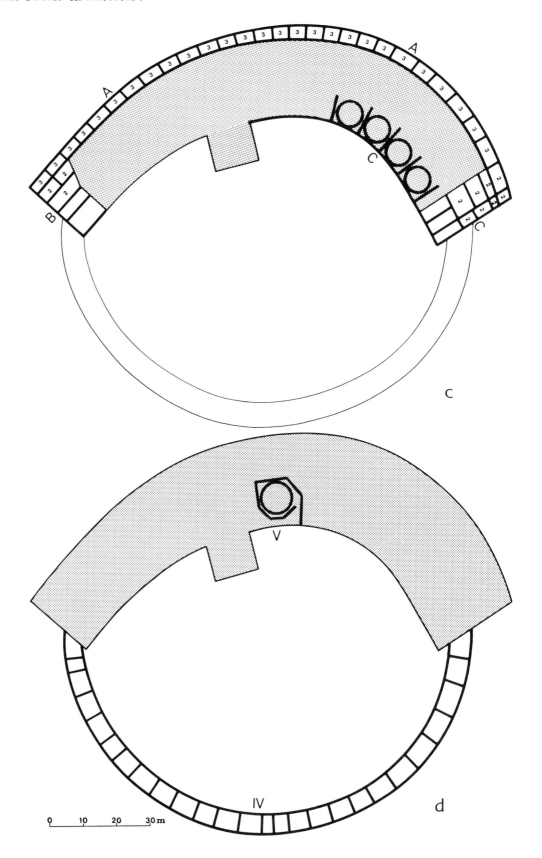

Figure 4.12    Peñasco Blanco, construction stages con't: (c) Stage III;
(d) Stages IV and V.

Figure 4.13.   Penasco Blanco, Kiva C and Room 19 foreground, looking west.

Figure 4.14.   Penasco Blanco, Rooms 31 to 34 foreground, looking southwest.

Figure 4.15.  Penasco Blanco, Rooms 15 and 19, foreground, looking northwest.

Figure 4.16.   Penasco Blanco, examples of masonry (frames are 70 cm x 70 cm.   Top row, left to right:   Room 40 NW wall; Room 12, S wall; Room 63, SE wall.   Middle row, left to right:   Room 3, W wall; Room 42, S wall; Room 92, S wall; Room 115, S wall. Bottom row, left to right:   Kiva C; "McElmo Ruin," N exterior wall; Retaining wall below "McElmo Ruin."

other Navajos excavated a number of rooms at Penasco Blanco, while in the employ of Richard Wetherill; a white man, not named, was in charge of the work (Judd 1954:345).

Wetherill did not claim responsibility for this work. Earlier, he had told Holsinger that the Navajos had dug in Peñasco Blanco looking for salable artifacts. A passage from Pepper does not resolve the Navajos' motives, but does describe their rewards:

During the period of our work in Pueblo Bonito some of our Navajo workmen cleaned out a number of rooms in Peñasco Blanco and in one of these a great many human bones were found. Some of these, including portions of the skull, were charred, and the majority of long bones had been cracked open... (Pepper 1920:378).

Sometime before the Navajo excavations, F. T. Bickford had also noted "...some fragments of skulls in Penasco Blanco. They lay among the rubbish of a fallen outer wall as if they had rolled from within" (1890:902). The debris of a cannibal feast was probably not the kind of buried treasure the Navajo excavators hoped to find. Hosteen Beyal, and others, had told Judd about sizable finds of turquoise at Penasco Blanco, and this may have inspired the unlikely looting of the site. In any event, the affected rooms probably included many of those which had intact roofs (and almost certainly Rooms 1, 2, 3, 7, 8, 31, 41, 46, 51, 61, 95, and 98).

In 1926, Frank H. H. Roberts, Jr. put a trench and two test pits in the trash mound (Roberts 1927). Roberts' work was the only scientific excavation at Peñasco Blanco until the limited testing of a prehistoric road south of the ruin by the Chaco Center.

Marty Mayer and W. E. Suddereth directed the only stabilization at Peñasco Blanco, which took place in 1971-1972. Mayer refilled the excavated rooms, obtained the first accurate map of the ruin and the first tree-ring samples with specific proveniences.

### Architecture

#### Stage I (900-915)

Stage I was an arc of 120 m in length, at least two- and probably three-rooms deep, and two stories tall (Figure 4.12a). The masonry was Type I. The rear row was a two-story line of small rooms, paired behind larger rooms of the front row. The rear rooms were consistently about 2.6 m wide, and averaged about 4.9 m in length (sd=0.4 m, N=11), with a floor area of about 12.7 m². Many of these small rooms had paired vents through the exterior wall on the second story. One pair of vents was exposed in the first story exterior wall of Room 98. Doors occurred in the first-story exterior walls of Rooms 32 and 43, but these probably represent Stage III modifications.

The row of larger rooms (Room 88 to the unnumbered room west of Room 19) may have been the original plaza-facing row of Stage I. In its final form, at least parts of this row were two stories, and as discussed below, these rooms may have been fronted by another single-story row of rooms. Doors from rooms of this row appear in some second-story walls, e.g., from the large rooms into rear row Rooms 56, 40, and 32. Plaza-facing, second-story doors (in Rooms 46, 52, and 45) probably reflect Stage III modifications. Walls are not preserved to a sufficient height to confirm the presence or absence of vents.

Rooms of this row were about 4.25 m wide and ranged from 9.1 to 12.0 m in length (discounting relatively insubstantial cross walls in Rooms 46-52 and 55-60). The average floor area was about 45.0 m², (sd=5.4 m², N=11), a little less than four times the floor area of rear row rooms. Since the rear row was two stories tall, each large room fronted four rear row rooms; thus the floor area of the large front room was about the same as the floor area of its associated rear rooms.

This row of large rooms may not have been the plaza-facing row of Stage I. The visible large rooms could been fronted by an almost identical one-story row (Room 89 to Room 21). No walls of this row are now standing, but rubble in this area appears to contain many chipped edge building stones, suggesting Type I masonry.

Stage I dates to about 900-915. Two dates (913r and 916cL; Table 4.2) in this span are definitely associated with Stage I; both were from lintels in the rear wall of Stage I, and were given a field provenience from Stage IIIA Rooms 30 and 96.

#### Stage II (1050-1065)

Stage IIA. Stage IIA is an extension of the north end of the Stage I arc, consisting of a block of six large rooms (Figure 4.12b).

All these rooms appear to have been two stories: the tall rear walls of Rooms 12, 15, and 19 (discussed below) rise to the top of the second story, but no further, and the few remaining walls of the front wall (e.g., the east wall of Room 13, the south wall of Room 20) remain to about 1 m above the first-story beams and offsets.

The second story of Stages II and III almost certainly rose well over the second story of Stage I. The first-story level of Stage II (and later Stage III) is probably well above the first-story level of Stage I. (See the discussion of Stage IIIA, below.)

The six large rooms average about 4.6 to 5.5 m wide and 8.0 to 9.4 m long, or about 40-45 $m^2$ in floor area. The four rear row rooms appear slightly irregular in length; the one measurable room is about 6.5 m long and 2.2 m wide (14.2 $m^2$ floor area).

Stage IIA includes the highest standing wall in the ruin (Figure 4.15); it is the second-story rear wall of Rooms 12, 15, and 19. This wall has been heavily stabilized, and currently visible features are largely rebuilt. It shows raised-sill doors from Room 15 into both of the smaller rooms behind it; the wall is sufficiently preserved to reveal evidence of similar doors, if originally present, leading into Rooms 12 and 19, but no such evidence is apparent. Also present are unusually low vents, paired on both sides of each cross wall of both the second and third (rear) row of rooms. Since these cross walls do not align, the rear wall of Room 15 is perforated by a remarkable number of vents and openings. At least one room in the rear row (Room 11) and perhaps two (Room 16) had room-wide platforms.

Stage IIA has three dates in the 1050-1065 span, and one beam which dates to 1087. The 1050-1065 beams from Stage IIA were considerably larger than the beam dated to 1087. The later beam probably was a repair, as it runs closely parallel to a larger, earlier beam in Room 15.

Stage IIB. The best-defined portion of Stage IIB (Figure 4.12b) is a block of rooms visible near the center of Stage I (Rooms 61-64). The first-story levels of Rooms 62 and 63 are of a masonry style very similar to that of Stage IIA, and a date of 1056 from Room 63 suggests that IIA and IIB were contemporaneous (1050-1065). Presumably the entire roomblock dates to this span. The row of single-story, plaza-facing rooms running north and south of this roomblock, along the front of Stage I, is speculative. The existence of these rooms themselves, later replaced by the elevated circular rooms of Stage IIIB, is suggested by the two-story height of Rooms 13, 14, and 20 -- the front row of rooms in Stage IIA. It is very likely that this two-story row terraced down to a single story, plaza-facing row; therefore, (Figure 4.12b) indicates such a plaza-facing row.

At the other end of Stage IIB (south of Rooms 61-64), the walls of the plaza-facing rooms are much too reduced to determine anything of the masonry style; however, massive sandstone of the type employed in the banded masonry of Stage III is very infrequent in the visible rubble, suggesting an earlier date. The rooms of the arc south of the roomblock were probably only one story tall, and of approximately the same size as the rooms directly behind them.

Little more can be said about this row. Parts of the central block (Rooms 61-64) were once exposed by illicit excavations. This unit was one story tall (a second story was added in Stage III) and must have replaced, in part, some rooms on the plaza-facing row of Stage I. The rooms are unusual in having their long axes perpendicular to the plaza.

Kiva G and its enclosure have been somewhat arbitrarily included in Stage IIB. The masonry of Kiva G, as far as it is visible, appears like that of other Stage II construction.

Stage III (1085-1090)

Stage III (Figure 4.12c) includes several substages: a rear row of rooms (IIIA); the rooms at the northeast and south ends of Stages I and II (IIIB and IIIC); and circular rooms along the north end of Stage I (IIID). Most of this architecture exhibits a well executed, banded, Type III masonry. Dating for Stage IIIA and IIIB, from 1085-1090, is fairly secure. Hawley dated "fine wide banded" masonry, the characteristic masonry of Stage III, to 1051-1062 at Peñasco Blanco (Senter 1938:6). I cannot reconcile Hawley's dating with mine.

Stage IIIA. A single row of three-story rooms was added to the original rear wall of the Stage I pueblo in Stage IIIA. To build the addition three stories tall, it was necessary to cap the Stage I rear wall with a third story of Stage III masonry. Ground floor levels of Stage IIIA

Table 4.2.  Tree-ring dates from Peñasco Blanco.

Room 1

| | | |
|---|---|---|
| PBL–29 | 1088r | |
| PBL–30 | 1088cL | |

Room 9

| | |
|---|---|
| PBL–39 | 1087rL |
| PBL–37 | 1087cL |
| PBL–44 | 1087cL |
| PBL–40 | 1088r |
| PBL–35 | 1088rL |
| PBL–97 | 1088rL |
| PBL–36 | 1088cL |
| PBL–38 | 1088cL |
| PBL–43 | 1088cL |
| PBL–45 | 1088cL |
| PBL–47 | 1088cL |
| PBL–95 | 1088cL |
| PBL–96 | 1088cL |

Room 11 (?)

| | |
|---|---|
| GP–2255 | 1052vv |
| GP–2256 | 1065v |

Room 12

| | |
|---|---|
| PBL–101 | 1058rL |
| PBL–102 | 1061rL |

Room 13

| | |
|---|---|
| GP–2252 | 1055vv |

Room 15/16

| | |
|---|---|
| PBL–51 | 1059r |
| PBL–52 | 1087r |

Room 20 (?)

| | |
|---|---|
| GP–2246 | 1061r |

Room 22 or 23

| | |
|---|---|
| GP–2244 | 1016vv |

Room 28 or 32

| | |
|---|---|
| GP–2238 | 1088r |

Room 30

| | |
|---|---|
| PBL–62 | 913r |

Room 31

| | |
|---|---|
| PBL–65 | 1088cL |

Room 35 (?)

| | |
|---|---|
| GP–2245 | 1018vv |

Room 36

| | |
|---|---|
| PBL–81 | 1120r |

Room 57 or 58

| | |
|---|---|
| GP–2234 | 1088r |

Room 61 (?)

| | |
|---|---|
| GP–2225 | 862vv |
| GP–2230 | 1051rB |
| GP–2226 | 1056r |

Room 63

| | |
|---|---|
| PBL–83 | 1056r |

Room 91, 92, or 93

| | |
|---|---|
| GP–2223 | 1080vv |

Room 96, vent lintel

| | |
|---|---|
| PBL–89 | 0916cL |

Room 98, vent lintel

| | |
|---|---|
| PBL–91 | 1088r |
| PBL–93 | 1088r |

Table 4.2 (continued)

Kiva F, enclosure

|  |  |
|---|---|
| GP-2241 | 1079vv |
| East end of arc | |
| GP-2263 | 1075vv |
| GP-2261 | 1085+r |
| GP-2264 | 1085+r |

No provenience

|  |  |
|---|---|
| PBL-24 | 898c |
| PBL-25 | 898c |
| PBL-7 | 915rL |
| PBL-21 | 916c |
| PBL-23 | 916c |
| PBL-1 | 984++vv |
| DPB-7 | 1030vv |
| PBL-106 | 1040r |
| DPB-6 | 1042vv |
| PBL-28 | 1045++r |
| DPB-8 | 1052vv |
| PBL-10 | 1052vv |
| DPB-11 | 1052v |
| DPB-10 | 1053vv |
| PBL-12 | 1055vv |
| BE-99 | 1056vv |
| PBL-13 | 1056rL |
| JPB-121 | 1057c |
| PBL-4 | 1059cL |
| DPB-9 | 1061r |
| PBL-27 | 1061r |
| PBL-5 | 1061r |
| PBL-3 | 1061c |
| BE-100 | 1061rL |
| PBL-2 | 1061cL |
| PBL-16 | 1065vv |
| PBL-22 | 1083r |
| K-9 | 1084cL |
| DPB-12 | 1087c |

Note:  All dates are probably from roof elements unless otherwise noted.
Key to symbols, see Appendix C.

are at least 1-1.25 m above the corresponding Stage I levels. The cross-wall pattern in the rear row of Stage I was continued in Stage IIIA. There is no evidence that this row continued as three stories behind Stage IIA. Perhaps the abbreviated first-story level was eliminated at the Stage I and Stage IIA junction, with the third-story of Stage IIIA continuing on the second-story level of Stage IIA. A similar situation is indicated behind Stage IIIB. Stage IIIA rooms averaged 4.3 m in length (sd=0.2 m, N=5), and were about 3 m wide, giving a floor area of about 12.9 m$^2$ (about the same as the rear rooms of Stage I). Stage IIIA rooms were 0.4 m longer than their Stage I counterparts, but the extra thickness of Stage III walls, when compared to Stage I cross walls, reduced the Stage IIIA floor areas to a figure comparable to the Stage I rooms immediately in front.

Other than the doors in the Stage I rear wall, probably cut in Stage IIIA, no first-story lateral doors were exposed in the partially excavated Rooms 31 and 95. No second- or third-story lateral openings were noted or reported; however, second-story doors, probably a modification made in Stage IIIA, opened from Rooms 30 and 37 perpendicularly into their Stage I counterparts. Stage IIIA is well dated to the 1085-1090 span by lintels in Rooms 30, 96, and 98.

Stage IIIB. Stage IIIB consists of the block of seven rooms at the south end of the Stage I and II arc. This addition was one room wide for the first three rows, which were probably terraced up to two stories in the third row, and two rooms wide in the rear two rows, which may have been three stories in height. Because the block was made to conform to the exterior south wall of Stage I, room sizes are irregular. The similarity of the banded masonry of Stage IIIA, and the symmetry of its placement with Stage IIIC, both suggest construction in the 1085- 1090 span.

Stage IIIC. Stage IIIC consists of a block of eight rooms (Rooms 1-4, 6-9) roughly comparable to Stage IIIB, but at the opposite end of the Stage I and II arc. Most of this building was constructed in banded masonry like the rest of Stage III. The block of eight rooms is two rooms wide and two stories tall; it is possible that the rear rooms were originally three stories, but their walls are not currently preserved to this height.

Several of the rooms in this block were once excavated, exposing first-story wall features that have been reburied.

Room 6, a large room in the front row, had doors in all four of its first-story walls; rooms behind Room 6 appear to have been connected by doors only in their north and south walls (i.e., those oriented perpendicular to the plaza). The situation in Rooms 1-4 is less clear. No lateral doors (either to Rooms 7-9 or to the exterior) are known except one door between Rooms 4 and 6. Only one north-south door, between Rooms 2 and 3, is known on the first-story level. Where walls of sufficient height are preserved, the pattern of doorways in these eight rooms seems to be repeated on the second story. Where visible (Rooms 6 and 7), vents are perpendicular to the plaza (i.e., east and west walls) on both stories.

Rooms 6-9 average about 6.0 to 6.5 m in length and decrease from front to rear rows from 5.75 to 2.25 m in width. Rooms 1-4 are about 2.25 to 2.30 m in width (east-west), but vary considerably in length (north-south). Rooms 3 and 4 are subdivided on the first story, but this may be a later modification of a room originally 4.80 m long. Room 1, on the other hand, appears to have been a cubicle about 2.25 m$^2$, with no known entry. This part of Stage IIIC is securely dated to the 1085-1090 span.

Stage IIID. The row of elevated, first-story round rooms (Kivas A-O) along the north end of the Stage I and II arc has also been assigned to Stage III. This assignment is on the basis of banded masonry exposed in the enclosure of Kiva D and again in Room 5, indicating a continuous wall of banded masonry enclosing these round rooms. The round rooms themselves appear to have been built of masonry employing predominately tabular sandstone, probably without banding. These round rooms are probably built over parts of Stage IIB, and even Stage I, construction. The dating of these units is speculative, and it is possible that Stage IIID is later than suggested here (see Stage V, below).

Stage IV (1090+)

Like Stage III, this one-room-wide, single-story, plaza-enclosing arc (Figure 4.12d) is also of banded masonry. It presumably postdates Stages IIIB and IIIC, but the similarity in masonry suggests that the difference in time was not great. This date is probably after 1090; I estimate 1090-1120.

The rooms are well preserved only near the center of the arc (Rooms 109-114); here measurements are about 5.25 m in length and 3 m in width in most rooms (with the exception of the subdivided Rooms 112 and 113). Average floor area would be about 15 m$^2$, since the curved long sides of the rooms are not equal in length.

A door opens into the plaza from Room 102. In the north corner of Room 112, there is an opening that may be the base of a partially blocked T-shaped door. No other features are visible in Stage IV walls.

Stage V (1120-1125?)

Stage V includes Kiva F and a few second-story walls to the south (Figure 4.12d). Kiva F is an elevated round room on the second-story level; it is not a Tower Kiva. The masonry of the round room enclosure is banded, much like that of Stage IIID. The date from Room 36 (A.D. 1120), a part of this enclosure, indicates a time period of 1120-1125 for this construction, later than other banded masonry at Peñasco Blanco.

Other Construction

There are at least four Great Kivas at Peñasco Blanco. Two are in the plaza, and two outside the main building to the south and northwest.

Just northeast of the main building, there is a large terrace or platform formed by two massive retaining walls. The full extent of this terrace cannot now be determined, but the two walls forming its downslope edges define a rectangle of over 20 m on a side. The terrace wall does not exceed 1.75 m in height.

Built upon this terrace is a small building referred to as the "McElmo Ruin." Six to eight rooms in an L-shaped block partly enclose a subterranean circular room. The visible walls are of massive "McElmo" style masonry. If, as seems likely, the terrace was prepared for the McElmo Ruin, this constitutes a great deal of site preparation for a rather small building.

PUEBLO BONITO

History

Pueblo Bonito (Figures 4.17-4.30) is the largest and best known building in

Chaco Canyon. It covered almost two acres and stood at least four stories tall. Pueblo Bonito, "beautiful town," was the name given by Carravahal, but the name was used as early as the 1840s by Josiah Gregg (apparently in reference to Pueblo Pintado). Edgar L. Hewett, rival excavator of nearby Chetro Ketl, took exception to this name: "It may be doubted if in the great days of the Chaco it (Pueblo Bonito) was distinguished among its neighbors for its great beauty. Several others probably surpassed it in this respect" (1936:32). Hewett preferred an Anglicized version of the Navajo name for Pueblo Bonito: Sabinei. The Navajo name referred to Threatening Rock (described below): "leaning rock" (Franstead and Wenner n.d.).

Pueblo Bonito was excavated over three decades, from 1896 to 1927, first by the American Museum of Natural History and later by the National Geographic Society. Pierson's (1956) account of the archaeological research at Pueblo Bonito needs no embellishment and is quoted here, in full:

In 1896 the Hyde Exploring Expedition was formed with one of its principle aims being the archeological excavation of Pueblo Bonito. Richard Wetherill, A Coloradoan, and guide, rancher, and amateur archaeologist, had interested two of his customers, B. Talbot B. Hyde and Frederick E. Hyde Jr., in exploring Pueblo Bonito. The Hyde brothers were wealthy New Yorkers, heirs to the Babbitt soap fortune, and had gained an interest in Southwestern archaeology partly through Mr. Wetherill. Wetherill had visited the canyon as early as 1895.

The Hydes contacted Professor F. W. Putnam of Harvard and the American Museum of Natural History for advice. Professor Putnam became scientific director of the expedition, although he spent very little time in the field. He appointed George Pepper, a student of his, as field director, Mr. Pepper directed the expedition's efforts in the summers of 1896-1899. Richard Wetherill served as excavation foreman with his four brothers assisting.

During the four seasons 198 rooms and kivas were excavated and backfilled. Most of the material, including several complete rooms, was donated to the American Museum of Natural History in New York City. The excavations started in the north central and northwest part of the building in 1896. In 1897 work continued in the northern or curved part of the building. Holsinger says that work also started in 1900 but there is no record as to whether this was the organization with Pepper or just the expedition going on its own.

Along with the expedition at various dates were experts in various fields, so that quite a bit of information was gathered over the years. In July, 1916, N. C. Nelson of the American Museum of Natural History and Earl H. Morris sank pits in the east and west trash mounds for stratigraphic tests. They also made a ground plan of Pueblo Bonito which, after checking by B. T. B. Hyde, was used by Pepper in his report. A glance at Pepper's (1920) report will serve to indicate the richness of the ruin and the amount of material removed.

In April of 1897 an expedition led by Warren K. Moorehead, Curator, Department of Archaeology, Phillips Academy, Andover, Massachusetts, arrived in Chaco Canyon. The excursion was paid for by Robert S. Peabody, ex-Phillips Academy student, and seems to have had as its principal objective the making of a collection of southwestern artifacts for the Phillips Academy Museum. Dr. W. N. Wallace of Farmington accompanied the expedition as interpreter. They left Farmington, New Mexico for Chaco with nine men, a large wagon and 5 horses. They dug and explored several rooms in Pueblo Bonito, securing some 2,000 artifacts in three weeks' time.

While in the canyon they also dug a small cemetery about a mile from Pueblo Bonito. Mr. Moorehead suggested that the government take over and protect the area. Stories have it that Moorehead was not particularly appreciated by the Wetherills, as the ruin was in the process of being excavated by them at the time that Moorehead did his digging. However, the land was unpatented government land, open to anyone with a shovel, so nothing could be done about it by the Wetherills.

During the summer of 1920 Neil Merton Judd, curator of Archaeology at the U. S. National Museum was asked by the National Geographic Society to make a preliminary study of Chaco Canyon and recommend a large house for archaeological exploration under their research program. Judd recommended Pueblo Bonito, and was appointed director of the Society's expedition, spending the summers of 1921 through 1927 digging Pueblo Bonito and Pueblo del Arroyo. The prime objective was the complete excavation, both for information and as an exhibit for the public. This entailed re-excavation in part of the backfilled rooms of the Hyde Expedition and some stabilization work. Except for a small collection in the National Geographic Society's Explorers' Hall, all of the material excavated by Judd in Pueblo Bonito is at present in the National Museum.

Excavations were commenced in May of 1921 with seven assistants and a mixed crew of 14 Zuni and Navajo Indians. Camp was set up directly in front of Pueblo Bonito along the edge of the arroyo. A water supply was developed and excavations were carried on in the central wing (Kiva A) and southeastern sections of the village. Fifty secular rooms, five kivas, and a number of refilled rooms were cleaned out. The west refuse mound was trenched.

The 1922 season lasted from May to September with seven assistants and about 20 Zuni and Navajo laborers. Excavations were carried out in the eastern wing and 35 rooms and six kivas were uncovered. The east refuse mound was trenched and three test pits, each 12 feet deep, were sunk in the alluvial fill of the valley floor in the vicinity of Pueblo Bonito to determine its composition and stratigraphy. In excavating beneath the floors of the east wing the remains of an earlier village were discovered. Railroad trams of the type used in small mines, and hoists with "A" frames were installed to aid in disposing of the tremendous amount of fill removed from the town.

Work was again resumed in the spring and summer of 1923 with excavations principally of the north section of Bonito. The crew consisted of several white assistants and 27 Navajo and Zuni. The rooms in the back section filled by the Hyde Expedition were redug and three new kivas and 26 new secular rooms were unearthed. The east courtyard was cleared to its original surface at the time of occupation and trenched in places. Expenditures for the year 1923, which included some work in Pueblo del Arroyo, totaled $18,700, a little over par.

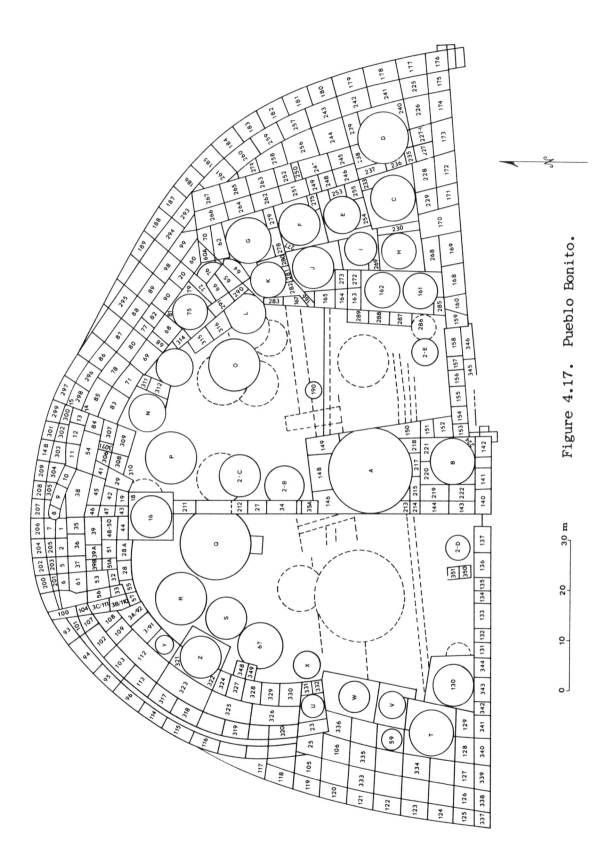

Figure 4.17.   Pueblo Bonito.

Figure 4.18.   Pueblo Bonito, looking northwest.

Figure 4.19.   Pueblo Bonito, looking northeast.

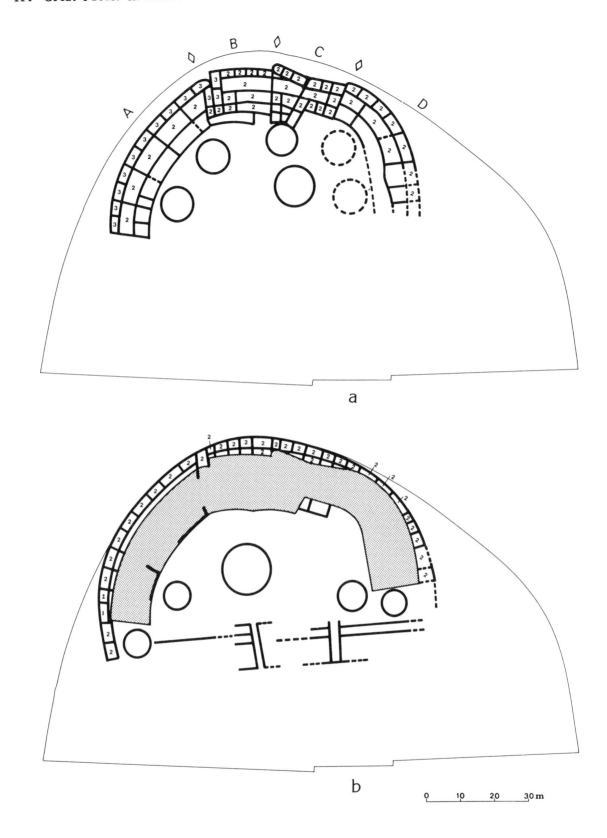

Figure 4.20.  Pueblo Bonito, construction stages.  (a) Stage I; (b) Stage
II.  All new construction is one story, unless otherwise
noted.

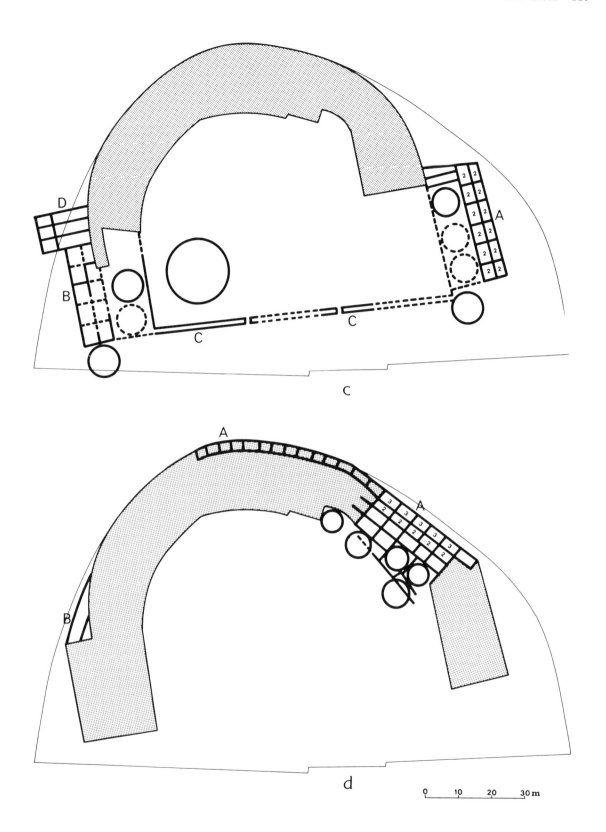

Figure 4.20    Pueblo Bonito, construction stages: (c) Stage III; (d) Stage
               IV.

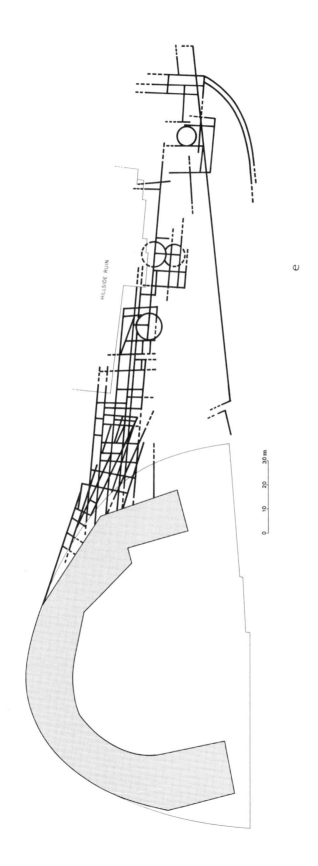

HILLSIDE RUIN

e

0   10   20   30 m

Figure 4.20   Pueblo Bonito, construction stages: (e) Stage V.

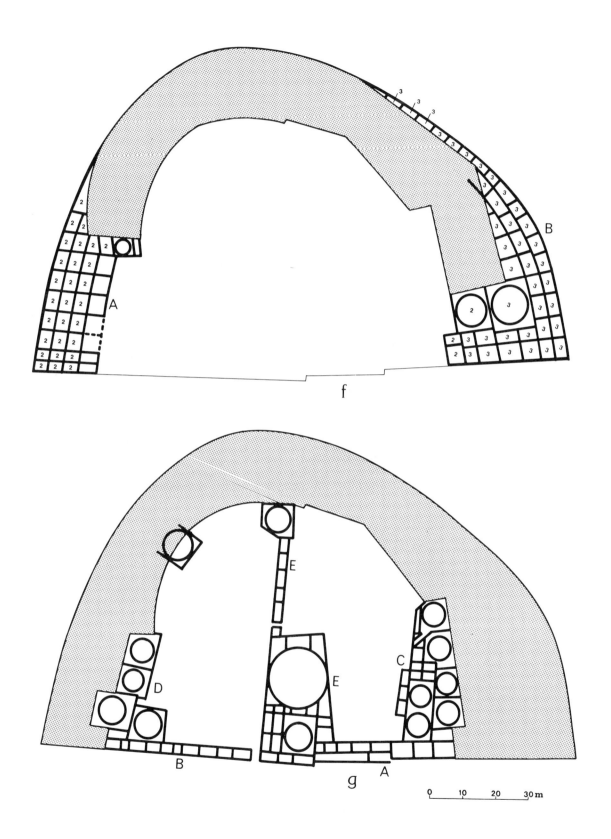

Figure 4.20   Pueblo Bonito, construction stages cont.:
(f) Stage VI; (g) Stage VII.

Figure 4.21.  Pueblo Bonito, southeast corner, looking northwest.

Figure 4.22.   Pueblo Bonito, Rooms 320, 326, and 330 foreground, looking
          southwest.

Figure 4.23.   Pueblo Bonito, Rooms 53 and 61 foreground, looking west.

Figure 4.24.   Pueblo Bonito, Rooms 188 and 294 foreground, looking northwest.

Figure 4.25.   Pueblo Bonito, Kivas K, L, and O foreground, looking northwest.

Figure 4.26. Pueblo Bonito, Room 333 foreground, looking south.

Figure 4.27. Pueblo Bonito, Exterior rear wall of Room 207 and rooms to the east, looking southeast.

Figure 4.28.  Pueblo Bonito, Rooms 171 to 175 foreground,
looking north.

Figure 4.29.    Pueblo Bonito, corner door in northwest corner of
Room 173, looking northwest.

Figure 4.30.  Pueblo Bonito, examples of masonry (frames are 70 cm x 70 cm.  Top row, left to right:  original exterior wall, outside Room 317; exterior wall, outside Room 100; exterior wall, outside Room 297.  Second row, left to right:  Room 247, S wall; Room 87, SW wall; Room 106, N wall; exterior wall, outside Room 123.  Third row, left to right:  Exterior wall, outside Room 189; exterior wall, outside Room 179; exterior wall, outside Room 172.  Fourth row, left to right:  Room 244, E wall; Room 229, S wall.  Bottom row, left to right:  exterior wall, outside Room 133; Room 151, N wall; Room 34, W wall.

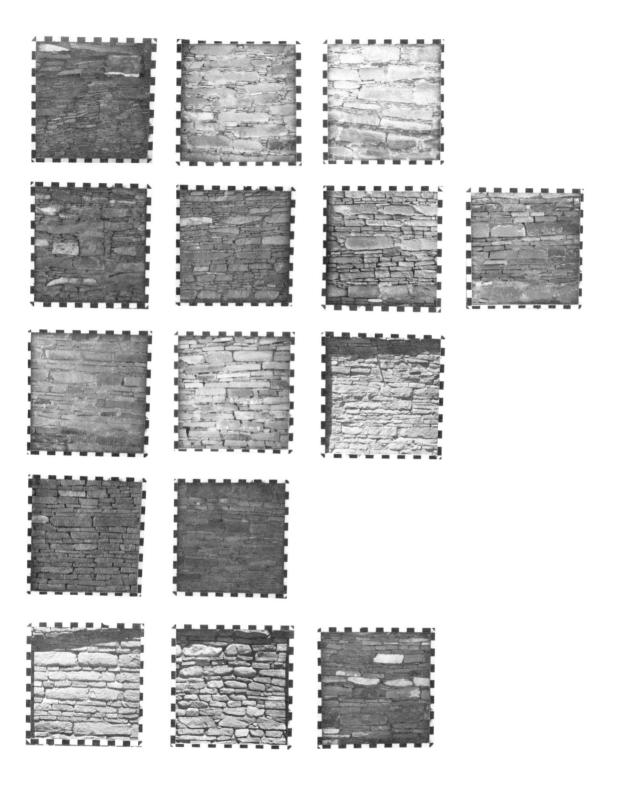

The summer months of 1924 saw work carried out in the west half of the village, in the foundation complex extending under and to the east of Pueblo Bonito, and in the west great kiva. The walls around the trash heap and a wall extending from the southeast corner of Pueblo Bonito in a northeasterly direction for 500 feet were delineated. Excavations in the eastern and northern sections of the village were completed. The crew this season consisted of six technical assistants plus four other whites and 37 Indians. The surface structures of Pueblo Bonito had been fairly well excavated by the end of the 1924 season.

During the 1925 season, 25 Indian laborers were employed at Pueblo Bonito and the concurrent dig at Pueblo del Arroyo. In Bonito the underlying structures were excavated and four deep stratigraphic trenches were made. Work in the substructures was continued in the 1926 season and sub-court walls in the west plaza were outlined in conjunction with the ceramic study of Dr. Roberts.

Some work was accomplished in the village in 1927, as eight laborers were employed, but most of Judd's time was spent in studying the various features on the mesa in back of Bonito and Chetro Ketl (Pierson 1956:24-28).

Since the National Geographic Society's fieldwork, excavation has been limited to operations incidental to stabilization (e.g., Vivian 1940).

Pueblo Bonito had attracted the interest of treasure hunters long before the first scientific excavation of the Hyde Exploring Expedition. The mounds in front of the ruin had been pitted over and over again -- particularly unfortunate in light of their unusual nature (discussed below). Nor were the members of the Hyde expedition themselves blameless. Wetherill's ranch buildings, trading post, and lodge were built in the flats just west of the ruin, and many of his timbers and much of his building stone came from the ruin. Seven of the presently dated beams from Pueblo Bonito came from Wetherill's buildings (Robinson et al. 1974), and these beams represent only a fraction of the timber removed from the ruin for use in historic buildings and campfires. Wetherill also repaired completely or rerofed several rooms in Pueblo Bonito.

The single greatest catastrophe to befall Pueblo Bonito -- if only because it was so long anticipated -- was the fall of Threatening Rock on January 22, 1941. Threatening Rock was a huge monolith of sandstone that had become detached from the cliff behind Pueblo Bonito. The threat to the pueblo was not lost on the town's original inhabitants, who apparently attempted to shore up the rock with posts, and built curtain walls around its base to prevent further erosion. Despite their efforts, and a flurry of National Park Service memoranda almost nine centuries later, Threatening Rock finally fell in 1941, leveling a large part of the northeast part of the building (Figure 4.18) (Schumm and Chorley 1964).

## Sources

Major sources on the architecture of Pueblo Bonito are Pepper's notes (1920), and Judd's monographs both on the architecture (1964) and, to a lesser extent, the artifacts (1954) of the site. Judd's notes, in the National Anthropological Archives, were also consulted for this study. Other sources include the accounts of Simpson (1850), Jackson (1878), and Holsinger (1901) and scale models, one prepared for the USGS by Jackson and another at the Brooklyn Museum, built under the direction of Herbert Spinden. Finally, the southeast third of the ruin was mapped and drawn in great detail by Herbert K. Boone, for the Historic American Building Survey (1940-1942). Boone's program began at the southeast corner of the site and did not reach the area below Threatening Rock until after the fall. Boone, in addition to being an superb draftsman, was no fool.

Neither Judd's nor Pepper's reports are easy reading. Using Judd's published data is more exegesis than archaeology. In general, this study follows Judd's (1964) outline of the growth of Pueblo Bonito; where divergences from his scheme are major, they are explicitly identified.

## Architecture

The plan of Pueblo Bonito, perhaps more than anything else, is responsible for its name. The tall curving exterior wall, viewed from ground level or from the cliffs above, offers a vista unique in the Southwest. Holsinger (1901:14), in a fanciful interpretation, compared the curve of the rear wall to the outline of the skull of its ancient builders. He appreciated, however, that the final layout was the culmination of a series of building stages and not a single construction, as have all other investigators of the ruin. At Pueblo Bonito, perhaps more than other Chacoan structures, the evidence of building stages is preserved in the layout (Figure 4.17).

Jackson and Holsinger examined the obscured layout of an unexcavated ruin, while Pepper touched on building stages only tangentially. So it was left to Judd, the final excavator and heir to Pepper's notes, to unravel the history of construction (Judd 1964). Unfortunately, Judd wrote his report under the influence of the studies of masonry facing styles that have long dominated Chacoan architectural studies. Judd defined four masonry styles during his fieldwork at Chaco, and in the climate of Hawley's and Roberts' work, he allowed these four styles to define four construction stages. That these stages, so defined, were frequently at odds with the evidence of layout and stratigraphy is clear again and again in Judd's report. Judd's types probably comprise a valid sequence, particularly if his third and fourth types are combined. The use of only one criterion, masonry style, to the nearly complete exclusion of other evidence, does not do justice to the series of building sequences so evident in the building's plan. This reanalysis, at 50 years distance, of course, also falls short of the true architectural sequence at Pueblo Bonito, but I believe that finer divisions than Judd's four are evident by combining masonry styles with dendrochronology, stratigraphy, visible wall abutments, and ground plan.

## Stage I (920-935)

"Old Bonito" was Judd's term for the earliest part of Pueblo Bonito, here called Stage I (Figures 4.20a, 4.22, 4.23). Stage I identified a semicircle of about 100 ground floor rooms, some reaching three stories, and at least three, and probably as many as five, round pit structures.

Stage I expanded along its arc in several segments, termed here Stages IA, IB, IC, and ID (Figure 4.20a). The western third, Stage IA, consists of a line of five large two-story rooms, each backed by a pair of smaller two- or three-story rooms, fronted by two round pit structures. Stage IA appears to have been constructed as a single unit. Central and east sections (Stages IB, IC, and ID), on the other hand, appear to

have been constructed in five or six segments, each segment consisting of one or two large front rooms backed by two to four smaller rooms, and perhaps fronted by a round pit structure. The pattern of growth is not clear, but construction of Stages IB, IC, and ID in a counterclockwise direction seems likely, at least up to the point of juncture with Stage IA outside Room 104. Stage IA may have been an independent, and possibly earlier, structure, eventually joined to the other sections of Stage I by a complex of small rooms (Rooms 3, 33, and 56), built over the north end of Stage IA. Alternately, these rooms could be a later remodeling of the completed Stage I. Judd concluded they represented part of the earliest "core" of Old Bonito (1964:58), but they may be later than other Stage I building.

Dendrochronology does not resolve this problem. The western arc has yielded the best dates from Stage I (Table 4.3). The earliest date (828) comes from Room 317, a small storeroom in Stage IA. Other rooms in the west arc (Rooms 320, 323, and 325) suggest construction from 920-935. In layout, the west arc indicates construction as a single unit, and because the 920-935 dates are tightly clustered, the 828 date is probably from a reused beam.

Stage IB structures have no dates, nor does the block of small rooms between the west and middle sections. From the small portion of the east arc that was not destroyed in Stage IVA, there is one date at 932 (Room 296), and several others in the 1040s (Rooms 85 and 296). These last probably date later (Stage II) modifications, which were extensive in this part of the building. On the basis of these few samples, Stage I may be dated from about 920 to 935, but questions of internal chronology remain moot.

In addition to growth in segments along the arc, rooms were added to the front of completed segments. This is particularly evident in the middle section, where up to three irregular rows of rooms were added in front of existing rooms. Abutments on Judd's maps and in the stabilized ruin are difficult to untangle, but the middle section of Stage I probably began as a large room (Room 61-37-36-35) with a jacal plaza-facing wall (later replaced by stone masonry), backed by four two-story smaller rooms (Rooms 1, 2, 5, 6). Two other large rooms (early versions of Rooms 38 and 54-84) adjoined on the east, with their own complement of smaller rear rooms. The jacal construction of the front wall of Room 38 and the small Stage I pit

Table 4.3.  Tree-ring dates from Pueblo Bonito.

Room 14B

| PB-5 | 1029L |
| PB-4 | 1138v |

Room 57

| JPB-48 | 1071v |

Room 97

| PB-12 | 897r |
| GP-2297 | 1068+vv |
| GP-2299 | 1073v |

Room 100

| PB-8 | 1024r |
| PB-9 | 1042rL |

Room 105

| GP-2310 | 1077+v |
| GP-2309 | 1077L |

Room 119

| GP-2308 | 1039v |
| GP-2307 | 1046+vv |
| GP-2306 | 1057v |

Room 172/228, intramural beam

| JPB-58 | 1061v |

Room 173

| JPB-03 | 1077v |
| JPB-2 | 1078cL |

Room 173/227, intramural beam

| GP-2319 | 1077L |

Room 227

| JPB-003 | 1053+v |
| JPB-22 | 1064vv |
| JPB-3 | 1075v |
| GP-2320 | 1077vv |
| JPB-23 | 1081r |

Room 227/235, intramural beam

| GP-2321 | 1078L |

Room 228

| JPB-55 | 1074+r |

Room 244

| JPB-5 | 1061++vv |
| JPB-7 | 1076v |
| JPB-6 | 1097vv |

Room 242

| JPB-24 | 1080+r |
| JPB-25 | 1081r |

Room 245

| ? JPB-1 | 1060++vv |

Room 251

| JPB-50 | 938+vv |

Room 256

| JPB-10 | 1051v |

Room 257

| JPB-16 | 1047vv |
| JPB-20 | 1055++vv |
| JPB-18 | 1080vv |
| JPB-14 | 1081r |
| JPB-19 | 1084r |
| JPB-15 | 1129vv |

Table 4.3 (continued)

| Room 261 or 267 | | | Room 320 (continued) | | |
|---|---|---|---|---|---|
| JPB–130 | 1073r | | PB–44 | 919r | |
| | | | PB–38 | 919r | |
| **Room 264** | | | PB–39 | 919r | |
| | | | PB–37 | 919c | |
| JPB–46 | 1040v | | PB–52 | 919c | |
| | | | PB–45 | 919c | |
| **Room 268, roof support post** | | | PB–49 | 919c | |
| | | | PB–42 | 919c | |
| JPB–27 | 1080vv | | PB–43 | 919c | |
| | | | JPB–107 | 919c | |
| **Room 290/291, intramural beam** | | | PB–47 | 919c | |
| | | | PB–48 | 919c | |
| JPB–79 | 1061r | | PB–46 | 919c | |
| | | | PB–51 | 919c | |
| **Room 293** | | | PB–40 | 919c | |
| | | | PB–33 | 919L | |
| JPB–67 | 920v | | PB–31 | 919L | |
| | | | PB–32 | 919L | |
| **Room 296** | | | PB–34 | 919L | |
| | | | PB–30 | 919L | |
| JPB–68 | 932rL | | | | |
| JPB–69 | 1047rL | | **Room 323** | | |
| | | | | | |
| **Room 300** | | | JPB–115 | 936r | |
| | | | JPB–114 | 936r | |
| GP–2313 | 1029v | | | | |
| GP–2314 | 1040L | | **Room 323, roof support posts** | | |
| GP–2315 | 1047L | | | | |
| | | | JPB–116 | 919r | |
| **Room 305** | | | JPB–117 | 919r | |
| | | | | | |
| JPB–83 | 1033rL | | **Room 325** | | |
| | | | | | |
| **Room 308** | | | JPB–120 | 902cL | |
| | | | | | |
| JPB–91 | 1045r | | **Room 325, roof support posts** | | |
| | | | JPB–106 | 919v | |
| **Room 314** | | | JPB–113 | 919c | |
| | | | | | |
| JPB–145 | 1082r | | **Room 327** | | |
| | | | | | |
| **Room 317** | | | JPB–118 | 876++r | |
| | | | | | |
| JPB–104 | 828r | | **Unnumbered room N of 295** | | |
| | | | | | |
| **Room 320** | | | JPB–76 | 1041r | |
| | | | | | |
| JPB–108 | 919r | | | | |
| JPB–109 | 919r | | | | |

Table 4.3 (continued)

Kiva C, pilaster

| | |
|---|---|
| JPB–38 | 1120r |

Kiva D, enclosure

| | |
|---|---|
| GP–2327 | 1064vv |

Kiva I, pilaster

| | |
|---|---|
| JPB–93 | 1011vv |

Kiva J, pilaster

| | |
|---|---|
| JPB–37 | 1080vv |

Kiva L

| | |
|---|---|
| JPB–81 | 1047c |
| JPB–70 | 1061r |

Kiva P, pilaster

| | |
|---|---|
| JPB–92 | 1102++vv |

Kiva X

| | |
|---|---|
| JPB–122 | 1034v |

Kiva 16

| | |
|---|---|
| K–8 | 977vv |

Room 162, pilasters

| | |
|---|---|
| JPB–31 | 963vv |
| JPB–33 | 996vv |
| JPB–34 | 1007vv |
| JPB–30 | 1029vv |
| JPB–28 | 1082vv |

Unnumbered round room below Room 286

| | |
|---|---|
| JPB–98 | 1058r |
| JPB–97 | 1088r |

North Wall, intramural beam

| | |
|---|---|
| JPB–206 | 1049v |
| PB–23 | 1077r |

No provenience

| | |
|---|---|
| GP–2275 | 986vv |
| DPB–15 | 1009vv |
| GP–2284 | 1029r |
| GP–2273 | 1036+vv |
| GP–2289 | 1043v |
| GP–2288 | 1044r |
| GP–2291 | 1061vv |
| GP–2330 | 1063vv |
| K–6 | 1063rL |
| K–3 | 1064c |
| K–5 | 1065cL |
| K–4 | 1065cL |
| K–7 | 1072rL |
| K–1 | 1073cL |
| GP–2329 | 1075vv |
| GP–2328 | 1095r |

Note:  All dates from roof elements unless otherwise noted.
      Key to symbols, see Appendix C.

structure partially fronting Room 54-84 both suggest that these rooms originally faced the plaza, and that the rooms in front of them (Figure 4.20a) were later additions. The few tree-ring dates from the rooms in front of Rooms 61-37-36-36, 38, and 54-84 are later than the suggested 920-935 period of initial Stage I building, but are so much later that they probably define Stage III and VII modifications and repairs.

The patterns of plaza-facing growth are less confused in Stage IA. The west section was apparently originally two rooms in depth, with the rear rooms being two or even three stories in height and the front rooms two. Running along the front of these rooms was a single story jacal wall, which later was replaced by stone masonry, becoming Rooms 3a to 330. In the west section, abutments in the repeatedly modified rooms of the final plaza-facing row suggest that many of their walls postdate the original plaza-facing row of large rooms. The roof beams of this later row are inserted into ventilators in the original plaza-facing wall, or run parallel to the plaza, again indicating that these roofs postdate the earlier rooms. The possible exception is Room 330, at the southwest end of Stage IA, which may have been part of the original construction.

Later Stage I pit structures were built just beyond this jacal wall, with the exception of a pit structure below Room 224 (a room in the jacal, plaza-fronting row). This pit structure may have been constructed in front of Room 323, and is comparable in size to a similar structure below Room 83 (both are about 4.9 m in diameter). Both of these small Stage I pit structures show that the west, as well as the middle, sections of Stage I were originally two rooms deep, with smaller, jacal ramadas added later over the earlier pit structures. The only problem with this reconstruction is Judd's classification of the masonry of the pit structure below Room 224 as his Type II, a type presumably postdating Stage I.

Very little can be said about the eastern section of Stage I. It probably resembled the middle more than the west section. Two rooms, 325 and 316, continued in use even when partially buried under Stage IV construction.

The large rooms of the original plaza-facing row include some of the largest in Chaco Canyon. They were generally about 3.4 to 4.0 m wide, but varied from 7.0 to 14.6 m in length. Room 61-37-36-35 was in excess of 50 m$^2$ in floor area; Room 323 was slightly over 40 m$^2$. Despite this very large size, Judd considered Room 323 "typical of its time" (1964:59).

Door patterns are very irregular. Some of the rooms of the original plaza-facing row have doors and vents along the line of the arc, but most doors were perpendicular to the arc (i.e., opening onto the plaza or into the rear row of rooms). Plaza-facing doors are difficult to characterize from the published accounts and visible remains. The only convincing T-shaped door in Stage I, opening from Room 109 into Room 3A, probably began as a plaza-facing door (Judd 1964:28). Interior doors appear to have had raised sills and rounded outlines.

Two centuries of subsequent use make any interpretation of floors and floor features difficult. With one or two exceptions, floors do not seem to have been prepared and plastered. In the well preserved Stage IA, only one large room (323) shows any evidence of original floor features: a single firepit and a series of five buried neck-banded jars, presumably used for storage. The neck-banded ceramic type would generally be consistent with Stage I dates (neck-banding continued until about 1000; T. Windes, personal communication, 1982). In the east section, numerous floor features were reported for Rooms 78 and 85, but these probably date from later stages. The features in Room 85 were built over thick layers of trash fill above the original floor (Pepper 1920: 270); in Room 78, only the earliest of the series of superimposed firepits may date to Stage I. A central, masonry-lined firepit in Room 315, at the extreme southeast end of Stage I, may be one of the few Stage I features to have survived (Judd 1964:73). In the middle section, no floor features are reported that could possibly be assigned to Stage I. Pepper's rather confusing descriptions of Rooms 38 and 54 may indicate room-wide platforms in the west ends of those rooms (Pepper 1920:184-186, 213-214). If these features were original, they would be the earliest known room-wide platforms at Chaco.

The rear row of rooms was a third to one-half the length and about two-thirds the width of the larger front row rooms. Judd (1964) also indicates lower ceiling heights in the rear row. Rear rooms in the middle section are smaller than their counterparts in the east and west sections. Middle section rear rooms average 8.1 m$^2$ (sd=2.8 m$^2$, N=10), while rear rooms in the east and west sections average 13.5 m$^2$ (sd=2.0 m$^2$, N=10). In Stage IA, with its regular ground plan, the ratio of large room to small room floor areas was approximately 3:1. Since each large room had two smaller rooms behind it, the ratio of ground floor area with one front and two rear rooms in a three-room unit would of course be 3:2. If we accept that the rear row was three stories, and the front row two, the ratio for all stories is about 1:1. That is, the total floor area in the small rear rooms was approximately equal to the floor area of the large rooms directly in front of them.

Doorways in the small rear row rooms are perpendicular to the plaza, opening into the large rooms in front. The rear row rooms do not connect laterally (with other small rooms) or to the exterior (through the rear wall of Stage I). Pepper (1920:Figure 7) shows a 0.12 m$^2$ opening through the second floor in the northwest corner of Room 1, one of the rear rooms in the middle section. When excavated, it was covered by a thin slab of sandstone. Judd states that rear row doors "were ordinarily equipped with a single secondary lintel pole about 5 inches below the main lintels and secondary jambs slanted to support a sandstone slab placed from the living room" (Judd 1964:59).

At least one rear room (320) had a flagstone floor. Almost all had plastered walls (as did most Stage I rooms) and in a few, the plaster was smoke-blackened. No rear row rooms had any evidence of floor features either in Stage I or later.

In the western section (Stage IA), the later plaza-facing rooms were approximately equal in depth to the large rooms behind them, but were apparently half or less the length of those larger rooms. Each of the later plaza-facing rooms had a floor area slightly less than half that of the larger rooms in the row behind, e.g., Rooms 328, 329, and 330 at the southwest end of Stage I. In two of these rooms (328 and 330) subfloor ceramics were of an assemblage consistent with Stage I dates (Roberts n.d.), suggesting that these floors and features on them may date to Stage I. All three rooms had a variety of firepits, bins, etc., of which the earliest could possibly date to Stage I. In particular, Room 328 had a firepit, deflector, and ventilator complex.

The warren of rooms in the front middle section of Stage I is one of the most confusing areas of Pueblo Bonito, both in the literature (Judd 1964:61-64) and the visible remains. Some rooms, particularly those bridging the middle and western sections, were of three stories, but most others were probably only two. The second-story level of Room 3 (which from Stage III on was at or below plaza level) was equipped with a firepit, deflector, and ventilator; the age of this complex of features is uncertain. Several other rooms in this area, such as 39 and 42, also had bins and firepits. A number of the larger rooms in the middle section were subdivided and used as late as the mid-1200s, as evidenced by the presence of Mesa Verde Black-on-white ceramics (Judd 1959:194, 1964:65). Doorway patterns in the front rows of the middle section are highly irregular, the result of extensive rebuilding and reuse over a fairly irregular block of Stage I rooms.

In the east section, surviving plaza-facing rooms include Rooms 71, 83, 315, and 316. A lower floor in Room 83 was lined with flagstones and had at least three firepits; these may belong in Stage I (Pepper 1920:269). On a lower floor of Room 71 there was a firepit, deflector, and ventilator complex. (Lower floors in both Rooms 71 and 83 were later sealed under featureless floors.) Both Rooms 315 and 316 had firepit, deflector, and ventilator complexes, which were apparently in use until late in the life of Pueblo Bonito; Room 315 also had a room-wide platform, probably a later addition (Judd 1964: 73).

## Stage II (1040-1050)

When the Late Bonitians came to dwell at Pueblo Bonito, their first conspicuous undertaking was to surround the crescent-shaped old village with a single, close fitting row of two-story houses ... remnants of cross-court building operations ... indicate that Late Bonitian architects were, from the time they assumed control at Pueblo Bonito, intent upon joining its two extremes into a compact whole (Judd 1964:78-93).

Between its Biblical opening and Taoist close, Judd's description provides a quaint, though accurate definition of Stage II. Stage II consists of three parts: first, a row of rooms surrounding the exterior of Stage I (partially razed in Stage IIIB, but projected from surviving foundations and wall stubs; second, a set of parallel walls running across the front of the plaza (from Judd 1964:Figures 4 and 5); and third, additions to and modifications of Stage I plaza-facing rooms and pit structures (Figure 4.20b). Dates associated with this construction (from Rooms 100, 300, 305 and possibly

Rooms 85 and 296) range from 1033 to 1047, with the most convincing dates toward the end of that range, or about 1040-1050 (Table 4.3). Stage II marks the introduction of Judd's Type II masonry, and another beam from a plaza-facing room modification of this type (Room 308) dates to 1045.

Stage II construction surrounded that of Stage I and created a building only slightly larger than the original Stage I. However, where Stage I was a series of small segments, the rear row of rooms and the plaza-enclosing walls of Stage II were built as coherent units in single, village-wide construction projects. Stage II construction differs rather dramatically in scale from Stage I.

The exterior row of rooms consisted of two parallel walls, about 2 m apart, surrounding the irregular rear wall of Stage I. Cross walls (between the long walls, and between these walls and the rear wall of Stage I) correspond exactly to the placement of cross walls in the rear row of rooms in Stage I. This suggests that this row of rooms is an extension of the small room pattern in Stage I. Stage II rooms in this exterior row were probably two stories tall.

The rear row of Stage II was built over up to 2 m of sand that had accumulated against the exterior wall of Stage I. This raised the ground floor level of Stage II to the level of the second floor of Stage I. Along the west arc of Stage I, the Stage I rear rooms were probably three stories in height and the Stage II addition two, so the roofs of both Stage I and II were on the same level. Along the middle section of Stage I, Stage II added a story above the existing, two-story Stage I rear rooms. Of course, not much of the Stage II rear row of rooms was standing when Pepper and Judd made their observations, and it is likely that the Stage II addition was three stories in the west section, making it uniformly one story taller than the Stage I rear wall it surrounded.

Stage II rooms in the west section (excluding the narrow dead space between the old exterior wall of Stage I and the newer building) average about 10.0 m$^2$ (sd=1.1 m$^2$, N=6), while those in the middle section (again excluding dead space) average only 6.5 m$^2$ (sd=0.6 m$^2$, N=6). If the west section was two stories tall, approximately 20.0 m$^2$ of floor space was added behind each Stage I rear room in the west arc. In the middle section of Stage II, the area added behind each Stage I room was slightly less, or about 13 m$^2$. Later, in Stage IIIB, a third story was added over the

middle section Stage II rooms, increasing the floor area behind each Stage I room to 19.5 m$^2$, a figure very close to the 20 m$^2$ area provided in Stage II for west arc rooms. This added floor space in the middle section may have rectified the inequities in the Stage II areas added behind the middle and west sections of Stage I.

The rear wall of Stage I had no doorways, so direct communication between the rear rooms of Stage I and the new arc of Stage II was not possible. Doorway connections in this 145 m long row of Stage II rooms were apparently entirely lateral (with the exception of doors into the interior Stage II rooms in the middle section). Doors were built in the exterior wall -- apparently in every room and on every story (Figure 4.27); however, both Pepper and Judd, who made their observations before stabilization, were convinced that all of the exterior doors were blocked with Type II masonry at the time of construction, that is, the exterior doors were blocked as soon as the rooms were finished. Other Chacoan buildings have doors in rear walls opening onto balconies, but this part of Pueblo Bonito showed no evidence of balconies.

The interpretation of the exterior doors in Stage II is rather difficult. The view often taken is that the blocked doors were expedient entrances and exits for use during construction, but the number of doorways involved (perhaps as many as 75) makes this difficult to accept.

Interior doorways, running the length of the addition, were fairly uniform, trapezoidal doors (lintels narrower than the sills) with a raised sill. None had secondary jambs or lintels. At least one preserved first story had a hatchway, and probably many other Stage II rooms did also. Communication from Stage I to Stage II may have been over the common roof level and through hatchways (where Stage I and II upper stories were on the same level) or perhaps through now-vanished third-story plaza-facing doors in the Stage II rooms, and then down through hatchways (where the Stage II upper story was higher than its Stage I counterpart).

Walls generally were not plastered, but floors apparently were. No floor features were reported. Room 14b, on both its first- and third-story levels, had a room-wide platform, as did the third floor of the unnumbered room (east of Room 297). Another feature, fairly specific to Stage II rooms at Pueblo Bonito, was a standardized ceiling type, using willow rod mats over the secondary timbers (Judd 1964:82; Pepper 1920:318).

The rooms between the main Stage II row and the rear wall of Stage I in the middle section were, of course, roofed at each level. Judd (1964:89) suggests that the narrow dead space between the Stage II rooms and the rear wall of the west section of Stage I was also roofed, but his evidence is less than compelling.

The second major Stage II building project was the erection of walls, subsequently razed, across the front of the plaza. Beyond noting that they (probably) existed, little can be said about these walls. They were more likely a line of rooms than double walls like those built in Stage III. They may have included a block of rooms near the central axis of the plaza -- perhaps mirrored later in the Kiva A enclosure of Stage VI.

Finally, in Stage II (and continuing into later stages) the plaza-facing rooms of Stage I were capped with a second story. Little is known about these additions. Their construction was irregular and associated floors were not preserved. This part of Stage II was much less systematic than the exterior row of rooms and the plaza-enclosing walls or rooms.

Round pit structures with Type II masonry (which generally equates with building Stage II, but may have continued in use through Stages IIIA and IIIB) include two which are clearly modifications of earlier Stage I pit structures (Kiva R and the unnumbered unit below Kiva 67). By its location, Kiva N was also a probable modification of an original Stage I structure.

Stage III (1050-1060)

Stage III is a marked departure from Judd's sequence. Stage III consists of four units (Figure 4.20c): IIIA, "a rectangular block (35 m long by 18 m deep) of east wing rooms that stand forth conspicuously on any ground plan of Pueblo Bonito" (Judd 1964:103); IIIB, a block of rooms symmetrical to IIIA, in the west wing; IIIC, plaza-enclosing double walls; and IIID, a block of six rooms planned, but perhaps never built, at the west end of Stage II.

Stage III preserved the azimuth of the axis of symmetry created in Stage I and maintained in Stage II, but shifted that azimuth slightly east. Stage IIIB, suggested by foundations and wall stubs, was razed and built over in Stage VA.

Stage IIIA. Stage IIIA, in its final form, consisted of a rectangular block of two-story rooms at least six rooms wide and two rooms deep, fronted by three elevated round rooms, the roofs of which formed a first terrace in front of the block of rectangular rooms. This block was repeatedly modified and rebuilt (Judd 1964:Figures 4, 5, and 6). Judd, who concluded that construction began with his Type II masonry, also shows entire walls built of his Type IV masonry. Despite its long history, I believe the final plan of a rectangular roomblock fronted by elevated round rooms was the original one, although the presently visible elevated round rooms are undoubtedly later versions of the original elevated round rooms. These may even have been preceded by earlier pit structures. The rectangular block was not incorporated in the curved Stage II building; it seems to have been appended from the Stage II southeast corner, almost as an independent unit.

If cross walls of obviously later construction are eliminated, the rooms in the rectangular block are very consistent in size. In the rear row, the cross wall between Rooms 247 and 252 originally existed on the second story level only; the first story below these rooms was a single, undivided room some 10.4 m in length. Room size (excluding first-story Rooms 247-252, and Rooms 62 and 70) averaged 15.5 m$^2$ (sd=1.5 m$^2$, N=12).

Doors on the ground floor are both parallel and perpendicular to the plaza. In addition to doors, the west wall of Room 245 was also equipped with an intramural stairway to the second story of Room 246. Ground floor doors opening toward the elevated round rooms are few, and those few are offset to permit entry into the corners of the round room enclosures rather than into the round rooms themselves. Some of these doors open into stairs and wells that lead to the first-story terrace on the roof level of the round rooms. Second-story walls above the terrace survive only in two rooms at the south end of the block. Of these, one had a T-shaped door, while the other has a sill that is probably the low part of another T-shaped door.

Late in the history of Pueblo Bonito, there may have been a line of ramadas on the terrace along the front of the roomblock. The evidence for these is the jacal wall on the terrace just west of Room 255 and the remains of the walls of Room 255, the only room in this area with a firepit, also on the terrace.

On the ground floor level, doors to the exterior were located in two rooms at either end of the block (north wall of Room 267, the south wall of 245) and in at least two rooms on the rear wall.

These doors probably were cut during one of the many rebuildings of Stage IIIA, but perhaps the south door in Room 245 was original (Judd 1964:109).

Floor features were generally absent on the ground level floors. The ground floor of Room 245 was of two levels, with the north half raised 0.7 m above the south. The lower south half was subsequently filled and covered creating a level floor. Below the lowest floors in Rooms 62 and 226 (at the north end of the block), there were several large trash-filled pits, containing pottery of both Red Mesa and Gallup Black-on-white assemblages. These pits probably predate Stage IIIA.

Walls of most if not all rooms in this block were plastered. The plastering may be contemporaneous or later than Stage IIIA.

Perhaps the most significant furniture in these rooms consisted of room-wide platforms, now represented by sockets in standing walls. On the first floor level, three rooms in the north end of the block (Rooms 62, 264, and 267) had platforms at one or both ends. Where the second floor has survived to a sufficient height (in the south end), three out of four rooms had platforms but on the second story only. Room 249, a later subdivision of Room 248-249, had a small room-wide platform which in its last use had supported half a dozen terminally hungry parrots (Judd 1964:107). Because of the extensive rebuilding in this area, these features cannot be assigned to a particular stage, but they clearly belong to Stage III or V.

There is one significant tree-ring date from Stage IIIA: 1040 from a first-story roof beam in Room 264. A 1060vv date, probably from a round room pilaster log, reused as a post step, set in the fill of the southern portion of the Room 245 floor (Judd 1964:109), and a third date of 928vv from Room 251 are almost certainly not associated with Stage III building.

Both Stages IIIA and IVA are bracketed chronologically by Stage II (1040-1050) and Stage VI (1075-1085), thus Stages IIIA and IVA fall in the span 1050-1075. Since Stage IIIA clearly precedes Stage IVA, Stage IIIA should fall in the first part of the 1050-1075 span, perhaps 1050-1060. This suggests that the single associated date of 1040 is too early, although this date may represent the poorly defined Type II masonry beginnings of Stage IIIA.

Subfloor ceramics from Rooms 251 and 252 include small amounts of "Chaco-McElmo" (Roberts n.d.), a type dated later than 1050-1060 (Thomas Windes, personal communication, 1982). However, in both rooms there are over 2 m of superimposed floors (Judd 1964:Figure 8). "Sub-floor" in this case, may refer to occupational deposits greatly postdating original Stage IIIA construction.

Stage IIIB. This construction is suggested by razed walls below the largely unexcavated Stage VIA. The plan appears to have been a rectangular block, three rows of rooms deep, fronted by one or more circular rooms (Judd 1964:Figure 5). If my interpretation of this fragmentary unit is correct, it is symmetrical in form and location, and one-third smaller than Stage IIIA. Presumably, it would have been built about the same time (1050-1060).

Stage IIIC. Stage IIIC combines Judd's Type II walls, running from Room 150 to the south wall of Stage IIIA (Judd 1964: Figure 4), with his Type III walls running from the center of Kiva T toward Room 214 (Judd 1964:Figure 5). Judd suggested that these formed a continuous wall (Judd 1964:119). They are double walls (similiar to the plazas at Chetro Ketl and Pueblo Alto) with possible openings both east and west of the later (Stage VII) Kiva A enclosure.

Stage IIID. This is an enigmatic block of rooms that Judd thought were begun but never finished (Judd 1964:125). The block was appended to the west end of Stage II. The exact sequence of construction of Stage IIID and later building in this area is difficult to determine. Judd believed (1964:125) that Stage IIID preceded my Stage IVB. If built, this unit would probably have consisted of nine rooms, with a probable orientation to the south. Measurable room sizes (N = 3) range from 8.9 to 16.4 $m^2$.

Stage IV (1060-1075)

Stage IVA. Stage IVA was a 35 m long rectangular block (Figure 4.20d) built over the razed east end of Stages I and II. It ran from the north end of Stage IIIA to the truncated east end of Stage II (along the line of Stage I Rooms 71, 78, and 86, and an unnumbered Stage II room north of Room 86). In its final form, Stage IVA was six rooms wide and four to five rooms deep, and terraced from three stories in the rear row to a single story in the two front rows. Stage IVA probably included Kiva 75 and the round rooms preserved in the curved northeast wall of Room 76. Kivas L and M may also have been associated with Stage IVA. The southeast end of Stage IVA is one of the most complex and confusing areas of Pueblo Bonito that is still exposed to view (Figure 4.25). Assignment of some of the rooms in this area to a particular stage is more a matter of faith, hope, and charity than concrete evidence. Judd classified the masonry of this area as his Type III, but this designation masks a great deal of variation. The round and rectangular rooms now visible from Kiva K to Kiva M may be later than Stage IVA. The three rows of rooms running northwest from Rooms 293, 99, and 60 are almost certainly original Stage IVA construction. The row of rooms between Room 69 and Room 76, fronting the first three rows, was heavily modified after their initial construction. It is impossible to determine if they originally paralleled in size and shape those behind them. Beyond the fact that they are an even later addition, little can be said about Rooms 64-66, and 290, 291, and 314.

Discounting the confusion of doors in the front two rows of rooms (290-314 and 76-69), some clear patterns of doors are apparent. Each room of the row from Room 20 to Room 80 had large T-shaped doors, both oriented toward the plaza and into the rooms of the next row to the rear (at least on the ground floor). In the second-story rear wall of this row, and in the two rows to the rear (beginning with Rooms 99 and 293), all doorways had raised sills. Many of these smaller doors were blocked with Type III masonry, but several which were not show secondary jambs and lintels, leaning into the rooms to the rear. Doorway connections were perpendicular to the plaza, except in the extreme southeast end of Stage IVA, where lateral doorways allowed access around existing (Stage IIIA) and Stage IVA construction. Vents were paired and were all perpendicular to the plaza.

Room area in the two rear rows is very uniform, and only slightly smaller than the average room size of corresponding rooms in Stage IIIA: about 13 m$^2$ (sd=0.7 m$^2$, N=6). The next (Rooms 60 to 80) row was much less regular in size, due mainly to variations in cross-wall spacing. These rooms average 12.9 m$^2$ (sd=4.5 m$^2$, N=6).

Several rooms had room-wide platforms. Both the first and second stories of Room 98 had two platforms, one in either end of the room. Other rooms with second-story room-wide platforms included Rooms 87, 88, and probably Room 89.

Floor features were absent in the rear two rows of rooms, and absent in most of the front (Rooms 77-82 to 60) row also. One exception was Room 90, in which Pepper (1920:294-296) reported a line of ten mealing bins.

The only tree-ring date from Stage IVA is a 920 date from Room 292. This date is clearly too early. Dates from Rooms 290 and 314, which clearly postdate initial construction are 1061 and 1082. This suggests that Stage IVA is no later than 1082. Since IVA is bracketed by IIIA (1050-1060) and VIB (1075-1085), a date of 1060-1075 is suggested.

At three stories tall, the rear row rooms of Stage IVA stood one story higher than the middle section of Stages I and IIIA. The row of third-story rooms over the middle section of Stage II (which are of Type III masonry) is probably an extension of Stage IVA over the earlier building.

Stage IVB. Stage IVB is a problematic alignment of foundations (Figure 4.20d) representing either razed walls or unused foundations (Judd 1964:Figure 5). These foundations suggest a building program similar to Stage IVA; however, they could also represent an early version of Stage VIA, as Judd suggests. As a parallel to Stage IVA, Stage IVB would have created three or four rooms, probably three stories tall, filling the reentrant between Stages II and IIIB.

Stage V (1070-1075?)

Stage V is the extensive series of foundations and razed walls (Figure 4.20e) extending southeast from the exterior walls of Stages IIIA and IVA. Judd referred to Stage V as the "northeast foundation complex," and repeatedly noted that the foundations were never used: "a complex of mud-and-stone foundations never built upon" (Judd 1964:143). However, limited testing by the Chaco Center, and several references in Judd, indicate that limited segments of the foundations were, in fact, built upon. In these sections, either the walls were stub walls or they were razed. The extent of the walls built on the foundation complex was limited (Judd 1964:Figure 11) and Judd was very emphatic that most of the complex of foundations never supported finished walls.

There are interesting differences in the construction of these foundations that may reflect their

intended use. Major northwest-
southeast foundations were generally
1.35 m deep and 0.75 m wide. Cross
wall foundations (southwest-north-
east) were much smaller: 0.15 to
0.50 m deep and 0.35 to 0.60 m wide
(Judd 1964:146).

Stage V extended at least 150 m east
of the southeast corner of Pueblo Bonito,
and undoubtedly continued under Hillside
Ruin. Its full extent is not known; Judd
did not excavate in the area between the
known foundations and the long wall running east from the southeast corner of
Pueblo Bonito. Nor did he extend his
search beyond the east end of the foundation complex as shown.

At least two major grid orientations
in the complex may represent two phases
of Stage V. These run on two different
azimuths, one about 110° east of north
and the other 120° east of north. Relative dating of the two phases is not possible from the published descriptions,
but the time between the two was probably
very short. The double wall (suggesting
a plaza-closing wall) that runs west from
the southeast corner of Stage VIB is
later than either grid (Judd 1964:Plate
49, lower).

Although Type III and IV masonry are
both represented in the small segments of
finished wall, the dating of Stage IV is
definitely between Stages IV and VI,
probably in the early 1070s.

Judd interpreted the "significance
of the complex" as follows:

Upon conclusion of our explorations
I could find but one reasonable
explanation for this whole vast
Northeastern Foundation Complex: It
was built to an extensive addition
planned for Pueblo Bonito, an addition altered repeatedly during the
planning stage but abandoned before
construction really began (1964:
151).

## Stage VI (1075-1085)

Stage VI created the final curved
exterior of Pueblo Bonito. This stage
has two substages (Figure 4.20f): Stage
VIA, built over the razed Stage IIIB, and
Stage VIB, built over the unused foundations of Stage V. Stage VIA is of Judd's
Type III masonry, while Stage VIB is of
his Type IV.

Stage VIA. This is the least excavated
area of Pueblo Bonito (Figure 4.26). Six

of about 30 rooms were never excavated,
and about 12 of those excavated were
reported by Pepper (1920:339) as "Minor
excavations ... nothing of special interest was developed" with no further elab-
oration. Whatever pearls Pepper discovered in these rooms, he did not choose
to cast them before the archaeological
profession. Judd excavated a few rooms
in this area, which are more fully documented than Pepper's work.

Stage VIA curved most markedly just
below its juncture with the rear wall of
Stage II (at Room 115) and so curved
beyond the southwest corner of Stage II.
Stage VIA presently does not stand over
two stories beyond that point. Doors on
the ground floor are all perpendicular to
the plaza, except at the extreme north
and south ends of the block. No complete
series of front-to-back, interconnected
rooms was excavated, so our view of room
features is somewhat spotty. Room 336
was probably originally a plaza-facing
room, as were the two rooms to the south,
and probably also the rooms replaced by
Kiva T. All three of the former rooms
had large T-shaped doors, but the two
excavated ones (Rooms 59 and 336) both
had round rooms built in at a later time.
In Room 356, the round room was subsequently removed, and a plastered living
room with firepit and bins was installed;
perhaps this restored the rooms's original function. Excavated Rooms 335, 333,
and 121 (behind the unexcavated plaza-
facing room south of 336) may represent
the other unexcavated interior rooms.
Room 335 was plastered, and has a room-
wide platform which Judd concluded was a
"post-construction" feature. Room 333,
next to the rear, was also plastered, and
had a low, masonry "bench" in the southwest corner. Room 121, the rear room in
the set, had "nothing of special interest." Room 334, behind the presumed
plaza-facing row, also had a T-shaped
door; it was plastered, but lacked any
floor features.

Room size in the first three rows was
fairly uniform, ranging from 18.9 to 20.5
m$^2$ (N=3). The smaller rooms in the
rear row were about two-thirds that size,
ranging from 1.5 m$^2$ to 13.9 m$^2$. The
six very small rooms at the south end of
Stage VIA represent rooms identical to
those in the rows to the north, though
half the size. Door patterns and wall
bondings suggest that these small rooms
are original, not later modifications.

The juncture between Stage VIA and
later Stage VIIB is conjectural. Judd
shows an abutment between Rooms 339 and
340 -- one room west of where this juncture is shown on Figure 4.20f. This butt
is not in the currently visible walls,

but neither is there evidence for a juncture between Rooms 340 and 341, as shown in Figure 4.20f. This boundary of Stage VIA is, in fact, a part of Stage VIA. Kivas T,V,W, and 130 (Stage VIID) are clearly additions and modifications of Stage VIA.

There are only three tree-ring dates from Stage VIA (Table 4.3): two in the late 1050s (Rooms 119 and 335) and one at 1077 (Room 105). Subfloor tests in Room 334 produced a Gallup Black-on-white ceramic assemblage, without later carbon-painted types (Roberts n.d.), an assemblage consistent with the earlier dates. However, directly beneath Room 334 were the remains of Stage IIIB (1050-1060). This sub-334 ceramic assemblage is very likely associated with Stage IIIB, and Stage VIA probably dates to the late 1070s.

Stage VIB. Stage VIB is characterized by the rectangular and round rooms surrounding the rear and south end of Stage IIIA. These consisted of a three-story tall, three-room deep arc behind Stage IIIA, two elevated round rooms (Kivas C and D) south of IIIA, and two rows of three-story rooms south of those round rooms (Rooms 176 and 177 to Rooms 171 and 229, and Room 170). The exterior wall running from the triple juncture of Stages II, IVA, and VIB (outside Room 297) to the southeast corner of Pueblo Bonito (Room 176) and the parallel walls between it and the rear wall of Stage IIIA were laid out together, continuing the lines of the long walls of Stage IVA and extending those lines out around the northeast wall of the Kiva D enclosure (Figure 4.20f). Judd thought that the northeast wall of Kiva D was earlier than Stage VIB, that is, perhaps an extension of Stage IIIA around an earlier version of Kiva D. The absence of doors in the ground-level west walls of Rooms 41, 241, and 242 supports the supposition of the presence of an earlier Kiva D. Prior to the construction of Stage VIB, the long walls of Stage VIB were continued around this enclosure and brought more-or-less parallel to the long north-south walls of Stage IIIA.

Although the long north-south axis walls were probably laid out in one operation, the placement of doors and ventilators in these long walls and east-west cross walls clearly proceeded from exterior to interior rows of rooms. The location of doors, which may have begun just above the foundation level (as discussed below), and vents, in all stories of both exterior and interior walls of the rear rooms, was determined in relation to the cross walls of that row. Similarly, the location of wall features in the next interior row (Rooms 261-175) was determined by the cross walls in that row rather than by those in the four rooms in their rear (Rooms 274-244).

Judd provided an illustration: a "previously completed ventilator was reduced to a width of 4" by the abutting south wall" in the southeast corner of Room 261 (Judd 1964:160). The location of the vent, in the east wall of the room, was evidently fixed and construction completed prior to construction of the south cross wall. This sort of error suggests division of labor between planners and builders -- and a certain amount of disinterest on the part of the builders, who apparently did not bother to look up while building the cross wall.

The three-story south leg of Stage VIB appears to have continued from the southeast corner of Pueblo Bonito at least as far west as Room 170 (Figure 4.28). Together, the existing Stage IIIA construction and additions to it in Stage VIB completely surrounded Kivas C and D.

Earlier versions of Kivas C and D were elevated, their roofs forming a terrace at the first-story level. The square enclosures around these two round rooms were heavily modified (mainly through extension upward) and the original round structures replaced by the presently visible Kivas C and D (on the second and third stories, respectively). In the north wall of Rooms 229 and 228, T-shaped doors that originally opened on the first-story terrace of the original Kiva C were blocked by the construction of the second-story round room.

Doorway connections in the ground story of the north arc of Stage VIB (the rows of rooms north of Rooms 177 and 225) are generally perpendicular to the plaza, with lateral connections in the extreme north end of the exterior row (behind the Stage IVA rear wall). Ventilators are paired, and are almost exclusively perpendicular to the plaza. A single corner door on the ground floor of the north arc at Stage VIB, from Room 257 to Room 258, appears to be a later modification.

In the second story of the north arc, doorways are both perpendicular and parallel to the plaza. In fact, almost every wall has a door (the major exceptions being the walls between Rooms 243 and 257, and between Rooms 180 and 181). Communication, which seems as though it would already have been fairly easy, was further facilitated by five corner doorways.

Third-story doorways, where present, appear to continue the pattern of the second story.

Although first- and second-floor doors in the north arc of Stage VIB were generally full-length doors, almost all were later partially blocked and transformed into raised-sill type doors. Many were subsequently completely blocked; the few open doors have secondary jambs and lintels, leaning away from the plaza.

Several doors in the south leg of Stage VIB are also full doors modified to raised-sill doors, but there are also several T-shaped doors. Two ground floor T-shaped doors are set off-center in the west walls of Rooms 226 and 227. Two other T-shaped doors, in the second-story north walls of Rooms 228 and 229, have been mentioned above in connection with Kiva C. Evidence of yet another T-shaped door remains in the third-story wall between Rooms 175 and 176. There were also two corner doors, in the southeast, second-story corners of Rooms 225 and 228.

While room sizes and shapes appear uniform in the rear two rows of the north arc of Stage VIB, the rear row rooms are actually slightly smaller, with an average size of about 16.5 m² (sd=1.4 m², N=10). Rooms of the next interior row are about one-fifth larger, with an average size of 20.9 m² (sd=1.1 m², N=7, excluding Rooms 175 and 261). Room sizes in the three rooms directly behind IIIA, of course, are quite variable, ranging from 19.7 m² to 30.1 m² (Rooms 258 and 24, respectively). Using Room 244 as a base, the ratio of ground floor room areas decreases from front to rear as follows: 1.00: 0.70 : 0.55. Room sizes and shapes in the south leg of Stage VIB are quite variable. Subdivision of Room 227/227-I was on the first floor only. During the replacement of Kiva C, the first stories of both Room 228 and Room 229 were quartered by stout masonry buttresses, presumably to support the walls against the filled first-story enclosure to the north. Disregarding the small compartments created by this quartering, room sizes in the south leg range from about 11.8 m² (Room 176) to 34.4 m² (Room 170).

Room 170 was probably no more than two stories. It was subdivided on its first story, creating a 2.25 m wide room at its north end that was subsequently filled. A vertical well was built into the fill behind the door through the partition wall, allowing access to the second floor at this point.

There are no records of floor features from Stage VIB, nor is there evidence of room-wide platforms.

Tree-ring dates (Table 4.3) from Stage VIB fall between an approximate range of 1075 to 1085, with two in the early 1070s (Rooms 228 and 261), one in the late 1070s (Room 244) and four in the early 1080s (Rooms 227, 242, and 257). A date in the late 1070s and early 1080s is supported by the subfloor ceramic assemblages in Rooms 179, 225, 241, and 243. These rooms, with the exception of Room 225, were built over earlier pit structures and plaza surfaces (Judd 1964: Appendix B). Subfloor ceramic assemblages in all rooms were primarily of Gallup Black-on-white with some carbon painted types -- an assemblage characteristic of the later 1000s (Thomas Windes, personal communication, 1982). A very late date (1129vv) from Room 257 may be from the late jacal wall dividing that room. Another late date of 1120, from Kiva C, probably dates the rebuilding of that round room. A span of 1075 to 1085 appears likely for Stage VIB.

## Stage VII (1085+)

Stage VII is a grouping of late rooms fronting Stages VIA and VIB, plus several rows of rooms enclosing and dividing the plaza (Figure 4.20g). Stage VII has been divided into five substages, each of which probably had a relatively complex internal construction sequence. With the exception of Stage VIIC, there is almost a complete lack of tree-ring dates for Stage VII. Moreover, Stage VII represents the last major building at Pueblo Bonito, and therefore lacks subsequent, dated building to bracket construction chronologically.

Stage VIIA. Stage VIIA consists of the line of single-story rooms extending across the south end of the east plaza, from Stage VIB to the enclosure of Kiva B. Within this stage, two distinct building episodes are evident: the first, three rooms extending west from Stage VIB (Rooms 159/160 to 169); and the second, the row of rooms extending from Stage VIIA to the Kiva B enclosure (Rooms 153 to 158). Judd classified the masonry of both as Type IV. The first unit of three rooms (Rooms 159/160 to 169) clearly precedes both the second unit and Stage VIIC. The second unit (Rooms 153-158) abuts the first; it also appears to abut the enclosure of Kiva B (Judd 1964:171), which suggests that at least the south portion of Stage VIIE preceded the west end of Stage VIIA. However, the east wall of the Kiva A enclosure abuts the north wall of Room 154, a room in this second section of Stage VIIA. Judd (1964:171) believed there were earlier versions of these rooms, a possibility supported by ceramic evidence. Subfloor ceramics from Room 153 were predominantly Red Mesa Black-on-white and associated types (Roberts interpreted this assemblage as indicating that Room 143 was built directly over the "old dump," [Roberts n.d.]). Subfloor ceramics from Room 156 were Gallup Black-on-white with little or no carbon painted types.

Rooms 159, 160, 168, and 169 are remarkable for the variety and number of doors in their north (originally plaza-facing) walls. Some doors were responses to subsequent building in Stage VIIIA, but probably each of these rooms had two or more doors at all times, including a possible corner door in the northwest corner of Room 169. Doors in Room 168 included one with steps leading to an unknown location below the later Kiva 161 and another with steps up to the terrace level of Kiva 161. The collection of doors in these rooms also included several T-shaped ones. The exact sequence of doors in any one room is now impossible to determine (but see Judd 1964:170-171). Floor area for these three rooms averaged 20.81 m$^2$ (sd=0.34 m$^2$). No floor features were recorded.

Rooms 153 to 158 also lack recorded floor features. These rooms averaged 7.8 m$^2$ (sd=2.8 m$^2$, N=6). Rooms 154 and 155 had doors to the plaza and also to the exterior; the doors toward the plaza were probably T-shaped, as was the door in Room 158. The form of doors to the exterior cannot now be determined.

As discussed below, Stage VII C may date to about 1095-1105. At least the first unit of Stage VII A (Rooms 159/160 to 169) should therefore date to the span between posited Stage VIB construction (1075-1085) and the beginning of Stage VIIC building, or about 1085-1095.

Stage VIIB. Stage VIIB consists of the long row of single-story rooms closing the south end of the west plaza. The conjectural nature of the western end of VIIB has been discussed above (Stage VIA).

There are no dates from Stage VIIB. It has been assigned to Stage VII on the basis of its symmetrical relationship with VIIA (see discussion of Stage VIIE).

Stage VIIB clearly precedes Stage VIID, and presumably follows Stage VIA. The rooms in Stage VIIB had doors into the plaza only. The multiple plaza-facing doors and the lateral doors (in Rooms

131, 343, and 344) were later modifications necessitated by the construction of Kiva 130 (Stage VIID). The only reported floor feature, a firepit in Room 343, was built over an internal modification related to construction of Kiva 130. Room size, in Stage VIIB's final configuration, was quite variable; floor area averaged 9.48 m$^2$ (sd=2.79 m$^2$, N=11).

Stage VIIC. Stage VIIC includes at least six separate constructions along the front of Stages IIIA and VIB. Kivas H and I appear to have been added to the plaza-facing wall (now obscured) of the earlier Kiva C and E enclosures. Kivas 161 and 162, along with the block of five rooms to their north (163-165, 272, 273) postdate Kivas H and I. These rooms abut Stage VIIA, and are presumably later than that Stage VII construction. The row of rooms added to the front of Kivas 161 and 162 (Rooms 286-289) is among the latest in Stage VIIC. Kiva K and its surrounding rooms were also included in Stage VIIC on the basis of the common plaza-facing wall, although Kiva K, in some form, may have actually originated in Stage IVA or even IIIA. Likewise, Kivas H, I, 161, and 162 cover and may have replaced earlier round pit structures (Judd 1964:Figures 4 and 5).

Judd classifies the masonry of the Stage VIIC unit as his Type III. This presents something of a problem for considering Judd's types as a sequence, since the Type III enclosures of Kivas 161 and 162, and Kiva H, are clearly later than the Type IV stonework of Stages VIB and VIIA, which they abut. Judd's use of Type III for Stage VIIC probably denotes the mixed use of both tabular and massive sandstones, rather than a banded facing pattern. In fact, the masonry of the Kiva 161 and Kiva 162 enclosures, and the rooms around them, is more like the masonry of the "McElmo" sites than any other masonry at Pueblo Bonito.

Room 268, located between the Kiva H enclosure and Stage VIIA, yielded a timber dating 1080vv (Table 4.3). Kiva J also produced an 1080vv date. A small round room below the "Room" 286 area produced a date of 1088 (JPB-97), while Kiva I has the latest date for this area, i.e., 1100vv. These dates suggest Stage VIIC construction no earlier than the late 1080s, with construction most likely taking place in the late 1090s and early 1100s. This span would follow closely on the heels of Stage VIB construction.

The round rooms of Stage VIIC may be associated with the rooms of Stage VIB, rather than the rooms of Stage IIIA to their immediate rear. Stage IIIA included both rectangular and round rooms;

Stage VIB had disproportionately few round rooms. If the three round rooms of Stage IIIA are associated with the 26-30 rectangular rooms of IIIA, the ratio of rectangular rooms to round rooms is about 9:1. If the five round rooms of Stage VIIA (H, I, J, perhaps K, 161, and 162) and the two Stage VIB round rooms (C and D) are associated with the 95-110 rectangular rooms of VIB, the ratio of round to rectangular rooms is comparable, or about 11.5:1.

The block of five rooms north of Kiva 162 (Rooms 163-165, 272, 273) apparently lacked floor features. The mean floor area of these single-story rooms was 7.45 m$^2$ (sd=1.86 m$^2$, N=5). Three (Rooms 164, 165, 273) had no direct access to the plaza; entrance was via the stairs built into the southwest corner of the Kiva J enclosure. Room 163 originally had a plaza-facing door, which was later blocked.

The enclosure of Kiva J is of particular interest because of a 1 m wide hallway running diagonally across its northwest corner. This hallway originally opened into the plaza, and was very similar to Kiva 16 and its southwest hallway across the plaza.

Kiva K, as noted above, could predate Stage VIIC. The rooms surrounding it, however, and the plaza-facing wall, almost certainly postdate the Kiva J enclosure, and consequently should be among the latest Stage VIIC building.

The row of rooms (286-289) fronting Kivas 161 and 162 is also late in Stage VIIC. Room 286 was a ramada and had a firepit. The three masonry rooms were built of "McElmo" style masonry, and averaged 8 m$^2$. Of these rooms, Room 287 had a firepit, as did Room 285, a small room in the southwest corner of the Kiva 161 enclosure. All these rooms may be associated with Kiva 2E, or perhaps with the trash fill of that unit, which had a Mesa Verde Black-on-white, McElmo Black-on-white, and Kayenta Polychrome ceramic assemblage (Judd 1964:307).

Subfloor ceramics in Kivas J and 162 were late Gallup Black-on-white with carbon painted types supporting a relatively late date. Surprisingly, the subfloor ceramics of Kiva C were early, with a predominantly Red Mesa Black-on-white assemblage.

Stage VIID. Kivas U, V, W, and 130 clearly postdate Stage VIA; Kiva 130, at least, also postdates Stage VIIB. These round rooms and their rectangular enclosures clearly abut the walls of Stages VIA and VIIB; moreover, the subfloor ceramics of Kivas T and V, and subfloor ceramics in Room 344 (in Stage VIIB, but reburied after the construction of Kiva 130) include small amounts of Mesa Verde Black-on-white. All four round rooms cover and may have replaced earlier round structures, possibly from Stages IIIB or VIA. If these round structures are associated with the 55-60 rooms of Stage VIA, the rectangular- to round-room ratio is approximately 1:14.

Stage VIIE. This stage includes the structures appended to the east side of the very wide one-story wall dividing the plaza into east and west halves (extending from Room 140, on the south, to Kiva 16, on the north). Not all of these structures were built at the same time. In Figures 5 and 6 (1964) Judd shows Great Kiva A, and its surrounding rooms, and Kiva 16 as Type III, and the row of rooms running between the Great Kiva A and Kiva 16 enclosure as Type IV. Judd believed that most of the Type III masonry was actually later here than Type III elsewhere in Pueblo Bonito (1964: 135).

The wide original north-south wall of Stage VIIE is clearly related to Stage VIIB, with which it forms a right angle. The juncture of the two (at "rooms" 138 and 139) formed an entry at the southeast corner of the west plaza. A similar gateway was built into the north-south wall near its center between Rooms 34a and 35.

The first construction appended to this wall was a row of long narrow rooms (Rooms 143, 144, 35a, to 211), which appears to have replaced an earlier, similar row (Judd 1964:Figure 5). The block of six rooms at the south end of Stage VIIE (corners defined by Rooms 219, 221, 222, and 224) was probably the next to be constructed. Kiva B was built into this block at a later time. As described in the discussion of Stage VIIA, this block predates the west end of Stage VIIA, while Stage VIIA itself predates the Kiva A enclosure, suggesting that the Kiva A enclosure is later than the block of six rooms. Probably the last construction in Stage VIIE, along with the Kiva A enclosure, was that of the three rooms (Rooms 140 to 142) at the south end of Stage VIIE. Kiva 16, which has not yet been discussed, may be earlier than any Stage VIIE construction, since the original north-south wall terminates at the Kiva 16 enclosure. In some form, this elevated circular structure may have originated in Stage VI, but was integrated in its final form into Stage VIIE, and is considered a part of the later stage here.

While Great Kiva A, the dominant feature of Stage VIIE, is a fairly typical Great Kiva, it has rather interesting peripheral rooms. Other Great Kivas have concentric peripheral rooms, however, those of Kiva A form a rectangular block into which the Great Kiva is set. The relative height of the Great Kiva wall is important for the interpretation of the surrounding one-story rooms. Judd (1964: 205-206) concluded that the Kiva A walls did not extend up to the roof height of the surrounding rooms, which led him to state that these rooms (Rooms 146-150, 213-218) were unroofed and open (unwalled) on the side toward Kiva A. This seems unlikely, but beyond expressing doubt, there is little more that can be added. In their final form, these rooms lacked floor features, with the exception of a single firepit in Room 218 and (if we believe Judd) roofs and walls facing Kiva A. The earlier floors of Rooms 213, 215, and 217 had firepits, though the relationship of these earlier floors to Kiva A itself is obscure.

Kiva B, just south of Great Kiva A, was a standard Chacoan elevated round room. Judd stated that several rooms surrounding Kiva B were also not roofed -- in particular Room 221, which had several very large firepits, and Room 220, which though featureless in its final form, had multiple firepits on an earlier floor. All other rooms north, east, and west of Kiva B were single story, but were built on the second story level over filled first stories. All except one (Room 144) had floor features; there were firepits and bins in four (Rooms 143, 151, 152, 219), and four probable mealing bins in one (Room 222). The three rooms south of the Kiva B enclosure (Rooms 140-142) were apparently featureless.

Doorway patterns and room sizes in the Kiva A-Kiva B block are highly irregular, and no clear patterns are evident.

The row of rooms running north from Kiva A (Room 34 to Room 211) was superimposed over Kivas 2-B and Q. The west wall of the row was supported on beams over Kiva Q; the beams subsequently collapsed. The floor of Room 34, to the south, one of the few in this row which survived more-or-less intact, had multiple firepits. No doorways were preserved in this row. The mean floor area for Rooms 27, 34, 143, 144, and 211 was 8.69 m$^2$ (sd=1.28 m$^2$; N=5).

There are no tree-ring dates from Stage VIIE. However, the Kiva A enclosure, in its final form, postdates the east end of Stage VIIA, Rooms 159 to 169 of which date no earlier than the later

1080s, and more likely the later 1090s to early 1100s. By extension, the last version of Kiva A and its enclosure should date to the latter part of the Stage VIIA span. Great Kiva A is remarkably like the Great Kiva at Aztec (Morris 1921), which dates to about 1115. In fact, a subfloor test in Kiva A produced both Mesa Verde and McElmo Black-on-white (Judd 1964:135; Roberts n.d.), but these sherds may relate only to the last floor of Kiva A, which was not extensively tested for evidence of earlier floors or structures. Subfloor ceramics from Rooms 143 and 144 are a late Gallup Black-on-white assemblage with some carbon painted types, a ceramic assemblage consistent with a date in the late 1000s.

Construction of the row of rooms along the large north-south wall, and perhaps also the block of rooms at the south end of Stage VIIE, obviously postdates the long wall, though perhaps not by a long time. Great Kiva A and its enclosure probably date even later.

## Other Construction

Great Kivas.   Great Kiva A was 13.7 m diameter at floor level and 17 m diameter in the exterior. This is almost certainly the latest Great Kiva at Pueblo Bonito, its last floor dating from the late 1100s or even later.

A huge, partially razed Great Kiva in the southwest plaza probably immediately preceded Kiva A. It shares the distinctive masonry pillars of Kiva A (see Judd [1964:201-202] for a discussion of Vivian and Reiter [1960] who described these pillars differently). The estimated diameter was about 16.3 m at floor level, and 19.4 m at the top of the walls. Judd "...guessed the razed stonework to have been of our third type, but it is more likely to have been of the second type and an early project of the Late Bonitian Builders" (1964:21). If so, the Great Kiva was outside of the Stage II enclosed plaza. I think it more likely that the southwest plaza Great Kiva was associated with Stage III, and was an intermediate form between Kiva Q and Kiva A. The southwest Great Kiva shared particular Great Kiva A features; however, like Kiva Q, it was fully subterranean while Kiva A was partially elevated in a roomblock.

Kiva Q, probably earlier than Kiva A, lies under the row of Rooms 34-211 associated with the final Stage VIIE Kiva A enclosure. It is the smallest of the three Great Kivas discussed so far, being 12.1 m diameter at the floor and with an exterior diameter of 14.6 m. Judd called its masonry Type III, but noted that "the masonry of Kiva Q does not fit into our local scheme" (1964:207). Its location places it in the plaza of Stage II; its use of wood posts, rather than masonry pillars, sunken rather than raised vaults, and its nondescript masonry all suggest that Kiva Q is earlier than both Kiva A and the razed southwest plaza Great Kiva. Kiva Q probably belongs to Stage II.

Perhaps the earliest Great Kiva at Pueblo Bonito is the unnumbered Type I pit structure later partly destroyed by Kiva 2-C (Figures 4.17, 4.20a). This structure, approximately 7 m diameter at the floor and almost 10 m in diameter at the exterior, was considerably larger than the contemporary Type I pit structures. The north third of the structure was preserved, but no floor features were reported (roof support posts should have been seen, if they were present). Judd (1964: Plate 23, right) shows a radial beam pilaster on the bench. In spite of the absence of some Great Kiva features, and the presence of one non-Great Kiva feature (the pilaster), the size and location of this structure make it a fair candidate for the earliest remaining Great Kiva at Pueblo Bonito.

Three other unexcavated subterranean pit structures at Pueblo Bonito are unusually large. An unnumbered pit structure (Kiva O) in the southeast plaza and another unnumbered pit structure remnant just northwest of Kiva O all have exterior diameters of about 11.3 m, over 1 m larger than the smallest excavated Great Kiva and Chacoan round room (see "Round Rooms"). Judd classified the first of these as Type II masonry, the second as Type III, and did not classify the third (1964:Figures 4 and 5). It should be noted that the exterior diameter of Chacoan Kiva R is about the same as these three unexcavated pit structures; Kiva R, however, has battered walls and an above-bench diameter of only 9.3 m.

"Shrines". Judd designated several features "shrines," and I am inclined to accept his interpretation. The most convincing is Room 190, in the middle of the east plaza. This room, excavated by Pepper, was "a flag-floored, sub-surface cylinder of sandstone masonry" (Judd 1964) with a diameter of about 2 m and a depth of about 0.75 m (Judd 1964:175-176; Pepper 1920:Figure 146).

There are two or perhaps three small masonry structures that Judd also considered shrines. He suggests that two

rectangular stepped platforms, one at the southeast corner of the building and another at the southeast corner of the Kiva A enclosure, were possible shrines. To these might be added a third one, a stepped platform at the southwest corner of the site (known only from a representation on the Brooklyn Museum model).

Trash mounds or platforms. About 15 m south of Pueblo Bonito were two large "trash mounds." Little of the extensive work in these units has been reported (Judd 1964; Nelson, in Pepper 1920; Windes 1980). Both the west mound (a rectangle some 30 m north-south by 60 m east-west) and the east platform (a less regular rectangle 25 m north-south at its west end, 17 m north-south at its east end and about 60 m east-west) were masonry enclosures standing over 2 m in height. The ground surfaces were probably leveled prior to construction of the masonry walls (Judd 1964:219, Figures 7 and 24) and the masonry enclosure was then filled to the tops of the walls with a combination of rubble, trash, and sand. In his profile of the east platform (Judd 1964:Figure 24, bottom) Judd shows a fill of "laminated silt" to the exclusion of other types of fill, but his text and notes make it clear that the predominant fill in both east and west platforms was trash and rubble (Figure 3.15). An interesting aspect of the east mound is that the south masonry wall was built on an adobe embankment some 1.5 m high -- an embankment very similar to that supporting the terrace below Threatening Rock (Judd 1964:Plate 42, left; Figure 24, station 50).

Profiles of both east and west platforms show a clear horizontal break in the strata, level with the tops of the enclosing walls of the platforms. This is particularly evident for the east mound (Figures 3.14, 3.15). Judd did not attempt to clear this surface, but it is almost certainly the horizontal surface of the walled platform. In both the east and the west mounds, deposition continued above this level. Whether this latter material is architectural, or simply trash disposal, is impossible to determine from the published data and unpublished notes.

Judd interpreted these units as refuse mounds, but then had to qualify this assessment by noting that neither an east nor west refuse mound was "normal" in the Southwest (Judd 1964:212). Windes (1980) noted that sherd densities in the east and west mounds were relatively low, compared to other trash deposition in the canyon. The Pueblo Bonito mounds differ from the mounds at other Chacoan sites in their configuration as platforms; neither Chetro Ketl nor Pueblo Alto mounds are walled, and neither show evidence of a level surface (Lekson 1983a; Roberts 1927; Windes 1980).

Windes (1980:9) dated the ceramic assemblages of both mounds at 1050 to 1100-1130. The alignment of the trash mound enclosure walls suggests construction of these walls in Stage VI, or later (1075-1105); however, Judd notes that considerable deposition had taken place in the mounds prior to the construction of these walls, perhaps during the building of Stages III, IV, and V (1050-1075).

HUNGO PAVI

History

Hungo Pavi is not a Navajo name. The Navajos have called this ruin "black house home" (Franstead and Werner 1974), "white house," "white rock house," "exploding rock house" (referring to rocks exploding when heated in a fire; Franstead and Werner 1974), or "high black post." Hungo Pavi is derived from none of these names. Hewett (1936:41) believed the name was a corruption of the Hopi town name Shungopovi. Jackson (1878) suggests it is a corruption of the Spanish for "hooked" or "crooked nose." Neither explanation is compelling.

Hungo Pavi (Figures 4.31-4.38) is unexcavated, and it is a classic example of the modern deterioration of these ancient ruins. In 1877, Jackson described the ruin "...portions of which are in quite perfect condition.... Many of the heavy pine logs which supported the flooring are still in position" (Jackson 1878). Nineteen years later, Holsinger noted that the ruin was "in the same condition as when visited twenty-four years ago by Jackson" (1901:47, Plate 41).

Hewett's photo, taken fewer than 35 years later, and the current state of the ruin (Henderson 1972; Lekson and McKenna 1979; Mayer 1972) document a sad record of deterioration. At the turn of the century, the rear wall carried most of its third story from the northeast corner to Room 6; in Hewett's photo, most of the third story has fallen, except in Room 4 and the corner of Rooms 5 and 6. In both Holsinger's and Hewett's photos, the north walls of Rooms 16 and 23 clearly rise to the third-story level; they are now truncated at the second-story level. The primary cause of this historic decay was probably the removal of Jackson's

"many heavy pine logs." Most of these appear to have vanished by the 1920s when dendrochronological sampling began; consequently, there are few in situ dates from Hungo Pavi (Table 4.4).

Architecture

Hungo Pavi is a remarkably symmetrical building. It consists of a main block with a central elevated round room (Kiva A), east and west wings, an arc of rooms enclosing the plaza, and a Great Kiva. The main block was three rooms deep, with the rear row standing three stories tall, the second row two stories, and the plaza-facing row one story. Kiva A was on the second-story level, and was fronted by a single-story room (Room 24) which jutted out into the plaza. The east and west wings were three rooms deep and probably two stories tall in second and rear rows, with a single-story plaza-facing row.

The front arc was probably one room wide and one story tall. The articulation of this arc with the east wing is a problem. Early maps show the arc joining the east wing, but more recent maps show the east end of the arc separated from the wing by a gap of about 5 m. This seems to be the actual condition of the ruin today.

A trash mound that Jackson thought he saw in 1877 (just outside the center of the arc) has either vanished completely during the last century or, more likely, never actually existed. There is no evidence for this feature today.

Primary beam sockets in the rear wall were spaced at about 1.75 cm intervals, without regard to cross-wall spacing. Some cross walls were built directly next to primary beams, and a few walls were actually built around the beams, changing the beams from primaries to intramural logs. First-story beam sockets (some of which have been incorrectly stabilized as vents) do not seem to correspond to the second and third-story pattern. A small opening (similar to "arrow slits" at Wijiji) ran through the rear wall, just above the third-story floor level of Room 4.

Few vents are visible. In the rear wall, vents appear to be paired, one high in each corner of the room.

Only two doors are exposed at Hungo Pavi, both in exterior first-story walls. The first is from the plaza into Room 24, the single story room in front of Kiva A. The second is in the west wall of Room 44. In the east wing, where walls

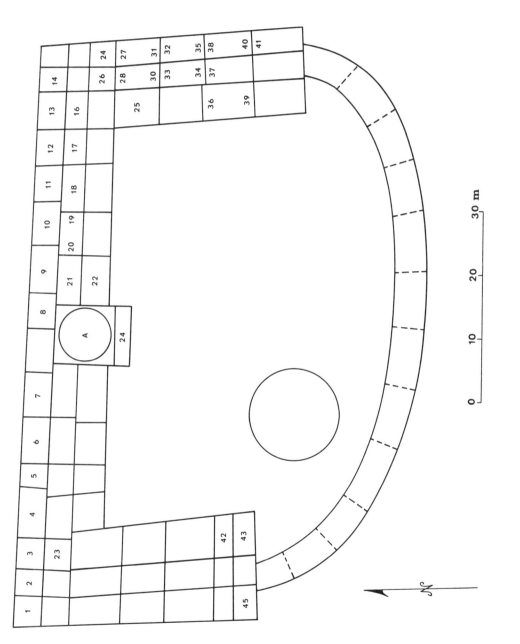

Figure 4.31. Hungo Pavi.

Figure 4.32.  Hungo Pavi, looking northeast.

Figure 4.33.  Hungo Pavi, looking west; Chaco Wash in middle distance.

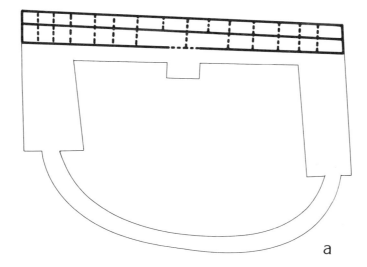

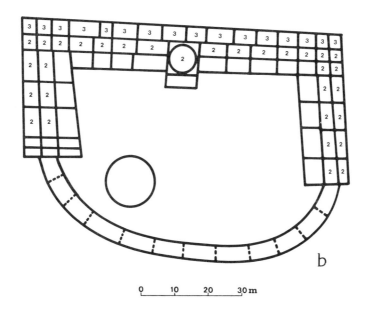

Figure 4.34. Hungo Pavi construction stages: (a) Stage I; (b) Stage II. All new construction is one story, unless otherwise noted.

Figure 4.35.   Hungo Pavi, looking southwest.   East wing left foreground, rear wall right.

Figure 4.36.   Hungo Pavi, looking north.

Figure 4.37.  Hungo Pavi, Room 28 foreground, looking northwest.

Figure 4.38. Hungo Pavi, examples of masonry (frames are 70 cm x 70 cm). Top row, left to right: exterior wall, outside Room 14; Room 3, N wall; Room 4, N wall. Bottom row, left to right: Room 16, N wall; Room 30, S wall; Room 37, E wall.

Table 4.4.  Tree-ring dates from Hungo Pavi.

Room 1

|  | HP-10 | 942r |
|  | HP-11 | 943r |

Room 1, 2, 3, 4, or 5

|  | HP-6 | 1063vv |
|  | DPB-3 | 1064r |

Room 3/4 (intramural beams)

| ? | HP-21 | 1004+rL |
| ? | HP-16 | 1005+r |
| ? | HP-27 | 1009r |

Room 13

|  | HP-13 | 989v |

Room 13 or 14

| ? | BE-91 | 1027vv |

Room 21/22 (intramural beams)

| ? | GP-2180 | 989r |
| ? | GP-2185 | 996v |
| ? | GP-2182 | 1004+r |

Room 24

|  | HP-12 | 1064rL |

Unnumbered room west of Kiva A

|  | GP-2184 | 1004v |

No provenience

|  | CNM-709 | 966vv |
|  | HP-1 | 1004+L |
|  | HP-3 | 1049vv |
|  | HP-5 | 1054L |
|  | BE-94 | 1059r |
|  | HP-7 | 1059r |
|  | DPB-3-1 | 1077rL |

Note:  All dates from roof elements unless otherwise noted.
       Key to symbols, see Appendix C.

perpendicular to the plaza are exposed, there are no doors in these walls.

Room sizes vary considerably (mean= 17.5 m$^2$, sd=7.0 m$^2$, N=9). In the north block, rear row rooms average about 9 or 10 m$^2$; plaza-facing and second row rooms appear slightly larger, ranging up to about 20 m$^2$. In this block, both length and width decrease away from the plaza. In the east and west wings, room size appears to decrease slightly from front to rear (e.g., second and third row rooms in the east wing average about 20 m$^2$, while the front row averages about 30 m$^2$), a function of room width.

## Chronology

Two first-story primary beams in Room 1 date 942 and 943 (Table 4.4). At the east end of the main block, in the first story of Room 13, another primary beam yielded a date of 989. A number of other dates from Hungo Pavi range from about 990 to 1010. Together, these dates indicate construction of the first and parts of the second story of the main block after about 945, and most likely from 990 to 1010. The masonry of the first story is not extensively visible today, but in 1877 Jackson noted that it differed from the other masonry only in the width of the walls. Late 900s-early 1000s building at Hungo Pavi will be referred to as Stage I (Figure 4.34). Stage I probably consisted of a large elongated rectangle, with a rear wall about 100 m long. A single date of 998 from the first-story roof of Room 35 suggests early 1000s construction of the east wing. I suspect, however, that this is a reused beam and the wings actually date somewhat later.

A second cluster of dates from 1059 to 1064 probably defines the construction period of the second story of the main block and the plaza-facing second-story wall of Kiva A. A single later date, at 1077, is without provenience. If construction at Hungo Pavi paralleled other Chacoan sites, the wings may have been added in the 1060s-1070s, and the 1077 date may actually refer to construction of the wings.

The arc was probably the last major construction; between Hungo Pavi I (990-1010) and the arc, there is little physical evidence for building stages at Hungo Pavi. The building is quite symmetrical and lacks obvious junctures, off-sets, or abutments. Its masonry is relatively homogeneous. Although Hungo Pavi may have been built in a series of discrete construction events, these cannot be

defined from the visible ruin. I suspect that Hungo Pavi was built in a series of stages from 1060 to at least 1080, but since these stages are not definable, all of the visible structure will be termed Stage II (1060-1080). Portions of Stage II construction probably used earlier Stage I structures for ground stories (Figure 4.34).

## CHETRO KETL

### History

The name Chetro Ketl is rather enigmatic. While most of the names of Chacoan ruins are either Spanish or Navajo, Chetro Ketl is of no known language. It was first reported by Simpson (1850), an Army officer who was relying on the knowledge of his native guides. Jackson (1878) translated Chetro Ketl as "Rain Pueblo," but did not identify his source. Recent Navajo names for the ruin include "house in the corner" (referring to Chetro Ketl's location in a small rincon), "covered hole," and "shining house" (Franstead and Werner 1974; Tietjens n.d.; Van Valkenberg 1941).

The excavation of Chetro Ketl (Figures 4.39-4.54) was the project of Edgar Lee Hewett. Hewett, then with New Mexico Highlands University, first visited Chetro Ketl in 1902. After securing backing from the Royal Ontario Museum of Archaeology and the Smithsonian Institution, he began preliminary studies in the fall of 1916, but this work was interrupted by the World War I (Pierson 1956:31).

In 1920, work resumed, beginning in the southeast corner of the site. "An area ninety feet square was laid off for excavations and a large outlying area staked off for examination" (Hewett 1936: 57). This included Rooms 1 to 7 and Kivas A to F. The trash mound was trenched, for the first of many times, along its long and short axes. The trenches were over 3 m wide (Hawley 1934:31).

The next season (1921) the work in the southeast corner was completed, and the Great Kiva was cleared. At the time, excavations in the Great Kiva were thought to be finished. From 1922 to 1928, work halted "to make way for another expedition," specifically Neil M. Judd's National Geographic Society excavations at Pueblo Bonito (Hewett 1936:- 60). While Hewett's forces awaited the departure of Judd from the canyon, Chetro Ketl remained largely untouched, except for the sampling of a few beams for dendrochronological study.

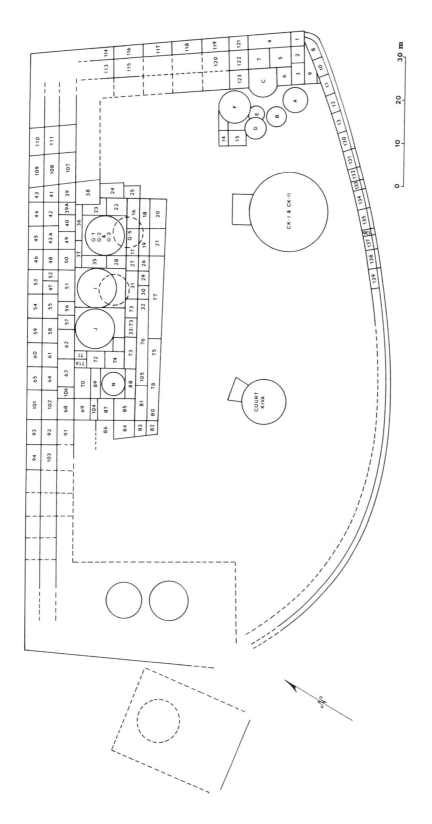

Figure 4.39. Chetro Ketl.

Figure 4.40.  Chetro Ketl, looking northwest.

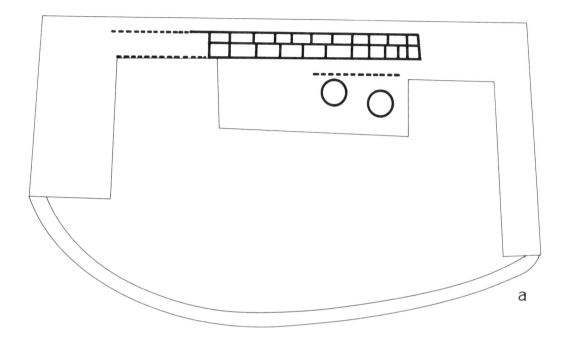

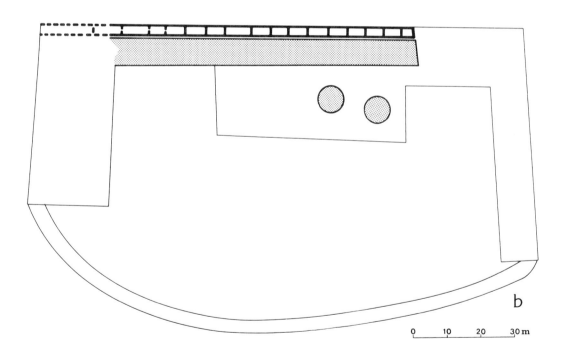

Figure 4.41.  Chetro Ketl, construction stages:  (a) Stage II; (b) Stage
III.  All new construction is one story unless otherwise
noted.

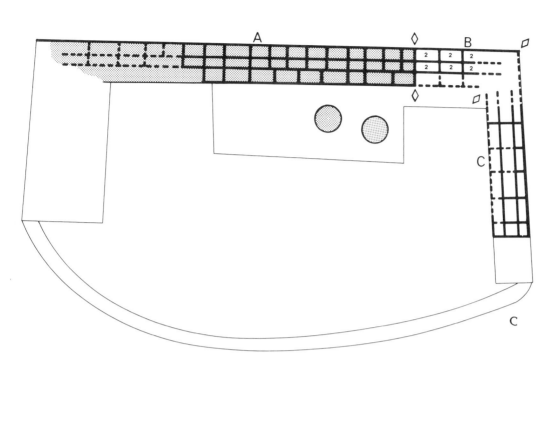

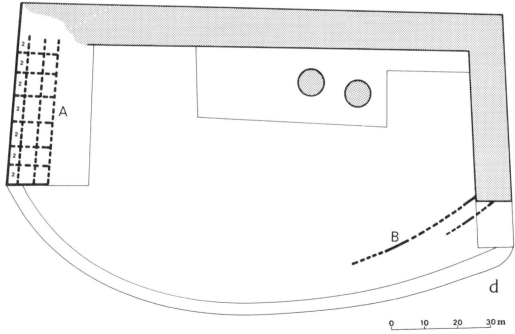

Figure 4.41.  Chetro Ketl, construction stages:  (c) Stage IV; (d) Stage V.

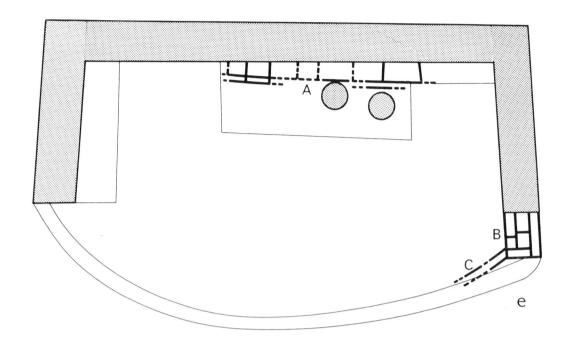

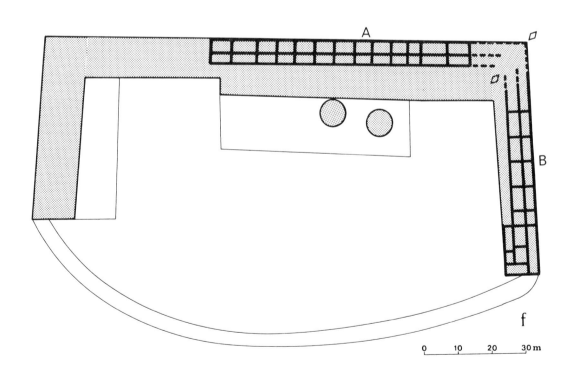

Figure 4.41.  Chetro Ketl, construction stages:  (e) Stage VI; (f) Stage VII.

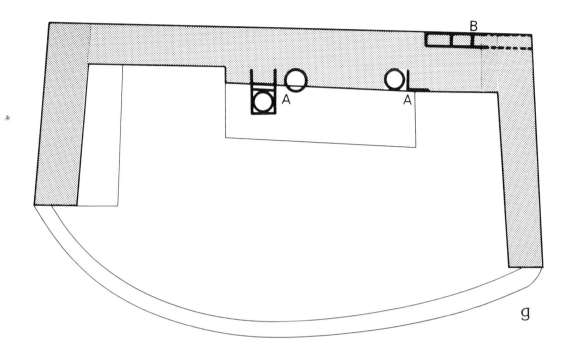

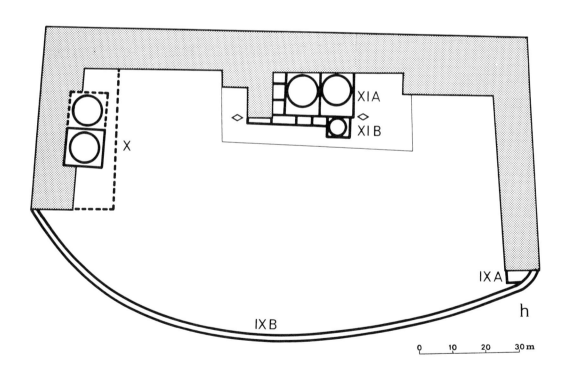

Figure 4.41. Chetro Ketl, construction stages: (g) Stage VIII; (h) Stages IX, X, and XI.

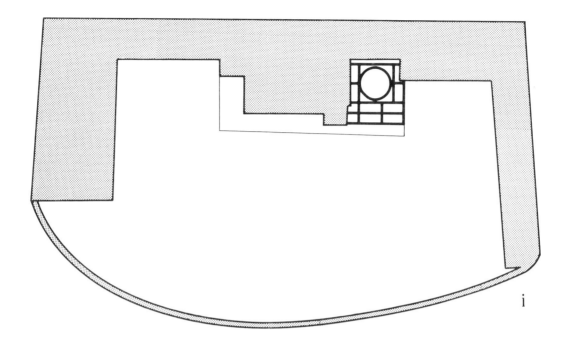

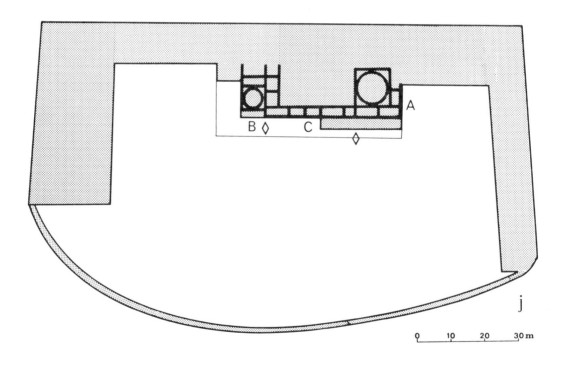

Figure 4.41.  Chetro Ketl, construction stages:  (i) Stage XII; (j) Stage XIII.

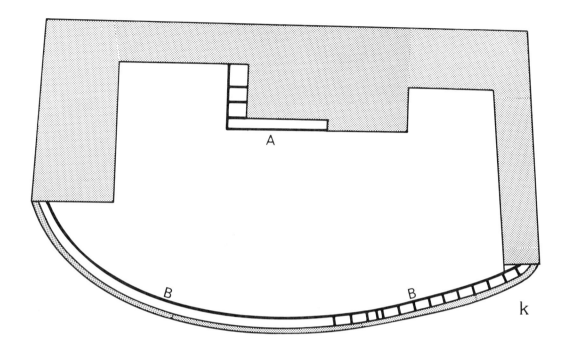

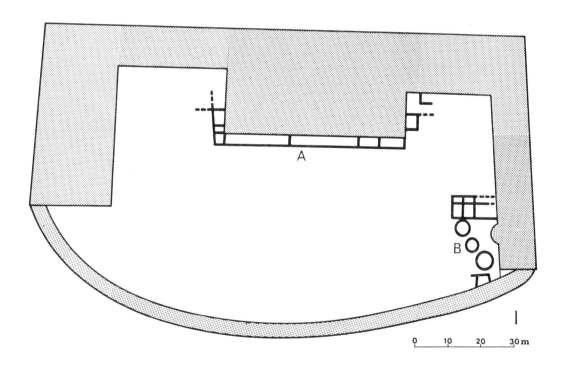

Figure 4.41.  Chetro Ketl, construction stages:  (k) Stage XIV; (l) Stage XV.

Figure 4.42.  Chetro Ketl, rear wall of Room 46 and rooms to the west,
looking southwest.

Figure 4.43.   Chetro Ketl, Room 65, east
wall in foreground, looking
northeast.

Figure 4.44.   Chetro Ketl, Rooms 63 and 64 foreground, looking east.

Figure 4.45.   Chetro Ketl, Rooms 46, 48, and 50, looking south.   Note
                double wall in foreground, room-wide platform at left
                (see also Fig. 3.3).

Figure 4.46. Chetro Ketl, multiple doors in south wall of Room 62.

Figure 4.47. Chetro Ketl, southeast corner of Kiva G complex; Rooms 24 and 25 foreground; Kiva G highest construction in middle of photo (note projecting stones), looking northwest.

Figure 4.48.   Chetro Ketl, Kivas I and J, looking west.

Figure 4.49.   Chetro Ketl, east wing from Room 134, looking northeast.

Figure 4.50.   Chetro Ketl, Rooms 4 and 7 foreground, looking southeast.

Figure 4.51.   Chetro Ketl, unnumbered round room in west wing, looking
              north.  Note Talus Unit in background, at base of cliff.

Figure 4.52.  Chetro Ketl Plaza-enclosing arc, Room 8 foreground, looking southwest.

Figure 4.53.   Chetro Ketl, Great Kiva
"Chetro Ketl I and II"
foreground, looking
northwest.

Figure 4.54.   Chetro Ketl, examples of masonry (frames are 70
cm x 70 cm.   Top row, left to right:   Room 63, E wall; Room
50, W wall; exterior wall outside Room 60.   Second row, left
to right:   Room 70, S wall; Room 38, E wall; exterior wall
outside Room 109; Room 108, S wall.   Third row, left to
right:   Room 73, W wall; Room 85, E wall; Kiva N.   Bottom
row, left to right:   Room 76, N wall; Room 22, S wall; Room
28, E wall; Room 19, S wall.

Figure 4.54   Chetro Ketl, examples of masonry (frames are 70
cm x 70 cm).  Top row, left to right:  Kiva G-5; Kiva G-2;
Kiva G-1.  Middle row, left to right:  Kiva I, Kiva J; Room
114, S wall; Room 119, E wall.  Bottom row, left to right:
Room 1, E wall; Room 7, S wall; exterior wall outside Room
4; exterior wall outside Room 117.

Hewett, at this time, associated with the School of American Research and the University of New Mexico, returned with the University of New Mexico Field School in 1929. Railroads and hoists left at Pueblo Bonito were appropriated for use at Chetro Ketl. As excavations reached greater depths, the removal of fill and the buttressing of precarious walls became more and more of a challenge; tipple car lines, aerial tramways, and intricate bracing systems were developed by Paul Reiter, Reginald Fisher, Sam Huddleson, and others. Work in the ruin shifted to the north block, particularly around Kiva G (Stubbs 1929). A pit was excavated in the center of the remaining portion of the trash mound by Anna Shepard (Hawley 1934:31). Hewett began to suspect that work had ceased prematurely in the Great Kiva, and tests confirmed that earlier floors lay beneath those cleared in 1920.

In 1930, subfloor excavations in the Great Kiva began in earnest, and continued for the next three summers under the direction of W.W. Postlethwaite. In the north block, work centered on Kiva G and the rooms to the north (Rooms 23, 39, through 45). "Trenches were put down both inside and outside [the north block] to discover the total number of stories" (Pierson 1956:32). A large series of dendrochronological samples was taken in this, and following, seasons by Florence Hawley, Roy Lassetter, and Paul Reiter.

Hawley also assumed direction of work in the trash mound in 1930. The work carried over into the next season. Hawley's (1934:32) description of the work follows:

It was decided to sink a trench 12 feet long through the west side of the dump, to examine the center with a single pit, and to carry a trench down the east slope from the old [1920] central cut to where the eastern edge met the present ground level. The depth of each excavation was to be determined by the level of the original valley floor...As time became an element before the planned excavations were completed, it was decided to carry the lower levels of excavation of the east trench to the bottom only in alternate sections, each section being four feet square ...The four foot sections mentioned above formed the horizontal unit adopted for the work. Vertically the material was to be taken out in 8 inch levels...(Hawley 1934:22).

During the next season, 1931, subfloor excavations in the Great Kiva continued and the first of the famous bead caches was found (Hewett 1936). The

Court Kiva was tested (Vivian and Reiter 1960; Woods 1934). Extremely difficult, deep excavations below Kiva G were begun by Fisher and Miller, and were not completed until the summer of 1934 (Miller 1937). Rooms 24 through 31, 35, 38, 46, 48, 50, and 77, and Kiva I were excavated in the north block.

In 1932, work continued in the deep excavations below Kiva G and the subfloor in Kiva I. Kiva J, and Rooms 32, 33, 47, 51 through 57, 60, 65, 83, 84, 88, and 89 were excavated. In the Great Kiva, excitement continued with the opening of a series of sealed niches each of which contained spectacular bead caches. Subfloor work in the Great Kiva also disclosed elaborate seating pits for the roof support beams and lower floor levels.

The next year, the focus of work shifted to Talus Unit, but some operations continued at Chetro Ketl. Kiva N (the "West Tower Kiva") and surrounding rooms were opened. Rooms along the rear wall were finished, and apparently much effort was expended in mapping and recording excavated units in the north and east wings. Postlethwaite finished work in the Great Kiva and explored the plaza area to the south of it, including about 30 m of the "moat" (the parallel walls running across the front of the plaza) and several of the rooms in the plaza-enclosing arc.

Hewett's last major season at Chetro Ketl was 1934. Miller completed his detailed study of the complex architectural sequence in and around Kiva G (Miller 1937). Janet Woods and Postlethwaite excavated the Court Kiva. Operations also continued at the Talus Unit (Lekson 1984a).

There was sporadic subsequent work by the University of New Mexico at Chetro Ketl. In 1936,

two rooms were cleared out in Chetro Ketl, a test hole dug, and a room (106) with murals on the wall was cleared..., [and the next year] Postlethwaite checked, by pits, the entire length of the moat across the front of the village (Pierson 1956: 34).

Excavations at Chetro Ketl by UNM and the School of American Research came to an end.

In 1940, Deric O'Bryan obtained a number of dendrochronological samples from Chetro Ketl for Gila Pueblo, the archaeological research institution founded by Harold S. Gladwin (Gladwin 1945).

"On the night of August 22, 1947, diversion from its usual channel of a flash flood resulting from torrential rains in the Chaco Canyon area caused serious damage to much of the excavated portion of Chetro Ketl," (Reed 1947:238; see also Vivian 1948a and Vivian and Lancaster 1947). Particularly affected were the rooms north of Kiva G:

A lake formed in the 'cellars' [the deep excavations in Rooms 39 through 60], water standing to the height of the adjacent ground level outside the walls--a depth of 6 to 15 feet. The 'mud' (adobe mortar) of the deep walls, thus immersed, dissolved; and the walls of some twenty rooms collapsed. A forty-foot segment of the exposed section of...the back wall fell inward. Large cracks developed in the adjacent high center section [north of Kiva G]...(Reed 1947:238).

Gordon Vivian, a veteran of UNM Field Schools at Chetro Ketl, was in charge of stabilization at Chaco Canyon. He supervised the extensive repairs necessary after the disaster and collected over 180 beams that had washed out of the collapsed walls (Bannister 1965:139; Vivian 1948a). The flood also lead to the excavation of the intact second story of Room 93. During this excavation, a remarkable collection of painted wood artifacts was discovered (Vivian et al. 1978).

Later excavations were also connected with stabilization requirements. About 1950, Vivian conducted fairly extensive excavations in Rooms 61, 62, and 63 (Vivian 1949). In 1964, Room 92 (directly in front of Room 93) was excavated to relieve pressure on the wall between those two rooms (Voll, in Vivian et al. 1978).

At the request of the Chaco Center, the Laboratory of Tree-Ring Research undertook an inventory of the dendrochronological samples in their possession from Chetro Ketl (Betancourt 1979). This lead to the complete resampling of all in situ wood at the site during the spring of 1979 (Dean and Warren 1983).

## Sources

The excavations at Chetro Ketl are reported in Edgar Hewett's The Chaco Canyon and Its Monuments (Hewett 1936). Several theses and dissertations resulted from this work, most notably that of Florence M. Hawley, The Significance of the Dated Prehistory of Chetro Ketl, (Hawley 1934), as well as studies by Reiter (1933), Leinau (1934), and Miller (1937). A final, comprehensive report was never prepared by the excavators.

Stabilization and excavations incidental to stabilization are reported in stabilization records on file at Chaco Canyon, and in a few publications (Vivian 1949; Vivian et al. 1978; Voll 1978).

Selected aspects of the architecture and dendrochronology of Chetro Ketl have appeared as parts of broader studies. The "colonnade" was discussed by Ferdon (1955), and the Great Kivas of Chetro Ketl were included in a study of that architectural form in Chaco Canyon by Vivian and Reiter (1960).

The dendrochronology of Chetro Ketl has been the subject of an interesting debate beginning with Hawley (1934). Harold Gladwin (1945) took exception to Hawley's interpretation, but Gladwin's analysis was later refuted by Bryant Bannister (1965).

Hewett's failure to produce a final report on his work at Chetro Ketl has been a major impediment to Chacoan studies. The Chaco Center attempted to alleviate this problem by synthesizing existing published and unpublished records, gathering architectural data from the ruin as it now stands, and sponsoring dendrochronological resampling and reanalysis by the Laboratory of Tree-Ring Research. This work (Lekson 1983b) is probably the most complete report to be expected; however, it falls discouragingly short of complete description and analysis of this important site. Detailed discussion of the tree-ring dates (Table 4.5) will be found in Dean and Warren (1983).

## Architecture

### Stage I (1010-1030)

Stage I is the incompletely known earlier building under the presently visible north block of Chetro Ketl. Stage I appears to have been a long, rectangular structure, underlying much of the later Stage II construction. Only the western third of one room (below Room 92) is currently exposed. This Stage I room was evidently open during the construction of Room 92. The wall of Room 92 was slightly offset over the wall of the Stage I room; the superimposed wall required a rough foundation which was veneered onto the Stage I wall. The Stage I room was later filled in, and the roof level of Stage I became the ground floor of Stage II. The foundation was plastered, which suggests that the Stage I room continued in use for some time after Stage II construction.

Table 4.5.  Tree-ring dates from Chetro Ketl.

Rooms 1 and 4

    Doorway in south wall
      CK-1115        1036+v
      CK-1114        1037+vv
      CK-1113        1039v
    Primary beams
      CK-1           1053r
      CK-130         1054v
    Secondary beam
      CK-2           1062cL
      CK-5           1062cL
    Second story crosswall
      CK-132         1053v
      CK-129         1063v
      CK-131         1103v
      CK-135         1041+v
    Intramural beam in west
    wall and the crosswall
      CK-1117        1061vv

Room 2

    "Ceiling beam"
      CK-68         1039cL
      CK-66         1053cL

Rooms 8/8A

    Passageway in east wall
      CK-128         1062v
    Primary beam
      CK-27         1076r

Room 9

    Primary beams
      CK-30         1061v
      CK-10         1072+v
      CK-9          1072r
    Secondary beams
      CK-25         1069r

Room 22

    Primary beam
      CK-53         1103L

Room 27

    Ceiling beams
      CK-308         1063vv
      CK-307         1077v
      CK-309         1100vv
      CK-306         1101+v
      CK-301         1103r
      CK-303         1117v

Room 28

    Ceiling beam
      GP-2207       1058vv

Room 31
    North wall intramural beam
      CK-148         1061r

Room 35

    Ceiling beam
      CK-321         1058vv
      CK-322         1058r
      CK-313         1082vv
      CK-314         1103r

Room 37

    Unknown
      CK-347         1027vv

Room 38

    Post
      CK-334         1022vv
    Unknown
      CK-323         1102r

Room 39

    Primary beam
      CK-336         1051+L
    Secondary beams
      CK-1232       1034+L
      CK-1251       1044+L
      CK-1228       1047+L

Table 4.5 (continued)

Room 39 (continued)

    Secondary beams (continued)
| | |
|---|---|
| CK-1231 | 1051L |
| CK-1248 | 1051L |
| CK-1226 | 1051L |
| CK-1237 | 1051L |
| CK-1249 | 1051L |
| CK-1235 | 1051L |
| CK-1224 | 1051L |
| CK-1238 | 1051L |
| CK-1247 | 1051L |
| CK-1239 | 1052L |
| CK-1234 | 1052L |
| CK-1225 | 1052L |
| CK-1233 | 1052L |
| CK-1229 | 1052L |
| CK-1250 | 1052L |

Sealed doorway in east wall
| | |
|---|---|
| CK-1253 | 1045L |

Upper doorway in south wall
| | |
|---|---|
| CK-1143 | 1050L |
| CK-1141 | 1054L |

Room 39A

    Ceiling beam
| | |
|---|---|
| CK-337 | 1038v |

Rooms 39-39A

    Ceiling Beam
| | |
|---|---|
| CK-174 | 1054rL |

Room 40

    Primary (?) beams
| | |
|---|---|
| CK-335 | 1037+v |
| CK-67 | 1053c |

    Secondary (?) beams
| | |
|---|---|
| CK-34 | 1037+r |
| CK-33 | 1051r |

Room 42

    Primary (?) beams
| | |
|---|---|
| CK-159 | 1027++vv |
| CK-166 | 1039r |
| CK-143 | 1066v |

Subterranean Room South of Room 42

    Ceiling (?) beam
| | |
|---|---|
| CK-100 | 1039rL |

Room 43

    Unknown
| | |
|---|---|
| CK-904 | 1035cL |

Room 43A

    Ceiling beams
| | |
|---|---|
| CK-36 | 942vv |
| CK-99 | 1037+v |
| CK-42 | 1059v |

    South wall, intramural beam
| | |
|---|---|
| CK-146 | 1029r |
| CK-147 | 1029r |

    West wall intramural beam
| | |
|---|---|
| CK-175 | 1033v |

    Unknown
| | |
|---|---|
| CK-872 | 1037+rL |
| CK-930 | 1038cL |
| CK-785 | 1039cL |
| CK-870 | 1042rL |
| CK-865 | 1045rL |
| CK-802 | 1045rL |

Room 44

    Primary beams
| | |
|---|---|
| CK-65 | 1039+vv |
| CK-64 | 1040+vv |
| CK-158 | 1040v |
| CK-103 | 1052rL |
| CK-141 | 1052cL |
| CK-37 | 1053r |
| CK-104 | 1061rL |

    Secondary beams
| | |
|---|---|
| CK-40 | 1052r |
| CK-38 | 1053cL |
| CK-112 | 1004+cL |
| CK-105 | 1009r |
| CK-109 | 1009r |
| CK-118 | 1010cL |
| CK-120 | 1037+c |
| CK-123 | 1039r |
| CK-119 | 1040cL |
| CK-117 | 1047rL |

Table 4.5 (continued)

Room 44 (continued)

Secondary beams (continued)
| | |
|---|---|
| CK-121 | 1048c |
| CK-106 | 1048c |

Sealed doorway in north wall
| | |
|---|---|
| CK-1158 | 1043vv |

Unknown
| | |
|---|---|
| CK-710 | 1038cL |
| CK-701 | 1039rL |
| CK-706 | 1039rL |
| CK-616 | 1044+cL |
| CK-617 | 1052cL |
| CK-615 | 1052cL |
| CK-705 | 1067+r |

Room 45

Unknown
| | |
|---|---|
| CK-908 | 1034+rL |
| CK-846 | 1036+rL |
| CK-933 | 1043+cL |

Rooms 45/43A/49

East wall,  intramural beams
| | |
|---|---|
| CK-907 | 995+rL |
| CK-814 | 1034+rL |
| CK-924 | 1038cL |
| CK-817 | 1038cL |
| CK-753 | 1039rL |
| CK-720 | 1039cL |
| CK-748 | 1040c |
| CK-839 | 1042cL |
| CK-913 | 1044cL |
| CK-718 | 1051r |
| CK-752 | 1051rL |
| CK-804 | 1052+rL |

Room 46

Primary beams
| | |
|---|---|
| CK-102 | 1041r |
| CK-101 | 1043+r |
| CK-95 | 1063rL |
| CK-94 | 1063cL |

Room 46 (continued)
Secondary beams
| | |
|---|---|
| CK-93 | 1053c |
| CK-89 | 1053cL |

Unknown
| | |
|---|---|
| CK-745 | 1008rL |
| CK-921 | 1037+rL |
| CK-833 | 1046rL |
| CK-618 | 1050r |
| CK-620 | 1052c |

Rooms  47(47/52)

Primary beams
| | |
|---|---|
| CK-165 | 1037+cL |
| CK-156 | 1038+cL |

Unknown
| | |
|---|---|
| CK-855 | 1000+rL |
| CK-805 | 1026r |
| CK-889 | 1026rL |
| CK-836 | 1026L |
| CK-741 | 1028rL |
| CK-811 | 1029rL |
| CK-879 | 1030cL |
| CK-931 | 1034cL |
| CK-778 | 1036+v |
| CK-773 | 1036+cL |
| CK-918 | 1037cL |
| CK-810 | 1038r |
| CK-782 | 1038+v |
| CK-760 | 1039rL |
| CK-880 | 1040cL |
| CK-853 | 1043cL |
| CK-891 | 1043cL |
| CK-854 | 1044cL |
| CK-775 | 1051cL |
| CK-784 | 1051cL |

Room 48

Roof beam (?)
| | |
|---|---|
| CK-169 | 1015+vv |
| CK-164 | 1027+vv |

Primary beams
| | |
|---|---|
| CK-75 | 1036++r |
| CK-144 | 1039v |
| CK-85 | 1052r |
| CK-82 | 1053r |
| CK-84 | 1053cL |
| CK-73 | 1061r |

Table 4.5 (continued)

| Room 48 (continued) | |
|---|---|
| Secondary beams | |
| CK-83 | 1039r |
| CK-81 | 1052c |
| CK-76 | 1052c |
| CK-80 | 1054r |
| Pole shelf across east end of room | |
| CK-1168 | 1039+v |
| CK-1167 | 1039+v |
| Unknown | |
| CK-914 | 1037+cL |
| CK-815 | 1045rL |

| Room 49 | |
|---|---|
| Primary beam | |
| CK-167 | 1039rL |

| Room 49/50 | |
|---|---|
| Unknown | |
| CK-808 | 1038cL |
| CK-797 | 1039+rL |
| CK-729 | 1039c |
| CK-769 | 1039cL |
| CK-772 | 1039cL |

| Room 53 | |
|---|---|
| Primary beam | |
| CK-149 | 1042v |
| CK-356 | 1043r |
| Secondary beams | |
| CK-154 | 1040r |
| CK-151 | 1040rL |
| CK-153 | 1047rL |
| Sealed doorway in north wall | |
| CK-1169 | 1033vv |
| CK-1170 | 1039vv |
| CK-708 | 1046cL |

| Room 54 | |
|---|---|
| Primary beams | |
| CK-1191 | 1040vv |
| CK-354 | 1043v |

| Room 54 (continued) | |
|---|---|
| Roof beam | |
| CK-355 | 1051v |
| Sealed doorway in north wall | |
| CK-1193 | 1051v |
| Unknown | |
| CK-702 | 1040+cL |
| CK-707 | 1042cL |

| Room 55 | |
|---|---|
| Unclassified roof beams | |
| CK-568 | 1016vv |
| CK-545-1 | 1050r |
| CK-543 | 1065r |
| CK-564 | 1036+vv |
| CK-567 | 1038+rL |
| Unknown | |
| CK-903 | 1021cL |
| CK-900 | 1034++r |
| CK-717 | 1037+cL |
| CK-902 | 1038rL |
| CK-704 | 1038r |
| CK-894 | 1039rL |
| CK-898 | 1043cL |
| CK-703 | 1049cL |
| CK-896 | 1104cL |

| Room 57 | |
|---|---|
| East wall, intramural beam | |
| CK-1196 | 1037v |
| Primary beam | |
| CK-1195 | 1038vv |
| CK-348 | 1052r |
| "Roof" | |
| CK-906 | 1016++c |
| CK-847 | 1036+cL |
| CK-746 | 1036+cL |
| CK-912 | 1036+cL |
| CK-938 | 1037+rL |
| CK-934 | 1037+rL |
| CK-920 | 1037+rL |
| CK-917 | 1037+cL |
| CK-911 | 1038rL |
| CK-910 | 1038cL |
| CK-909 | 1038cL |

Table 4.5 (continued)

| Room 57 (continued) | | Room 58/59 | |
| --- | --- | --- | --- |
| "Roof" (continued) | | | |
| CK-905 | 1038cL | Unknown | |
| CK-700 | 1038cL | CK-923 | 989rL |
| CK-779 | 1039rL | CK-842 | 1015cL |
| CK-928 | 1039cL | CK-850 | 1018rL |
| CK-929 | 1039cL | CK-886 | 1020r |
| CK-876 | 1039cL | CK-862 | 1020cL |
| CK-838 | 1040rL | CK-901 | 1021rL |
| CK-935 | 1044cL | CK-758 | 1023v |
| CK-875 | 1049cL | CK-791 | 1024rL |
| | | CK-919 | 1037+rL |
| Room 58 | | CK-828 | 1037rL |
| | | CK-927 | 1038rL |
| Roof beams | | CK-806 | 1038cL |
| CK-353 | 1040vv | CK-744 | 1039cL |
| CK-541 | 1052r | CK-844 | 1039cL |
| CK-542 | 1066+rL | CK-777 | 1045cL |
| CK-566 | 1029c | CK-821 | 1046cL |
| CK-565 | 1039v | | |
| Unknown | | Room 59 | |
| CK-878 | 990rL | | |
| CK-883 | 994rL | Primary beams | |
| CK-916 | 1020r | CK-525 | 1043v |
| CK-937 | 1020rL | GP-2201 | 1043+v |
| CK-825 | 1021cL | Roof beams | |
| CK-834 | 1026cL | CK-357 | 1048r |
| CK-890 | 1029cL | CK-361 | 1060rL |
| CK-712 | 1033rL | Doorway in north wall | |
| CK-809 | 1033rL | CK-1175 | 1043vv |
| CK-774 | 1034+rl | CK-1176 | 1046v |
| CK-796 | 1037+v | Unknown | |
| CK-735 | 1037rL | CK-711 | 1051rL |
| CK-726 | 1038+rL | | |
| CK-738 | 1039rL | Room 60 | |
| CK-776 | 1039rL | | |
| CK-877 | 1039cL | Primary beams | |
| CK-816 | 1039cL | CK-533 | 1041+v |
| CK-739 | 1040rL | CK-534-2 | 1041v |
| CK-723 | 1040rL | | |
| CK-740 | 1040cL | Rooms 60/61 | |
| CK-843 | 1044+rl | | |
| CK-743 | 1045rL | Unknown | |
| CK-831 | 1047rL | CK-714 | 1021c |
| | | CK-892 | 1020cL |
| | | CK-926 | 1021rL |
| | | CK-893 | 1021cL |
| | | CK-721 | 1036+cL |

Table 4.5 (continued)

Room 60/61 (continued)
    Unknown (continued)
        CK-869            1039+cL
        CK-789            1039cL
        CK-766            1039cL
        CK-882            1041cL
        CK-826            1043+rL
        CK-866            1043rL
        CK-737            1043c
        CK-965            1044cL
        CK-724            1045cL
        CK-832            1046v
        CK-359            1046rL
        CK-848            1046rL
        CK-861            1046rL
        CK-884            1046cL
        CK-786            1047c
        CK-936            1047rL
        CK-781            1047rL
        CK-857            1047cL

Room 61

    Primary beams
        CK-535-2          1038L
        CK-536            1038L
    Roof beam
        CK-535-1          1061cL
    West wall intramural beam
        CK-540            1035+v

Room 64

    Primary beams
        CK-1210           1036+vv
        CK-534-1          1038+v

Room 65

    Primary beams
        CK-1180           1063vv
        CK-1181           1066vv
        CK-531            1072r
    Unknown
        CK-734            1008rL
        CK-783            1009rL
        CK-829            1043+rL
        CK-887            1043rL
        CK-849            1044rL
        CK-771            1045cL
        CK-868            1046rL

Room 70

    Primary beams
        CK-538            1048L
        CK-539            1050vv
        CK-120            1051+v
        CK-1215           1056v
    West wall intramural beam
        CK-536-2          1045+v

Room 71A

    Sealed doorway in south wall
        CK-1214           1037++vv
        CK-1213           1049L

Room 88

    First story doorway, west wall
        CK-1259           1076+v
    Second story secondary beams
        CK-1265           1062v
        CK-1263           1075+v

Room 89

    East wall intramural beam
        GP-2199           1060vv
    Primary beam
        CK-1222           1069+L
    Unknown
        GP-2198           1065+v

Room 91

    Primary beam
        CK-1275           1033L

Room beneath 92

    Primary beam
        CK-1274           963vv

Room 92

    Unclassified roof beams
        CK-973            1007vv
        CK-1047           1029vv
        CK-1032           1033cL

Table 4.5 (continued)

| Room 92 (continued) | | Room 93 (continued) | |
|---|---|---|---|
| Unclassified roof beams | | Secondary beam (continued) | |
| (continued) | | CK-1098 | 1048++L |
| CK-974 | 1033rL | CK-1063 | 1050+L |
| CK-979 | 1034++LGB | CK-1070 | 1050+L |
| CK-977 | 1039+cL | CK-1073 | 1050L |
| CK-972 | 1043cL | CK-1072 | 1051L |
| CK-970 | 1046cL | CK-1059 | 1051L |
| CK-1048 | 1050rL | CK-1060 | 1051L |
| CK-1050 | 1052v | CK-1065 | 1051L |
| CK-1044 | 1052rL | CK-1066 | 1051L |
| CK-999 | 1052rL | CK-1067 | 1051L |
| CK-1031 | 1053r | CK-1068 | 1051L |
| CK-992 | 1053r | CK-1069 | 1051L |
| CK-987 | 1053rL | CK-1071 | 1051L |
| CK-990-2 | 1054r | CK-1075 | 1051L |
| CK-1018 | 1054cL | CK-1076 | 1051L |
| CK-990-1 | 1054cL | CK-1077 | 1051L |
| CK-1014 | 1054cL | CK-1078 | 1051L |
| CK-1013 | 1054cL | CK-1080 | 1051L |
| CK-1025 | 1054cL | CK-1081 | 1051L |
| CK-985 | 1054cL | CK-1084 | 1051L |
| CK-976 | 1056rL | CK-1085 | 1051L |
| CK-955 | 1065v | CK-1086 | 1051L |
| CK-1012 | 1066v | CK-1090 | 1051L |
| CK-1022 | 1066v | CK-1062 | 1052L |
| CK-1028 | 1067v | CK-1064 | 1052L |
| CK-1024 | 1067r | CK-1074 | 1052L |
| CK-1026 | 1067rL | CK-1082 | 1052L |
| CK-1023 | 1067rL | CK-1083 | 1052L |
| CK-975 | 1069cL | Recess in south wall | |
| CK-1029 | 1070r | CK-1058 | 1047L |
| | | Ventilator in south wall | |
| Room 93 | | CK-1096 | 1041v |
| | | CK-1095 | 1045L |
| Primary beams | | Sealed doorway in north wall | |
| CK-1054 | 1036++L | CK-1093 | 1020++L |
| CK-1052 | 1041L | CK-1094 | 1045L |
| CK-1053 | 1043L | Eastern ventilator in north wall | |
| Secondary beams | | CK-1097 | 1043vv |
| CK-1079 | 1037+L | Shelf across east end of room | |
| CK-1099 | 1041++L | CK-1056 | 1051L |
| CK-1061 | 1043++L | CK-1057 | 1064L |
| CK-1100 | 1044++L | | |
| CK-1089 | 1048++L | | |

Table 4.5 (continued)

Room 94

    Primary beam
        CK-1270           1038vv
    Doorway in north wall
        CK-1272           1048L
        CK-1273           1051+vv
        CK-1271           1087vv

Second room west of Room 94

    Doorway in north wall
        CK-1187           1052L

Room 101

    Doorway in north wall
        CK-1183           1037+L

Room 104
    Sealed doorway in south wall
        CK-1257           1080vv

Room 106

    Primary beams
        CK-1294           1032L
        CK-1308           1033L
        CK-1303           1033L
        CK-1292           1033L
        CK-1300           1033L
        CK-1304           1033L
        CK-1306           1033L
        CK-1295           1034L
        CK-1307           1034+L
        CK-1309           1034+L
        CK-1302           1034+L
        CK-1305           1036+L
        CK-1291           1050L
    Sealed doorway in south wall
        CK-1311           1066L

Room 107

    Primary beam
        GP-2210           1053v

Room 108

    Doorway in north wall
        CK-1131           1047L
        CK-1134           1047L
        CK-1130           1050vv
        CK-1133           1050L

Room 113 or 115

    Unclassified roof beam
        GP-2208           1053vv

Room 118

    Unclassified roof beam
        CK-325            952vv
        CK-326            1007vv

Room 119

    Unclassified roof beam
        CK-327            1034vv

Room 121

    Unclassified roof beam
        CK-140            1051v

Unnumbered NW corner room

    Unknown
        CK-713            1045cL

Kiva A

    Unclassified roof beams
        CK-13             1058v
        CK-14             1070v

Kivas G-1 and G-2

    Pilaster
        CK-316            912vv
        CK-311            952vv
        CK-312            957vv

Table 4.5 (continued)

| Kivas G-1 and G-2 (continued) | | Room 87 | |
| --- | --- | --- | --- |
| Corner buttresses | | Subterranean structure (continued) | |
| CK-55 | 1037+L | CK-1104 | 1003++vv |
| CK-63 | 1047vv | CK-1101 | 1073vv |
| CK-136 | 1049v | CK-1102 | 1079vv |
| CK-72 | 1049rL | | |
| CK-126 | 1049rL | "Northern part of site | |
| CK-56 | 1053v | Deep excavations" | |
| CK-138 | 1066L | | |
| CK-137 | 1098v | GP-2438 | 1033r |
| CK-168 | 1098r | GP-2437 | 1034+rL |
| CK-60 | 1099r | GP-2441 | 1034+rL |
| CK-57 | 1099L | GP-2443 | 1034r |
| CK-61 | 1100v | GP-2442-1 | 1045v |
| CK-58 | 1100v | GP-2440 | 1045rL |
| Unknown | | | |
| CK-606 | 1099r | Flood logs from north central | |
| | | part of site | |
| Kiva G-5 | | CK-944 | 1006+rL |
| | | CK-940 | 1021rL |
| Unknown | | CK-946 | 1024cL |
| CK-330 | 931vv | CK-827 | 1028v |
| CK-333 | 1028vv | CK-858 | 1028rL |
| CK-400 | 1029v | CK-840 | 1028cL |
| | | CK-956 | 1028cL |
| Kiva I | | CK-939 | 1032++cL |
| | | CK-947 | 1036+rL |
| Pilaster | | CK-952 | 1036+cL |
| GP-2206 | 1061vv | CK-949 | 1037+cL |
| Wainscotting (?) | | CK-819 | 1038cL |
| CK-170 | 1087r | CK-941 | 1038+cL |
| | | CK-950 | 1039rL |
| Kiva J | | CK-942 | 1039cL |
| | | CK-945 | 1039cL |
| Pilaster | | CK-951 | 1039cL |
| CK-522 | 1040vv | CK-955 | 1039cL |
| Unknown | | CK-943 | 1040rL |
| CK-571 | 1033vv | CK-959 | 1040rL |
| CK-572 | 1039+vv | CK-835 | 1040rL |
| CK-524 | 1043v | CK-871 | 1040cL |
| | | CK-759 | 1040+cL |
| Kiva N | | CK-873 | 1042+rL |
| | | CK-874 | 1043cL |
| Unclassified roof beam | | CK-867 | 1045rL |
| CK-319 | 1100vv | CK-958 | 1045rL |
| Doorway in wall beyond north wall | | | |
| CK-1283 | 1074L | | |
| Subterranean structure below Room 87 | | | |
| CK-1106 | 883vv | | |
| CK-1103 | 909vv | | |

Table 4.5 (continued)

Flood logs from north central part
  of site (continued)
    CK-800              1045cL
    CK-824              1045cL
    CK-953              1045cL
    CK-823              1046rL
    CK-841              1046rL
    CK-856              1046rL
    CK-864              1046cL
    CK-954              1046cL
    CK-813              1047rL
    CK-733              1050rL
    CK-761              1051rL

Southeast section roof
  ("Hewett Scrap Pile")

    JPB-140             1070v
    JPB-141             1072vv

Northeast quarter

    JPB-143             1053v

Middle east side

    JPB-144             1050vv

No provenience

    CK-317              1005+vv
    CK-A-11             1024vv
    CK-12               1025vv
    CK-10               1033r
    CK-546              1046+v
    CK-548-1            1049vv
    CK-613              1049v
    CK-587              1050r
    CK-556              1051rL
    CK-547              1052vv
    CK-589              1052vv
    CK-612-1            1052vv
    CK-555              1052v
    CK-549              1054v
    CK-373              1061cL
    CK-557              1064rL

Note:  Key to symbols, see Appendix C.
       All dates from roof elements unless otherwise noted.

Only one date (963vv) is directly associated with Stage I building. Clusters of dates from 1008 to about 1030 from beams used in later building may also be attributed to Stage I (Table 4.5).

## Stage II (1035-1040)

Stage II (Figure 4.41a) consists of at least two rows of single story rooms, extending over 60 m west from Rooms 39 and 41. Only two rows of rooms are currently visible, but another plaza-facing row probably was present. Kiva G-5, and a similar structure beneath later Kiva I, indicate a row of large subterranean round rooms along the front of Stage II. These round pit structures would have been at some distance from the presently visible Stage II rooms. The space between the visible rooms and the pit structures was probably filled with work areas, ramadas or, as suggested here, a row of plaza-facing rooms.

Subsequent building greatly altered many of the exposed rooms of Stage II. Rooms of the remaining front row (39 to 68) were subdivided and modified. At the east end of this row (Rooms 39, 39A, 40, 49, and 50), it is difficult to determine whether cross walls are original or later introductions. Doors are centered between cross walls (which is not the case in Room 56-57); it appears that these rooms were in fact designed as small square rooms. These small square rooms, along with Room 41 (a similar room in the rear row), form the east end of Stage II. The mean floor area is 11.56 m$^2$ (sd= 2.98 m$^2$, N=6).

Some of the other Stage II rooms were also later subdivided, but when the later cross walls are disregarded, the larger front row rooms average 22.95 m$^2$ (sd=0.66 m$^2$, N=5); and the rear row rooms (excluding Room 41) average about half that, 12.00 m$^2$ (sd=1.45 m$^2$, N=10). The size difference between front and rear row rooms is a difference of both length and width.

Stage II has, of course, undergone extensive later modification, but at least six and perhaps seven discrete room suites can be defined from doorway patterns. Each consists of one or two large front row rooms and from one to three smaller rear row rooms. Connections within the posited plaza-facing row are, of course, unknown.

Within the front row, as already noted, there are formal differences between the small square rooms (39, 39A, 40, 49, 50) at the east end of the front row, and the larger rooms to the west (beginning with Rooms 51, 56-57, etc.). There are several other differences (in addition to size) between these two classes of rooms. While primary roof beams in the larger rooms are perpendicular to the plaza, primary beams in smaller rooms run parallel. In both cases, primary beams span the short axis of the room.

Doors in the front walls of the larger rooms were very tall and broad (only the tops of these doors are visible above room fill). The small, square rooms each have two doors in front walls: the first, and presumably the original, is a short rectangular raised-sill door, centered in the wall between the cross walls, and between the floor and ceiling. The second door is considerably higher (the lintels were just below the ceiling level) and offset toward one cross wall. These doors were all later blocked.

Presumably the second, larger doors in the smaller rooms postdate the first (e.g., the upper door in Room 39 dates to about 1054 while the room itself dates about 1035-1040). This sequence of doors may demonstrate modification of the rooms to allow access to a higher level to the front, the older Stage II rooms having become partially subterranean through the accumulation of plaza or construction surfaces. (This situation is also encountered in Old Bonito.) The apparently tall doors in the larger rooms might be later, higher remodeling (like those added to the small, square rooms) rather than unusually tall original doors; however, their great breadth remains distinctive.

It is likely that the smaller, raised-sill doors of the small square rooms opened into the posited plaza-facing row. This row was razed and for some length of time prior to Stage VIA (see below), the currently visible front rooms of Stage II may have opened directly onto a plaza; hence the larger doors open onto a surface considerably higher than the ground floor level of the room.

Paired vents (one vent in each upper corner of a wall) are known from the rear walls of a few rear row rooms; however, in the front row, only the rear wall of Room 50 is definitely equipped with paired vents. Probably none of the plaza-facing walls of the front row had vents.

Along the entire rear wall of Stage II, there is only one doorway (Room 47-52). In my opinion, this door is an artifact of post-flood stabilization. Very likely, the rear wall of Stage II was penetrated only by vents, as indicated above, and an odd "window" in Room 48. This 60 cm square opening (doorway) was constructed just like a large vent. Its function must have been related to the room-wide platform in the east end of Room 48, since the feature is centered directly above the platform's surface. One other rear row room (92) had room-wide platforms, in both east and west ends, but no "windows." One remarkable door not yet mentioned goes diagonally from front row Room 39A to rear row Room 41. This corner door seems to have been original, and if so it is the earliest corner door known at Chaco. Almost nothing is known of Stage II floor features. In a few rooms with relatively complete notes, none is mentioned.

Most of Stage II is built masonry remarkably similar to masonry used in the initial construction at Pueblo Alto (1020-1040).

## Stage III (1045-1050)

About 10 years after the initial construction of Stage II, a single row of one-story tall rooms was added to the rear of the existing building (Figures 4.41b, 4.42, 4.43). The construction of this addition is rather unusual (Figure 4.45). Instead of seating the new primary beams in the parapet of the older rear wall, the addition was built as an independent unit, with two long walls. One formed the new rear wall of the building, and the other was built directly alongside the older rear wall, creating a double wall between Stages II and III. Much of this double wall fell during the 1947 flood, but it originally ran the entire length of Stage III. In most, and probably all, Stage III rooms, the double wall included a large rectangular void or niche (about 1.60 m wide by 1.00 m tall and 0.95 m deep), centered between the cross walls and about 70 cm above the floor. The sides and floor of the niche were evenly finished, and the top was supported by large beams, like the lintels of a very large door. The exterior face of the older Stage II wall formed the rear of the niche. In at least three (and perhaps all) rooms, a second equally distinctive feature accompanied the large niche. This was a second rectangular void at the west end of the double wall, serving as a shaft for vertical access from the ground floor to the roof level.

What was the function of the double wall? At least four explanations have been offered:

1. The wall provided lateral support to the rear wall of Stage II.
2. The wall increased support for upper-story building.
3. The wall supported Stage III primary beams, either, because (a) Stage II was already two stories tall, and lacked a parapet in which to seat new beams, or (b) the beams stockpiled for Stage III construction were too short for the designated span.
4. The double wall allowed the construction of the large niche and access shaft.

These suggestions are not mutually exclusive. They will be discussed individually in the order presented.

Lateral support for the rear wall of Stage II seems reasonable in light of similar construction at Pueblo Bonito, Kin Bineola, and elsewhere; however, the rear wall of Chetro Ketl Stage II shows no evidence of uneven settling or movement.

The second argument, increased support for eventual upper-story building, suggests long term planning, for, in fact, the second story over Stages II and III was built 5 to 10 years after Stage III. Two arguments can be made against this interpretation. First, the rear wall of Stage III, which would also have been needed to support any upper story building, is a wall of normal width. Second, when the second story was added over the double wall, it was built over the original Stage II rear wall, rather than the thicker Stage III double wall.

The sequence of upper story construction also suggests that the double wall was not an alternative to punching beam sockets in an existing two-story wall, since the wall was evidently not two stories in height when Stage III was built.

This leaves the last two suggestions, which I believe are the most likely: either the wall represents a compromise between a selected span and the available beams, or the wall was designed to allow construction of the large niche and vertical shaft features, or both.

The large niches, the vertical shaft, and the double wall itself are very unusual features. The double wall technique is seen infrequently at other Chacoan sites. The intramural shaft is even more rare. The large niches are probably unique to Chetro Ketl Stage III; their occurrence in every Stage III room is a strong argument for centralized design.

One room (93) of this series also had a room-wide platform. The few pre-flood photos that remain do not show room-wide platforms in other Stage III rooms. The double wall in at least one room (number unknown) had a trio of smaller niches east of the distinctive large niche.

Rooms in Stage III are very uniform in size (mean=11.23 m$^2$, sd=1.81 m$^2$, N=12), and fairly close to the average size of rear row rooms of Stage II. The double wall covered any major openings in the Stage II rear wall (e.g., the "window" in Room 48, and the door, if real, in Room 47-52), although some, and perhaps all, vents present in the Stage II rear wall were continued through the Stage III double wall. All Stage III rooms had small raised-sill doors and paired vents in their rear walls, and lateral doors through most probably all cross walls. The doors in the Stage III rear wall were all subsequently blocked.

These interconnected rooms form a suite, but clearly do not represent the same kind of unit as the 2-5 room Stage II suites. Stage II rooms connected laterally, but did not have doors cut through to the older suites.

## Stage IV (1050-1055)

In the early 1050s, second stories (Stage IVA) were added over existing Stage II and III rooms (Figure 4.41c). The second story extended east, at least in the rear two rows of rooms, as part of a three-room deep addition (Stage IVB) to the east end of Stages II and III. There is a legendary change in the masonry type (admired on every Chetro Ketl tour) between the second stories of Stages IVA and IVB. Despite this evident break (greatly enhanced by modern repairs), the second stories of both date to 1050-1055.

While the second story of Stage IVB is dated to 1050-1055, the dating of the first story below it is problematic. Since this first-story construction abuts Stage III (1045-1050), the first and second stories of IVB must be essentially contemporaneous. It must be noted that the east door of Stage II Room 39, which opens into the front row of Stage IVB, may date to 1045. While this date at least supports the separation of Stage IVB from Stage II, it also could support an earlier date for the first story of Stage IVB. While no conclusive argument can be made for either dating, I have assumed that first and second stories are

contemporaneous, to allow articulation of the first stories of both the north block (Stage IVB) and east wing (Stage IVC).

Stage IVA. Many ceilings in Stage II and III rooms were substantially strengthened with new beams in the early 1050s, probably in preparation for Stage IVA construction. Modification and repair may have anticipated higher live loads on the first-story roofs which were to become second-story floors. At about the same time, several rooms in the front row of the existing building were subdivided. Cross walls of smaller rooms in the older ground floor rooms were not continued into the new second story, notably first-story Rooms 39 and 39A became a single larger room on the second level, a situation also likely over Rooms 49 and 50. In the front row of Stage IVA, then, mean size (22.82 m$^2$) is about the same as the Stage II front row rooms (sd=0.62 m$^2$, N=6), while second and third row room sizes remained almost identical to those of the earlier rooms on the first story, i.e., 11 to 12 m$^2$.

All rooms probably had a single raised-sill door and paired vents in each rear wall, but the lack of alignment of cross walls from the first to the second row necessitated off-center and occasionally multiple doors in the wall between them (e.g., the rear walls of Rooms 56-57 and 60). The second-story, plaza-facing walls (i.e., those in the front wall of the front row) apparently had large, multiple doors in each wall, including at least one T-shaped door (Room 62).

The rear row of rooms interconnects laterally, while the middle row rooms do not. Only two pairs of front row rooms are laterally connected (Rooms 62 and 63, and Rooms 51 and 56-57), both with unusually broad doors (of which only the blocked basal portions remain).

There were two corner doors in Stage IVA. The first may have opened to the exterior from the southeast corner of Room 56-57, and the second was an internal door between the second row room (47-52) and rear row room (46).

The only floor features reported from Stage IVA were in Room 39. The first story of Room 39 had been filled, perhaps intentionally, with trash, and thus the floor of the second story was intact when excavated. The second-story floor of Room 39 had been rebuilt three times. On the first and last floor, there were corner firepits, while the middle floor had a central firepit.

Stage IVB. Stage IVB includes most of the northeast corner of Chetro Ketl. Only a few rooms are visible here, most having been badly reduced prior to any archaeological research and then further obscured by an extensive backdirt embankment created during the excavation of the north block. Only a few rooms in the rear row on the second-story level are visible; first-story rooms are entirely buried. The rooms appear to be uniformly large, (i.e., almost twice as large as rooms of the same rows in Stage IVA (mean=19.68 m$^2$, sd=1.93 m$^2$, N=4). With the exception of the rear wall of the building, which had only paired vents, every wall parallel to the plaza had a raised-sill door and paired vents. Cross walls also have lateral doors but no vents. No other wall features, and of course no floor features, are known from Stage IVB.

Stage IVC. Stage IVC was the ground floor of the northern two-thirds of the east wing. Only the uppermost portions of some walls are visible, e.g., Rooms 114, 116, 118, and 119). Stage IVC was presumably three rooms deep, and one story in height. There is a suggestion of decreasing room size from front to rear. Rear row rooms average 16.47 m$^2$ (sd=1.24 m$^2$, N=4), about 40% smaller than the single measurable middle row room (Room 115, 25.94 m$^2$).

The masonry of Stage IVC is a form of Type II, more like that of Stage IVA than that of IVB, with which Stage IVC presumably articulates in the northeast corner of the building.

Stage V (1050?-1075?)

Stage VA. The plaza-enclosing arc at Chetro Ketl is unusual in that it seems to curve around the west wing and terminate at the west end of the north block (Figure 4.39). This suggests that at some point, Chetro Ketl may have been "L" shaped, much like Una Vida, Pueblo Pintado, or perhaps Pueblo Alto (see Pueblo Alto, Stage IV). If so, the west wing superimposed on the plaza-enclosing arc was probably relatively late.

Other lines of argument may indicate that the two wings were more or less contemporaneous. In its final (post-1130?) form, Chetro Ketl was marked by the asymmetry of its two wings, the east wing being about 14.5 m longer than the west. The east wing as it appeared in the mid-

1050s (i.e., Stage IVC) was almost exactly the same length as the west, which suggests that the west wing paralleled the east in construction. The west wing lacks tree-ring dates and, with the exception of one or two elevated round rooms and an odd corner here and there, is completely reduced. I suspect that most of the west wing was built at the same time as Stage IVC, and I have postulated that this construction (Stage VA) was similar in form to the earliest east wing: that is, three rooms deep and about six rooms long (Figure 4.41d). The west wing was evidently two stories tall, although, like the earliest portions of the north block and the east wing, the rising plaza level eventually made the second story the ground story. Extending the east wing-west wing analogy to the construction of stories, the first story may have been built in the early 1050s and the second in the 1060s or early 1070s.

Stage VB. A pair of razed walls, running southwest from Room 123 and Kiva C, and beneath the Great Kiva, suggests an arc of plaza-enclosing rooms running from Stage IVC to the southeast corner of the west wing, both of which may date to the early 1050s. The depth of the razed walls, relative both to each other and to Room 123 and Kiva C, is unknown; the walls are about 4 m below the present plaza surface. If these segments do represent a continuous arc, the fact is of considerable significance to the dating of the Great Kiva, which must then postdate that arc. Similar parallel plaza-enclosing walls at Pueblo Bonito date about 1045-1060.

Stage VI (1050-1060)

Stage VIA. Stage VIA consists of a line of large single-story rooms either added to, or more likely replacing, a razed plaza-facing row of Stage II rooms, and perhaps a second line of very narrow rooms running along the front of the large rooms (Figure 4.41e). The pattern is best illustrated by Rooms 70, 89, and 104. Room 70 is a large rectangular room added to the front of the first story of Stage II with a double wall (very much like that employed in Stage III). There are at least two doors in the front wall of Room 70, opening into Room 89. Room 89 is a very narrow room which faced the plaza. The first story of neither Room 70 nor 89 is currently exposed, but perhaps the open first story of Room 104, a narrow room west of Room 89, is representative. Room 104 had a large, much modified door opening into the plaza, and room-wide platforms at both ends. It is impossible to say if room-wide platforms were standard features in Stage VIA plaza-facing rooms, and in fact these features in Room 104 may be later introductions paralleling those in nearby, but later, upper stories of Rooms 88 and 89 (see Stage XIV).

Stage VIA probably includes Rooms 69 and 104, and Rooms 70 and 89. Evidence for the continuation of Stage VIA to the east may be found in the razed walls beneath Kiva I and Kiva G (constructions G-3-1a and G-3-1d in Miller [1937]), and Rooms 25 and 38. The bases of these razed walls are at a depth comparable to that of the floor of Room 104, and beneath Kiva G-3 they also show the large room-narrow room pattern. This pattern probably characterizes much of Stage VIA.

Room 70 is about 26.6 m$^2$ in floor area, larger than the Stage II rooms behind it; the projected rooms to the east of it are larger still. The front row rooms of Stage IVA seem to be equal in width to the larger rooms behind, but only about one third as deep.

Stage VIB. Stage VIB (Figure 4.41e), a single story extension of the east wing (Stage IVC), consists of a block of four square rooms (Rooms 5, 6, 7 and the fourth under the later Kiva C), and two extremely long, narrow rooms to the rear and to the south of this block (Rooms 1-4 and 2-3). The small square rooms measure about 4 m x 4 m (mean area=15.71 m$^2$, sd=3.45 m$^2$, N=3). The long, narrow rooms (Rooms 1-4 and 2-3) are each about 3 m wide, and about three to four times longer than they are wide.

The only portion of Stage VIB presently exposed is the first story of Room 1-4. A single door is located at the south end of this room, originally opening to the valley floor outside the plaza. Apparently no doors connected Room 1-4 with Rooms 2-3 and 5. Beyond this, we know nothing of wall or floor features from Stage VIB.

Stage VIC. Stage VIC (Figure 4.41e) is limited to a pair of razed walls running southwest from Stage VIB, partially buried beneath later Kiva A. The depth of Kiva A places Stage VIC on about the same level as the floor of Stage VIB. The walls are probably the remnants of an early plaza-enclosing arc.

Stage VII (1060-1070)

Between 1060-1070 (and probably within the first five years of that span)

third-story rooms were added to the two rear rows of the north block (Stage VIIA), and second-story rooms were added over the rear rows of the east wing (Stage VIIB). These rooms naturally continued the form of the lower stories, with a slight increase in floor area reflecting a slight decrease in wall width (Figure 4.41f).

Stage VIIA. Very little remains standing of the third story over earlier Stage IVA in the north block; most of it was lost in the 1947 flood. The exterior (rear) wall probably included paired vents and a raised-sill door for each room, doors which opened onto a long balcony along the second-story ceiling level of the rear wall. The third story over north block Stage IVB collapsed prior to the 1947 flood, but it appears in photographs taken by the Mindeleffs and Pepper in the 1880s. These early photos and the small amount of remaining wall show no doors in the rear (exterior) wall over Stage IVB; however, interior walls parallel to the plaza had raised-sill doors and paired vents. Remaining cross walls also have raised-sill doors. Both of the rear row rooms for which there are data (Rooms 109 and 110) had room-wide platforms.

Stage VIIB. Stage VIIB includes two rows of rooms built on the second story level, over the middle and rear rows of the east wing. What remains is largely the rear, exterior wall. This wall shows paired vents, but no doors, in each room. Rear row rooms had doors in plaza-facing walls, and none in lateral walls. The visible cross walls of the middle row had lateral doors. Nothing is known of doors in plaza-facing walls of this row.

Stage VIIB building is both more visible and more complex over Stage VIB at the south end of the east wing (Figures 4.49, 4.50). The excavators believed that the older first story, (Stage VIB) was intentionally filled prior to or during VIIB construction, but this may not be correct (Dean and Warren 1983).

Except for the rear, exterior wall, doors occur in all walls parallel to the plaza, but in no walls perpendicular to the plaza. Rooms 5, 6, and 2-3 have numerous wall niches, but these may date to later modifications of the area that include the subdivision of Rooms 1-4 and 2-3 and the introduction of Kiva C (Stage XIVC).

Stage VIII (1070-1075)

Stage VIIIA. Stage VIIIA (Figure 4.41g) is a poorly known modification of the plaza-facing rooms of the north block (Stage VIA) that took place about 1070-1075. The dendrochronology of the only two dated units, the Kiva N complex and Room 38, is less definite than could be wished (see Dean and Warren 1983). In the Kiva N complex, equivalent stories of Room 89 (second story) and Kiva N (first story) were probably built about this time, as was the second story of Room 70. Room 38 is dated between 1054 and 1090. In this one case, I accept Hawley's unconfirmed date of 1073. This date is listed as coming from the second story; however, since Room 38 is but a single story, the date must come from the first.

Kiva N began as a small elevated round room; in Stage XIII, a second story was added to Kiva N and it became one of the fewer than one-half dozen Chacoan Tower Kivas. As built in Stage VIIIA, Kiva N had a large T-shaped door to the exterior (west) and a smaller door north into Room 89. A partition wall apparently ran a short distance in from the T-shaped door, but other features are not known. A large (1.25 m diameter) and mysterious solid masonry column stands against the wall in the southeast quarter of Kiva N, but this is very likely a later addition, perhaps part of the metamorphosis from circular room to Tower Kiva.

Room 38 is a square room with at least two floors. The lower had a central firepit and possibly a vent running below the large T-shaped door through the south wall, and the upper floor had both central and corner firepits.

Stage VIIIA may have consisted of only isolated construction, such as Kiva N and Room 38; however, I believe that much subsequently obscured construction between these two units may also date to this span. Two elevated round rooms (the razed remains of Kiva G-8 and the unnumbered round room preserved in a short arc in the west wall of Room 72), on about the same level as Room 38 and Kiva N, were probably part of this construction. Each of these round rooms was about the same diameter as Kiva N. Most of the area probably occupied by Stage VIIIA was not excavated to sufficient depth to expose remains, if present.

Stage VIIIB. Around 1075 a fourth story was added over the existing (Stage IVB) rear row of rooms in the northeast corner of the building (Figure 4.41g). There is no evidence that this fourth story continued west beyond Room 109. The rooms of Stage VIIIB collapsed relatively recently (see Stage IVB). Only paired vents in walls parallel to the plaza are evident in early photographs of Stage VIIIB. Nothing is known about floor or other wall features.

Dating is largely conjectural. Stage IVB, upon which VIIIB was built, dated to 1060-1070, providing an approximate building date for Stage VIIIB. Since there is little evidence of any major construction after 1075 in the main roomblocks, I have assumed that Stage VIIIB was built prior to 1075. A likely span, then, is 1070-1075.

## Stage IX (1075-1085)

Stage IXA. Stage IXA (Figure 4.41h) is a one-story room (Room 8-9) added to the the south end of the east wing, on the same level as VIB. This construction evidently took place between 1075-1085, but subsequent modifications of the room (particularly the addition of Stages IXB and XIVB) and heavy stabilization have confused both architecture and dendrochronology.

Stage IXB. The "Moat," two parallel walls about 0.6 m apart and standing up to 2 m tall, runs from east wing to west across the front of the plaza (Figures 4.41h). The walls were finished on both interior and exterior faces, and the narrow passage between had a well plastered floor. This floor, plus a vent in the wall opposite Room 135, suggests that the Moat was roofed. There were no cross walls.

## Stage X (1075-1115?)

Stage XA. Probably after 1075, two elevated round rooms and several plaza-facing rectangular rooms were added to the west wing (Figures 4.41h, 4.51). If this construction was analogous to similar construction in the north block, the round rooms date to about 1080-1090, and the rectangular rooms to 1080-1105.

The round rooms were constructed on the second story of the existing west wing (Stage VA). At the time of Stage X construction, the floor of the old second story was probably at plaza level. Other construction in Stage X was probably on the same level as the round rooms, i.e., on the present plaza level.

Stage XB. The dendrochronology of the trash mound suggests deposition from about 1075 to sometime after 1110 (Robinson et al. 1974:22). This range of dates is compatible with the ceramic content of the mound (Windes 1980).

Stage XI (1080-1090)

Kivas I and J and the rooms immediately around them (Figures 4.41h, 4.48) probably date about 1080-1090. Rooms along the plaza-facing walls of Kivas I and J (i.e., Rooms 29 through 31, 33, and 88) may be slightly later in time; these I have called XIB, while Kivas I and J and the three rooms separating Kiva J from the Kiva N complex are Stage XIA.

Stage XIA. Kivas I and J and their square enclosures were built at one time. Rooms 71, 72 and 74, to the west, were probably built at the same time. These rooms were most likely one story, as were the two round rooms, but the ground or plaza level on which they were built corresponds to the second-story construction of earlier building in the north block. (The three square rooms were eventually two stories in height, but the additional story was probably added along with the second story of the Kiva N complex, Stage XIIIB.) Rooms 71, 72, and 74 average about 10.89 m$^2$ in area (sd=2.46 m$^2$, N=3). Only Room 71, subdivided by a north-south wall into two very small, narrow rooms, was excavated. The one on the west end has a very small, elaborate door in its south wall which leads into an odd, narrow passage along the west side of Room 72, the ground floor of which was partially filled with the remains of earlier construction (see Stage VIIIA). Lateral communication from Rooms 71 through 71A into the second story of earlier Room 70 was possible through raised-sill doors. To the rear, Room 71 connected with older Room 62 through an existing T-shaped door, which was subsequently blocked.

Kivas I and J were fairly typical Chacoan round rooms. Both overlie earlier constructions. The southwest corner of the Kiva J enclosure was converted into a small room behind Room 73, and this room, like Room 73, is probably part of Stage XIB construction.

Stage XIB. The line of rooms along the plaza-facing walls of Kivas I and J may be slightly later than those two units, but in view of subsequent building (Stage XII), Stage XIB cannot have been very much later than XIA. Rooms 33, 33/73, and 73 are single story rooms; 33 and 33/73 are each about 10.30 m$^2$ in area, 73 was 60% larger (16.56 m$^2$). Each of these rooms had a large door centered in the plaza-facing wall, definitely a T-shaped door in Room 33/73 and very likely T-shaped doors in the other two rooms. As noted above, Room 73, the largest of the three, also connects with the

small room in the southwest corner of Kiva J.

Rooms east and west of these three are fairly different in form. Room 88, to the west, can be seen as a later addition to the Kiva N complex, mirroring Room 89 in size, shape, and perhaps function. Room 88 is a long, very narrow room, divided (perhaps during Stage XIV) into upper and lower compartments (each a little over 1 m in height) by a secondary ceiling or continuous room-wide platform. Each of these long, low compartments has a separate door from Room 85. The lower compartment was subdivided by a thin cross wall, with its own door. Access into the far reaches of these compartments must have been on hands and knees.

Rooms 29 through 31 are a second distinct unit that apparently began as a small circular room (5.50 m in diameter). This round room may originally have been two stories in height, making it a "Tower Kiva." The upper story was later razed and converted into three rectangular rooms by building a foundation wall across the south half of the round room and filling in the first story (Stage XIIIC).

Stage XII (1090-1095)

About 1090-1095, a major addition, the Kiva G complex, was made to the existing north block (Figure 4.41i, 4.47). This complex was constructed over the filled-in Kiva G-5 and the remains of other earlier round and rectangular rooms.

As first built, Stage XII consisted of a single story block of rectangular rooms surrounding the rectangular enclosure of Kiva G-3. Stage XII was very similar to Stage XI Kivas I and J, and in fact differences between Stages XIA and XII are minor: Kiva G-3 was slightly smaller than Kivas I and J; the floor level of Stage XII is slightly higher than that of Stage XI (the floor of Kiva G-3 was about on the level of the benches of Kivas I and J); and the masonry of the Kiva G complex is of a "McElmo" type.

The rooms surrounding Kiva G-3 are one deep on the north, east, and west sides, and two deep on the south. Rooms 36 and 37, on the north, originally were a single, very long, narrow room. We know nothing about Room 36-37 beyond its size and shape, and the fact that it connected with the Stage II rooms located to the rear of it. It is possible that it functioned either as dead space or as "buttressing," familiar features of round rooms and their enclosures; however, it may have been similar to Rooms 88, 89, or 104 (see Stages VIA and XIB).

Rooms 28 and 35, separating Stage XII from Stage XI to the west, were built around a blocky masonry buttress for Kiva I. Room 35, the northern of these two rooms, had a set of mealing bins, a possible room-wide platform, and a very high door to the roof terrace level of Kiva I (comparable to Room 55 at Pueblo del Arroyo). Other doors in Rooms 28 and 35 open into the rooms south of Kiva G-3.

Rooms east of Kiva G-3 are squeezed between the G-3 enclosure and the remnants of Stage VIIIA (i.e., Room 38). Room 23 connected by way of a raised-sill door to plaza-facing Room 22, which had a single exit, a T-shaped door into the plaza.

Four of the rooms south of Kiva G-3 form two non-communicating suites: first, Rooms 16 and 18, and second, Rooms 17 and 19. These rooms are similar in shape and size (about 15 m$^2$), and had doors in all plaza-facing walls. Strangely, all these doors seem to have been of the raised-sill type. All four of these rooms were featureless, except for a room-wide platform in the west end of Room 18 -- probably a later addition.

In the southwest corner of Stage XII are two small (about 9.5 m$^2$) square rooms (Rooms 26 and 27), connecting the four rooms just described with the two rooms west of Kiva G-3 (Rooms 28 and 35). The plaza-facing room of this pair (Room 26) may or may not have had a door into the plaza; if so, it was of the raised-sill type, while the rear door of Room 26, opening into Room 35, was full length. Room 27 had a corner firepit and slab-lined cist.

The average floor area of Stage XII rooms, excluding Room 36/37, is 13.04 m$^2$ (sd=2.76 m$^2$, N=10). Rooms with doors into the plaza were generally larger than those without doors.

## Stage XIII (1095-1105)

A series of second-story additions were made over the plaza-facing rooms of the north block (Figure 4.41j). These consisted of XIIIA, second-story construction over the Kiva G complex; XIIIB, upper story construction over the Kiva N complex; and XIIIC, second-story building over the plaza-facing rooms between Kivas G and N. This building created a large terrace over the roofs of Kivas I and J that was surrounded by second- and third-story rooms.

Stage XIIIA. Construction of Kivas G-1 and G-2 over Kiva G-3 occurred about 1095-1105. These circular rooms were built over the relatively intact walls of the earlier Kiva G-3, raising the later kivas to the second-story level. Presumably the second stories over Rooms 16, 17, 22, and 23 were also built at this time. There is no evidence for a second story over Rooms 28 and 35, but a second story probably was built over Room 36/37. Where data exist, wall and floor features are absent.

Stage XIIIB. This stage consists of the second story of Kiva N and the third story of Room 89. Dean and Warren (1983) date this construction to the early 1100s.

The addition of a second story over Kiva N created a Tower Kiva. Floor features of the second-story room are unknown; a bench with a recess to th east remains and a door (perhaps T-shaped) opens through Room 74 onto the Kiva I and J terrace.

Stage XIIIC. Rooms 31, 33, and 71-73 probably acquired their second stories at this time. Walls are very reduced, but at least one room (31) had a door opening onto the Kiva I and J terrace, while other rooms had lateral doors (i.e., Room 31 into Room 27, Room 72 into Room 74). The second story of Room 31, preserved over the filled first story (see Stage XIB), had a central firepit. Other floor and wall features are not known.

## Stage XIV (1105+)

Stage XIV is a series of very late constructions added to the plaza-facing walls of the existing building (Figure 4.41k). The ground floor level of Stage XIV and the last plaza surface are on the second-story level of earlier north and east wing building. None of this construction can be dated directly by dendrochronology.

Stage XIVA. A row of single-story rooms added around the west and south sides of the central north block were butted onto Stages VII and XI. Along the west plaza-facing wall of the Kiva N complex, Stage XIVA consists of at least two and perhaps three large square rooms, all about 18 m$^2$ in area (Rooms 85, 87, and a similar room over Rooms 69 and 104).

Both Rooms 85 and 87 have doors into the plaza, but there was no door between the two. Room 87 had multiple doors north into the postulated room over Room 69/104. Both Rooms 85 and 87 have doors to the rear: Room 85, double doors into the upper and lower portions of Room 88; and Room 87, the T-shaped door into the first story of Kiva N (partially blocked by the wall between Rooms 85 and 87), and a second door into Room 104. In addition, Room 85 has a raised-sill door into the Colonnade (described below), but this was probably a later addition. Both Rooms 85 and 87 had unusual floor features. Room 87 had a firepit and deflector complex, while Room 85 had a series of bins and firepits, and several small wall niches.

Possible suites incorporate rooms built during earlier stages. The two suites in this stage are nearly identical, each consisting of the large square rooms (85 and 87) with elaborate firepits and bins, each connected to an interior, long, narrow room with multiple room-wide platforms (88 and 104). This pattern is not particularly common at other Chacoan sites. Suites in contemporary Chacoan building (Pueblo del Arroyo, parts of Pueblo Bonito, and Aztec and Salmon ruins) more often consist of four or more square to rectangular rooms connected perpendicularly to the plaza.

The famous Colonnade (Rooms 75, 77, 78, and 80) was apparently constructed as part of Stage XIVA. The Colonnade consists of at least 13 square masonry columns, spaced about 1.3 m apart, forming the plaza-facing wall of a long narrow room. The Colonnade was not intended to facilitate access from plaza to interior, since the columns are built on a low, stub wall about 0.80 m tall. The spaces between columns were subsequently blocked, and the long narrow room behind them subdivided into several smaller rooms. While it is impossible to date these modifications, they probably occurred long after Stage XIVA.

Stage XIVB. The arc of single-story rooms along the interior of Stage IXB was built on the upper surface level of the plaza (Figure 4.52). The rooms were built over the early parallel walls of the Moat (Stage IXB). Each room had a door towards the plaza; not enough of the exterior (rear) walls remain to determine if these, too, had doors. At least four of these rooms, and probably more, had firepits and bins. The rooms average about 11.61 m$^2$ in area (sd=2.62 m$^2$, N=11).

Stage XV (1105+)

Stage XVA. A row of irregular and poorly constructed rooms was added to the front of the Colonnade, perhaps when the spaces between the columns were filled (Figure 4.411). Other obviously late construction in this area (Rooms 24 and 25) is also included in Stage XV, as are similar constructions in the southeast plaza. Obviously, the contemporaneity of these structures is conjectural, but all clearly dates later than 1105.

Rooms 20 and 21 are considered part of Stage XV, since they probably postdate Stage XII behind them, but they are much more substantially built than other Stage XV rooms (Figure 4.47). Rooms 20 and 21 are almost exactly the same size and proportions of the rooms behind them. Both rooms have doors in their east walls, but neither had doors in its south (plaza-facing) wall. Room 20 had a firepit.

Stage XVB. Some of the late construction in the southeast plaza has also been included in this stage (Figure 4.411). Although exact contemporaneity cannot be demonstrated, Stage XVB construction all seems to be associated with the uppermost plaza surface. Little is known about this maze of round pit structures and plaza features. It is likely that Kiva F was the earliest of the group, and may in fact date as early as Stage VIIB.

PUEBLO ALTO

Thomas C. Windes

History

Because of its location high on the mesa overlooking Chaco Canyon, Pueblo Alto was the next to the last Great House to be discovered and named. Simpson's trek through the canyon missed Pueblo Alto, and it was left to the photographer William Jackson, in 1877, to name and map Pueblo Alto after noticing the low mounds while exploring Peñasco Blanco (Jackson 1878:446-448). Jackson noted a few of the long walls extending from Pueblo Alto, but he failed to associate these with prehistoric roads.

Unlike many other Great Houses in the canyon, Pueblo Alto (Figures 4.55-4.62) has long enjoyed minimal disturbance from looters, archaeologists, and other curious folk primarily because of its mounded condition with little standing architecture. The earliest reference to work at Pueblo Alto relates to some pottery being collected by an A.P. Davis in 1887 or 1888 (Powell 1892:xxxix). John Wetherill reported that a few graves were dug in one of the mounds near Pueblo

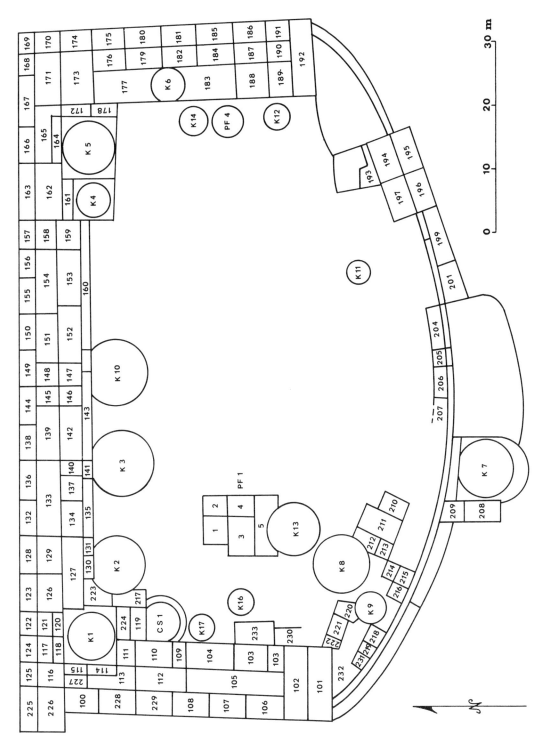

Figure 4.55.  Pueblo Alto.

Figure 4.56.   Pueblo Alto, looking northwest.   Note New Alto, top center
               right; trash mound, bottom center.

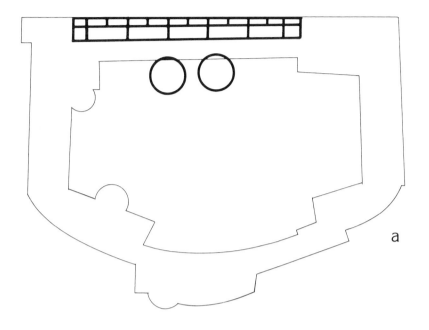

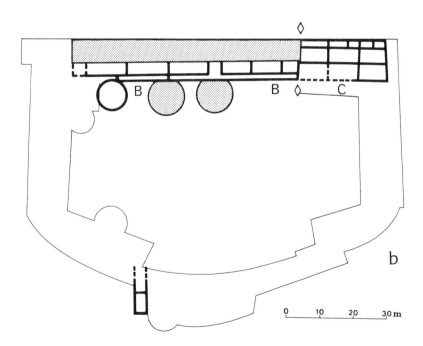

Figure 4.57. Pueblo Alto, construction stages: (a) Stage IA; (b) Stages
    IB and IC. All new construction is one story unless
    otherwise noted.

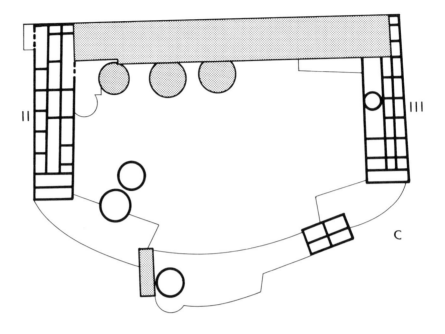

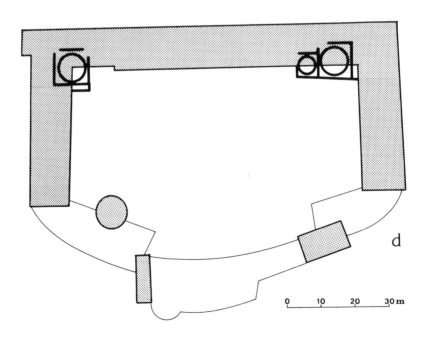

Figure 4.57   Pueblo Alto construction stages:  (c) Stages II and III; (d) Stage IV.

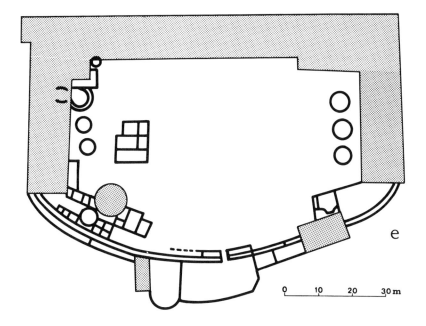

Figure 4.57    Pueblo Alto construction stages:    (e) Stage V.

Figure 4.58.  Pueblo Alto, Room 142 with foundations of earlier Rooms 50 and 51 (lower right), vertically.

Figure 4.59.  Pueblo Alto, exterior wall of Rooms 186 and 191, looking southwest.  Note partially excavated firepit at base of wall.

Figure 4.60. Pueblo Alto, Kiva 15,
looking south.

Figure 4.61.  Pueblo Alto, Room 103,
              looking south.

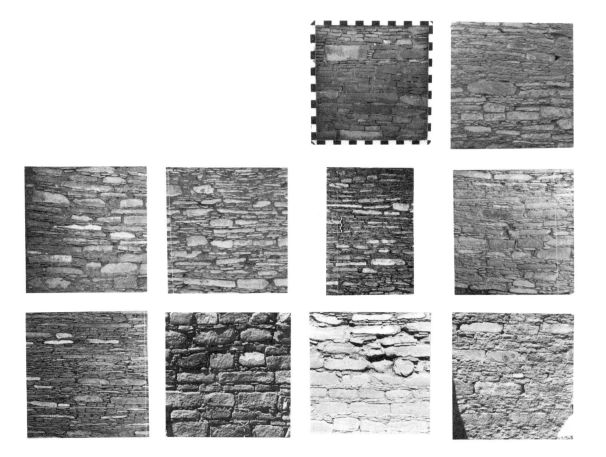

Figure 4.62. Pueblo Alto, examples of masonry (frames are 70 cm x 70 cm. Top row, left to right: Room 102, S wall; Room 103, S wall. Middle row, left to right: Room 112, N wall; Room 112, W wall; Room 112, S wall; Room 229, S wall. Bottom row, left to right: Room 142, W wall; exterior plaza-facing wall outside Kiva 5; exterior plaza-facing wall outside Room 183; E exterior wall.

Alto about the turn of the century (Wetherill Mercantile Co. 1904). One of these graves yielded a hunch-backed human effigy vessel, possibly the one that F.W. Putnam donated to the Peabody Museum. These mounds also yielded the two cylindrical jars and four pitchers in the Wetherill Collection at the Chicago Field Museum of Natural History (Martin and Willis 1940:152, Plate 69).

It is not known whether these excavations actually occurred at Pueblo Alto. The trash mound normally would have attracted relic seekers, but trash mounds at Chaco have been notoriously devoid of burials and spectacular artifacts, and the mound at Pueblo Alto has proven no exception. It would seem unlikely that such material could have been found at Pueblo Alto, but it is impossible to be sure. On the other hand, sites "near" Pueblo Alto are few and lack refuse mounds. One must go a kilometer or more to find sites with the potential for yielding burials. Furthermore, Judd (1920) reports on his first inspection of Pueblo Alto that "not much digging has been attempted although holes have been dug here and there." In a later note appended to a fairly accurate map of Pueblo Alto he states that "little or no digging has been done perhaps because of the unimposing character of the ruin" (Judd 1920).

The earliest documented excavations at Pueblo Alto were done in 1926 by Frank H.H. Roberts, Jr. He placed two trenches across the short axis of the trash mound while working on ceramic studies for Neil Judd (Roberts 1927). For the next 41 years there is little to report about Pueblo Alto. The parking lot at Pueblo Alto, which must have added to the disintegration of the Parking Lot Ruin, was present at least by the 1930s (Robert Lister, personal communication, 1979).

Not until 1967 and again in 1970 and 1971 is archaeological work recorded for Pueblo Alto. During that span, Gwinn Vivian and Robert Buettner investigated water control structures and roads at Pueblo Alto (Vivian 1972).

After that, Pueblo Alto became the focus for several remote sensing experiments. Prehistoric roads had been recognized running north from Pueblo Alto to the Escavada Wash and beyond to the San Juan River as early as the turn of the century according to Mrs. Richard Wetherill (cited in Vivian [1948b] and Holsinger [1901]). The interest in roads around Pueblo Alto prompted further investigation by Ware and Gumerman in 1972 (1977). From aerial imagery they were able to pinpoint a possible entry in the wall running east from the northeast

corner of the building from which a number of roads radiated north from Plaza 2. The entry and several of the roads were verified by testing.

In 1974, Richard Loose tested the jog in the wall that connected Pueblo Alto to nearby East Ruin. This jog was thought to indicate the presence of a small room or part of a ramp leading over the wall; however, the results of the examination were inconclusive. A year later he tested for structures in the main plaza following subsurface radar experiments (Vickers et al. 1976). Loose's work verified the existence of features detected by the radar and resulted in the discovery of a shrine-like structure in the center of the plaza and a probable trash-filled pit structure that yielded, among other things, a copper bell. The Chaco Center initiated large-scale testing at Pueblo Alto in 1976 and concluded it in 1979.

### Chronology

Many construction timbers were recovered as a result of wall clearing, but these could not be dated primarily because of the short ring series. Only a single cutting date (1021r) is directly associated with construction at Pueblo Alto (Table 4.6), although at least two constructional events are evident from clusters of tree-ring dates (at 1045 and 1056) recovered from secondary deposits. The size and species involved indicate initial use in roof construction (Table 4.6); however, their exact association with any particular building stage is unknown. A number of C-14 and archeomagnetic dates (not reported here) were also obtained from Pueblo Alto. While at times the dates yielded by these chronometric methods were contradictory, overall they proved useful.

### Architecture

#### Earliest Construction

The earliest construction at Pueblo Alto was a pair of contiguous rooms (50 and 51) built directly below Rooms 142, 143, and 146 (Figure 4.58). This pair appeared to represent a typical living room/storage room unit with an associated plaza. Their orientation was due east, that is, the living room (51), containing three floors and several features including a firepit, was east of the attached room (50) directly behind it, which had but a single feature for two floors. A large firepit, an equally large heating

Table 4.6.  Tree-ring dates from Pueblo Alto.

TRASH MOUND from one or more roofs
that burned in a single episode.
(Layer 16)

| | | | |
|---|---|---|---|
| CNM-424 | 0979vv | CNM-454 | 1045vv |
| CNM-428 | 1015vv | CNM-468 | 1045vv |
| CNM-399 | 1016vv | CNM-407 | 1045v |
| CNM-409 | 1016vv | CNM-411 | 1045v |
| CNM-439 | 1017vv | CNM-413 | 1045v |
| CNM-425 | 1017vv | CNM-410 | 1045v |
| CNM-467 | 1017vv | CNM-465 | 1045r |
| CNM-426 | 1017vv | CNM-396 | 1045r |
| CNM-403 | 1022vv | CNM-406 | 1045r |
| CNM-401 | 1024vv | CNM-395 | 1045r |
| CNM-464 | 1024vv | CNM-438 | 1045r |
| CNM-400 | 1027++r | CNM-447 | 1045r |
| CNM-444 | 1028vv | CNM-394 | 1045r |
| CNM-423 | 1030++r | CNM-420 | 1045r |
| CNM-419 | 1031vv | CNM-442 | 1045r |
| CNM-449 | 1034vv | CNM-453 | 1045r |
| CNM-429 | 1038+vv | CNM-392 | 1045r |
| CNM-437 | 1039vv | CNM-450 | 1045r |
| CNM-412 | 10039+r | CNM-455 | 1045r |
| CNM-440 | 1040vv | CNM-415 | 1045r |
| CNM-391 | 1042vv | CNM-397 | 1045r |
| CNM-460 | 1043r | CNM-446 | 1045r |
| CNM-441 | 1044vv | CNM-448 | 1045r |
| CNM-398 | 1044r | CNM-452 | 1045r |
| CNM-436 | 1044r | CNM-462 | 1045r |
| CNM-402 | 1044r | CNM-463 | 1045r |
| CNM-451 | 1044r | CNM-435 | 1045r |
| CNM-417 | 1044r | CNM-456 | 1045r |
| CNM-461 | 1044r | CNM-422 | 1045r |
| CNM-393 | 1044r | | |

Room 110, North wall, intramural beam

    CNM-667        1021r

Room 142, Floor 1, fill

    CNM-385        1004v

Room 142, Floor 1, posthole

    CNM-386        1016vv

Room 143, Floor 1, posthole

    CNM-675        0911vv

Room 166, fill (roof?)

    CNM-320        0966vv

Room 188, outside west wall
  (intramural beam?)

    CNM-475        0949vv

Room 190, fill (roof?)

    CNM-338        0935vv

Kiva 12, upright above
  ventilator tunnel

    CNM-486        1044vv

PLAZA FEATURE 1

Room 3, Floor 1, fill (roof?)

| | |
|---|---|
| CNM-631 | 0915+vv |
| CNM-622 | 0965vv |
| CNM-625 | 1010++vv |
| CNM-628 | 1013++vv |
| CNM-626 | 1018+vv |
| CNM-623 | 1023vv |
| CNM-621 | 1024vv |
| CNM-627 | 1026++vv |

Note:  All dates from roof elements unless otherwise noted.
      Key to symbols, see Appendix C.

pit, and three postholes just east of Room 51 mark a probable associated ramada in the plaza.

Evidence for additional rooms is lacking. Nearby, in Plaza Grid 8 to the south is a deep hole in the bedrock filled with trash. The ashy, soft nature of the trash, dominated by Red Mesa Black-on-white and plain gray (with no Gallup Black-on-white), suggests household refuse generated from Rooms 50 and 51. The pit is such that an abandoned pit structure is suspected, although the room orientation suggests that another pit structure should be located to the east.

This early complex should not be dismissed as unrelated to Pueblo Alto. Early buildings in the area (e.g., on the mesa top) are extremely rare and the location of this one may not be fortuitous. Archeomagnetic and C-14 dates suggest use of the two rooms immediately prior to the main Pueblo Alto construction (Stage I) so that a hiatus may not exist. Furthermore, the wall foundations for the two rooms are wide (50 cm) and not unlike those of the Stage I construction. An early 1000s date is reasonable for this early unit.

It should be noted that earlier, presumably outdoor, surfaces marked by several large basin-shaped pits exist under Rooms 50 and 51. A single archeomagnetic date of 980±48 was obtained from one of the pits overlain by the main complex walls. This is the earliest date from the site and is not unreasonable considering its stratigraphic position.

## Stage I (1020-1040)

Stage IA. The wall abutment study shows a continuous outside wall along the east, north, and west sides of Pueblo Alto (Figure 4.55). This is also true (with three exceptions) of the next wall parallel to the outside wall(s). The overall impression of the site, then, is of a single constructional event, including East and West Wings and the Central Block.

However, there are some discrepancies in this suggestion which lead to alternative interpretations. First and foremost is the deposition of trash in the rooms dominated by Red Mesa Black-on-white and plain gray and without Gallup Black-on-white. In the West Wing, the assemblage lies under the lowest defined floors (in excavated Rooms 103, 110, 112, and 229). Constructional debris occurs on the lowest floors or above, not with the underlying material. Conversely, in the Central Block the same ceramic assemblage lies on the lower floors in association with wall construction debris (in Rooms 138 and 139).

Second, there is a marked change in the room symmetry near the east and west ends of the Central Block. The assumption here is that symmetry is more likely to be maintained during a single period of building (and thus reflect a unit of planning) rather than across construction episodes. Near the east end, this architectural change coincides with some discontinuities in the wall construction (e.g., walls are butted and change alignment). The same can be seen at the west end although it is less clear.

From this, it seems likely that the earliest great pueblo building at Pueblo Alto consists of the outer two rows of rooms in the Central Block (Figure 4.57a), from Rooms 121 and 122 east to Rooms 157 and 158. This plan contains five major suites of rooms, each with a huge room oriented to the plaza and backed by two smaller rooms. Floor areas for the five huge rooms average 37.9 m$^2$ (sd=2.8 m$^2$) and for the ten small rooms 9.8 m$^2$ (sd=0.8 m$^2$).

In addition, at each end of this linear plan of suites is a small two-room unit containing a square plaza-facing room backed by a smaller rectangular room (mean floor area = 7.75 m$^2$, sd=0.9 m$^2$). No lateral movement was possible among any of these seven suites; all initial wall ventilators and doorways were orientated north-south with access to and from the plaza. Doors in excavated rooms are all raised-sill types; several had secondary jambs and lintels.

The lowest floors in the excavated rooms of Stage I were probably associated with its construction. These floors had numerous shallow and irregular heating pits. The first plastered floors in these rooms were on the Stage IB floor level (see Stage IB), and were featureless.

The size and symmetrical layout of two of the large plaza-facing round pit structures suggest their association with Stage IA. Kiva 3 and Kiva 10, the largest two at the site (11 m and ca. 10 m diameter, respectively), are located just astride an arbitrary north-south division of the Stage IA rooms. In plan, at least, this creates two equal subdivisions of Stage IA which may reflect social or political divisions of the initial site population. There is still plaza space separating the two pit structures from the initial suites -- an early trait that is later modified as round rooms are incorporated into the roomblocks.

Kiva 2 may also be associated with Stage I; if included, it violates the apparent symmetry of Stage IA. Tests in the open space fronting the eastern suites revealed sterile soil without a trace of companion pit structures. Kiva 2 is also smaller (8.6 m across) than Kivas 3 and 10, although its present size could simply reflect remodeling of an earlier (larger) structure. At this point, there is not good evidence for inclusion or rejection of Kiva 2 into Stage IA.

The masonry style associated with Stage IA is Judd's Type II or a variation thereof. Essentially it is composed of thin, lenticulate, well indurated dark sandstone, chipped along the ends and edges. Larger stones are common, but overall the style is one of masses of long, thin stones with little mortar in between. From the ceramic evidence, and some absolute dates, the suggested period of construction is in the early 1000s, perhaps as late as 1030 or 1040.

Stage IB. A second set of large plaza-facing rooms was apparently added shortly after completion of Stage IA (Figure 4.57b). Ten of the eleven cross walls in this unit are butted to the Stage IA section and several do not follow the alignment of the initial construction. At least in the excavated suite, there is also a sharp rise in the native soil level directly south of Stage IA which results in higher wall foundations for the new addition. The north-south foundations in Rooms 142 and 146 butt the foundations of Stage IA. It is clear, then, that there is a break in the planning and construction between Stages IA and IB, although probably a very short one.

The new construction nearly mirrors in plan the string of huge rooms in Stage IA. Several cross-wall subdivisions of these huge rooms are clearly later additions and these are not included here. There were five large new rooms added to the five original suites, as well as an additional small square room appended at each end. The average floor area of the Stage IB rooms is 37.6 m$^2$ (sd=5.4 m$^2$). The western three rooms are similar in size to their counterparts in the next row (41.4 m$^2$, sd=2.1m$^2$), but the eastern two are smaller (31.4 m$^2$, sd=0.5 m$^2$) and do not quite align with those to the back. The latter more closely resemble the large rooms in Stage IC. The single excavated large Stage IB room (Room 142) had room-wide platforms, which may be later additions, in both ends of the room.

The irregularity in the size of the eastern and western rooms may be due to the space left between the two additions at the expense of the central suite (the one excavated). This left a square area in the plaza (later Room 147) that may have forced a shift in room alignments to similar floor areas for both huge rooms. Doors that led into the plaza from the surrounding rooms would have provided access into or across Kiva 10, a structure which nearly articulates with the new section. A similar room arrangement may account for the subdivisions behind Kiva 3, allowing access into or across Kiva 3 from Room 140 or an earlier plaza square underneath.

Both Kivas 3 and 10 are still used in this and nearly all succeeding stages. Kiva 2 may have been contemporaneous if not earlier. Sections of plaza-facing corridor rooms were also probably added at this time. Corridor rooms exhibit a distinct masonry style of dark, long, thin tabular stone, chipped along the edges and ends, a style which matches that in the south walls of the new huge rooms. Foundations (at least in Room 143) are bonded to those of the larger rooms.

The corridor rooms may not have been completely enclosed, however. Room 143 was originally left open at the east end, possibly to facilitate easier movement into Kiva 10 or the plaza space directly behind (later enclosed to form Room 147). Wall abutments suggest a similar plan behind Kiva 3 where corridor Rooms 131 and 135 might have opened towards the east. The extension of the corridor room walls over the two pit structures would have forced their modification. With Kiva 10 this was indeed the case and we suspect a similar fate for Kiva 3 and perhaps also Kiva 2 by Stage III.

The upper floor of the corridor room had several heating pits, possible storage pits, and a room-wide platform. There are fewer such features on lower floors, and some had none at all. Sockets for the platform beams are irregular and crude, suggesting that they were late (perhaps final) additions to the room.

Rooms 208 and 209 in the southern arc enclosing Plaza 1 exhibit a masonry style similar to that in the Stage IB corridor rooms. There may once have been a larger block of rooms associated with a pit structure in this arc. A prehistoric road from Pueblo Bonito apparently entered Pueblo Alto along the west side of these rooms. Later arc walls have obscured any entrance, but this unit and the associated road are postulated to be of Stage IB or Stage IC construction.

Stage IB, overlying Rooms 50 and 51, is still associated with a Red Mesa ceramic assemblage (without Gallup Black-on-white). A roof support post in Room 142 was tree-ring dated at 1016vv while a charcoal fragment (perhaps from the roof) on the upper floor was 1004v. These suggest construction of Stage IB after 1016 and probably closer to the 1030s or 1040s. Undoubtedly, Stage IB quickly followed Stage IA, because the Stage IA doors are too high (160 cm) to permit reasonable passage between rooms without raising the floors. The raised floors in the Stage IA section excavated are level with those of the later Stage IIB floors in front, thus providing reasonable access through the units.

Stage IC. A block of rooms at the east end of the Central Block suggests a third stage of construction (Figure 4.57c). A few butted walls, smaller rooms, and a shift in east-west wall alignments hint at a discontinuity between Stages IB and IC. Parts of Stage IC exhibit a masonry style identical to that in the Stage IB corridor rooms, although it is disconcerting that not all of Stage IC shares these properties. The six large rooms in Stage IC are similar in form and size to the eastern two rooms of Stage II. The north wall of this unit appears continuous with that of Stage IA. Although there are certain characteristics that parallel events in Stage IB, there are enough differences to postulate a separate period of construction. Obviously, if the north wall is continuous, Stages IA and IC are contemporary.

Six large rooms (mean area=33.8 m², sd=1.4 m², N=4) in two rows of three each are backed by five to six smaller rooms (mean area=12.0 m², sd=4.0 m², N=4). There is a north-south wall segment sandwiched between Kivas 4 and 5 which duplicates the masonry of the fine corridor room. The wall does not follow the projected plan, for it is butted on the north end, which suggests a later subdivision of the western large room in the section. Two of the large rooms have been cut by the later additions of Kivas 4 and 5.

Where does Stage IC terminate? The critical outside corner is probably between Rooms 168 and 169, but it could not be located. Nevertheless, Stage IC stands fairly well by itself, although it may have included more than is presented here.

There has been no excavation in this section and no dates have been obtained other than a meaningless tree-ring date of 966vv from Room 166. The masonry styles, variations of Type II, are

similar to Stage II and suggest construction around 1020 to 1040.

## Stage II (1020-1050)

Stage II is represented by the West Wing (Figure 4.57d). A number of large plaza-facing rooms were built and then backed by rooms of the same size with a single exception (Room 105). A string of six north-south oriented rooms (mean=17.5 m², sd=0.8 m²) connected by doors was added to the back of these and then two huge rooms (35.8 m² and 36.6 m²) were appended to the south end of the wing. The string of exterior rooms had no door connections to inner rooms until a late door was created between Rooms 112 and 229. The five large plaza-facing rooms average 25.2 m² in area (sd=0.8 m²); the three behind them (except Room 105) average 26.0 m² in area (sd=1.9 m²). Overall the eight rooms average 25.5 m² (sd=1.2 m²). If subdivided, the double-length room (Room 105) behind plaza-facing Rooms 103 and 104 would fit into these categories.

The north end of the wing has been partly obscured by the later addition of Kiva 1 and its buttresses (Rooms 114, 115, 118, 120, and 224); however, wall abutments plainly indicate the presence of larger early rooms extending under Kiva 1. Two room pairs are evident: one directly north of Rooms 110 and 112 that consists of Room 111 (partly under the kiva) and Room 113/114; and a second pair of rooms within the space of Rooms 117 and 118 and the northwest quarter of Kiva 1, and a back room incorporating Rooms 115, 116, and 227.

Examination of wall foundations suggests the inner- and outermost were set first, then the inner two longitudinal foundations were added along with the cross-wall foundations. All foundations are bonded. Evidently a hiatus of unknown duration then occurred allowing a layer of clean sand to accumulate before wall construction began. The exterior row of rooms may have been added after the plaza-facing rooms despite the conjectured priority of the former's foundation. Cross walls of the outer rooms abut the next row of rooms and generally do not align with the latter. A trace of Gallup Black-on-white under the lower floor of Room 229 and on the lower floor of Room 103 also suggests that the construction of the entire wing was not simultaneous.

The wing terminates in two very large rooms set perpendicular to the plaza. The wall abutment sequence is unclear; however, I suspect that these were the last major additions to the wing during Stage II. Their size is nearly identical to a similarly positioned very large room in the East Wing (Stage III).

A pair of rooms jutting westward at the northwest corner of the wing mar the apparent symmetry of the building. The critical corners of these rooms (225 and 226) were collapsed, and their temporal relationship is unclear. The size and position of the paired rooms indicate that they are associated with the prehistoric road from Pueblo Bonito that passes a few meters away. The rooms are believed to be associated with Stage III.

Identifying the original suites in the West Wing is difficult. Rooms 103 and 104 appeared to be paired. Room 105, directly behind these, might have formed a pair with Rooms 103 and 104 except no doors provided access. Although its great size (53.6 m$^2$) would suggest that it was once two rooms of equal size, there testing yielded no evidence of a cross wall. Thus, despite its departure from our perceived symmetry of the wing, Room 105 must be accepted as a single large room.

Rooms 110 and 112 were originally paired as a unit front-to-back and not side-by-side like Rooms 103 and 104. The door leading into Room 229 from Room 112 was a late addition. Doors do not lead south from this pair (110-112), but they do go north into the next rooms. At this point, we were unable to confirm additional doors between the large north rooms because of the Kiva 1 buttresses. Thus, we are left with several possibilities for suite arrangements, from paired units to a single unit incorporating all six rooms.

On the floors above the surfaces associated with room construction, the two excavated plaza-facing rooms (103 and 110) had a variety of features indicative of habitation. Numerous heating pits, storage pits, postholes, wall niches and sets of mealing bins were associated with the occupational floors in Rooms 103 (Figure 4.61) and Room 110. Curiously, formal firepits were intermittently used during occupation of both rooms. Room 103, during most of its use life, had no firepit at all.

There are two small round pit structures (Kivas 16 and 17) just in front of Rooms 103 and 104, but these are Stage V additions. The spatial proximity of plaza Kiva 8, at the south end of the West Wing, and its size (9.3 m in diam-

eter) suggest that it was built in conjunction with the wing and may have served its inhabitants. Kiva 13, later built over by Plaza Feature 1, may also have been built at this time or earlier. Kiva 8 may have replaced Kiva 13.

The masonry style of the later cross walls in the components of Stages IA and IB (e.g., in Rooms 134/137/140, 139/145, and 142/146) suggests that these were in place by no later than Stage II. The masonry style in the West Wing is similar to that observed in Stages IA and IC. Basically, it is Type II or a variation of it.

There is a single tree-ring date from the West Wing despite numerous logs salvaged during wall clearing. A date of 1021r was obtained from a log built into the north wall of Room 110 (Table 4.6) and indicates construction of the north part of the wing, at least, by 1021 or later. The absence of Gallup Black-on-white in the Red Mesa assemblage on some lower floors suggests construction between 1021 and 1040; however, the trace of Gallup Black-on-white in Rooms 103 and 229 suggests that some construction might be slightly later by a decade or so (e.g., 1050).

Stage III (1040-1060)

The East Wing (Stage III) parallels the West Wing in its positioning, form, and layout (Figure 4.57e); however, the former is distinct and exhibits a different masonry style, either Type III or IV (Figure 4.59). The West Wing's eastern orientation (i.e., living rooms facing east onto the plaza) suggests that it is the earlier of the two. Perhaps, the West Wing's position relative to the Central Block replicates the L-shaped plan of Una Vida and Pueblo Pintado. There is no precedent for the construction of a western-facing roomblock (and living rooms) that is not balanced by an eastern-facing block of rooms. If the wings at Pueblo Alto are not contemporaneous, the West (Stage II) probably predates the East (Stage III).

The primary block in the East Wing appears to be two suites of two large rooms (46.1 m$^2$, sd=2.8 m$^2$) each backed by two smaller rooms (14.2 m$^2$, sd=0.7 m$^2$) -- a pattern common to the Central Block (Stages IA, IB, and IC). These suites are connected by doors leading front to back (or toward the plaza) without allowing lateral movement. It appears that a later round room separates the two large rooms, although it is difficult to explain the positioning of this round room over the projected cross wall shared by both rooms. Instead, Kiva 6 might be part of the initial wing construction; its walls are bonded with those of Rooms 177 and 183. The suite room doors reflect the spatial presence of Kiva 6, (i. e., the doors are offset) as if it were part of the initial planning. If so, the large rooms would be somewhat diminished in size (42.8 m$^2$, sd=4.6 m$^2$). The small size of Kiva 6 (4.75 m in diameter) and its unusual position within the wing suggests it may have been a tower or Tower Kiva (see Chapter 3).

Like the West Wing, a separate but probably nearly contemporary unit of seven to nine rooms (11.7 m$^2$, sd=2.6 m$^2$, N=9) was added along the wing's exterior with doors running north-south. The variation in size is greatly reduced (12.5 m$^2$, sd=1.0 m$^2$, N=7) by the elimination of the two end rooms. Communication and access toward the interior plaza were limited to a single door in Room 186. There were several outside doors leading to exterior plazas that are crossed by prehistoric roads. It is suggested that these exterior rows of wing rooms are associated with the road.

The south end of the wing contains two or three more possible suites of small rectangular rooms and a large room (Room 192, 35.0 m$^2$) that mirrors two others in the West Wing. Rooms 189-191 once may have comprised a second large room identical to Room 192, but there is no hint of that in the wall abutments. Only one suite allows access across the entire wing (Rooms 186-188).

The sequence of construction appears to parallel that in the West Wing. The longitudinal walls were built first and then the cross walls added. The latter are butted to the longitudinal walls or tied only in the core. The style of masonry banding is similar to that of Type III.

Although three small round pit structures (Kivas 13 and 14, and Plaza Feature 4) are located in the interior plaza next to the East Wing, they may not be of this stage. Their size and shape indicate possible construction during Stage V.

A block of four rooms (Rooms 194-197) located in the eastern half of the southern wall arc enclosing the interior plaza stands apart from the surrounding architecture on the basis of wall abutments, door connections, and masonry style. The masonry is similar to

that of the East Wing and, therefore, is included in this stage on those criteria alone. The four rooms (two paired suites) are located just east of a prehistoric road from Chetro Ketl that enters the interior plaza from the south. The existence of this road was verified by the presence of a doorway through the arc in the exact position predicted from aerial imagery. The position of the small roomblock suggests an association with an earlier arc not now visible.

There are additional blocks of paired rooms of identical size associated with prehistoric roads on the east and west sides of the site. These, Parking Lot Ruin (west of the main building) and East Ruin, might be contemporaneous with Rooms 194-197 and reflect major expansion or remodeling of the road system around Pueblo Alto (see Windes 1982).

This period or the next might also include the remodeling of Rooms 225 and 226 that now jut west from the northwest corner of the house. Room 225 is slightly smaller than Room 226; nevertheless, both can be considered part of a functional unit by virtue of a connecting doorway. The pairing of these rooms of slightly different size and of their respective areas is nearly identical to that of each of the paired-room units comprising the Room 194-197 block, the East Ruin, and the Parking Lot Ruin. The orientation of the Room 225-226 unit, like the others, is also perpendicular to a prehistoric roadway. The masonry style of Rooms 225 and 226 is consistent with the construction of this period.

The masonry style of the eastern addition to Room 143 suggests that it too belongs to this stage of construction. Because the addition extends across Kiva 10, it must have been remodeled at the same time. It is likely that the space north of Kiva 10 was then enclosed to form Room 147. Possibly, similar building took place at Kivas 2, 3, and 7 forcing a reduction in their sizes.

Two tree-ring dates were obtained from the East Wing wall clearing: 949vv from Room 188 and 935vv from Room 190 (Table 4.6). Neither is useful for interpreting construction events.

Several large firepits were built along the outside wall of the wing near the end of the occupation at Pueblo Alto (Figure 4.59), probably during Stage V. The fuel remains, evidently from roofing material removed from the building, were ponderosa pine, Douglas fir, and white fir. The proximity of the firepits to the East Wing rooms naturally suggests that

the source for the wood was at hand.
There is relatively little fir in the
assemblage, as opposed to the frequency
of its occurrence in the West Wing and
Central Block. Based on this tentative
data, it is proposed that the firewood
was gathered from the East Wing. The
many dates from this wood indicate some
construction at approximately 1056. Considering the masonry style and the very
tentative dates, the wing's construction
can best be assigned to the period of
about 1040- 1060.

## Stage IV (1080-1100)

The last major addition to the main
roomblock is the placement of three round
rooms and their associated buttresses
into the northwest and northeast corners
of the building (Figure 4.57f). By this
time, Kiva 13 (south of Plaza Feature 1)
had been abandoned and filled with trash
dominated by Gallup Black-on-white. Kiva
10 also appears to have been abandoned at
this time or shortly thereafter, and
then, after a short hiatus, used as a
trash dump during Stage V. Ceramics from
the trash are dominated by Gallup, Chaco-
McElmo, McElmo, and Puerco Black-on-
whites.

There are no chronometric dates for
this period. Based on tree-ring dates
from other Chacoan ruins this period can
be assigned to about 1080-1100.

## Stage V (1100-1140)

There are a host of late additions
to Pueblo Alto, primarily along the south
side of the interior plaza between the
two wings (Figure 4.57g). Possibly the
earliest of the late construction is
Plaza Feature 1 and Room 119. The placement of Kiva 15 within Room 110 (Figure
4.60) may also occur during this early
period. The southern enclosing arc is
either modified or constructed for the
first time, with additions (e.g., the
outer wall) completed subsequently. A
cluster of small rooms, added along the
inside of the arc in the southeast and
southwest corners, continues north from
the southwest corner to butt against the
Stage IV rooms. One or more small round
pit structures are built within the maze
of small rooms in the plaza corners.
Another is built inside Room 223 and possibly the ones in the East Ruin (Rooms 6
and 11) are added as well. Also, the
crude large block masonry, double-walled
structure (Circular Structure 1, Figure

4.55) is built against the plaza-facing
rooms in the northwest corner.

Numerous tree-ring dates from huge
firepits in Plaza Feature 1 suggest the
use of the firepits in 1132 (Table 4.6).
The late dates are derived solely from
piñon while the earlier dates came solely
from ponderosa and white fir, presumably
ripped from abandoned room roofs. Piñon,
a common fuel at Chaco is presumed to
have been obtained locally just prior to
its use in the firepits. Numerous
archeomagnetic dates from the firepits
and from Kiva 15 indicate a late 1100s
use, but these are probably 50 to 70
years too late. The construction for
Stage VII probably takes place about
1100-1140.

## Latest Occupation

Unlike several other buildings at
Chaco, there is no evidence of an occupation at Pueblo Alto utilizing Mesa Verde
Black-on-white. The final occupation at
Pueblo Alto, then, is assumed to terminate in the twelfth century, probably
between 1130 and 1150. After considerable deterioration had taken place, there
appears to have been a brief reoccupation
of the site. Evidence for this is based
upon the discovery of large, crude slab-
lined firepits built high in the post-
occupation rubble fill in Room 103 and
Kiva 14. Both were sampled for archeomagnetic dating and yielded an estimated
date, for the former, and an absolute
date, for the latter, of about 1365. The
time in question overlaps the mid-1000s
on the archeomagnetic curve, but in this
instance that time period is improbable.
Similar large firepits were also found in
the post-occupational room deposits at
Pueblo Bonito and Kin Kletso (Vivian and
Mathews 1965:61, 64) and also must be
very late.

The dearth of roofing timbers at
Pueblo Alto probably can be attributed to
their reuse as firewood by the late occupants at the site. Dismantling of the
roofs clearly marks the termination of
Pueblo Alto's role in the Chacoan system.

## PUEBLO DEL ARROYO

### History

Pueblo del Arroyo sits just above
the modern channel of the Chaco -- a fact

reflected in both its Spanish and Navajo names. Pueblo del Arroyo, "town of the gully," is approximately the same as the Navajo name "home beside water's edge" (Franstead and Wenner 1974).

The first recorded excavation at Pueblo del Arroyo (Figures 4.63-4.71) was Holsinger's diggings, in the front arc of rooms. Holsinger, a Government Land Office agent investigating illegal excavations at Chaco, found the lure of the spade impossible to resist. He engaged in "a little prospecting with a pick and shovel" and thought he had located a gateway or entrance in the middle of the arc (Holsinger 1901:51). His gateway was not confirmed in later excavations.

A little over half of Pueblo del Arroyo was excavated by the National Geographic Society. Neil M. Judd, the director of the Society's work at Chaco, mistook the Tri-wall behind the ruin for an earlier structure (Judd 1959:109). The stratigraphic potential intrigued him, so Judd decided to excavate part of the ruin. He placed Karl Ruppert in charge of the operations, which began in 1923 and continued for three years.

During 1923 debris from the south and west sides of the ruin was removed and one kiva and 20 rooms were excavated. The south wing and extra-mural habitations were excavated during 1923 and 1924; and in 1925 work was concentrated in the middle portion of the building and the plaza was tested, but not cleared to its original court pavement. The final season of 1926 was confined to the structure at the rear of del Arroyo, which turned out to be series of rooms and a tri-wall kiva. The north wing and the series of rooms across the front of the village were untouched (Pierson 1956:34).

In 1950, Gordon Vivian and Leland Able reexcavated and stabilized the Tri-wall (Vivian 1959). During this work, several previously unexcavated rooms associated with the Tri-wall were tested and mapped. Stabilization was also the justification for the partial excavation of Kiva L, in the north wing, by Gordon Vivian in 1959.

## Architecture

### Stage I (1065-1075)

Judd believed that the east wall of Rooms 35, 44, 47, 52, and 55 was the original plaza-facing wall of the building (Judd 1959:73). The three rows of rooms behind this wall are included here in Stage I (Figure 4.66a). The south end of Stage I was preserved in the construction of later Stage IIA; that is, the south walls of Rooms 34 and 35 appear to have been part of Stage I rather than a part of Stage IIA. There is a vertical break in the masonry of the rear exterior wall of Pueblo del Arroyo that corresponds to the south end of Stage I, at the southwest corner of Room 33. (This break, now heavily stabilized, has been interpreted as the remains of an intruded bond of a wall from Stage IVB.) The lack of alignment of the north walls of Rooms 53, 54, and 55 suggests that these walls are not the original north end of Stage I. Instead, it is very likely that the north end of Stage I was either razed for or incorporated into Stage IIB. The north end of the rear exterior wall of Pueblo del Arroyo is too far reduced to evaluate this possibility.

The rear two rows of rooms in Stage I were two stories, while the original plaza-facing rooms were probably only one, with a second story added in Stage IIIA. The area around later Kiva E was modified and rebuilt several times, but a T-shaped door survives that would have opened from the second story of Room 46, in the second row, onto the roof of the single story Room 47, in the plaza-facing row. In general, other doorway connections in Stage I appear to have been perpendicular to the plaza.

Only three rooms of the Stage I plaza-facing row were excavated, but two of these rooms (44 and 55) had floor features. Room 44 was originally longer than it appears on our map. Its north wall was a later modification. The original floor in Room 44 was observed only in limited tests, and no floor features were noted. A second, later floor had a firepit and a storage bin. The third and last floor had only a firepit (Judd 1959: 33).

Room 55 was considerably longer than the rooms behind it; there is no indication that the north and south walls are not original. Both of the floor levels had lines of mealing bins running the length of the room. The first floor probably also had a firepit (Judd 1959: 45). The mealing bins on the second, or later, floor were imaginatively restored by Judd's Zuni workmen (Judd 1959:45). The east, plaza-facing wall of both Rooms 44 and 55 showed a series of blocked, replaced, and modified doors. Although multiple doors may reflect the fact that this wall was originally an exterior wall, they were certainly also a response to subsequent building in Stage IIIA. In

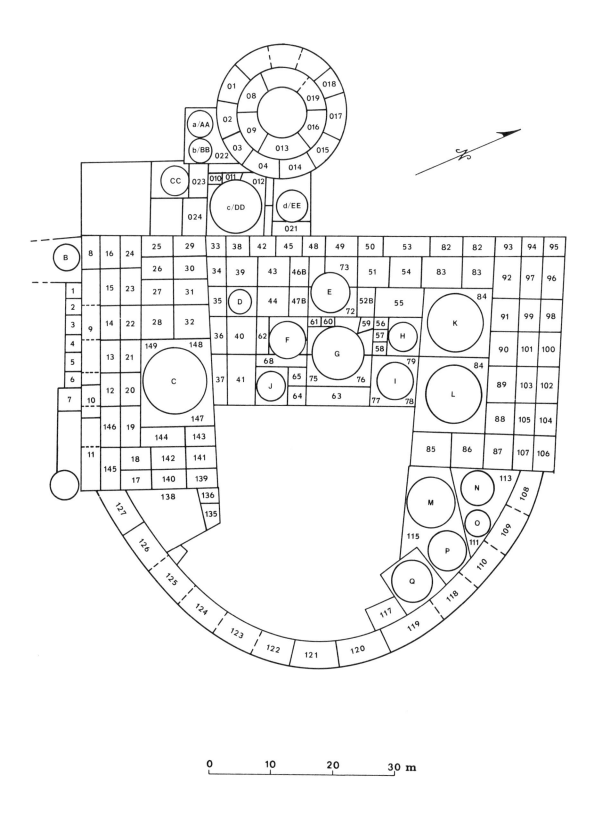

**Figure 4.63.   Pueblo del Arroyo.**

Figure 4.64.  Pueblo del Arroyo, looking north.

Figure 4.65.  Pueblo del Arroyo, looking southwest.  Chaco Wash, line of
trees in middle distance; South Gap, far distance.

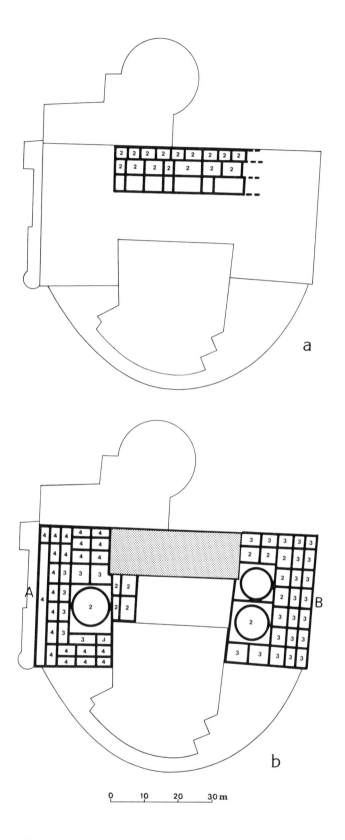

Figure 4.66.  Pueblo del Arroyo, construction stages:  (a) Stage I; (b)
Stage II.  All new construction is one story unless
otherwise noted.

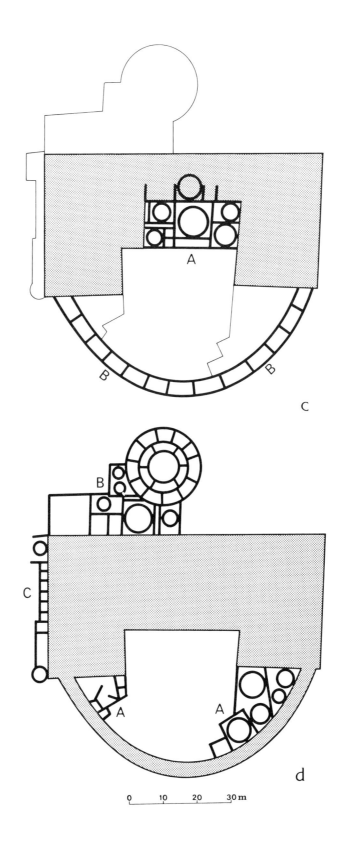

Figure 4.66    Pueblo del Arroyo, construction stages:  (c) Stage III; (d)
Stage IV.

Figure 4.67.  Pueblo del Arroyo, looking northwest.  South wing in foreground, north wing to right.

Figure 4.68.  Pueblo del Arroyo, Kiva C foreground, looking west.

Figure 4.69.  Pueblo del Arroyo, Room 41 foreground, looking north.

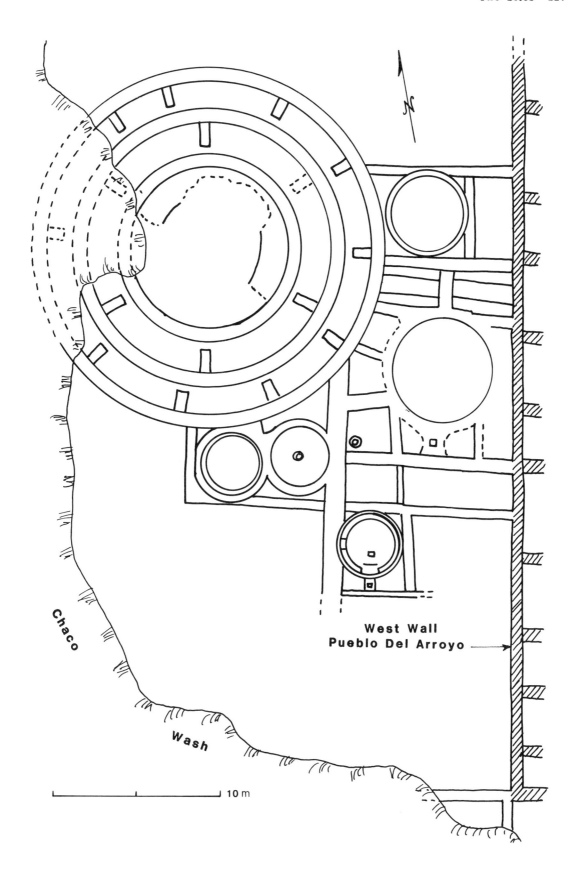

Figure 4.70.  Pueblo del Arroyo Tri-wall (after Vivian 1959: Fig. 48).

Figure 4.71.  Pueblo del Arroyo, examples of masonry (frames are 70 cm x
            70 cm.  Top row, left to right:  exterior wall outside Room
            45; Room 44, N wall; Room 43, E wall; Room 43, N wall.
            Second row, left to right:  exterior wall outside Room 25;
            Room 55, S wall; exterior wall outside Room 4.  Third row,
            left to right:  Room 15, W wall; Room 19, S wall; Room 27, N
            wall; Room 41, W wall.  Fourth row, left to right:  exterior
            wall outside Room 82; exterior plaza-facing wall outside
            Room 85; Kiva L enclosure.  Bottom row, Room 13, W wall.

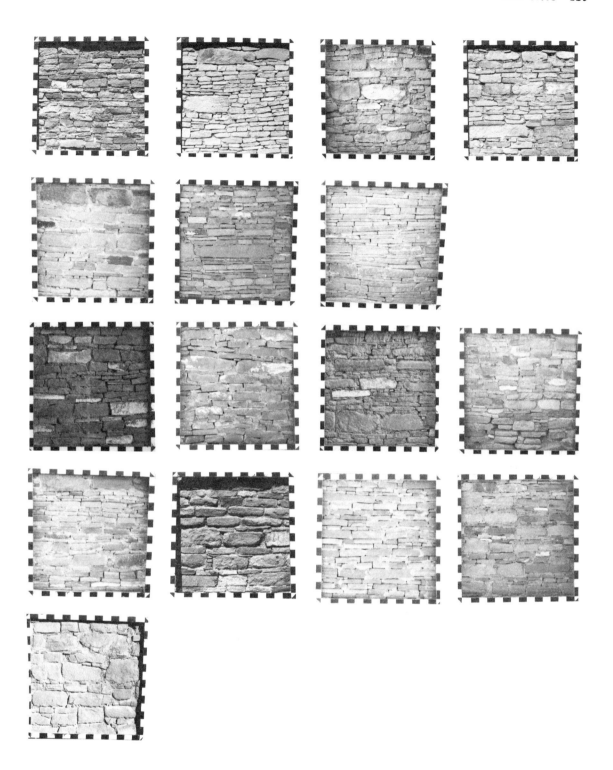

fact, both of these rooms retained direct access to Stage IIIA circular room roofs through the use of stairs and wells.

Five rooms in the second row were excavated to ground floor levels, and only one of these five (Room 51) had floor features. Room 51 had a solitary firepit.

None of the eight Stage I rear rooms was excavated. Where doors into the rear row rooms were exposed through the excavation of rooms in the second row, these had raised sills and secondary jambs and lintels.

Because cross-wall spacing is not regular, room sizes in the rear row are variable. Average floor area for this row is about 11 m² (sd=1.7 m², N=7) excluding Room 53 where a cross wall has probably fallen. Cross-wall spacing in the second row, where it has not been obscured by later building (e.g., Kiva E) is more regular, and room sizes are all about 18.7 m² (sd=0.1 m², N=4), excluding 10 m² Room 34 at the south end of this row.

Rooms of the original plaza-facing row are quite variable in area, ranging from 10 m² (Room 35 at the south end of the row) to 19 m² (Room 44) to the largest, 32 m² (Room 55). Although doorway patterns run from front to back, there is no clear pattern in the arrangement of the rooms connected by those doors: first row Room 43 is backed by an identical room in the second row, which is itself backed by two rear row rooms that are approximately half the size of either Rooms 43 or 44; the large Room 55 is backed by second row Room 54 (about half the size of Room 55), which probably connects to a single rear row room (much like Rooms 51 and 50). The total floor area represented by both the Room 44 and 55 suites is similar, i.e., about 90-100 m².

Ventilators occur in no obvious pattern in interior Stage I rooms; however, ventilators, in some cases paired ventilators, do occur regularly in exterior walls, e.g., the rear exterior wall and the presumed south exterior walls of Rooms 34 and 35.

Stage I dates (Table 4.7) at 1066, as obtained from the primary beams of two rooms in the original plaza-facing row (Rooms 44 and 47). The dating of Room 47 is complex; it was modified several times and yields dates at 1066, 1076, and 1086. The 1066 date comes from the butt of a

primary roof beam cut off near the wall to allow for later construction of a round room. This round room, a forerunner of Kiva E, was probably built in 1086, a date yielded by a horizontal log pilaster. A second-story partition wall was built over this circular room (after construction of Kiva E), and that partition wall was supported on a (reused?) beam dating 1076. Although these dates suggest that the plaza-facing row of Stage I was built about 1066, the second row of Stage I has rooms with primary beams dating in the early 1070s (JPB-126 and -131). The only dates from the rear row come from Room 82, which may actually belong in Stage IIB rather than Stage I. These samples are probably from primary beams, and are dated at 1065 and 1075, thus indicating a construction period for Stage I of 1065-1075.

## Stage II(1095-1105)

The second major construction at Pueblo del Arroyo was the addition of north and south wings to Stage I. These wings were remarkably similar in plan (Figure 4.66b). Each consisted of one (IIA) or two (IIB) large elevated round rooms surrounded by blocks of rectangular rooms three to four rows deep (Figure 4.68). As noted above, Stage IIB may have been built, in part, over the north end of Stage IA; however, Judd (1959:16, 25) states that "there were no subfloor walls" below the south wing (IIA).

Stage IIA. Stage IIA reached four stories at its east and west ends, and was probably entirely four stories except in the rooms facing Kiva C, which were three stories. Two unusual features of Stage IIA were the long first-story room (Room 9-10-11) on its south side and the block of four rooms appended to its north. Ignoring these for the moment, the ground floor rooms of Stage IIA were all featureless, except for one firepit in the floor of Room 20, which was pronounced to be "plainly of later introduction" (Judd 1959:21). Though the walls of the first story were not plastered, at least some of the upper-story walls were.

Door connections, generally perpendicular (away from) Kiva C (except in the gallery, discussed below), were repeated on every floor. The remaining doors all appear to have been of the raised sill type, generally without secondary jambs and lintels. Doors opening on the roof level of Kiva C were not preserved. A

Table 4.7.  Tree-ring dates from Pueblo del Arroyo.

Room 8B

    JPB–62     1105cL

Room 9

    GP–2339   1100v
    JPB–88     1100v
    JPB–89     1100c
    JPB–87     1100cL
    JPB–63     1101cL
    JPB–85     1102c
    JPB–84     1102c
    GP–2340   1103v

Room 12

    JPB–59     1102c
    JPB–60     1103c
    JPB–61     1103cL

Room 16

    JPB–66     1101cL
    GP–2341   1103+v

Room 20

 ? DPB–2336  1080v
    JPB–101    1095+c
    JPB–100    1096c

Room 34

    JPB–125    1073+vv

Room 37

    JPB–136    1051vv

Room 38 or 39

    JPB–124    1062vv

Room 39, 43, or 46B

    GP–2342   1066r

Kiva C pilaster

    JPB–102    1064vv

Kiva C, enclosure

    JPB–146    1103+r
    JPB–147    1103rL

Kiva I, enclosure

    JPB–139    1091vv

Room 42, 45, 48, or 49

    GP–2338   1041vv

Room 43

    JPB–126    1075cL

Room 44 or 47

    GP–2334   1066+v
    GP–2333   1066+v

Room 44

    JPB–129    1066+cL

Room 46

    JPB–131    1073+c

Room 46, roof support post

    JPB–132    1052v

Room 47

    JPB–133    1066+r
    JPB–134    1076v
    JPB–135–2 1086cL

Room 53

    JPB–153    1065c

Room 53 – Unnumbered room north
  of Room 53 (intramural beam)
    JPB–148    1029cL
    JPB–151    1089c
    JPB–149    1103r

Unnumbered room north of Room 53
    JPB–154    1057cL
    JPB–152    1101c

Room 63 or 64, intramural beam

 ? JPB–137    1074r

Tri–wall, Room 1

    JPB–205    1109c

No provenience

    GP–2332   1045v
    DPB–2      1080vv
    JPB–11     1092++r

Note:  All dates from roof elements unless otherwise noted.
      Key to symbols, see Appendix C.

single, ground floor, T-shaped door in the west wall of Room 24 was the only door in the rear wall of the building. Ventilators were located only in exterior walls (i.e., north, south, and west walls on Stage IIA).

Room 9-10-11, later subdivided into Rooms 9, 10, and 11, was a 33 m long ground floor room along the south of Stage IIA. These later subdivisions of Room 9-10-11 had multiple firepits. There is no information on features of the floor of the earlier, unsubdivided room.

The second story of Room 9-10-11 was originally subdivded into rooms continuing the cross-wall pattern of Stage IIA (Rooms 12-24). Several of the second-story rooms also had firepits, judging from the smoke-blackened walls and an intact firepit in Room 9B-III. However, both first- and second-story features were probably associated with the last construction in this area (Stage IVC) rather than Stage IIA.

The exterior wall of Room 9-10-11 began to tilt outward shortly after -- or perhaps during -- construction. Eight low buttresses were built along the exterior wall (see Stage IVC). These must have been effective since the tilting walls are still standing to the middle of the second story. The second-story exterior wall was pierced by two T-shaped doors, from Rooms 9B-III and 10B, probably indicating a balcony on the first floor level (compare Stage IIB).

The rooms on the second story of Room 9-10-11 were the smallest of all Stage IIA rooms (mean=10.1 m$^2$, sd=0.9 m$^2$, N=6); the two rooms just west of Kiva C were the largest, both being about 23.6 m$^2$. All other rooms varied between 1.3 and 1.5 times the size of the smallest rooms: Rooms 12-24 averaged 13.1 m$^2$ (sd=0.3 m$^2$, N=10) while Rooms 25-27 and 29-31 (behind the two largest rooms, 28 and 32) averaged about the same (mean=14.5 m$^2$, sd=0.9 m$^2$, N=6).

The block of four rooms (36, 37, 40, 41) attached to the north edge of Stage IIA were built over a razed or unfinished round room which may have fronted Stage I (Judd 1959:26). These rooms were two stories in height. Ground floor features were found in two rooms: two firepits in Room 40 and three mealing bins and a firepit in Room 41.

Rooms 40 and 41, larger rooms with living room features, are each about 23.6 m$^2$ floor area. Rooms 36 and 37 (behind Rooms 40 and 41) are each about 15 m$^2$ in area.

Stage IIA is well dated to about 1095-1105, with dates from Rooms 9, 12, 16, and 20.

Stage IIB. The north wing, Stage IIB, is very similar to Stage IIA, except that there are two elevated round rooms (the western on the first, and the eastern on the second-story level), rather than the single round room of Stage IIA. The two wings are very close in size and shape, but the north wing (IIB) may have stood three stories tall -- one story less than Stage IIA. Photographs of the north exterior wall of Stage IIB show beams projecting 1.50 to 1.75 m along the third-story floor level (Mindeleff 1891). These beams are the remains of a balcony (which was probably matched on the second-story level of the south exterior wall of Stage IIA). Judd was not enthusiastic about balconies, and pointed out that no exterior door remained to allow access to the Stage IIB balcony (Judd 1959:53). Today, both the beams and the walls behind them are gone. Despite Judd's naysaying, there probably were balconies at both the north and south ends of Pueblo del Arroyo -- perhaps with limited access, as indicated by only two doors in the south exterior wall and no remaining doors in the north.

Room sizes in Stage IIB repeat the range of sizes seen in Stage IIA (excluding the small rooms above the unusually narrow Room 9-10-11). Since IIB is unexcavated, nothing can be said about door connections.

Stage IIB produced dates of 1029, 1089, 1101, and 1103 (Table 4.7). These may all have come from the same room (probably Room 102), suggesting construction about 1103. On the basis of these dates, and Stage IIB's similarities to Stage IIA, a construction span of 1095-1105 seems reasonable.

## Stage III (1105+)

Stage IIIA. Stage IIIA consists of the late, plaza-facing structures added to the front of Stage I, and much of the second-story construction on the earlier front row of Stage I (Figures 4.66c and 4.69). Stage IIIA may mask a considerable amount of earlier building. Few Stage IIIA rooms were excavated to the Stage I ground floor level. What is currently visible is probably late, and consists of rectangular enclosures for Kivas F, G, H, I, and J, and a number of irregularly shaped rooms in the corners of those enclosures.

The final plaza-facing wall of this part of Pueblo del Arroyo may have been built mainly to enclose Kivas G, I, and J. Stage IIIA, in its final form, was a maze of irregular rooms in and around these circular rooms. The floors of most Stage IIIA rooms were found high in the fill of the circular room enclosures. Room 63, the long plaza-facing room fronting Kiva G, had a firepit on its final floor, but other rooms lacked features.

Stage IIIA has only two tree-ring dates, both of dubious provenience. Both may be from the plaza-facing wall of Stage IIIA, with dates of 1074 and 1091vv (Table 4.7). This suggests Stage IIIA construction in the 1090s. Most Stage IIIA construction clearly postdates Stage II, that is, it is post-1105.

Stage IIIB. Stage IIIB is the plaza-closing arc of rooms (Figure 4.66c), which could have been built any time after Stage II. Holsinger, as noted above, thought there was a gate or opening near the middle of the arc, but Judd denies it (1959:7). The arc was probably only one room wide and one story tall. The rooms, as shown by Judd (1959:Figure 2) are about 24-25 m² in floor area.

Stage IV (1110+)

Stage IVA. The maze of round and small, irregularly shaped rooms built into the corners of the front arc and Stages IIA and IIB (Figure 4.66d) was obviously built after Stage IIIA. Beyond that temporal placement, little can be said about the architecture and features of these units.

Stage IVB. Stage IVB includes the Tri-wall and perhaps some of the rooms to its south (Figures 4.66d, 4.70). These were excavated by Judd (in 1926) and by Vivian (in 1950). Each prepared a report, and the reports were published the same year (1959) with apparently no communication between their authors. There is gratifying agreement on most details of stratigraphy and architecture.

The Tri-wall was razed prehistorically, but enough was left to show two concentric rows of rooms, each row connected circularly by raised-sill doors. The rooms surrounded a central circular room or court. The circular room or court was at least partially paved with sandstone slabs. No floor features were observed in either the central court or its surrounding rooms.

The complex of rooms between the Tri-wall and the main building includes a variety of round rooms. There is one large Chacoan round room, (Judd's Kiva "C" and Vivian's Kiva DD) with a floor level slightly lower than that of the Tri-wall. All other rooms in Stage IVB had considerably higher floor levels than Kiva "C." This round room might predate the Tri-wall, but neither Judd nor Vivian drew this conclusion.

Vivian states that the Tri-wall and Stage I were built on the same original ground surface, but interprets this as follows:

...Pueblo del Arroyo proper was in use for some time before the triple walled building was erected. During this time interval some 6 feet of soil was deposited against the rear wall of the pueblo...When the triple walled building was constructed an excavation was made, kiva fashion, through the sandy layers to the adobe ("undisturbed hardpan") and the walls were based on this level ...(1959:64-65).

Both Vivian and Judd agree that the rooms between the Tri-wall and the rear wall of the main building are later than either (Judd 1959:118; Vivian 1959:64).

There is a single tree-ring date of 1109 (JPB-205) from the Tri-wall. There is no reason to consider this date unduly early for the Tri-wall (Lekson 1984b). The rooms between the Tri-wall and the main building postdate the Tri-wall, but probably not by a very great length of time. The whole Stage IV complex probably dates to the early to middle 1100s -- perhaps 1110 to 1140.

Stage IVC. Judd described Stage IVC with particular relish (Judd 1959:Chapter IV). Stage IVC (Figure 4.66d) consists of mean and ordinary little rooms, built between and around the series of low masonry buttresses along the south exterior wall of Stage IIA. There are seven rectangular and two circular rooms, presumably contemporaneous. Most of the rooms had firepits and/or mealing bins. An archeomagnetic sample from a firepit in Room 3 produced a date of about 1140±21 (Thomas Windes, personal communication, 1982), suggesting construction before that date, most likely between 1105 and 1140.

WIJIJI

History

The name Wijiji is an approximation of the Navajo "black greasewood" (Franstead and Wenner 1974). The ruin has also been called "Blue House" (Franstead and Wenner 1974) or, similarly, "Turquoise House" (Hewett 1936:41).

At least two rooms (9 and 127) were cleared and partly refilled in the past, but no records survive. Major stabilization programs were undertaken in 1940-1941 by Gordon Vivian, in 1959 by Joel Shiner, in 1975 by Steve Adams, and 1978 by Jim Trott. Wijiji has poorly bonded walls and was built over a 1.5 m thick layer of clayey sand that expands when wet, a situation which has caused a great deal of damage through parted corners and fallen walls (West 1978). During the winter of 1958-1959, the rear (north) wall from Room 42 to Room 57 fell. The wall broke cleanly and fell more or less intact, and Shiner was able to rebuild it stone-by-stone to approximately its original condition (Shiner 1959). Other walls have fallen between the time of the first photo of Wijiji and the fall of the north wall.

Architecture

Wijiji (Figures 4.72-4.78) was three stories tall along the rear row of rooms and two stories over most of the remainder, with rooms surrounding the plaza being one story. Room size is extremely uniform (mean=5.4 m$^2$, sd=1.2 m$^2$, N=25). There is a tendency toward slightly larger rooms near the plaza, which may be a function of the thinner walls in one-story plaza-facing rooms, compared to the thicker walls in multi-storied rooms of essentially the same size. Round room diameters are about 8.7 m. There is no Great Kiva in the plaza, no plaza-enclosing arc of rooms, and no trash mound.

Holsinger was among the first to note a peculiar series of holes along the back wall of Wijiji:

...a series of loop holes, extending along the entire north, outside wall in the second story, about two feet below the small windows [beam sockets] referred to by Jackson. These apertures were 2 by 3 inches and unquestionably loop-holes for the purpose of discharging

arrows in case of assault on the inmates. The apertures extend diagonally through the wall and alternated regularly from north-east to north-west, thus giving the archers full command of about three hundred yards of the base of the bluff (1901:45).

Two "loop holes" remain, both in the third story north wall of Room 37. One is rectangular in section, about 6 cm by 6 cm, and points downwards about 30°. The ground surface visible through this opening is only about 3 m x 4 m. The second appears slightly rounded on its interior (like a beam socket) and is horizontal through the wall but about 10° off the perpendicular. These are not particularly convincing as "loop holes," for the "field of fire" is restricted because the openings have parallel rather than expanding sides.

Masonry at Wijiji is very uniform (Figure 4.78). The stone used is almost entirely the darker, thin-bedded sandstone which has been stripped off the top of the sandstone cliff behind the ruin.

Wijiji shows no evidence of more than one construction stage (Figure 4.75). The symmetry of the plan, the most perfect of any Chacoan ruin, also suggests a single construction event. (A possible small round room just northwest of Kiva A, by its very asymmetry, is prably an isolated later addition.)

Doorways are almost exclusively perpendicular to the plaza, in both the first and second stories. Exceptions include the first-story rooms around Kivas A and B, where doorways allowed circulation around the kivas, and the extreme south ends of the east and west wings, where door patterns may have been parallel as well as perpendicular to the plaza. Vents are virtually absent. There appears to be a pattern of small rectangular niches usually on one side, but occasionally on both sides, of doorways, just below the level of the lintels. This pattern is particularly noticeable in the central section of the east wing.

Chronology

There is a single tree-ring date from Wijiji (Table 4.8), probably from either the second-story door lintels in the north wall of Room 50, or the first-story door lintels on the east wall of Room 85. "The earlier date [1027] published by Hawley (Senter 1938) was not

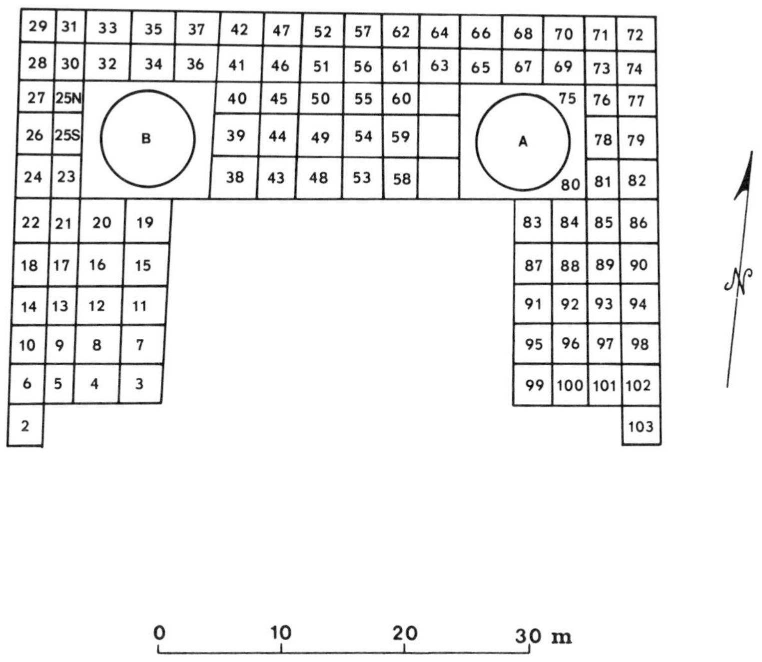

Figure 4.72. Wijiji.

Figure 4.73.  Wijiji, looking northeast.

Figure 4.74.  Wijiji, looking southeast.  Note timbers bracing collapsing
walls.

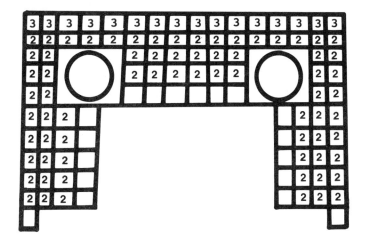

Figure 4.75. Wijiji, construction in one stage. All construction one story unless otherwise noted.

Figure 4.76.  Wijiji, looking northwest.  East wing right, west wing left.

Figure 4.77.  Wijiji, east wing from northeast corner, looking south.

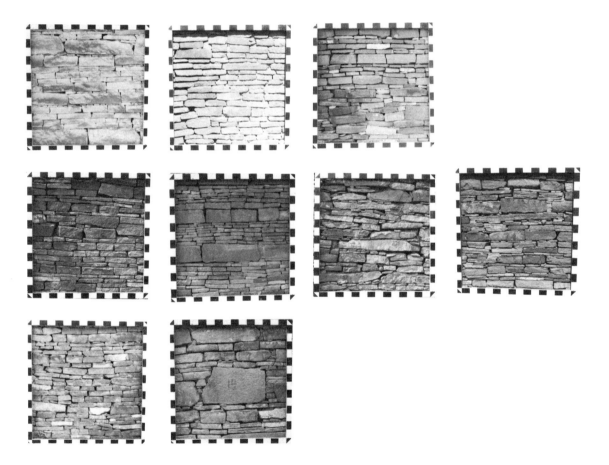

Figure 4.78.   Wijiji, examples of masonry (frames are 70 cm x 70 cm).  Top row, left to right:  exterior wall outside Room 42; exterior wall outside Room 31; exterior wall outside Room 74.  Middle row, left to right:  Room 35, N wall; Kiva B enclosure, N wall; Room 50, N wall; Room 72, E wall.  Bottom row, left to right:  Room 81, S wall; Room 16, S wall.

Table 4.8.   Tree-ring dates from Wijiji, Tsin Kletzin, Chiquita,
and Kin Kletso.

WIJIJI

Room 50 or 85

  ?  WIJ–5       1110c

TSIN KLETZIN

Room 1 or 8

  ?  T–1       1112rL

No Provenience

     T–2      1111rL
     T–3      1113v

CASA CHIQUITA

Room 3

    CCH–1     1063rL

Northwest corner

   JPB–160–1   1058vv

No Provenience
   JPB–160    1064r

KIN KLETSO

Room 11/12, intramural beam

    CKK–7    1123c

Room 21

    CKK–11   1077r

Room 32

    CKK–9    1059c

Room 32/36, intramural beam

    CKK–10   1124v

Room 37/50, intramural beam

    CKK–8    1124c

Room 50

    CKK–5    1076c
    CKK–6    1076c

No provenience

    CKK–4    1063v
    CKK–2    1124c

Note:   All dates from roof elements unless otherwise noted.
Key to symbols, see Appendix C.

confirmed" (Robinson et al. 1974:45). Wijiji gives every appearance of having been built in a single, very short construction program. Based on one tree-ring date, the suggested span is 1110-1115.

## TSIN KLETZIN

### History

This ruin was first described by Holsinger (1901:32). He translated the name as "house in the beautiful wood." Given Tsin Kletzin's location atop barren, windswept South Mesa, this is an unlikely appelation. The ruin had also been called "Hermoso" ("beautiful") from as early as 1914 (Bradford 1981:5; Judd 1964:3). Hewett (1936:37) translated Tsin Kletzin as "black wood, or charcoal, place," which may be a little closer to reality than Holsinger's translation. The ruin has also been called "house on top" by local Navajos (Franstead and Werner 1974).

Tsin Kletzin (Figures 4.79-4.85) has never been excavated, although Room 1 was partially cleared by unknown parties. The ruin was stabilized first in 1971 (Mayer 1971) and again in 1981 (Bradford 1981).

The unusual location of Tsin Kletzin appears to have been fixed by the intersections of several lines-of-sight (Hayes and Windes 1975:152-154; Hewett 1936:37; Holsinger 1901:34). From Kiva A (the highest part of the building) six other major buildings are visible: Pueblo Alto, Peñasco Blanco, Kin Kletso, Kin Klizhin, Bis sa'ani, and Kin Ya'a. A shift of 10 m in any direction would have made these multiple views impossible.

### Architecture

Tsin Kletzin is asymmetric in plan. It consists of a main roomblock, a west wing, a plaza enclosed by an arc of rooms (Figure 4:83), and a large rectangular enclosure defined by a low wall behind (to the north of) the main block. There is a low trash mound in the sand dunes to the southeast and southwest of the building (Windes 1980).

A "gateway" (Figure 4:84) about 1 m wide is evident in the center of the plaza-enclosing arc. The north enclosure, which was formed by a low wall, shows no evidence of any entrances.

Masonry at Tsin Kletzin is uniformly "McElmo" in style (Figure 4.85). The building was probably two stories tall in the main block, and one story in the west wing and front arc. The two round rooms in the main block (Kivas A and B) were elevated to the second floor level.

The building is much reduced and wall patterns within the main block and the east wing cannot be clearly defined. Holsinger's 1901 map (when more walls may have been standing), Bradford's map (1981), and our maps show an unusual pattern of rectangular rooms apparently subdivided along the long axis. The approximate area of the undivided rectangular rooms ranges from 9 to 11 m². Subdivisions would then be about 4 to 5 m² in floor area. Bradford (1981:12) noted a range in rectangular room sizes from 4 to 9.68 m². Rooms in the arc average about 6.2 m² with the exception of the two slightly smaller ones, flanking the gateway (4.5 m²).

The diameter of the largest round room (Kiva A) is slightly over 8 m. The smaller round room in the main block (Kiva B) is about 6 m in diameter, as is the round room in the west wing (Kiva C). No vents are currently visible. Bradford describes the few doorways which are visible:

Four rooms (8, 41, 42, and 45) provide evidence of doorways. In Room 8, the doorway provided access into Room 10. The three other rooms are in the arc which encloses the plaza. All three doorways are located in the plaza-facing walls. Door widths ranged from 53 to 60 cm wide; heights are unknown. In addition, Mayer (1961: 25) mentions a doorway between Rooms 47 and 6 (1981:12).

The plan suggests more than one construction event (Figure 4.81). Very likely, the first construction was the square unit surrounding Kiva A, probably followed by the remainder of the main block and the addition of the west wing, and then the arc. The round room and surrounding rooms built into the reentrant of the west wing and the plaza-enclosing arc were probably the last rooms added. The north enclosure, of course, could have been built at any time after the construction of the main block.

### Chronology

There are three dates from Tsin Kletzin (Table 4.8). A date of 1112rl from the "1st floor" (Bannister 1965:195) may come from an intramural beam in the

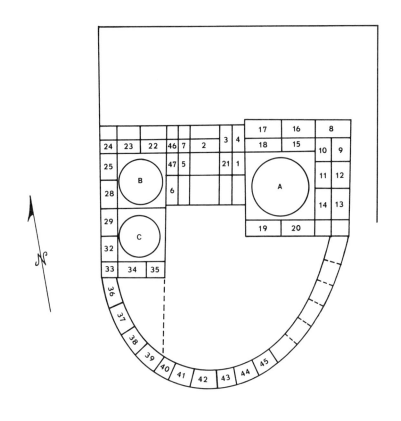

Figure 4.79.  Tsin Kletzin.

Figure 4.80. Tsin Kletzin, looking northeast.

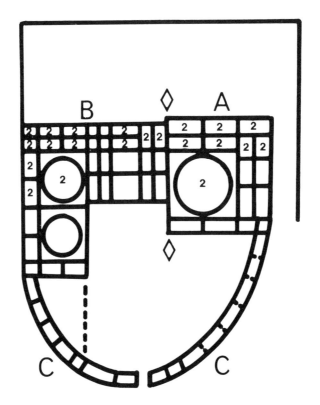

Figure 4.81.   Tsin Kletzin, construction in three sub-stages.  All
construction is one story unless otherwise noted.

Figure 4.82.  Tsin Kletzin, looking east.

Figure 4.83.  Tsin Kletzin, arc, exterior walls of Rooms 40 to 44, looking
north.

Figure 4.84.  Tsin Kletzin, arc, plaza-facing walls of Rooms 42
and 43, looking south.  Note "gateway" at left
center.

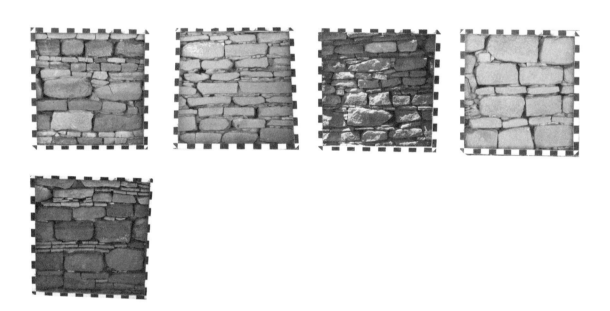

Figure 4.85.   Tsin Kletzin, examples of masonry.   Top row, left

to right:   exterior wall outside Room 16; Room 4,

W wall; plaza-facing wall outside Room 41.

Bottom row: Kiva A.

first floor, south wall of Room 8, or from the now refilled Room 1. This date agrees with two other dates that lack specific provenience and suggests construction of the block around Kiva A at about 1110-1115. The uniformity of masonry suggests that the remainder of the main block and the west wing were built somewhat contemporaneously. Although multiple construction events are possible, I believe the entire building dates to the early twelfth century.

## KIN KLETSO

### History

Kin Kletso (Figures 4.86-4.93) was originally known simply as "Ruin Number 8," a designation given to it by Simpson; later Holsinger recorded the name as "kin'klet'soi." The use of light-colored sandstone masonry is undoubtedly responsible for this Navajo name, which means "yellow house" (Franstead and Werner 1974).

In the 1890s, the Hyde Exploring Expedition removed a considerable amount of building stone from the rubble of Kin Kletso. The stone was reused in bunk houses, store rooms, etc. The Hyde Expedition must have preferred the larger blocks of massive sandstone over the smaller tabular stones of Pueblo del Arroyo, immediately behind their buildings (Holsinger 1901:53).

The first scientific excavations at Kin Kletso were carried out by Edwin Ferdon in 1934 for the School of American Research. He cleared Kivas A and B and Rooms 8, 9 and 23, and partially cleared Rooms 1, 12, 14, 17, 20, and 35. Excavation and stabilization were completed in 1950 and 1951 (with limited testing outside the ruin in 1953) by Gordon Vivian and Tom Mathews of the National Park Service. Their report (Vivian and Mathews 1965) is the basic reference on Kin Kletso.

### Architecture

The masonry of Kin Kletso is of massive, light-colored sandstone almost exclusively, with blocks shaped by pecking (the "McElmo" style) (Figure 4.93). This style of masonry is fairly uniform at Kin Kletso, with the exception of several walls of banded masonry (e.g., the exterior north wall of the kiva and Rooms 20 and 22).

Kin Kletso's sequence of construction seems straightforward, but this simplicity may be deceptive. Vivian and Mathews (1965:53-54) initially outlined a series of three construction events: two major construction programs (our Stages I and II), each constituting half of the main building, with a third, very minor addition (our Stage III). Vivian and Mathews' construction sequence was defined on several grounds: (1) vents in the east wall of Stage I with other vents at Kin Kletso occurring in exterior walls; (2) lack of a ceiling ledge or offset on the east (exterior) face of this wall; and (3) clear abutment of Stage II walls on the Stage I east wall (Vivian and Mathews 1965:53).

However, the dendrochronology of the site (Table 4.8) suggested to Bannister (1965)--and Bannister suggested to Vivian and Mathews--that the upper stories of the ruin represented a separate major construction stage, built after the first story of the building. My building stages follow Vivian and Mathews' original analysis of construction, prior to their discussion of Bannister's tree-ring dating (1965:53-54 and Figure 31).

### Stage I (1125-1130)

Stage IA. Stage IA (Figure 4.89a) was a square block of rooms surrounding the elevated Kiva E. Vivian and Mathews imply that Kiva A, a Tower Kiva, might have been a later addition to this block, but since this tower is built over a huge sandstone boulder incoporated in the first story of the building, it was probably part of the original plan. Kiva E was a large Chacoan round room built on the first-story level. Rooms to the north and south were two rows deep, three rows deep to the west, and one row deep to the east. The rooms north and west of Kiva E reached three stories, and were probably terraced down to the Kiva E roof level. Rooms along the south edge of Stage I are currently only two stories. The single row of rooms east of Kiva E was two stories tall. The orientation of Stage I was evidently to the east, rather than south.

Rooms are generally square and average 8.55 m$^2$ (sd=1.43 m$^2$, N=27). The largest ground floor rooms are located in the single row east of Kiva E. Doorways tend to run north-south; ventilators are located only in the exterior east wall. A vertical shaft connects the ground floor of Room 55 to the roof level of Kiva E.

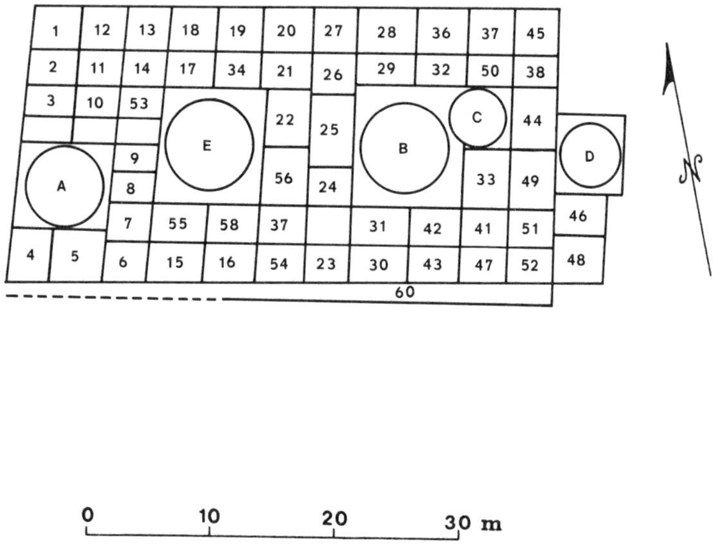

Figure 4.86.  Kin Kletso.

Figure 4.87.  Kin Kletso, looking east.

Figure 4.88.  Kin Kletso, looking west.  Roof over Kiva D.

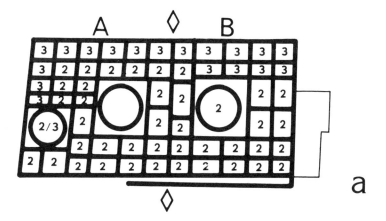

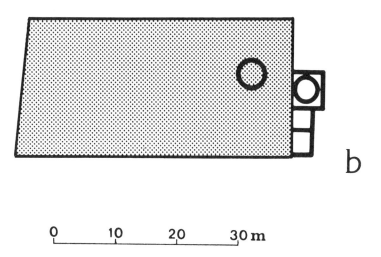

Figure 4.89. Kin Kletso, construction stages: (a) Stage I;
(b) Stage II

Figure 4.90.  Kin Kletso, Rooms 54, 23, and 30 foreground,
looking north.

Figure 4.91.   Kin Kletso, Room 54 (foreground right center) and Room 23
          (right, looking northwest).

Figure 4.92.   Kin Kletso, Room 60 from southeast corner of building,
          looking northwest.

Figure 4.93.   Kin Kletso, examples of masonry (frames are 70 cm x 70 cm. Left to right:   Room 12, W wall; Kiva E enclosure, N wall; Room 22, W wall; Room 38, W wall.

The most prominent feature of Stage IA was Kiva A, a two-story cylinder with a T-shaped door in the east wall of its first level. It was built over a huge boulder, which appears to have been surrounded by a filled enclosure. Kiva A was thus raised to the second story level, and, with its upper story, it towered over Kiva E (Vivian and Mathews 1965:Figure 25). The inclusion of the boulder in the ground plan of Kin Kletso has led some critics to suggest that the builders were forced to use the last available square meter of non-agricultural land in the canyon. This disparaging argument fails to account for the subsequent expansion of the site 20 m to the east in Stage IB, when a shift in the original ground plan only 10 m to the east avoided the boulder in question. The site was probably selected specifically because of the boulder, for its use in raising the base level of Kiva A.

Only Rooms 2 and 7 in Stage IA had floor features, e.g., firepits occurred in both. Room 2 is in an exterior row (although there were no ventilators or other openings to the exterior), while Room 7 was an interior room. Vivian and Mathews reported a slab-lined and covered "drain" running north-south below the floor of Room 6, just south of Room 7. They considered this to be an earlier, unrelated construction (1965:44), but it may have been a ventilator shaft running to the firepit in Room 7.

Stage IB. Stage IB (Figure 4.89b), a mirror image of Stage IA, was a square block of rooms surrounding an elevated Chacoan round room (Kiva B, just above the second-story level), apparently oriented to the west, toward Stage IA. Rooms surrounding Kiva B were two rows deep and three stories tall on the north, and two deep and two stories on the east and south. On the west, the single row of rooms was two stories tall. Rooms were relatively square, with an average size of 9.4 m² (sd=2.4 m², N=25). The largest rooms were in the single row west of Kiva B. Doors tend to run north-south, except in the south rows, where they run east-west. Vents occur only in the east exterior wall. Rooms 38 and 49, in the easternmost row, had firepits.

A puzzling situation exists regarding the south wall of Room 23. As Kin Kletso now stands, there is no south wall for this room, thus creating a small re-entrant in the south exterior wall of the building (Figure 4.90). The southeast exterior corner of Room 54 and the southwest exterior corner of Room 30 are well finished, and show no signs of collapsed

wall bondings. A south wall is shown by Vivian and Mathews (1965:Figure 15), who also state that all exterior walls stood high enough to carry door openings "except possibly the southwest corner" (1965:40). Our map (Figure 4.86) shows a wall present, following Vivian and Mathews' map, but the wall is not there now.

The low wall (Figure 4.92) running parallel to the south exterior wall of Stages IA and IIB probably belongs to Stage IB. The wall, faced on the exterior side only, was about 0.6 m from the south wall of the main building. At 1.2 m intervals, there were "rough, unfaced partition walls" (Vivian and Mathews 1965:44). (Compare the similar construction at Casa Chiquita.)

Stage II (1130+)

Stage II (Figure 4.89c) consisted of two single story rooms and a round room added to the east exterior wall of Stage IB, and Kiva C. These rooms are comparable in size to those of Stages IA and IB. Room 48ad a firepit.

Chronology

Bannister (1965) and Vivian and Mathews (1965) interpreted Kin Kletso tree-ring dates as indicating construction of the first stories of Stages IA and IB between 1059-1079 (favoring the later end of that span) and construction of the upper stories of both Stages IA and IB in or about 1124. This interpretation was required to avoid "retreating to that overcrowded refuge, the reused beam" (Vivian and Mathews 1965:53). Rather than an overcrowded refuge, the "reused beam" should be a standard interpretive consideration at Chaco.

What evidence is there for construction of the upper stories of these two stages? The Tower Kiva, Kiva A in Stage IA, was anticipated on the ground floor by the inclusion of a huge boulder. Kiva A rose to the third-story level, suggesting that at least three stories were planned from the initial construction of Stage IA. Similarly, Kiva B (the central round room of Stage IB) was probably planned from the inception of the Stage IB ground floor; Kiva B is elevated above the second-floor level. It seems unlikely that Kiva B and its enclosure were built a story above the surrounding rooms, and those rooms brought up to its level fifty years later. Finally, the vertical shaft in the northwest corner of Room 55 allowed direct access from the ground floor of this room to the roof level of Kiva E. It is likely that this shaft would not have been built unless a second story over Room 55 was planned at the time of first-story construction.

Architecturally, the evidence indicates that Stages IA and IB were coherent units, with multiple stories built in single construction events. The homogeneous masonry and identical plans of Stages IA and IB also suggest that these two units were built almost contemporaneously. I suggest that the beams producing 1059-1079 tree-ring dates (Table 4.8) are, in fact, reused, as are so very many other beams in late construction at Chaco. Stages IA and IB were both built between 1125 and 1130.

## CASA CHIQUITA

### History

Casa Chiquita (Figures 4.94-4.98) was originally numbered by Simpson ("Ruin Number 9"), but later became known by its Spanish name, "Little House." This is also one of its names in Navajo (Franstead and Werner 1974). Another Navajo name, "rock crack house" (Franstead and Werner 1974) refers to either its location at the mouth of Cly's Canyon or to the twisted and eroded cliff at its rear.

Jackson, in 1877, described the north and west walls of "Ruin Number 9" as three or four stories tall, standing 18 feet (Jackson 1878). Since Holsinger, only 24 years later, reported the ruin much as it looks today, Jackson probably was talking about Kin Kletso (which he called "Ruin Number 8").

Casa Chiquita is unexcavated. Some room fill was removed, probably to obtain tree-ring dates, in 1927. Considerably more debris was removed to clear the south and west exterior walls, and to expose the tops of interior walls during stabilization in 1964 (Voll and Mayer 1964).

The site may also have been altered during the construction of the old road up Cly's Canyon. In particular, a 3 m tall pile of debris east of Casa Chiquita may be spoil from road building. Jackson, on his map of Ruin 9 (clearly a map of Casa Chiquita) does not indicate the presence of this mound.

### Architecture

Casa Chiquita was an imperfectly square block of rooms surrounding a central elevated round room. The rooms were three-deep on the west, two-deep on the north, probably two-deep on the east side of the round room, and one-room deep south of the round room. The south row was two stories tall, and the west rooms were three. The north and east rows were probably at least two stories, but the site of Casa Chiquita makes this difficult to determine. Casa Chiquita was built over and around talus and a low clay knob. The building is probably terraced up this knob, with the elevated round room, on the second-story level, excavated into a natural surface. The east and north wings may have reached the third-story level, with their second stories actually resting on the natural slope.

Masonry at Casa Chiquita is "McElmo" in style, using pecked blocks of massive light-colored sandstone (Figure 4.98). Some of the third-story masonry in the west rooms is in a banded variation of this style.

Room sizes average about 4.2 m$^2$ (sd=0.9 m$^2$, N=12), but the remains of a door in the south wall of Room 15 suggest that this room, at least, may have been twice that size on the second story. This is the only door visible at the ruin.

Along the front of the south exterior wall, Voll and Mayer found

...a parallel wall which stands one story high...at an average distance of 2.0 feet [from the south exterior wall]...The space between the two walls is divided into rectangles about 4.5 feet long (1964:7).

The feature was exposed outside Room 3, but the excavators concluded that it ran the length of the south wall of the building. This structure was identical to one found at Kin Kletso.

There is a separate structure of two or more rooms and perhaps another round room attached to the northeast corner of the main building. These are much reduced, and, beyond the fact that a small structure is present, little can be said about it and its relation to the main building. The rooms may be similar to Stage III at Kin Kletso.

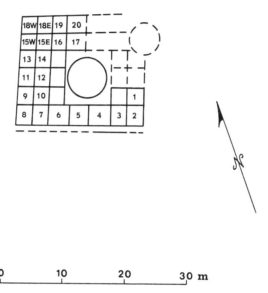

Figure 4.94.  Casa Chiquita.

Figure 4.95.  Casa Chiquita, looking northeast.

Figure 4.96.  Casa Chiquita, southwest corner, looking northeast.

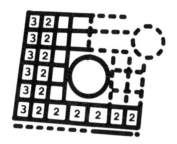

0        10        20        30 m

Figure 4.97.   Casa Chiquita, construction in one stage.   All construction
one story unless otherwise noted.

Figure 4.98.  Casa Chiquita, examples of masonry (frames are 70 cm x 70 cm.  Left to right:  Room 5, W wall; Room 14, N wall.

## Chronology

Casa Chiquita, with the possible exception of the rooms northeast of the main building, appears to represent a single phase of construction. There are three tree-ring dates (Table 4.8), only one of which has a specific provenience, i.e., the date of 1063 came from Room 3 (CCH-1). This and the two other dates of 1064 and 1058vv seem to indicate construction in the early 1060s. Although there are grounds for arguing a much later date, in the early 1100s, Casa Chiquita is one of the "McElmo" sites discussed in Chapters 3 and 5. Kin Kletso, the best dated of these sites, dates to about 1125-1130. Based on its similarity to Kin Kletso and other dated "McElmo" masonry units, Casa Chiquita probably dates to the early twelfth century, probably between 1100 and 1130.

## NEW ALTO

### History

Pueblo Alto ("high town" in Spanish) refers to two separate ruins: the first is the larger and heavily reduced Pueblo Alto (Alto Grande, as Hewett called it); the second is the smaller but better preserved New Alto (or Alto Chiquita). In this study, Pueblo Alto will be reserved for the larger building. Hayes (1981: Table 1) lists a Navajo name of "Ki-a-a" for New Alto, but no translation is given. Other Navajo names for New Alto are discussed in the section on Old Alto, some of which may also apply to the more visible New Alto.

New Alto (Figures 4.99-4.104) was first described by Jackson in 1878:

> ...a small square building in a better state of preservation than the larger ruin. It is 75 feet square, divided into six equal apartments on each side thus making 36 rooms in all,

four of which, however make room for an estufa [circular room]. This was probably three stories in height, for the walls are now standing to the top of the second story. The masonry resembles that of Ruin Number 9 [Casa Chiquita] (Jackson 1878:448).

New Alto has never been excavated. Major stabilization occurred in 1947 (Vivian 1947) and again in 1966 (Morris and Kayser 1966). The Chaco Center excavated a long wall running just north of New Alto in 1976.

### Architecture

The building was two stories tall except for the front (south) row of rooms, which was only one story. The masonry, which is "McElmo" in style (Figure 4.104), also includes a small amount of banding in the walls facing the circular room.

Room size is very uniform. First floor rooms average about 7.1 m$^2$ (sd=1.1 m$^2$, N=14), with second-floor areas ranging from about 1 to 2.5 m$^2$ more per room. Second-floor doorways have raised sills, and open north-south behind the circular room, and east-west on either side of the circular room (i.e., doorways are perpendicular to the round room). First-story doors are known only between Rooms 12 and 7; however, if collapsed masonry in the second-story walls is any clue to the openings below, first-story doors in the rooms behind the round room may run east-west as well as north-south. There is only one definite ventilator, high in the north end of the first-story wall between Rooms 7 and 16.

The round room, with an exterior diameter of about 7.75 m., was elevated with the roof at the first-story level. Several of probably six masonry pilasters are visible. There are no tree-ring dates from New Alto. The closeness in form and technical similarities to Kin Kletso suggest a date of about 1100-1130 (see discussion at "McElmo" sites, Chapters 3 and 5).

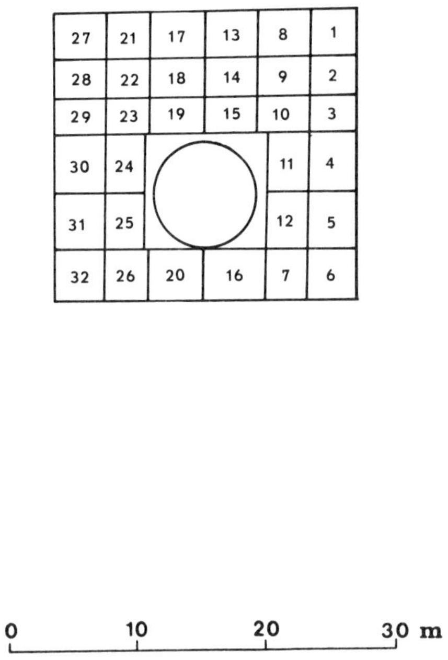

0      10      20     30 m

Figure 4.99.  New Alto.

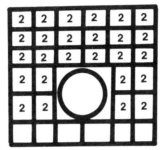

0        10        20        30 m

Figure 4.100.   New Alto, construction in one stage.   All   construction is
                one story unless otherwise   noted.

Figure 4.101.  New Alto, looking west.

Figure 4.102.  New Alto, Room 25 foreground, looking northeast.

Figure 4.103.   New Alto, Room 12 foreground, looking northwest.

Figure 4.104.   New Alto, examples of masonry (frames are 70 cm   x 70 cm.
Left to right:  Room 15, W wall; Round   room   enclosure, E
wall.

# Chapter Five

# Conclusions

The questions guiding this research were two. First, what were the social ramifications of construction? And second, what were the social correlates of form? This chapter addresses these questions. My arguments will buttress the narrow perspective of architecture with other kinds of data; however, for the grand synthesis, the reader must await the conclusions of the Chaco Center's research, of which this study is a minor part.

## SOCIAL IMPLICATIONS OF CONSTRUCTION

Almost every description of Chacoan architecture includes an appreciation of the labor represented by the buildings; however, few authors can agree upon the implications of these expenditures of energy and skill. Hewett, ever the New World democrat, insisted that the

> prodigious task...was no unwilling work under the lash of priestly or kingly task masters. It was the spontaneous impulse of a virile people, comparable to the heaping up of great mounds far in excess of actual needs, by insect communities (Hewett 1936:23).

Recent opinion has swung more in favor of the priestly task master; lashless perhaps, but still a figure or institution controlling the deployment of labor.

Labor is tantalizingly quantifiable. It can be measured metabolically as energy expended (e.g., at Chaco, [Shimada 1978]). It can also be measured in person-hours (PH), that, is, the length of time required to complete a specific task. The second approach is taken here In the estimates that follow, all Chacoan building is reduced to a few basic ele-

ments: masonry walls with foundations and two types of roofs -- flat and domed. Admittedly, this simplifies Chacoan building, but walls and roofs account for the majority of construction in the canyon, and in themselves show surprisingly little variation.

Labor estimates of this sort are discouraging exercises. Beyond the problems of developing appropriate labor rates, (Appendix B, Tables 1-7) there are certain imponderables both crucial and inherent to the situation of work. The first is productivity (see general note, Appendix B); the second is the length of both work day and work year. Person-hour (PH) estimates alone are of little meaning unless placed in a daily or seasonal context.

For example, a ten-hour work day is not an impossibility; a five-hour day is equally possible and quite a bit more pleasant to contemplate. Days of ten hours or days of five hours will produce very different translations of PH into person/days and person/years. The length of the working day is not routinely discernible from the archaeological record. Because fundamental problems of this sort greatly limit the precision of our reconstructions, I have not allowed myself to become too dismayed with relatively crude labor rates. Increased precision would be misplaced.

### The Scale of Construction Events

The number of person/hours required for each construction stage defined in Chapter 4 was calculated from the labor constants developed in Appendix B. The value for each stage is plotted on Figure 5.1 with an approximate mid-point date of each stage (beginning date plus ending date, divided by two). To anticipate the following discussion, there appear to be

257

four general classes of construction events (Table 5.1), based on the number of person/hours. These are shown on Figure 5.1 as Classes I, II, III, and IV. Large roomblocks (groups of rectangular rooms at least two rooms wide and two rooms deep, with or without associated round rooms) are indicated on Figure 5.1 by dots; all other construction (e.g., clusters of round rooms, incidental rooms, plaza-enclosing arcs) are idicated by circles.

Three large roomblocks are excluded from Figure 5.1 because they almost certainly represent more than one actual stage. These are the poorly defined Peñasco Blanco I, Peñasco Blanco IIB, and Hungo Pavi II (Chapter 4). In addition, four small clusters of round and incidental rooms (Peñasco Blanco IIID, Pueblo del Arroyo (IIIA, Pueblo Bonito VIIC and VIIE) have also been excluded from Figure 5.1. These would fall at the upper boundary of Class I, but again are almost

Table 5.1.  Construction stage classes.

| Class | range in PH | mean | sd | N | % PH |
|---|---|---|---|---|---|
| I | 5,000- 55,000 | 24,876 | 14,098 | 59 | 41.3 |
| II | 55,000- 90,000 | 75,368 | 10,741 | 14 | 35.1 |
| III | 117,000-130,000 | 121,726 | 6,521 | 3 | 9.4 |
| IV | 170,000-192,000 | 183,787 | 11,453 | 3 | 14.2 |

Note:  %PH refers to the proportion of the total PH.

Table 5.2.  Labor requirements in months for a 30-person work force over 10 years.

| | 1 | 2 | 3 | 4 | 5 | 6 | 7 | 8 | 9 | 10 |
|---|---|---|---|---|---|---|---|---|---|---|
| Cutting | 1 | | | | | | | | | |
| Transporting | | 1.2 | 1.2 | 1.2 | 1.2 | 1.2 | | | | |
| Quarrying | | | | | | | 3 | | | |
| Constructing | | | | | | | | 3.6 | 3.6 | 3.6 |

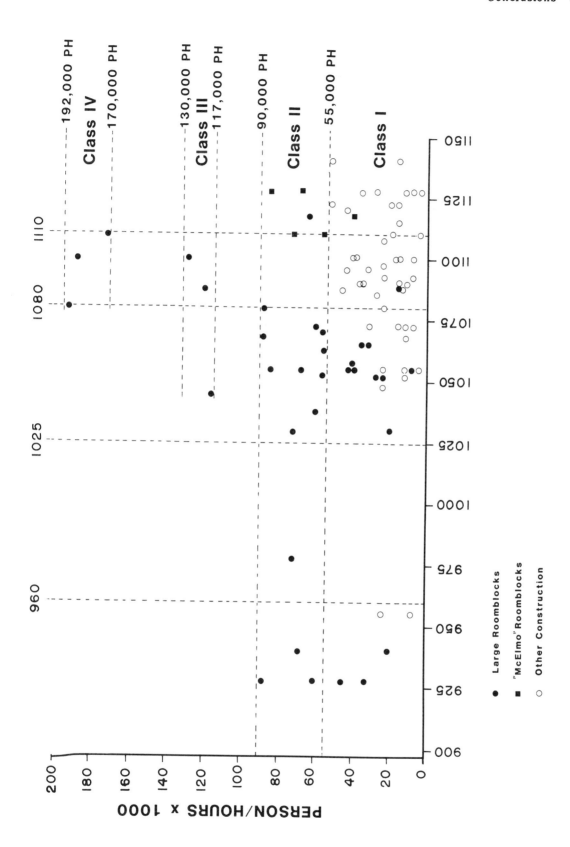

Figure 5.1. Construction labor by event, building stage. Solid circles are large room blocks, solid squares are "McElmo" sites, hollow circles are other construction.

certainly composed of multiple smaller construction events.

Two groups of very large construction stages are immediately obvious: three events ranging from 170,000 to 192,000 PH (Class IV), and three from 117,000 to 130,000 PH (Class III). Class III includes two almost identical units (Pueblo Bonito II and Peñasco Blanco IIIA), each consisting of a multistoried row of rooms built around the exterior of an arc-shaped early 900s structure. The third Class III stage, Pueblo del Arroyo IIB, is a wing symmetrical in form with Pueblo del Arroyo IIA (Class IV). The two wings at Pueblo del Arroyo are almost identical in plan; the main difference between them lies in the estimated number of stories. It is quite possible that the standing walls of the smaller unit, Pueblo del Arroyo IIB, under-represent its original height. I would not be surprised to find that Pueblo del Arroyo IIB originally carried as many stories as IIA. If this were true, then Class III would include only the two strikingly similar rear-row additions (Pueblo Bonito II and Peñasco Blanco IIIA).

To summarize, Class IV includes very large wings added to existing buildings (Pueblo Bonito VIB and Pueblo del Arroyo IIA) and one complete structure (Wijiji). The very size of these units immediately suggests that they may be incorrectly defined, but these five stages are less ambiguous than most in their formal evidence for coherent construction. By the criteria used in this study to define construction stages, Wijiji, Pueblo Bonito VIB, and Pueblo del Arroyo IIA are very convincing single episode units.

All other construction stages (Classes I and II, with over 75% of the total PH in Figure 5.1) are less than 90,000 PH each. It appears that events under 90,000 PH can be divided into two ranges, Class I (5,000 to 55,000 PH) and Class II (55,000 to 90,000 PH). Construction of 55,000 to 90,000 PH (Class II) is limited entirely to large roomblocks.

Over three-quarters of the construction stages fall into Class I (5,000 to 55,000 PH), which includes a few large roomblocks, numerous small roomblocks, round rooms, incidental rooms, and plaza-enclosing arcs. Arcs, in particular, are a convincing confirmation of the class. Arcs almost certainly represent single event construction. The mean amount of labor in arcs, 25,772 PH (sd=8,888, N=10), is nearly identical to the Class I mean excluding arcs (24,490 PH; sd= 14,380, N=49). Another building type that arguably represents a single con-

struction event is the Great Kiva. The labor requirement for the first Great Kiva at Chetro Ketl (a relatively large Great Kiva) was about 29,135 PH (including excavations). This estimate is perhaps less reliable than the estimates for other types of construction, since Great Kivas involve unique material and technical problems; nevertheless, the similarity of this figure to the mean for arcs and the mean for Class I building supports the division between the two classes at 55,000 PH.

## The Timing of Construction Events

The dating of Class I events is almost uniformly poor, and no analysis of temporal patterns or intervals of Class I building is possible. After about 1020, Class I building was probably a relatively constant process at Chaco, perhaps year round, every year, or perhaps one or two Class I units every two to four years. In any event, Class I building was probably a more or less constant background to the larger scale construction of Classes II, III, and IV.

There are fourteen large roomblocks in Class II. While the mid-point dates of these units are not an entirely accurate indication of the date of their construction, there is nonetheless an intriguing temporal pattern evident in Figure 5.1. In Class II construction, there is a gap from about 1080 to 1110 (Figure 5.1), which corresponds almost exactly to the mid-point dates of five of the six largest construction stages (Classes III and IV, Figure 5.1).

The average interval between mid-point dates of Class II, III, and IV events is about seven years (simultaneous events and the 960 to 1040 hiatus excluded). This figure suggests rather more precision in dating than is actually possible with these events as the average dated span for these events is over 9 years. For Class IV construction alone, the interval is slightly higher, about 7 to 10 years. However, it appears that patterns of Class II, III and IV building change through time. Dating here uses the mid-point dates of Figure 5.1; therefore, the spans given in the following discussion differ slightly from the spans of formal change presented in Chapter 3.

### A.D. 900 to 1040

Class II building during this earliest period occurs in a temporal series with apparently minimal overlap. As shown on Figure 5.1, these are (from early to late) Peñasco Blanco, Pueblo Bonito, Una Vida, Hungo Pavi, Pueblo Alto, and Chetro Ketl. Pueblo del Arroyo (1065-1075) may actually be the last in this series. The intervals between events are not well defined; however, the dates do indicate relatively short spans (at most, 20 years) between the first three events (Peñasco Blanco, Pueblo Bonito, and Una Vida) and between the last two or three events (Pueblo Alto, Chetro Ketl, and perhaps Pueblo del Arroyo).

## A.D. 1040 to 1080

Class II and Class III construction was mainly confined to Pueblo Bonito, where a series of large events culminated in Pueblo Bonito VI, one unit of which (VIA) is Class II, while the other (VIB) is the earliest Class IV event. At the same time, much smaller Class II and the ubiquitous Class I building events continued at other sites (Chetro Ketl, Peñasco Blanco, Una Vida, Pueblo Alto, and probably Hungo Pavi). This period is clearly dominated by a series of very large and probably continuous construction events at Pueblo Bonito.

## A.D. 1080 to 1110-1115

Class II building ceased, and was replaced by large-scale building (Classes III and IV). The period begins with massive building at Pueblo Bonito, continues with equally massive events at Peñasco Blanco and Pueblo del Arroyo, and ends with construction of a completely new site, Wijiji. These events appear to have been sequential, although symmetrically paired events (such as construction of the wings at Pueblo Bonito VI and Pueblo del Arroyo II) were arguably the products of a single plan.

## A.D. 1110-1115 to 1140+

Construction reverts to Class II events, which take place mainly at new sites (Tsin Kletzin, New Alto, and Kin Kletso). Additional building at sites begun during previous periods is limited to smaller roomblocks, incidental rooms, round room groups etc.

## Analysis of Class IV Construction

Pueblo Bonito VIB, Pueblo del Arroyo IIA, and Wijiji were the three largest construction events in the Chaco se-

quence. They were almost identical in their labor requirements. The amount of masonry estimated for these three events varies only plus or minus one percent. Pueblo Bonito VIB required the most labor, and in this section the construction of this single event is analyzed in terms of a hypothetical labor scheduling.

Construction labor can be divided into four general types representing an approximate sequence: cutting and processing beams, transporting beams, quarrying stone and procuring other masonry materials, and actual construction.

We have no method for establishing the actual span of the Pueblo Bonito VIB construction event (which probably occurred sometime between 1075 and 1085). Hints at this type of information come from other sites, e.g., most or all of the wood used in one well sampled room at Chetro Ketl was cut over a very short period of time, perhaps a matter of weeks (Bannister and Robinson 1978). The minimum number of years for construction of Pueblo Alto I was perhaps three, with activities occurring mainly in the spring, as determined by faunal remains with construction debris in the Pueblo Alto trash mound (Akins 1982). It is clearly impossible to accurately reconstruct the sequence of events involved in building Pueblo Bonito VIB. I hope here only to offer a plausible scenario that will illustrate what the PH in such a construction might mean.

Pueblo Bonito VIB required a total of 192,862 PH. Only 50% of this total represents actual construction (laying and shaping stone, mixing and carrying mortar, installing roofs). The other 50% comprises tree cutting and transport and masonry material procurement.

For a hypothetical reconstruction of the sequencing of this labor, I have assumed a 10-hour work day and a 30-day work month. I have further assumed that construction events occurred in a 10-year period (the probable interval between Class IV building, as noted above, was about 7-10 years).

Evidence from Chetro Ketl suggests that wood cutting took place over a matter of weeks. If all timber for Pueblo Bonito VIB was cut and processed in one month, it would require about 30 workers, or 30 person/months. Thirty person/months will serve as a basic unit for all other activities. In terms of 30 person/month units, Pueblo Bonito VIB had the following requirements:

Cutting/processing trees    1
Transporting beams          6
Quarrying, etc.             3
Constructing               10.8

Assuming that all building activities were completed in ten years, but that actual construction took only three, these labor requirements can be apportioned as in Table 5.2.

In words, a 30-person crew could cut and transport beams for about 1-1.2 months a year over a 6-year period, and quarry and construct for 3.6 (more likely, three to four) months a year over a 4-year period, and build the single largest construction event in the Chacoan record.

General Trends in Construction Labor

It is almost certain that several different construction events were simultaneously in progress; thus, total construction labor in the canyon during Pueblo Bonito VIB was more than the levels described above. To understand the implications of simultaneous building, we must analyze canyon-wide trends in construction labor.

Labor expended in individual construction stages was apportioned into five-year increments ("half-decades") over the span of each stage. Totals from all construction stages were then summed for each half-decade. Finally, labor estimates in PH were computed by multiplying the total measures for wall and roofs by the constants in Appendix B.

Raw PH figures are graphed on Figure 5.2 in a dashed line. Marked fluctuations are evident, especially after 1050 (e.g., peaks at 1055, 1090, 1100, and 1130). These peaks are separated by very short periods of lessened PH expenditure -- periods of as little as five years. I greatly mistrust these remarkable variations in amplitude; I suspect they are largely a function of my erroneous short-dating of several construction stages. A second presentation of labor values, employing a weighted moving average, is shown on Figure 5.2 in heavy solid line. This averaged line, and the values it represents, should correct minor errors in dating.

The half-decade with the highest PH figure was 1095 - 1100, with 278,224 PH, or an average of 55,645 PH/ year -- about three times the yearly levels for Pueblo

Bonito VIB (above).   What does 55,645 PH/year mean?

The figure (55,645 PH) represents 5565 10-hour person/days; if Chacoan builders worked a 365-day year, 5565 person/days could have been generated by a labor force as small as 16. Of course, this intensity of labor is extremely unlikely; it illustrates the reductio ad absurdum possible in the analysis of labor estimates divorced from cultural context.   Ford (1968) estimated the yearly labor requirements of San Juan Pueblo for ca. 1890. Although San Juan Pueblo is far removed from Chaco, the budget of labor at San Juan is instructive in creating a scale for the evaluation of Chacoan building. Ford assumed a total population of 400, and a work force of 212. Two hundred and twelve workers represent a total of 1,857,120 hours per year (212 x 24 x 365). Ford details the number of hours spent sleeping, sitting, working (subsistence, crafts, housework, etc.) and participating in ceremonies. The largest organized labor event at San Juan was the annual cleaning of the irrigation ditches, an activity requiring more than 100 workers for four long (10-hour) days, or about 0.23% of the work force's total time.   At a 0.23% rate, 55,645 PH/year represents a population of about 2762 workers. Given the ratio of 212 workers in a total population of 400, this indicates a total population of about 5211. This is alarmingly close to Hayes' (1981:51) peak population estimate for Chaco of 5652. This near agreement should not be taken too seriously; for example, many of the rooms and buildings included in Hayes' peak population calculations were not yet built at 1100.

There are other, more fundamental difficulties with direct extrapolation from San Juan ditch clearing to Chacoan building.   Ditch clearing represents a single continuous task, while building represents several discrete tasks, some of which must be done simultaneously while others can be performed in sequence. A comparison of Chacoan labor requirements to Ford's somewhat idealized San Juan labor budget at least indicates that Chacoan building could have been supported by a relatively simple socioeconomic substructure. Even if the labor requirements summarized above are underestimated by a factor of two or three, they would still make no impossible demands on a population of around 4000 - 5000 with the organizational characteristics of Ford's San Juan Pueblo.

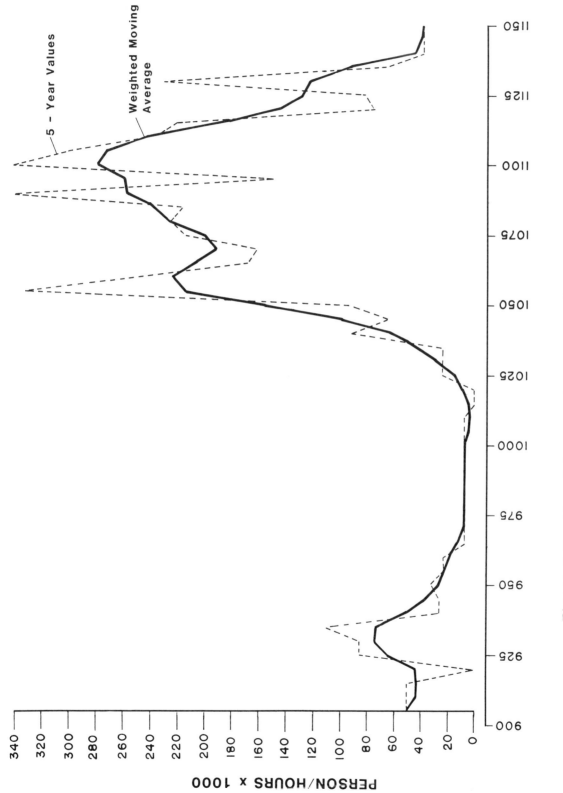

Figure 5.2.   Mean labor requirements by 5-year intervals.

## SOCIAL CORRELATES OF FORM

Previous work by the Chaco Center (Judge et al. 1981; Schelberg 1982) suggests that Chaco Canyon was the center of a regional system of marked complexity. Whatever the exact nature of the society centered on Chaco, two independent lines of evidence support arguments for socio-political complexity: regional settlement (Marshall et al. 1979; Powers et al. 1983) and intra-canyon burial data (Akins and Schelberg 1981). Does the architecture of Chaco Canyon also reflect this complexity?

The formal sequence at Chaco can be usefully divided into three periods: the first, from 900 to about 1050; the second, from 1075 to about 1110-1115; and the third, from about 1110 to the cessation of major building about 1140. Form was relatively homogeneous prior to about 1050; after that time, the number of building types multiplied, culminating in the extreme variety of building forms of the early 1100s. The period from 1050 to 1075 was one of transition in Chacoan building. The beginning and end of this transition are more clearly defined than the transition (the gap from 1050-1075).

### A.D. 900 to 1050

Chacoan buildings of the early 900s were formally identical to the small site domestic structure, scaled up and augmented by upper stories. The basic form continued into the early to middle 1000s, disappearing about 1050. What were these buildings? Extensive midden and room-fill trash at Pueblo Bonito, Peñasco Blanco, and Una Vida suggest that these structures housed some domestic functions from the early 900s on.

The west arc of Pueblo Bonito I is the least disturbed and best documented of the early 900s buildings. Most domestic floor features would be expected in the ramada and plaza-facing rooms of the west arc; however, two centuries of subsequent use and Neil Judd's disinclination to destroy later structures to expose earlier levels limits any possibility of evidence remaining of tenth century domestic features here.

The architectural shell of the west arc, however, remains. The total floor area of the west arc, including a projected ramada, is about 1060 m$^2$, while the total floor area of the subterranean round rooms associated with this arc is about 114 m$^2$. The ratio of round room floor space to rectangular room floor space is thus about 1:9.3. These ratios at small domestic structures bracketing the construction span of Pueblo Bonito IA are as follows (Marcia Truell, personal communication, 1982):

| Sites | Date | Ratio |
|---|---|---|
| 627 & 724 | 800s | 1:2.7 |
| 627 | middle 900s | 1:3.6 |
| 627 | early 1000s | 1:6.0 |

In this sequence, the early 900s Pueblo Bonito ratio (1:9.3) is anomalous. The Pueblo Bonito room floor area is over three times the values of the small sites of the 800s, and over two and one-half times those of the middle 900s. If semi-subterranean round rooms at large sites parallel in function the pit structures of smaller sites, then there is proportionately much more rectangular room space in larger buildings than at small sites.

"Excess" space in rectangular rooms at Pueblo Bonito could be interpreted in at least two ways: First, if space-per-person is the same at both large and small sites, the excess may represent architectural space designed for non-domestic uses. Second, space per person may vary among formal subsets of a domestic architecture. In other words, space per person may vary with more space per person in large sites than at smaller sites.

From the evidence of the buildings alone, no good case can be made for either alternative. Nor do we have reliable independent data on population size, which would inform us about space per person.

Our interpretation of these structures must depend not so much upon the internal evidence from the buildings themselves as on their place in the canyon's settlement pattern. Hayes (1981) provides a summary of Chacoan settlement information.

At the beginning of Great Pueblo building in the late 800s, there were well defined clusters of small domestic structures at three places in the canyon: one in the Fajada Gap-Gallo area, a second in and around South Gap, and a third above the Chaco-Escavada confluence (Figure 1.1).

Construction of large structures began in the early 900s, where major side drainages enter the canyon: Una Vida across from Fajada, Pueblo Bonito opposite South Gap, and Peñasco Blanco on the bluffs overlooking the confluence of the Chaco and the Escavada.

Small site communities continued, though "slightly reduced" (Hayes 1981: 28), e.g., South Gap and the Fajada-Gallo Wash area. Around Peñasco Blanco, small sites were so few as to preclude definition as a cluster; thus, Pueblo Bonito and Una Vida were central to communities of small sites, while Peñasco Blanco appears to replace the previous site cluster.

Although this thumbnail sketch greatly simplifies Hayes' interpretations, two important trends are clear. First, early 900s large-scale building occurred in areas of existing small site clusters; and second, large-scale construction corresponds to the decreasing definition of small site clusters.

Which of the alternative interpretations of early 900s building do these data support? If large sites replaced site clusters (as appears to be the case at Peñasco Blanco), the populations from those smaller structures might have aggregated in the larger buildings. This would suggest that early 900s buildings are simply a new form of domestic architecture, perhaps with more persons per rectangular room and a change in the function of round rooms.

Pueblo Bonito and Una Vida did not replace site clusters, but instead formed central places for communities of smaller structures. It is important to note that Hayes' work around Peñasco Blanco was limited by the park boundaries. The absence of an early 900s community around this site may more nearly reflect the parameters of the survey than the pattern of settlement.

The simplest interpretation is that early 900s buildings are scaled-up domestic structures located at strategic confluences, housing groups which are themselves of some importance and centrality to their surrounding communities. The three earliest Chacoan buildings may have housed local (intra-canyon) elite groups that made up no more than 10% of the canyon population (based on the number of round rooms). They were in some sense "central places" within the canyon settlement system, or more accurately, within two and probably three distinct settlement systems. This suggests that early 900s building reflects the status symbolism and storage requirements of emerging "big men" -- a primus inter pares whose standing depends on show and display, the accumulation of material goods, and most importantly on the creation (through family extension and recruitment) of a large domestic labor force. All these aspects of "big man" political maneuvering would be consistent

with the increased labor input, the increased scale of component forms, and the increased total size of early tenth century building.

The evidence is ambiguous, since Peñasco Blanco, as currently known, favors a scenario of aggregation, while Pueblo Bonito and Una Vida suggest a development of architectural complexity. Incomplete survey data around Peñasco Blanco may indicate that Pueblo Bonito and Una Vida more accurately represent the prehistoric situation. There is also extra-canyon confirmation of the Pueblo Bonito and Una Vida pattern, in the communities found around almost every major outlier (Marshall et al. 1979; Powers et al. 1983). The existence of contemporaneous communities of small sites around most outliers suggests that large-scale building was not an architectural expression of simple aggregation, but that the functions and people housed in the buildings were in fact distinct from those housed in smaller sites.

Hungo Pavi, the next major construction in the late 900s and early 1000s, was located at the mouth of Mockingbird Canyon, the next largest tributary to the Chaco after the three already occupied. Although small sites were present at Mockingbird and across the canyon at the mouth of Werito's Rincon, there were no concentrations of smaller structures comparable to those around Pueblo Bonito and Una Vida. In the early 1000s there seem to have been changes in the context and probably in the function of Chacoan buildings, demonstrated most clearly by slightly later construction at Chetro Ketl and Pueblo Alto. Chetro Ketl was built within the existing Pueblo Bonito cluster area. Pueblo Alto is isolated on the mesa top, with no contemporaneous community of any kind. Neither could have been a "central place" for intra-canyon small site clusters.

What are the early 1000s structures? They are formally very similar to the early 900s buildings and presumably were designed to solve similar problems. If our surmises about the early 900s buildings are correct, the early 1000s buildings should house elite groups, but the placement of the buildings does not suggest centrality to any local cluster of sites. At Pueblo Alto, with its many road terminii, and at Chetro Ketl and Hungo Pavi which both lack associated communities, we see our first hints of the extra-canyon ramification of the Chacoan system. Only hints appear in the early 1000s; more convincing evidence must await the formal developments of the later 1000s.

## A.D. 1050 to 1110-1115

During the third quarter of the eleventh century, only one new structure was begun (Pueblo del Arroyo). Otherwise, construction was limited to additions to existing buildings: wings, asymmetrical extensions, etc. The early 900s plan disappears. Increasingly from 1050 to 1075, building consists mainly of rear-row rooms, upper stories over existing rear row rooms, and massed blocks with many interior and few exterior rooms.

The most massive construction in all Chacoan building was undertaken in the last quarter of the eleventh century and the earliest decades of the twelfth (1075-1115). The building of 1075-1115 added rooms to three existing structures, and created an entirely new building (Wijiji), well away from the central canyon area (Figure 1.1). The additions were massive blocks; the east wing of Pueblo Bonito is up to five rows deep and four stories tall. Most of the rooms created would not have had direct access to the exterior. Some construction retained a front-to-rear pattern that recalls the earlier units (e.g., Figure 3.8), and at each building several of these units seem to be associated with an unusually large round room. However, most rooms interconnnect in both axes, and size differences from front to rear are minimal. The exception to this pattern of massive blocks is Peñasco Blanco, where 1075-1115 building added a row of rear rooms apparently without corresponding plaza-facing construction.

Presumably, interior rooms were not used for domestic activities. They are generally labeled storage, and this seems a reasonable guess. From 1075 to 1115, a great amount of potential storage space was created. When compared to earlier ratios of domestic to storage space, this was an amount much in excess of contemporaneously constructed "domestic" rooms. Chacoan architecture was changing from the construction of elite residences to that of large storage facilities. These storage rooms were built in the most costly, planned construction events in the Chacoan sequence.

If we assume that the large Chacoan buildings continued a local elite residence function, the settlement hierarchy at Chaco in the late 1000s and early 1100s was very top heavy; there are about as many rooms in large sites as there are in all the smaller buildings. It is, however, probably incorrect to equate a room in a large site with a room in a smaller site as a population index. If

new rooms equal new population, from 700 to about 1140 the annual rate of population growth for Chaco Canyon was approximately 0.3% (data from Hayes [1981], using his population estimates as the maximum for each phase). However, the rate at large sites, considered separately, was much higher. At Pueblo Bonito, the annual growth rate (similarly estimated) was about 2.25%. Neolithic growth rates usually range from 0.1 to 0.5% (Hassan 1981:201). While the canyon as a whole falls within this range, growth at the larger sites cannot be attributed to internal population increase alone. The construction of rooms at larger sites presumably equates with something other than new population. After 1075 (and perhaps before), a great many of the rooms at larger sites were probably neither domestic units nor storage rooms directly associated with domestic units, a circumstance which may indicate an added public function to that of elite residence.

Hayes (1981) suggests a population of 2763 for the large sites, based on the number of rooms. Using an index based on the numbers of round rooms (Lekson 1981c), I estimate only 1300. Even with this lower population estimate, however, the elites housed in the larger sites comprise a disproportionate segment of the canyon population. It is difficult to continue to see them as only local elite.

At some point, the centrality of the larger Chacoan sites expanded beyond the canyon and its immediate surroundings. The architectural evidence for this shift points to a period between 1050 and 1075; the latter date marks the beginning of the most massive construction programs, suggesting that a regional system was already in full operation, (i.e., one that both required the addition of centralized storage space and supported its construction). Chaco had become the center of a region, and the functions of the larger buildings at Chaco had shifted from being central places within the canyon to buildings within a cohesive larger settlement, itself central to both a core area around Chaco and a much larger area approximating the San Juan Basin (Marshall et al. 1979; Powers et al. 1983).

This settlement was, of course, not limited to large structures. Also present were approximately 300 smaller buildings (Hayes 1981; Truell 1983). In the past, the differences between the large and small buildings have been dichotomized into towns and villages (Vivian 1970). Many studies have addressed the "town - village problem" (e.g., Brand et al. 1937; Gladwin 1945; Grebinger 1973; Hayes 1981; Vivian 1970; Vivian and Mathews 1965).

The size differences are real, but the "town" and "village" terminology is unfortunate, and has distorted the published conceptions of settlement pattern in Chaco. Although a hierarchy of "towns" and "villages" is appropriate to a regional landscape, Chaco Canyon itself is hardly a region. Several "towns" are literally a stone's throw apart, and the "villages" are crowded between them. Rank-order analyses and site size hierarchies that consider Pueblo Bonito, Chetro Ketl, and Pueblo del Arroyo separately are misguided. These buildings -- together with the numerous other structures in the central canyon -- should be considered a single analytical unit. It becomes necessary to shift our concern from "towns" and "villages" to the canyon itself, especially the central area around South Gap, as a larger settlement of significant complexity.

Numerous eleventh century communities (Marshall et al. 1979; Powers et al. 1983) were scattered around the San Juan Basin, of which Chaco was the geographic center. Typically, these communities consisted of 20 to 40 small structures, each of 5 to 15 rooms, with an associated subterranean round room and a midden. The small houses were clustered in a settlement of perhaps 2 km$^2$; the central feature of the settlement was a massively constructed "Chacoan" building. Each of these communities, which could not have had a population much greater than 500, would in most parts of the world be considered a large hamlet or small village. Each of the small structures would be termed a house.

In Chaco Canyon, however, the individual small structures have been termed "villages"; thus, there are 300 separate but nearly continuous "villages" in a 17 km length of canyon. If each of the larger buildings is a "town," we have the unlikely concentration of three of the largest "towns" within a 0.75 km radius, almost close enough to be connected by a single additional building unit. This usage of "town" may have been intended to reflect such peculiarities of Puebloan settlement as the Hopi-Tewa situation on First Mesa, but "towns" and "villages" can only confuse those not familiar with Chaco and its archaeology.

## A.D. 1110-1115 to 1140+

Chacoan building of the early 1100s has traditionally been referred to as the "McElmo" phase (Vivian and Mathews 1965). This phase was originally defined in southwestern Colorado (McElmo Creek, from which the phase took its name, runs just north of Mesa Verde), and is dated there to 1075-1200 (Hayes and Lancaster 1975:184). It is defined by the following architectural and ceramic characteristics (Hayes 1964:97-100):

1. Incorporation of round rooms into the house block.
2. Predominance of McElmo Black-on-white pottery.
3. Increasing refinement in building stone dressing.
4. Beginnings of multiple-storied building.
5. Beginning of round towers.

Vivian and Mathews (1965), in their important report on Kin Kletso, introduced the McElmo phase to Chaco Canyon. Vivian and Mathews believed that Kin Kletso represented an intrusive McElmo phase unit from the Mesa Verde area (Vivian and Mathews 1965:110). They also identified Casa Chiquita, New Alto, Tsin Kletzin, and the house block adjoining the Pueblo del Arroyo Tri-wall as similar McElmo intrusions. The architectural and ceramic criteria that they proposed for the "McElmo" phase at Chaco (Vivian and Mathews 1965:109) included:

1. Compact, multistory plan, round rooms enclosed in house blocks.
2. One period site with no development in place.
3. Cored, thin wall...Occasional "banded" areas are rare, typical is the facing of large blocks of soft stone, pecked and "dimpled," with chinking between stones.
4. The Great Kiva is absent; was a probable association with the tri-walled structure adjacent to Pueblo del Arroyo. The earliest small kivas were...similar to those in the Bonito Phase...Later kivas...were the general San Juan style.
5. Tower Kiva: One present at Kin Kletso.

Vivian dated the Chacoan "McElmo" phase to 1050 to 1124+ (Vivian and Mathews 1965:109). I have suggested beginning dates around 1110-1115, and end dates about 1140 for the Chaco Canyon "McElmo" sites. This dating is more in line with the McElmo phase in the Mesa Verde area, but as we shall see, the Chacoan "McElmo" phase is probably not an intrusive manifestation of the Mesa Verde McElmo phase.

The similarities between the McElmo phase at Mesa Verde and the "McElmo" phase at Chaco are evidently (1) the enclosure of round rooms in the room block, (2) multiple story building, (3) the ground plan, (4) pecked stone facings, and (5) ceramics. These features will be examined in some detail.

Two of the suggested architectural characteristics of the intrusive "McElmo" phase are multistoried building and round rooms elevated and enclosed in the room-block. Multistoried building at Chaco dates at least as early as 900; elevated enclosed rooms date as early as 1050. Both multiple stories and round room placement predate "McElmo" building by at least half a century, and it is difficult to see how they could be "intrusive."

The Chacoan "McElmo" ground plan is distinct and consistent (Figure 3.13); the square plan with an elevated round room enclosed by one, two, and three rows of small square rooms is evident at each site, and in each of the two construction stages at Kin Kletso. The "McElmo" ground plan appears with intriguing frequency at road-related sites (Kincaid 1983). The formal, most visible Chacoan roads were probably constructed in the 1100s (John R. Stein, personal communication, 1983), contemporaneous with the "McElmo" sites in the canyon. At Chaco, sites with this plan are located next to larger buildings with longer construction histories, at Pueblo Alto (New Alto), Peñasco Blanco (the "McElmo ruin"), Pueblo Bonito (Kin Kletso), and Chetro Ketl (the small room block appended to the west wing). All of these sites are terminii of roads. In addition, other "McElmo" sites are located at strategic points related to canyon access and presumably roads (Casa Chiquita, Tsin Kletzin).

Oddly enough, the Chacoan "McElmo" plan is frequently seen in Chacoan "outliers" of the Mesa Verde area. Perhaps the best example is Escalante Ruin (Hallasi 1979), which is practically identical to New Alto and Kin Kletso IA or IB (Figure 3.13). Escalante, dating to about 1130, illustrates a fundamental problem with Vivian and Mathews' concept of the "McElmo" phase as a cultural intrusion in Chaco. Escalante is apparently anomalous and considered Chacoan: "The architecture and layout of the Escalante Ruin is identifiable as being of Chaco style" (Hallasi 1979:231). Similar structures are evident at the central unit at Yucca House and East Ruin at Aztec, both of which are often cited as Chacoan outliers. The "McElmo" ground plan is a San Juan/Mesa Verde intrusion at Chaco, but it is a Chacoan intrusion in the San Juan and Mesa Verde areas.

It is illuminating to compare layouts of real McElmo phase sites at Mesa Verde to contemporary sites at Chaco. One good example of a large McElmo phase site in Mesa Verde is Big Juniper House, a pueblo of about 30 rooms dating to the late 1000s and early 1100s (Swannack 1969). A glance at the ground plan of Big Juniper House (Figure 3.13g) shows that the McElmo phase in Mesa Verde more closely resembles the "Bc" sites (Figure 3.13h) of the old Hosta Butte phase, than the Chaco "McElmo" phase.

Pecked stone facings were partly a response to the decreasing availability of tabular sandstones. This is particularly true in the central canyon area, where easily obtainable tabular stone was probably exhausted by the early twelfth century; late construction at Wijiji, in an area where no large-scale construction had depleted the stone, was with tabular stone in a simple rubble facing style. The pecked stone facing with gallet spalls is also certainly a style; however, the "McElmo" style was not limited to "McElmo" sites. Pecked stone was used in facings as early as the mid-eleventh century; the "McElmo" style itself was definitely present in some of the later sections of Pueblo Bonito (Pueblo Bonito VIIC), Chetro Ketl (particularly the Kiva G complex, Chetro Ketl XIIA), and Pueblo del Arroyo (Pueblo del Arroyo IIIA). Pecked stone facings seem more indicative of the time of construction than of "site unit intrusion."

Vivian and Mathews mention two additional specific architectural criteria to describe and define the Chacoan "McElmo" phase: Tower Kivas and absence of Great Kivas. Tower Kivas and Mesa Verde McElmo towers are not particularly close analogues, nor are Tower Kivas a definitive characteristic of Chacoan "McElmo" sites. One was found at Kin Kletso, but more are known from other late, non-"McElmo" sites. Great Kivas are neither found at "McElmo" sites nor are they constantly associated with other large Chacoan buildings.

Ceramics were a major factor in Vivian's interpretation of the "McElmo" sites. The ceramics at Chacoan "McElmo" sites were carbon-painted, as were those of the Mesa Verde McElmo phase. Although ceramics are beyond the scope of this study, a brief digression is necessary to address this particular problem.

Chacoan carbon-painted ceramics subsume a broad variety of types (Toll et al. 1980) including increasing amounts of San Juan wares (i.e., McElmo Black-on-white) in the time periods corresponding to "McElmo" site construction. It is gratifying that these ceramics in Chaco are roughly contemporaneous, and not earlier than their Mesa Verde counterparts (as Vivian and Mathews' dating, 1050-1124, of the Chacoan "McElmo" phase would require).

This complex of carbon-painted types, supposedly characteristic of Chacoan "McElmo" phase sites, occurs at every large site at Chaco. The assemblage is temporally defined, rather than specific to a particular class of site within the canyon; thus the predominance of carbon paint at Kin Kletso, for example, does not indicate an intrusion of makers of carbon-painted pottery but rather reflects Kin Kletso's dates of construction and use. Since the Chacoan "McElmo" sites are (by definition, Vivian and Mathews [1965:110]) single component, the ceramics present reflect only this late occupation.

On every point, the Chacoan "McElmo" phase seems invalid. Carbon-paint ceramics are not specific to these sites, nor is pecked masonry, nor are enclosed elevated round rooms, nor is multistoried construction. There remains a coherence among the buildings listed by Vivian and Mathews in plan, masonry style, in their construction de novo, and in their late date of construction. If we look at these sites as late construction within the Chacoan building tradition, rather than intrusive forms from the San Juan area, these shared characteristics begin to make sense.

The period from 1115 to 1140 saw the construction of a number of separate buildings, characterized by many small interior rooms and comparatively few round rooms. Following the arguments for construction of the preceding periods, these could be interpreted as specifically designed storage facilities. Was there that much more to store? Or was the storage function of the older structures being transferred to specially designed buildings? I suspect the latter was the case.

What effect would the removal of public storage functions to these new buildings have on the existing buildings? For one thing, it would make available a lot of previously encumbered rooms. The residents would be able to use these now abandoned rooms for other purposes. In historic pueblos, abandoned rooms are often used for trash disposal. This happened at Chaco in the late 1000s and

early 1100s. Trash-filled rooms were common at Pueblo Bonito: "Indeed, there is probably not a ground floor room in the entire village that escaped the bearer of trash" (Judd 1954:20).

Kin Kletso is one of the posited storage facilities. According to the excavators, 10 of the building's 55 ground floor rooms were also trash-filled. "The amount of refuse in the rooms varied greatly; Room 5 was filled above the ceiling level..." (Vivian and Mathews 1965:59, Figure 32). Trash-filled rooms in storage facilities may seem fatal to my argument, but "trash-filled" rooms at Kin Kletso differed from the trash-filled rooms at Pueblo Bonito and the other habitation structures.

For a number of practical reasons, the most accessible index for trash is decorated sherds. At Kin Kletso, only 6061 black-on-white and redware sherds were recovered from the entire site (Vivian and Mathews 1965:65). Late trash-filled rooms at Pueblo Bonito routinely produced from about 1500 to over 5000 decorated sherds per room (Judd 1954:Figure 4; Roberts n.d.).

Room 5 at Kin Kletso, "filled above the ceiling level ... one of the heaviest deposits in the site" (Vivian and Mathews 1965: 59), has a volume of a little of over 33 m$^3$. A single test trench, removing about 11 m$^3$ of fill, in a trash-filled round room at Pueblo Alto produced over 4000 decorated sherds. This is two thirds of the total number of decorated sherds at Kin Kletso from one third the volume of Room 5.

No doubt a few of the rooms at Kin Kletso were trash-filled; however, most of the 10 trash-filled rooms at Kin Kletso contained only very small deposits or a rather anemic brand of trash, perhaps the "background noise" sherds ubiquitous in any room fill. Limited excavation data and surface examination of other late, presumably storage structures suggests that none had extensive trash deposits either in room fill or in extramural middens. For example, at Wijiji one looks almost in vain for any sherds.

POPULATION, ARCHITECTURE, AND COMPLEXITY

At the inception of this study, the best population figure available was Hayes' (1981), developed from his survey data. Converting numbers of rooms to numbers of people, Hayes estimated a total population of about 5600. Basing large site population on the number of round rooms -- a more appropriate architectural indicator of habitation than rectangular rooms -- I later lowered this to 4100 (Lekson 1981c). Windes (1981), who has been doing the major work on this problem at the Chaco Center, would like to go even lower than that.

The culmination of this trend is an emerging notion that Chaco was a periodic population center, largely empty for most of the year. Judge (1983) recently proposed such a model of Chaco, which he sees as a basin-wide ceremonial center. Judge suggests a very small year-round resident group at Chaco, joined at intervals by a sort of grand gathering of the clans from all corners of the basin.

Decreasing the population estimates solves a major, long-standing difficulty in Chacoan archaeology, i.e., feeding people. Population levels of 4000 or 5000 would seriously tax local farmland (Schelberg 1982) and would probably require movement of foodstuffs on a scale quite out of line for the Puebloan Southwest. The lower the population, the less we are troubled by specters of non-Puebloan economic systems, but as a consequence, the greater looms the problem of construction, and the difficulty of organizing labor to get things built. Lower population estimates or a semi-permanent settlement may solve the problem of too many mouths to feed, but these remedies introduce equally serious problems of too few hands to make work light.

Labor requirements are more or less fixed. If we decrease the resident population -- the available labor force -- then we must change our perspectives on the social complexity required to organize that labor force. If the canyon population was significantly less than the 4100 to 5600 level, labor requirements for construction would have posed an increasing challange for work force mobilization and coordination. Although the estimated labor requirements were low enough that the conclusions presented above should stand against all but the most radical population reduction, I suspect that the "empty ceremonial center" model is sufficiently radical. If the canyon was largely depopulated for most of the year, the organization of labor must have been altogether different than the San Juan ditch-clearing parable.

Does Chacoan construction technology contribute to the solution of the population question? Not really! The technology is in some ways ambiguous. In the Southwest, permanence of the building technology is often used as a gauge of permanence of settlement. Sites without architecture are not habitations, sites with ephemeral architecture are temporary camps, and sites with substantial building are permanent residences. Though this formula is far too simple, if it were applied to Chaco, it would certainly indicate permanent settlement. Chacoan construction is without question the most permanent of any Anasazi building tradition.

On the other hand, their remarkable permanence suggests that the buildings were something other than "normal" housing. Perhaps the buildings were designed to stand for long periods of the year without maintenance. The contemporary small site would require nearly constant care, particularly after the inevitable but unpredictable thunderstorms. If the large structures were primarily designed to survive long periods of neglect, this might support the idea of Chaco as a periodic population center.

What about form? Obviously, lower population estimates leave us with many empty rooms and buildings. If the buildings were not inhabited, for what were they being used? In the empty ceremonial center model, the large sites are mainly residential facilities designed to accommodate the large periodic influxes. There is, however, little evidence that most of the rooms in the big buildings were ever residential. In fact, it was the paucity of living area features that first spurred the wave of population reductions (e.g., Windes 1981). Perhaps people were content to live without the customary features and furniture at periodic gatherings, but then why go to the trouble of building exaggerated, tremendously expensive shells? It seems odd to labor over massive walls and carry beams (the size of telephone poles) all over northwest New Mexico, and then balk at building a simple firepit. We are still faced with the problem of many empty rooms, and the fewer people we conclude lived at Chaco, the more empty rooms we have to explain.

Architecture is our most accessible archaeological index of population, but at Chaco, architecture is not an index but an issue. Perhaps the best independent measure of population is the burial record, particularly in areas which have been extensively excavated. Chaco has been excavated, and the record of burials is notoriously slim. There are over 300 documented burials from Chaco, but this is fewer than we would expect from a large resident population. However, Nancy Akins, of the Chaco Center, examined notes and collections in a number of eastern and western institutions, and concluded that the published numbers are too low:

> The most often cited figures fall between 300 and 325 ... However, with the inclusion of isolated and unpublished materials this number is now approximately 700. In addition we are certain that many more burials were removed but were never systematically recorded or curated (Akins and Schelberg 1981).

This is not the kind of hard evidence we would like, but at least we can say that the burial record at Chaco probably does not indicate an uninhabited empty canyon.

The wide variety of building types suggests a heavy investment in permanent facilities; and in very real terms, an increasing institutionalization of the socioeconomic systems the facilities served. Massive construction and permanence of the facility (whatever its implications for population levels) almost certainly indicate that the problem being solved was perceived as a long term one, far longer than the average life of the contemporary small house. In monumental building, that kind of permanence addresses fairly ethereal requirements, but there is little Chacoan architecture that could seriously be considered monumental. Perhaps mounds and Great Kivas are monumental, but rather along the lines of the Hohokam construction that David Wilcox has termed "modestly monumental." Large Chacoan buildings were probably in almost every sense utilitarian. But what were they?

From 900 to about 1040, it is clear that major Chacoan buildings were scaled-up domestic architectural forms. Trash middens, floor features, and burials testify that people were living in these structures. Formally, it is difficult to see large Chacoan structures as anything but very expensive housing.

During this period, the division between large and small houses is fairly apparent; the blurring of that distinction occurs later. Because of the clear division, and the proportions of the population (presumably) living in each dwelling type, "stratified housing" seems to accurately describe the architectural situation. Stratification in housing presumably reflected social distinctions in the population.

Between 1050 and 1075, additions to the large buildings, while less obviously domestic in form, are in part blocks of rear and exterior rooms. The older resi-

dential structures apparently were beginning to acquire new, centralized storage functions. People were still living in the large buildings, although we are unable to specify how many, or for how long. (Intriguingly, occupation of small houses may actually decrease from about 1050 to about 1100 [Thomas Windes, personal communication, 1983], but this interesting idea is still a matter of debate.)

After 1075, several massive additions to the older buildings, and many new buildings are constructed that are obviously not domestic building. These structures had many small, interior or rear-row rectangular rooms but very few round rooms. We assume that these small interior rooms were storage rooms, and, presumably, the additions were designed primarily for storage. This construction is contemporaneous with the formalization of the Chacoan regional network, and it is difficult to maintain that the two developments were simply coincidental.

At its architectural peak (early 1100s), there is abundant evidence for occupation of both large and small residential structures at Chaco. This last-use of the structures (actually, last extensive use) is demonstrated not by trash mounds but by numerous trash-filled rooms, at Pueblo Bonito, Chetro Ketl, and elsewhere. There are some interesting ideas associated with trash-filled rooms. Archaeologists seem to believe that this untidiness signals the end of the Chacoan weltanschauung: when life was good, trash went into a tidy trash mound and Chaco was at its peak; when people started leaving evidence of life in the great empty halls, the society was on the wane.

The patterns of trash disposal have been used as a basis on which to judge the level of complexity of Chacoan society. Sometimes this criterion seems to be inconsistently applied. During the tidy period, we argue that no evidence of life in the buildings suggests a low population level, and therefore Chacoan society was simpler than its architecture suggests. In the following messy era, when we have abundant evidence of people living in the buildings, the society may have been deteriorating; therefore, Chacoan society was simpler than its architecture suggests.

Actually, the end of the Chacoan sequence was perhaps its most dynamic period. The architecture has been described. The early 1100s also produced some of the most compelling evidence for long-distance trade. Most of the macaws found at Pueblo Bonito were found, dead of disease or starvation, on their perches (4 or 5 in Room 249, Judd 1964:

107; at least 13 in Room 38, Pepper 1920: 194), as they were also at Pueblo del Arroyo (3 in Room 63, Judd 1959:127). These birds were probably alive during the early 1100s use of the building. Copper bells are less well provenienced, but many (probably most) of these at Pueblo Bonito and Pueblo del Arroyo were found in late trash, or in "last-use" contexts (Judd 1954:109, 1959: 24, 86).

Rather than signalling decay of a failing system, the architectural patterns of the late 1000s and early 1100s suggest that Chaco was reaching new levels of complexity. The "McElmo" storage structures and the plethora of contemporary specialized building types (triwalls, road ramps, etc.) indicate physical differentiation of functions previously incorporated in the older stratified housing, and -- presumably -- increasing institutionalization of the social systems the new buildings served. Administration of these systems may have been alienated from existing local elite groups, the occupants of the older habitation structures, and removed to a higher level, just as the older intra-canyon central places merged into a basin-wide central place, a single settlement.

How many people lived in the settlement at Chaco Canyon? We return to the question of population. We have discussed estimates of 5600 and 4100, based on survey data from the entire canyon. I suspect that the entire survey area -- over 110 km$^2$ is not relevant to the question at hand. We should instead focus on the dense concentration of building around Pueblo Bonito. In an 8 km$^2$ area were Pueblo Bonito, Chetro Ketl, Pueblo Alto, New Alto, Pueblo del Arroyo, Kin Kletso, Talus Unit, Hillside Ruin, Casa Rinconada, and literally hundreds of smaller houses. Roads, low boundary walls, and irrigation features crisscrossed the landscape. This well defined architectural concentration was a distinct settlement -- the largest in the Chacoan region.

Using Hayes' estimates for small sites, but correcting his large site formula for round rooms only, rather than total room counts, I estimate that between 2100 and 2700 people resided in downtown Chaco.

How does this compare to other Southwestern settlements? The ten most populous Rio Grande Pueblos averaged about 400 residents each during the eighteenth and nineteenth centuries; the western New Mexico Pueblos averaged about 1000 residents during the same period (Simmons 1979: Table 1; Zubrow 1974:

Table 2). After the Revolt of 1680, no Pueblo was ever larger than about 1500, except Zuni, which occasionally peaked at 2500 (but which averaged about 1500). These figures are useful measures of the Pueblo societies that we are accustomed to use as ethnographic models for Chaco and other Anasazi archaeology.

If the 2100 to 2700 figure is correct, this population was five to six times greater than the average Rio Grande Pueblo. Chaco was considerably larger in scale than the ethnographic Pueblos. At the same time, Chaco was roughly the same size as the largest population ever recorded at the largest modern Pueblo. Although the Pueblos may be a reasonable baseline for thinking about Chaco, population and architecture suggest that Chaco Canyon was something more.

With their enclosed plazas and inward-looking orientations, Chacoan buildings of the 900s and early 1000s suggest a settlement of separate elite groups. By the early 1100s, Chaco was transformed into a coherent settlement, delineated by roads, walls, mounds, and myriad public buildings, with new administrative functions realized in separate facilities. The organization of labor to reshape the settlement, the construction of those new facilities, and the institutionalization of the systems they served, suggest a level of socio-political complexity considerably beyond that of the ethnographic Pueblo world.

The major problem in studying Chacoan architecture has always been keeping the subject in focus. The ruins are spectacular, so striking that at first it seemed as if they must have been built by Toltecs, not the predecessors of the Pueblos. When the inevitable reaction struck, the interpretation of Chaco as a Toltec outpost was challenged by the view of Chaco as a prehistoric example of the modern Pueblos. Academic lines were drawn, and the battle has raged ever since. Pity the poor Park Service, waffling along, trying to find a formula that nodded to the polarized archaeological opinion but still fit that lowest common denominator, the trail guide.

Debate continues but on slightly altered premises. For Toltec, we now read "polities," "low-level states," "stratified society" or other complexities that transcend the ethnologic Pueblos. Although the mechanism has changed, the issue is the same: was Chaco qualitatively different from the historic Pueblos?

Are the Pueblos the highpoint, or have there been episodes in their prehistory which exceeded the ethnographically documented social and political complexity?   Obviously, I think there were such episodes, and Chaco was one. Since we lack the archaeological tools to unambiguously identify the lower boundaries of complexity -- and by any construction, we are dealing with lower boundaries -- the subject has been more debated than researched.   In any debate, it is always easy to find polar positions, to slip to extremes.   We labor under constricting, all-or-nothing definitions of complexity.

It is essential to keep the subject in focus.   Chaco was never a Toltec empire, but it must have been more complex than the modern Pueblos.   By my reading of the architecture, somewhere near the lower end of the gap between Pueblo and Toltec is a reasonable place to look for Chaco.

Architecture alone cannot satisfactorily answer the questions we would like to ask of Chaco.  The arguments presented here will have to be judged against other lines of inquiry and evidence.   That, happily, is not my task -- at least in this study.  Journalist Ernie Pyle, after visiting Chaco in the thirties, concluded that its ruins "are exasperating.  They raise a question and leave it unanswered."  Half a century later we can answer some of our questions about the ruins, but the big ones still get away.

# Appendix A
# Glossary

ABUT  Walls not integrally tied at corners.

BLOCKED  An opening (door, vent) filled with masonry.

BOND  Walls integrally tied at corners.

CIST  A slab-lined pit.

CLOSING MATERIAL  Layer(s) of material resting on the roof beams, supporting the mud mortar, etc., of the floor/roof (see Figure 2.2).

CORE  A misnomer.  The interior of a faced or core-and-veneer wall.

CORNER DOOR  A door running diagonally through the intersection of two walls.

COURSE  A line of stones in the vertical plane.  Compare WYTHE.

CORBELLED  A dome built up of layers of beams, each layer consisting of beams set end to end in, e.g., hexagonal or octagonal rings.  The ends of each beam in a given layer are supported on the mid-point of two beams of the layer below.  Thus, beam length and roof span decrease in each layer from the base of the dome to the top of the cribbing (see Figure 2.7).

CRIBBED  When applied to round room roofs, a misnomer.  See CORBELLED.

DOUBLE WALL  An unusual building technique, in which two structurally independent walls are parallel and contiguous (see Figure 2.5).

FACINGS  The exposed stones in the wall surface.

FIREPIT  A stone- or plaster-lined pit used for containing fire.

HEATING PIT  An unlined pit used for containing fire or embers (see Figure 3.2).

INTRAMURAL BEAM  A log enclosed in or built into the core of a masonry wall, usually horizontal, rarely vertical (see Figure 2.3).

JACAL  A wall or partition built on a framework of vertical poles or posts, connected with horizontal rods or purlines.  The rods are not woven through the posts.  Mud is applied over this framework to form a solid wall.  Compare WATTLE AND DAUB.

LINTEL  Members, almost always wood, spanning the top of a wall opening and supporting the wall above it.  These are usually a series of parallel small beams (see Figure 2.3).

MEALING BIN  A pit, usually rectangular and slab-lined, in which metates were set for use (see Figure 3.2).

NICHE  On a wall face, a rectangular or irregular recess (see Figures 2.3, 2.6).

PAIRED VENTS  On a wall face, vents in both upper corners (see VENT).

PIER-TYPE PILASTER  In round rooms, masonry piers or buttresses built up vertically from the rear of the bench (see Figure 3.4).

PLAZA  A large, open area enclosed on two or three sides by the building and, often, on the remaining side by a single row of rooms.

POLE-AND-WATTLE  Architectural wickerwork.  Compare JACAL.

PORTAL  A ramada attached to the front of a building, a porch( see Figure 2.3).

PRIMARY BEAM  The large main roof beams, which support secondaries.  Also called viga (see Figure 2.2).

RADIAL BEAM PILASTER  In round rooms, a short log section set radially and horizontally on the bench, usually enclosed in a masonry box-shaped construction (see Figures 3.4, 3.6).

RAISED–SILL DOOR   A small rectangular door with a sill above floor level (see Figures 2.3, 2.6).

RAMADA   A post and beam frame structure with a light roof and no walls.

RING HOLES   On a wall face, small holes on either side of a door, corresponding to small yucca rings through which a bar or pole could be set, closing the door.

ROOMBLOCK   A linear or rectangular structure consisting of multiple rectangular rooms built as a unit.

ROOM-WIDE PLATFORM   A large, deep shelf, built into and spanning one end of a room.  Usually, the platforms are at mid-wall height and are about one-third the room length in depth.  The platform structure exactly parallels that of a roof, with primary beams, secondary beams, etc. (see Figures 2.3, 3.3).

SECONDARY BEAM   Smaller roof beams set perpendicular to and supported by the primaries.  Also called latillas (see Figure 2.2).

SECONDARY LINTEL AND JAMBS   In a raised sill door, an inset of wood (secondary lintel) and masonry (secondary jambs) serves as a collar for a large slab of stone or wood.  The slab, resting against the secondary sill and jambs, closed the door (see Figures 2.3, 2.6).

SHAKE   A long, narrow, thin piece of wood, split out of a log.

SILL   The floor of a door; usually stone slabs, occasionally closely set wood beams or planks (see Figure 2.3)

STRINGER   See INTRAMURAL BEAM.

SUITE   Rooms interconnected by doors.

T-SHAPED DOOR   A door with a rectangular upper portion wider than its lower portion (see Figures 2.3, 2.6).

TOWER KIVA   Round room with more than one story.

VENT   A small rectangular opening in a wall, usually placed just below roof level (see Figures 2.3, 2.6).

VENTILATOR   In a round room, a tunnel running from the exterior to the area of the firepit (see Figures 3.4, 3.6).

VENEER   A misnomer.  See FACING.

WAINSCOTTING   In a round room, pole-and-wattle construction built from and around the rear of the bench (see Figures 3.4, 3.7).

WALL PLATE   An intramural beam partially supporting the ends of the primary beams.

WALL TIE–POLES   Small poles running through contiguous parallel walls.

WATTLE–AND–DAUB   Pole-and-wattle construction covered with mud plaster (daub).  Compare JACAL.

WYTHE   A line of stones in the horizontal plane.  Compare COURSE.

# Appendix B
# Construction Rates

Tables B.1-7 detail labor estimates in person-hours (PH) for various elements of Chacoan building. These estimates are most applicable to building from 1025 to 1105.

Labor rates are very rough approximations. As with all crafts, construction rates will vary greatly with individual proficiency. Masons, in particular, are notoriously variable in production. Highly skilled brick masons can produce at a level two to three times higher than reference book rates. Table B.1, Notes 1 and 2, describe variation in the work of National Park Service stabilization crews: a "fast" crew can be over three times as productive as a "slow" crew. These tables use "average" rates when a range was evident.

Some figures in the tables are partly arbitrary. For example, the source of timber for Chacoan building has been a topic of extensive argument and speculation (but see Betancourt et al. 1984). At present, it seems likely that small stands of ponderosa pine were present at the heads of rincons as far downstream as Pueblo Bonito, but extensive forests were probably limited to the higher elevations of Lobo Mesa, Mount Taylor, and the Chuska Mountains. As noted in Table B.2, Note 4, a procurement distance was set at 50 km, the distance between Pueblo Bonito and Lobo Mesa at Kin Ya'a. Similar decisions have been made for other aspects of the tables, e.g., distance to rock sources. The source of rock is not nearly as mysterious as the source of timbers, but the actual distance from rock sources to the several construction sites varies considerably.

Most sources on labor rates were in English measure; all have been translated into metric units. Steve Adams' observations of National Park Service crews (Steve Adams, personal communication, 1982) have been manipulated and remanipulated from his data sheets; errors or incongruities should not be blamed on Adams. Erasmus' (1965) figures for Maya stone work, used in earlier labor estimates (Lekson and Judge 1978), are much higher than the rates used here; however, Erasmus' rates for excavation seem reasonable and are used here. Transportation rates for bulk materials (soil and rock) were taken from Aaron and Bonsignore (1975), based on formulas developed for the United Nations. These formulas determine the time required for a defined task, given a work load, transport distance and length of work day. Person-hours per unit of material are estimated by assuming a 10 hour day and then solving for the rate in PH per unit moved. Transport rates for timbers are described in Table B.2, Note 4.

The rates used are neither minimal nor maximal. They represent judgments (my own, and those of the authorities cited) of reasonable production by competent craftspersons and laborers. Since we can assume that Chacoan builders were at least competent, this clearly was not a situation for modern experiment and replication. The author has done stabilization masonry work, and is painfully aware that to become moderately competent would take several years of training and practice. Although becoming a patient mason would provide a comfortable backup for the tenuously employed archaeologist, it could not be justified for this research. A pity.

Table B.1.  Type III walls, Unit = $m^3$.

|  | Quantity | Rate | Subtotal | Notes |
|---|---|---|---|---|
| Stone | 0.6 $m^3$ | 14.0 PH/$mx^3$ | 8.4 PH | 1; see Table B.5 |
| Mortar | 0.4 $m^3$ | 4.4 PH/$mx^3$ | 1.7 PH | 1; see Table B.6 |
| Labor | 1.0 $m^3$ | 28.25PH/$m^3$ | 28.5 PH | 2 |

Total = 36.6 PH/$m^3$

Notes:

1. Proportions of materials in wall: 60% stone, 40% mortar.  Compare Tsegi phase walls, northeastern Arizona: 40% stone, 60% mortar (Steve Adams, personal communication, 1982).  Compare brickwork (3/8" joints): 75% brick, 25% mortar (Page 1959).

2. Adams (personal communication, 1982) estimated rates for "laying, minor shaping and mortar mixing" in Type III wall construction:

| Slow | 47.09 PH/$m^3$ |
|---|---|
| Average | 28.25 PH/$m^3$ |
| Fast | 14.13 PH/$m^3$ |

The average rate of 28.25 PH/$m^3$ is used here.  Compare 40.44 PH/$m^3$ (cited in Shimada 1978) and 47.09 PH/$m^3$ (National Park Service "rule of thumb," which includes other types of labor, probably established at Chaco.)

Rates for laying only have been estimated as follows:

| Slow | 11.11 PH/$m^3$ | (Steve Adams, personal communication, 1982) |
|---|---|---|
| Fast | 5.00 PH/$m^3$ | (Steve Adams, personal communication, 1982) |
| Fast | 4.56 PH/$m^3$ | (Cecil Werrito, personal communication, 1982) |

Mean of these three values is 6.89 PH/$m^3$.  Compare brickwork laying at 6.52 PH/$m^3$ (Page 1959).

Shimada (1978) measured rates for laying core and facing stones as follows:

| Facing | 17.65 PH/$m^3$ |
|---|---|
| Core | 7.06 PH/$m^3$ |

Using a ratio of 66% facing and 33% core, these rates produce a composite rate of about 13.98 PH/$m^3$; this compares with the "slow" rate given above.

Recently (December 1983), the stabilization crew at Chaco built masonry cases for new exhibits at the Visitors Center.  This provided an opportunity to observe Type III construction of new walls, rather than estimate construction rates from the stabilization and repair of existing walls.  Rates derived from this construction for laying only averaged 13.25 PH/$m^3$, slightly slower than Adams' slow rate.

Table B.1 (continued)

In modern brickwork, the mason's helper (hod carrier) contributes 60 to 100% of the mason's PH for each cubic meter (Page 1959).  Assuming that the ratio of mason's activities (laying) to helper's activities (mortar mix and transport) is approximately similar in Type III work, and that Type III laying requires 6.89 PH/m$^3$, 80% (an arbitrary "average" of 60% and 100%) of labor is about 5.51 PH/m$^3$.  Labor in "minor shaping" can then be estimated:

$$29.82 - 6.89 - 5.51 = 17.42 \text{ PH/m}^3$$

That is, about 60% of labor is expended in "minor shaping" and related activities.  Clearly, more substantial shaping requirements (e.g., grinding) will greatly increase labor estimates.

Table B.2. Flat roof, Unit = 5 $m^2$.

| Beams: | Quantity | Procure | Process | Transport | Install |
|---|---|---|---|---|---|
| Primary | 1 | 0.7 PH | 2.1 PH | 53.4 PH | 0.5 PH |
| Secondary | 15 | 3.0 PH | 9.0 PH | 45.0 PH | 1.0 PH |
| Subtotal | | 3.7 PH | 11.1 PH | 98.4 PH | 1.5 PH |
| Notes | 1 | 2 | 3 | 4 | 5 |

| Surface: | | | | | | Notes |
|---|---|---|---|---|---|---|
| Closing material | ? | ? | ? | ? | 12.0 PH | 6 |
| Adobe | 0.25 $m^3$ | --------1.1 PH------------ | | | incl.above | 7 |
| Dry soil | 0.5 $m^3$ | --------1.7 PH------------ | | | incl.above | 7 |

Total, beams = 3.7 + 11.1 + 98.4 = 113.2 PH
Total, surfaces = 1.1 + 1.7 + 12.0 = 14.8 PH

Total = 128 PH/5 $m^2$

Notes:

1.   Number of primaries and secondaries in 5 $m^2$.  The minimum length of secondaries was determined from the spacing of primaries, which equals the minimum span of the supported secondary.  Mean spacing of primaries is 1.66 m (sd=0.28 m, N=100); thus the mean length of secondaries is about 1.7 m.  The mean length of exposed primaries should equal mean room width. Mean room width is 2.61 m;  however, this statistic reflects numerous subdivisions of earlier rooms, and hence is not a reliable measure of primary beam length.  A more accurate measure was derived from the distance between parallel walls of major building stages.  This produced a mean of 3.00 m (sd=0.31 m, N=76), which is used here.

Given a secondary span of 1.7 m and a primary span of 3.0 m, the area of roof between primaries is 5.1 $m^2$, or about 5 $m^2$; thus, there is one primary beam for each 5 $m^2$ of roof area.  To determine the number of secondaries, it is necessary to estimate the number of secondary beams supported on each primary.  Mean secondary diameter is about 10 cm (see Note 2, below); 30 secondaries can then be supported on a 3.0 m span.  Intact roofs and beam sockets suggest that secondaries were positioned either alternately or in alternate pairs on primaries; therefore of 30 supported secondaries, only one-half, or 15, would support the 5 $m^2$ of roof between primaries.  Thus for each 5 $m^2$ of roof area, there should be 1 primary and 15 secondaries.  Note that in a 15 $m^2$ roof, this formula estimates 3 primaries;  one of these would be coincident with a cross wall. Measurements for mean primary spacing did not include primaries within 40 cm of cross walls, which are not infrequent.

To illustrate the use of these figures, they can be compared to the "average" Chacoan room.  Mean room length is 4.73 m; mean room width is 2.61 m.  In a room 4.73 m long, we would expect 3 spans of secondaries on 2 primary beams (4.73/1.70 = 2.8, or 3 spans).  In a room 2.61m wide, we would expect 26 secondaries resting on each primary (2.6m/0.1m = 26); with alternate placement, each span of secondaries would consist of 13 beams; 3 spans thus equal 39 secondaries.  These figures, 2 primaries and 39 secondaries, agree closely with the numbers derived by the formula.

2.   Procurement refers only to cutting down trees.  Rates for this operation were determined by using the formula for cutting with stone axes given in Carneiro (1979:48),

Table   B.2   (continued)

Time in hours = (2.3 x diam in feet) x (1.3 x specific gravity of the wood)

The diameters of primary and secondary beams are (cf. Dean and Warren 1983: Table V:12):

|           | mean     | sd      | N  |
|-----------|----------|---------|----|
| Primary   | 21.95 cm | 1.76 cm | 76 |
| Secondary | 9.22 cm  | 1.17 cm | 73 |

The specific gravity of ponderosa pine is 0.39.  Using Carniero's formula, a primary could be cut down in 30 minutes and a secondary in 2 minutes.

An alternate estimate was derived from data in Sarayadar and Shimada (1971): in this experiment, maple (specific gravity 0.57) was cut at a rate of 4.6 cm in 16 minutes.  Assuming that efficiency of cutting varies inversely with specific gravity of the wood, a rate for pine was estimated at about 6.8 cm in 16 minutes.  Using this rate, estimates for cutting were derived as follows: primary, 52 minutes; secondary, 21 minutes.  Estimated rates were established by taking the average of the two estimates, thus:

|           | Carneiro | Sarayadar & Shimada | Average    |
|-----------|----------|---------------------|------------|
| Primary   | 30       | 52                  | 41 minutes |
| Secondary | 2        | 21                  | 12 minutes |

The rate used here for secondaries (12 minutes) compares with a time of 6 minutes reported by Morris (1939:137) for cutting and trimming a cottonwood 10 cm in diameter.  Morris noted that pine, being harder than cottonwood, would require more time.

Coles (1979:102) summarizing several tree-felling experiments, concluded "...any tree up to about 20 cm in diameter can be knocked down by a stone ax in under 15 minutes, while larger trees can take three or four times as long."

3.  Processing simply triples the procurement rate.  This arbitrary estimate presumably includes topping, trimming, bark stripping, reduction of knots, and cutting ends flush.

4.  Transport rates were determined by using a 3 km/hr rate loaded and 5 km/hr rate unloaded for the most likely sources for beams, i.e., Lobo Mesa behind Kin Ya'a.  Lobo Mesa is the nearest existing ponderosa forest; the distance from Pueblo Bonito through Kin Ya'a and to the nearest extensive stands of ponderosa pine on Lobo Mesa is 48 km, measured along the South Road.

Secondaries were assumed to be 1.70 m long (see Note 1).  Primary length was determined by the average span (3 m) plus two times half the average wall width (0.6 m) for beam seating.  Thus total primary length was 3.60 m.  Weight of dry ponderosa primaries was about 15.92 kg/m; secondaries were 2.90 kg/m.  Total weight for a primary is thus 57.31 kg; total weight of a secondary is 4.93 kg.

The exact method of transportation is unknown.  I have assumed that beams were carried rather than dragged, even though dragging would be more efficient.  For a single primary, a team of two would each have a load of approximately 30 kg.  Multiple secondaries could have been carried by a single person; with a 44 kg load (Aaron and Bonsignore 1975), one person could transport 9 secondaries.

Using these loads, the following PH values were calculated for individual primaries and secondaries:

| Primaries:       |         |
|------------------|---------|
| 2 persons/beam   | 53.4 PH |
| Secondaries:     |         |
| 9 beams/person   | 3.0 PH  |

5.  Installation PH requirements from A.D. Parra (personal communication, 1982).

Table B.2 (continued)

6.  Closing materials are highly variable, and can include willow rods, juniper splints, boards, rush mats, bark, etc.  Most roofs included at least one layer of juniper splints.  Ill defined variability in closing materials and lack of controlled rates for production of those materials made labor estimates impossible.  Installation labor was estimated by Adams, see Note 7.

7.  Quantity of adobe was estimated at 5 cm thick over 5 m$^2$, or 0.25 m$^3$.  Quantity of dry soil was estimated at 10 cm thick over 5 m$^2$, or 0.5 m$^3$.  For rates see Table B.5.  Installation rates for adobe, soil, and closing material are for a roof slightly more elaborate than most Chacoan roofs (Steve Adams, personal communication, 1982).

Table B.3.  Dome roofs, Unit = 1 dome room.

|  | Quantity | Procurement | Transport | Processing |
|---|---|---|---|---|
| Primary | 90 | 61.2 PH | 4806.0 PH | 183.6 PH |
| Secondary | 105 | 21.0 PH | 315.0 PH | 63.0 PH |
| Subtotals |  | 82.2 PH | 5121.0 PH | 246.6 PH |

Total = 82.2 + 5121.0 + 246.6 PH = 5449.8 PH

Note:

Quantities of timber required for domed (corbelled) roofs were computed by reference to the intact roof of Kiva L at Pueblo Bonito (Judd 1964:180) Judd's description allows the estimation of minimal timber requirements by (1) setting each set of beams as far forward (towards the center of the room) as possible; and (2) by measuring lengths from point-of-contact to point-of-contact (assuming minimum overlap) except as noted by Judd (i.e., "each layer above the three lowest was braced both ways by a longer member" reaching the wall, [Judd 1964:180]), and (3) assuming a 'nominal' 10 cm diameter for all beams.  With these assumptions and the data in Judd (1964: 180), the roof of Kiva L was reconstructed (on paper), and included the following beams:

| Length in meters | N |
|---|---|
| 1.25-1.75 | 79 |
| 1.75-2.25 | 14 |
| 2.25-2.75 | 12 |
| 2.75-3.25 | 12 |
| 3.25-3.75 | 12 |
| 3.75-4.25 | 52 |
| 4.25-4.75 | 14 |

For ease of computation, beams 1.25 to 2.75 m in length (mean length= 1.68 m, sd=0.34 m, N=105) were considered to be secondaries, and beams 2.75 to 4.75 m in length (mean length=3.88 m, sd=0.43 m, N=90) were considered to be primaries.  Labor requirements for each were taken from Table B.2.

Kiva L had a diameter of 7.0 m; mean round room diameter for Chaco-style round rooms is 7.2 m (see Chapter 3).  Because Kiva L was very near the mean in size, the timbering of Kiva L was used as a standard for all round rooms.

Roof area over round rooms is also included under roof area totals for flat roofs.  Given a diameter of 7.0 m, the roof area of Kiva L was about 38.48 m$^2$.  Using the formula developed in Table B.2, this area translates into 7.7 primaries and 116 secondaries -- close to the "135 shorter pieces completing and leveling the fourteenth or uppermost layer" (Judd 1964: 180).  Thus roof requirements for round rooms include both the flat roof area (Table B.2) and the domed roof constant (Table B.3).

Construction labor could not be estimated, so it is not included.

Table B.4.   Stone, Unit = 1 m$^3$.

| Method | Procurement | Transport | Total | Notes |
|---|---|---|---|---|
| Quarry | 7.1 PH/m$^3$ | 7.0 PH/m$^3$ | 14.1 PH/m$^3$ | 1,2 |
| Collect | ----------14 PH/m$^3$---------- | | 14.0 PH/m$^3$ | 3 |

Rate = <u>14.0 PH/m$^3$</u>

<u>Notes</u>:

1.  The labor estimate for quarrying surface rock with wooden prying tools is derived from Erasmus (1965).  Erasmus noted 1700 kg limestone in beds about 70 cm thick were quarried in 5 hours:  1700 kg of limestone at 2.4 gm/cm$^3$ (Winkler 1973) equals 0.71 m$^3$ stone; 0.71 m$^3$ in 5 hours equals 0.14 m$^3$ per hour, or 7.14 PH/m$^3$.

2.  Transport rates from Aaron and Bonsignore (1975) using 44 kg load, 230 m distance and no vertical gain.  A mean distance from each site to either talus or exposed bedrock was calculated at 229 m (sd=233 m, N=11).   In fact, sandstone was sometimes quarried from specific locations on exposed bedrock, and in other cases collected from talus at the base of the cliffs. Forty-four kilograms is equivalent to a block of sandstone measuring about 50 cm x 20 cm x 20 cm.

3.  Labor estimates for collection from talus materials are derived from Adams (personal communication, 1982); Adams' measurements are from Betatakin (talus immediately adjacent to work) and include both selection and transport.

Table B.5.  Mortar, Unit = 1 m³.

| | Quantity | Procurement | Processing | Transport | Notes |
|---|---|---|---|---|---|
| Earth | 1.0 m³ | 1.9 PH/m³ | included in wall labor | 1.4 PH/m³ | 1,2,3,4 |
| Water | 0.3 m³ | -- | included in wall labor | 1.1 PH/m³ | 1,3,4 |

Subtotals:

1.9 PH/m³                    2.5 PH/m³

Rate = 1.9 + 2.5 = 4.4 PH/m³

Notes:

1.  Materials in 1 m³ mortar: 1 m³ earth, 0.33 m³ water (from Steve Adams, personal communication, 1982; Eyre 1935:Table 7).

2.  The rate for earth procurement (excavation) is from Erasmus (1965): 1.9 PH/m³ for excavation with digging stick.  Compare 2.08 PH/m³ for hand excavation (medium soil, dry) with pick and shovel (Page 1959).

3.  Processing (mixing) included in rate for wall labor, Table B.1.

4.  Transport rates from Aaron and Bonsignore (1965), assume on-site procurement, using 22 kg load, and no vertical gain, 50 m distance.  Two hundred, 50-meter rates for earth and water would be 7.0 and 6.0 PH, respectively.  A 22 kg load for water would require 5.5 jars of an 8 liter capacity total in each load.  A 22 kg load for earth equals a cylindrical container about 40 cm diameter by 15 cm height.

Table B.6. Lintels, Unit = 1 door.

| | Quantity | Procure/Process/Transport/Install |
|---|---|---|
| Lintel | 8 | 30.9 PH |

Note:  Average number of lintel beams per door is about 8 (mean=8.18, sd= 1.60, N=50).  Labor rates taken from Table B.2, assuming that one lintel equals one secondary beam (in fact, lintel beams are slightly smaller than secondaries).  The number of doors is computed by dividing the linear meters of wall by 7.34, a constant devised from all excavated ruins.

Table B.7. Foundations, Unit = 1 linear meter of ground floor wall.

| | Quantity | Excavation | Construction |
|---|---|---|---|
| Foundation | 0.5 x 0.5 x 1.0 m | 0.5 PH | 10.0 PH |

Rate = 0.5 + 10.0 = 10.5 PH/m

Note:  Rate for excavation taken from Table B.5, Note 2.  Rate for one construction taken as identical to rate for Type III wall, Table B.1.

# Appendix C
# Key to Tree-Ring Dating Symbols

B — bark present

G — beetle galleries are present on the surface of the specimen

L — a characteristic surface patination and smoothness, which develops on beams stripped of bark, is present

c — the outermost ring is continuous around the full circumference of the specimen. This symbol is used only if a full section is present

r — less than a full section is present, but the outermost ring is continuous around available circumference

v — a subjective judgment that, although there is no direct evidence of the true outside on the specimen, the date is within a very few years of being a cutting date

vv — there is no way of estimating how far the last ring is from the true outside

+ — one or more rings may be missing near the end of the ring series whose presence or absence cannot be determined because the specimen does not extend far enough to provide an adequate check

++ — a ring count is necessary due to the fact that beyond a certain point the specimen could not be dated

The symbols B, G, L, c, and r indicate cutting dates in order of decreasing confidence, unless a + or ++ is also present.

The symbols L, G, and B may be used in any combination with each other or with the other symbols except v and vv. The r and c symbols are mutually exclusive, but may be used with L, G, B, +, and ++. The v and vv are also mutually exclusive and may be used with the + and ++. The + and ++ are mutually exclusive, but may be used in combination with all the other symbols.

Note: From Robinson et al. (1974:4-5).

- - - - - - - - -

? — tentative provenience, this study only (not a Laboratory of Tree-ring Research symbol).

# References

AABERG, STEPHEN, and JAY BONSIGNORE
1975    A consideration of time and labor expenditure in the construction process at Teotihuacan Pyramid of the Sun and Poverty Point Mound. IN Three papers on Mesoamerican archaeology, edited by J.A. Graham and R.F. Heizer, pp. 39-78, Contributions of the University of California Archaeological Research Facility 24.

AKINS, NANCY J.
1982    Analyses of the faunal remains from Pueblo Alto, Chaco Canyon. On file, Division of Cultural Research, National Park Service, Albuquerque.

AKINS, NANCY J., and WILLIAM B. GILLESPIE
1979    Summary report of archaeological investigations at Una Vida, Chaco Canyon, New Mexico. On file, Division of Cultural Research, National Park Service, Albuquerque.

AKINS, NANCY J., and JOHN D. SCHELBERG
1981    Evidence for organizational complexity as seen from the mortuary practices at Chaco Canyon. Paper presented at the 46th annual meeting of the Society for American Archaeology, San Diego.

ALEXANDER, CHRISTOPHER
1964    Notes on the synthesis of form. Harvard University Press, Cambridge.

BANNISTER, BRYANT
1965    Tree-ring dating of the archaeological sites in the Chaco Canyon region, New Mexico. Southwest Parks and Monuments Association Technical Series 6(2).

BANNISTER, BRYANT, and WILLIAM J. ROBINSON
1978    The dendrochronology of Room 93, Chetro Ketl. IN Wooden ritual artifacts from Chaco Canyon, New Mexico: The Chetro Ketl Collection, by R. G. Vivian, D. N. Dodgen, and G. H. Hartman, Appendix E. Anthropological Papers of the University of Arizona 22.

BETANCOURT, JULIO
1979    Inventory and provenience check: Tree-ring specimens from Chetro Ketl, Chaco Canyon. On file, Division of Cultural Research, National Park Service, Albuquerque, and the Laboratory of Tree-Ring Research, Tucson.

BETANCOURT, JULIO, JEFFREY S. DEAN, and HERBERT M. HULL
1984    Prehistoric long-distance transport of spruce and fir construction beams, Chaco Canyon, New Mexico. Ms. on file, Laboratory of Tree-Ring Research, University of Arizona, Tucson.

BICKFORD, F. T.
1890    Prehistoric cave-dwellings. Century Magazine 40:896-911.

BRADFORD, JAMES
1981    Historic Structure Report, Tsin Kletzin ruin, Chaco Culture National Historical Park, New Mexico. Southwest Cultural Resources Center, National Park Service Southwest Regional Office, Santa Fe, New Mexico.

BRADLEY, ZORRO A., and WILFRED D. LOGAN
1969 Prospectus: Chaco Canyon Studies. National Park Service, Washington, D.C. On file, Division of Cultural Research, National Park Service, Albuquerque.

BRAND, DONALD D., FLORENCE M. HAWLEY, and FRANK C. HIBBEN
1937 Tseh So, a small house ruin, Chaco Canyon, New Mexico. Preliminary report. University of New Mexico Bulletin 308, Anthropological Series 2(2).

BRETERNITZ, CORY DALE
1976 An analysis of axes and mauls from Chaco Canyon, New Mexico. On file, Division of Cultural Research, National Park Service, Albuquerque.

CARAVATY, RAYMOND D., and HARRY C. PLUMMER
1960 Principles of clay masonry construction. Structural Clay Products Institute, Washington, D.C.

CARNIERO, ROBERT L.
1979 Tree felling with the stone ax. IN Ethnoarchaeology, edited by Carol Kramer, pp 21-58. Columbia University Press, New York.

COLES, JOHN M.
1979 Experimental archaeology. Academic Press, New York.

DEAN, JEFFREY S., and RICHARD L. WARREN
1983 Dendrochronology. IN The architecture and dendrochronology of Chetro Ketl, Chaco Canyon, New Mexico, edited by Stephen H. Lekson, pp. 105-240. Reports of the Chaco Center 6.

DiPESO, CHARLES C.
1974 Medio period architecture. IN Casas Grandes, a fallen trading center of the Gran Chichimeca 4. Amerind Foundation Series 9, by C.C. DiPeso, J.B. Rinaldo, and G.J. Fenner. The Amerind Foundation and Northland Press, Dragoon and Flagstaff.

DRAGER, DWIGHT L., and THOMAS R. LYONS
1984 Remote sensing, photogrammetry in archaeology: The Chaco mapping project. Remote sensing: A handbook for archaeologists and cultural resource managers: Supplement 10. Division of Cultural Research, National Park Service, Albuquerque.

ERASMUS, CHARLES J.
1965 Monument building: Some field experiments. Southwestern Journal of Anthropology 21(4):277-301.

EYRE, THOMAS TAYLOR
1935 The physical properties of adobe used as a building material. University of New Mexico Engineering Series Bulletin 263, vol. 1 (3).

FERDON, EDWIN N.
1955 A trial survey of Mexican-Southwestern architectural parallels. School of American Research Monographs 21.

FERGUSON, C. W.
1959 Growth rings in woody shrubs as potential aids in archaeological interpretation. The Kiva 25(2): 24-30.

FORD, RICHARD I.
1968 An ecological analysis involving the population of San Juan Pueblo, New Mexico. Unpublished Ph.D. dissertation, University of Michigan.

FRANSTEAD, DENNIS, and OSWALD WERNER
1974 The ethnogeography of the Chaco Canyon area. On file, Division of Cultural Research, National Park Service, Albuquerque.

GLADWIN, HAROLD STERLING
1945 The Chaco Branch: Excavations at White Mound and in the Red Mesa Valley. Medallion Papers 33.

GLADWIN, HAROLD STERLING, and WINIFRED GLADWIN
1934 A method for the designation of cultures and their variations. Medallion Papers 15.

GREBINGER, PAUL
1973 Prehistoric social organization in Chaco Canyon, New Mexico: An alternative reconstruction. The Kiva 39(1):3-23.

HALLASI, JUDITH ANN
1979 Archeological excavation at the Escalante site, Dolores, Colorado, 1975 and 1976. Part 2, The Archeology and Stabilization of the Dominguez and Escalante Ruins, Cultural Resources Series 7. Bureau of Land Management, Denver.

HASSAN, FEKRI A.
1981 Demographic archaeology. Academic Press, New York.

HAWLEY, FLORENCE M.
1934  The significance of the dated pre-
      history of Chetro Ketl, Chaco Can-
      yon, New Mexico. Monographs of
      the School of American Research,
      2.

1938  The family tree of Chaco Canyon
      masonry.  American  Antiquity
      3(3):247-255.

HAYES, ALDEN C.
1964  The  archaeological  survey  of
      Wetherill Mesa.  National Park
      Service  Archaeological  Research
      Series 7A. Washington, D.C.

1981  A survey of Chaco Canyon archeo-
      logy.  IN Archeological surveys of
      Chaco Canyon, New Mexico, by A. C.
      Hayes, D. M. Brugge, and W.J.
      Judge, pp. 1-68. National Park
      Service Archeological Series 18A:
      Chaco Canyon Studies.  Washington,
      D.C.

HAYES, ALDEN C., and JAMES A. LANCASTER
1975  Badger  House  community,  Mesa
      Verde  National  Park.  National
      Park  Service  Publications  in
      Archeology  7E:  Wetherill  Mesa
      Studies.  Washington, D.C.

HAYES, ALDEN C., and THOMAS C. WINDES
1975  An Anasazi shrine in Chaco Can-
      yon.  IN Collected papers in
      honor of Florence Hawley Ellis,
      edited by Theodore R. Frisbie, pp.
      143-156.  Papers of the Archaeo-
      logical Society of New Mexico 2.

HENDERSON, SAM R.
1972  Hungo Pavie Ruin, Chaco Canyon
      National  Monument,  New  Mexico,
      Stabilization Report - 1971.  Ruins
      Stabilization Unit, National Park
      Service Arizona Archeological Cen-
      ter, Tucson.

HEWETT, EDGAR L.
1936  The Chaco Canyon and its monu-
      ments.  Handbooks of  Archaeo-
      logical History, University of
      New Mexico Press, Albuquerque.

HODGE, FREDERICK WEBB
1923  Circular kivas near Hawikuh, New
      Mexico.  Contributions from the
      Museum of the American Indian 7
      (1).

HOLSINGER, S.J.
1901  Report on prehistoric ruins of
      Chaco Canyon, New Mexico. Ordered
      by General Land Office Letter "P,"

December 18, 1900, General Land
Office.  Ms. on file, National
Archives, Washington, D.C.

JACKSON, WILLIAM H.
1878  Report  on  the  ancient  ruins
      examined in 1875 and 1877.  IN
      Tenth Annual Report of the U.S.
      Geological and Geographical Sur-
      vey.  Washington, D.C.

JUDD, NEIL MERTON
1920  National  Geographic  Society
      reconnaissance of Chaco Canyon,
      New  Mexico:  Diary of Neil M.
      Judd, Papers of Neil M. Judd,
      Box 6.  Smithsonian Institution
      National  Anthropological  Ar-
      chives, Washington, D.C.

1927  The architectural evolution of
      Pueblo Bonito.  Proceedings of
      the National Academy of Sciences
      13 (7):561-563.

1954  The material culture of Pueblo
      Bonito.  Smithsonian Miscellan-
      eous Collections 124.

1959  Pueblo del Arroyo, Chaco Canyon,
      New Mexico.  Smithsonian Miscel-
      laneous Collections 138.

1964  The  architecture  of  Pueblo
      Bonito.  Smithsonian Miscellan-
      eous Collections 147(1).

JUDGE, W. JAMES
1983  Chaco Canyon - San Juan Basin.
      Paper presented at the School of
      American Research Seminar "Dy-
      namics of Southwestern Prehis-
      tory," School of American Re-
      search, Santa Fe.

JUDGE, W. JAMES, H. WOLCOTT TOLL,
WILLIAM B. GILLESPIE, and
STEPHEN H. LEKSON
1981  Tenth  Century  Developments  in
      Chaco Canyon.  IN Collected
      papers in honor of Erik Keller-
      man Reed, edited by A. H.
      Schroeder, pp. 65-98.  Archaeo-
      logical Society of New Mexico
      6.

KIDDER, ALFRED VINCENT
1958  Pecos, New Mexico:  Archaeo-
      logical notes.  Papers of the
      Peabody Foundation for Archae-
      ology 5.  Phillips Academy, An-
      dover.

KINCAID, CHRIS (editor)
1983  Chaco Roads Project Phase I.
      Bureau of Land Management, Santa
      Fe.

KLUCKHOHN, CLYDE, and PAUL REITER
(editors)
1939 Preliminary report on the 1937 excavations, Bc 50-51, Chaco Canyon, New Mexico. *University of New Mexico Bulletin* 345, *Anthropological Series* 3:2.

LEINAU, ALICE
1934 *Sanctuaries in the ancient pueblo of Chetro Ketl*. Unpublished M.A. thesis, University of New Mexico, Albuquerque.

LEKSON, STEPHEN H.
1981a Cognitive frameworks and Chacoan architecture. *New Mexico Journal of Science* 21 (1):27-36.

1981b *Architecture in archaeology: A critical bibliography of sources for theory*. On file, Division of Cultural Research, National Park Service, Albuquerque.

1981c Standing architecture and the interpretation of local and regional organization of Chaco Canyon. Paper presented at the 46th Annual Meeting of the Society of American Archaeology, San Diego.

1983a Chacoan architecture in continental context. IN *Proceedings of the Anasazi Symposium 1981*, compiled by J.E. Smith, pp. 183-194. Mesa Verde Museum Association, Mesa Verde, Colorado.

1983b The architecture and dendrochronology of Chetro Ketl, Chaco Canyon, New Mexico. *Reports of the Chaco Center* 6. Division of Cultural Research, National Park Service, Albuquerque.

1984a *The architecture of Talus Unit*. On file, Division of Cultural Research, National Park Service, Albuquerque.

1984b Dating the Hubbard Tri-wall and other tri-wall structures. *Southwestern Lore* 49 (4):15-23.

LEKSON, STEPHEN H., and W. JAMES JUDGE
1978 Architecture of the Bonito Phase of Chaco Canyon. Paper presented at the American Anthropological Association Annual Meeting, Los Angeles.

LEKSON, STEPHEN H., and PETER J. McKENNA
1979 *Wall elevations of major Chacoan ruins*. On file, Division of Cultural Research, National Park Service, Albuquerque.

LISTER, ROBERT H., and FLORENCE C. LISTER
1981 *Chaco Canyon: Archaeology and archaeologists*. University of New Mexico Press, Albuquerque.

LOVE, MARIAN F.
1974 A survey of the distribution of T-shaped doorways in the Greater Southwest. IN Collected papers in honor of Florence Hawley Ellis, edited by Theodore R. Frisbie, pp. 296-311. *Papers of the Archaeological Society of New Mexico* 2.

MARSHALL, MICHAEL P., JOHN R. STEIN, RICHARD W. LOOSE, and JUDITH E. NOVOTNY
1979 *Anasazi communities in the San Juan Basin*. Public Service Company, Albuquerque, and the Historic Preservation Bureau, Santa Fe.

MARTIN, PAUL S.
1936 Lowry Ruin in southwestern Colorado. *Field Museum of Natural History, Anthropological Series* (23) (1).

MARTIN, PAUL S., and FRED PLOG
1973 *The archaeology of Arizona: A study of the Southwest region*. Natural History Press, Garden City.

MARTIN, PAUL S., and ELIZABETH S. WILLIS
1940 Anasazi painted pottery in the Field Museum of Natural History. *Anthropology Memoirs, Field Museum of Natural History* 5.

MARUCA, MARY
1982 *An administrative history of the Chaco Project*. National Park Service, Washington, D.C. On file, Division of Cultural Research, National Park Service, Albuquerque.

MAYER, MARTIN T.
1971 *Tsin Kletzin--Pueblo Bonito Stabilization Report*. Ms. on file, Chaco Culture National Historical Park.

1972 *Stabilization of Hungo Pavi, 1972*. Ms. on file, Chaco Culture National Historical Park.

McLELLAN, GEORGE E.
1969  The origin, development, and typology of Anasazi kivas and Great Kivas. Unpublished Ph.D. dissertation, University of Colorado, Boulder.

McNITT, FRANK
1957  Richard Wetherill: Anasazi. University of New Mexico Press, Albuquerque.

MILLER, JAMES MARSHALL
1937  The G kivas of Chetro Ketl. Unpublished M.A. thesis, University of Southern California, Los Angeles.

MINDELEFF, VICTOR
1891  A study of Pueblo architecture: Tusayan and Cibola. IN Eighth Annual Report of the Bureau of Ethnology 1886-1887. Washington, D.C.

MORENON, E. PIERRE
1977  Architectural analysis and intra-site variation: A case study. Unpublished Ph.D. dissertation, Southern Methodist University, Dallas.

MORRIS, DON, and DAVID W. KAYSER
1966  Ruins stabilization of New Alto, Chaco Canyon National Monument, New Mexico. Ruins Stabilization Unit, National Park Service Arizona Archaeological Center, Globe, Arizona.

MORRIS, EARL H.
1919  The Aztec Ruin. Anthropological Papers of the American Museum of Natural History 26(1).

1921  The house of the Great Kiva at the Aztec Ruin. Anthropological Papers of the American Museum of Natural History 26(2).

1928  Notes on excavations in the Aztec Ruin. Anthropological Papers of the American Museum of Natural History 26(5).

1939  Archaeological studies in the La Plata District. Carnegie Institution of Washington Publication 519.

OUTWATER, J. ODGEN, JR.
1957  The Pre-Columbian stone cutting techniques of the Mexican Plateau. American Antiquity 22(3): 258-264.

PAGE, JOHN S.
1959  Estimator's General Construction Man-hour Manual. Gulf Publishing Company, Houston.

PIERSON, LLOYD M.
1956  A history of Chaco Canyon National Monument. Chaco Center Archive #726. On file, Division of Cultural Research, National Park Service, Albuquerque.

PEPPER, GEORGE H.
1920  Pueblo Bonito. Anthropological Papers of the American Museum of Natural History 27.

POWELL, J.W.
1892  Ninth annual report of the Bureau of American Ethnology to the Secretary of the Smithsonian Institution 1887-1888. Government Printing Office, Washington, D.C.

POWERS, ROBERT P., WILLIAM B. GILLESPIE, and STEPHEN H. LEKSON
1983  The outlier survey, a regional view of settlement in the San Juan Basin. Reports of the Chaco Center 3. Division of Cultural Research, National Park Service, Albuquerque.

REED, ERIK K.
1947  Flood damage to Chetro Ketl. El Palacio 54(10):238-240.

REITER, PAUL
1933  The ancient pueblo of Chetro Ketl. Unpublished M.A. thesis, University of New Mexico, Albuquerque.

1946  Form and function in some prehistoric ceremonial structures in the Southwest. Unpublished Ph.D. dissertation, Harvard University, Cambridge.

ROBERTS, FRANK H.H., JR.
n.d.  Papers of F.H.H. Roberts, miscellaneous collections #4851, Smithsonian Institution National Archives, Washington, D.C. Chaco Center Archives #2099 and #2108. On file, Division of Cultural Research, National Park Service, Albuquerque.

1927  The ceramic sequence in the Chaco Canyon, New Mexico, and its relation to the cultures of the San Juan Basin. Unpublished Ph.D. dissertation, Harvard University, Cambridge.

1938  Chaco Canyon masonry. American Antiquity 4(1):60-61.

ROBINSON, WILLIAM J., BRUCE G. HARRILL,
and RICHARD L. WARREN
1974 Tree-ring dates from New Mexico
G: Chaco-Gobernador Area. The
Laboratory of Tree-Ring Research,
University of Arizona, Tucson.

ROHN, ARTHUR H.
1971 Mug House. National Park Service
Archaeological Research Series
7D. Washington, D.C.

ROYS, LAWRENCE
1936 Lowry Ruin as an introduction to
the study of Southwestern
masonry. IN Lowry Ruin in southwestern Colorado, by Paul S.
Martin, pp.115-142. Field Museum
of Natural History, Anthropological Series 23(1).

SARAYDER, STEPHEN, and IZUMI SHIMADA
1971 A quantitative comparison of
efficiency between a stone ax and
a steel ax. American Antiquity
36(2):216-217.

SCHELBERG, JOHN DANIEL
1982 Economic and social development
as an adaptation to a marginal
environment in Chaco Canyon, New
Mexico. Ph.D. dissertation
Northwestern University, Evans-
ton.

SCHUMM, S.A., and R.J. CHORLEY
1964 The fall of Threatening Rock,
American Journal of Science 262
(9):1041-1054.

SENTER, FLORENCE H.
1938 Southwestern dated ruins: IV.
Tree-Ring Bulletin 5 (1):6-7.

SHELLEY, PHILLIP H.
1980 Chacoan tree felling. IN
Investigations at the Salmon
site: The structure of Chacoan
society in the northern Southwest
3, edited by Cynthia Irwin-
Williams and Phillip H. Shelley,
pp. 115-121. Eastern New Mexico
University, Portales.

SHIMADA, IZUMI
1978 Behavioral variability and organization in ancient constructions:
An experimental approach. IN
Papers on the economy and
architecture of the Ancient Maya,
edited by Raymond Sidrys, pp.
209-235. Institute of Archaeology, University of California,
Los Angeles.

SHINER, JOEL
1959 Stabilization of Wijiji, 1959.
National Park Service Regional
Stabilization Unit, Globe,
Arizona.

1961 Excavation of a Chaco-type kiva,
Chaco Canyon, New Mexico. Chaco
Center Archive # 2769. On file,
Division of Cultural Research,
National Park Service, Albuquer-
que.

SIMMONS, MARC
1979 History of the Pueblos since
1821. IN Handbook of North
American Indians 9, edited by
Alfonso Ortiz, pp. 206-223.
Smithsonian Institution, Washington, D.C.

SIMPSON, J.H., LT.
1850 Journal of a military reconnais-
sance from Santa Fe, New Mexico,
to the Navajo country. Report of
the Secretary of the War, 31st
Congress, 1st Session, Senate Ex.
Doc. 64, Washington, D.C.

STUBBS, STANLEY
1929 The east tower of Chetro Ketl,
1929. Ms. on file at Laboratory
of Anthropology, Museum of New
Mexico, Santa Fe. Chaco Center
Archive #2125. On file, Division
of Cultural Research, National
Park Service, Albuquerque.

SULLIVAN III, ALLAN P.
1974 Problems in the estimation of
origin room function: A tentative solution from Grasshopper
Ruin. The Kiva 40(1-2):93-100.

SWANNACK, JERVIS D., JR.
1969 Big Juniper House, Mesa Verde
National Park, Colorado. National Park Service
Archaeological Research Series
7E: Wetherill Mesa Studies.
Washington, D.C.

TIETJENS, JANET
n.d. Chaco Canyon place names. On
file, Division of Cultural
Research, National Park Service,
Albuquerque.

TOLL, H. WOLCOTT, THOMAS C. WINDES, and
PETER J. McKENNA
1980 Late ceramic patterns in Chaco
Canyon: The pragmatics of model-
ing ceramic exchange. IN Models
and methods in regional exchange,
edited by R.E. Fry, pp. 95-117,
Society for American Archaeology
Papers.

TRUELL, MARCIA
1983 A summary of small site architecture in Chaco Canyon, New Mexico. On file, Division of Cultural Research, National Park Service, Albuquerque.

VAN VALKENBERG, RICHARD F.
1941 Dine Bikeyah. Window Rock, US Department of the Interior, Office of Indian Affairs, Navajo Science.

VICKERS, ROGER, LAMBERT DOLPHIN, and DAVID JOHNSON
1976 Archaeological investigations at Chaco Canyon using a subsurface radar. IN Remote sensing experiments in cultural resource studies, assembled by T. R. Lyons, pp. 81-101. Reports of the Chaco Center 1, Division of Cultural Research, National Park Service, Albuquerque.

VIVIAN, R. GORDON
1936 Letter to Edgar Hewett. Chaco Center Archive # 2124. On file, Division of Cultural Research, National Park Service, Albuquerque.

1940 New rooms and kiva found in Pueblo Bonito. Southwestern Monuments Report, supplement for February 1940:127-130.

1947 Ruins Stabilization, Chaco Canyon National Monument, Pueblo Alto (New Alto), 1947. National Park Service Mobile Unit, Southwestern National Monuments, Globe.

1948a Chaco Canyon National Monument, Chetro Ketl emergency stabilization, 1948. Ms. on file, Chaco Culture National Historical Park, New Mexico.

1948b Memorandum for superintendent McNeill, Chaco Canyon. Chaco Center Archive #657. On file, Division of Cultural Research, National Park Service, Albuquerque.

1949 Pre-historic handy man. New Mexico Magazine 27(6):14, 39-41.

1959 The Hubbard site and other tri-wall structures in New Mexico and Colorado. National Park Service Archaeological Research Series 5.

VIVIAN, R. GORDON and JAMES A. LANCASTER
1947 Ruins stabilization, Chaco Canyon National Monument, Chetro Ketl Ruin, 1947. Ms. on file, Chaco Culture National Historical Park, New Mexico.

VIVIAN, R. GORDON, and TOM W. MATHEWS
1965 Kin Kletso: A Pueblo III community in Chaco Canyon, New Mexico. Southwest Parks and Monuments Association, Technical Series 6(1).

VIVIAN, R. GORDON, and PAUL REITER
1960 The Great Kivas of Chaco Canyon. School of American Research Monographs 22.

VIVIAN, R. GWINN
1970 An inquiry into prehistoric social organization in Chaco Canyon, New Mexico. IN Reconstructing Prehistoric Pueblo Societies, edited by William A. Longacre, pp. 59-83. University of New Mexico Press, Albuquerque.

1972 Final technical report for prehistoric water conservation in Chaco Canyon. On file, Division of Cultural Research, National Park Service, Albuquerque.

VIVIAN, R. GWINN, DULCE N. DODGEN, and GAYLE H. HARTMAN
1978 Wooden ritual artifacts from Chaco Canyon, New Mexico: The Chetro Ketl collection. Anthropological Papers of the University of Arizona 22.

VOLL, CHARLES B.
1978 The excavation of Room 92, Chetro Ketl. IN Wooden ritual artifacts from Chaco Canyon, New Mexico: The Chetro Ketl collection, by R.G. Vivian, D.N. Dodgen, and G.H. Hartman, Appendix E. Anthropological Papers of the University of Arizona 22.

VOLL, CHARLES B., and MARTIN T. MAYER
1964 1964 stabilization of Casa Chiquita Ruin, Chaco Canyon National Monument, New Mexico. Ruins Stabilization Unit, National Park Service Southwest Archaeological Center, Globe, Arizona.

WARE, JOHN A., and GEORGE GUMERMAN
1977 Remote sensing methodology and the Chaco Canyon prehistoric road system. IN Aerial remote sensing techniques in archeology, edited by Thomas R. Lyons and Robert K. Hitchcock, pp. 135-167, Reports of the Chaco Center 2:135-167. On file, Division of Cultural Research, National Park Service, Albuquerque.

WETHERILL MERCANTILE COMPANY
1904 Letter to George Dorsey. American Museum of Natural History, accession number 198. On file, Division of Cultural Research, National Park Service, Albuquerque.

WHEELER, RICHARD P.
  1965  Edge-abraded flakes, blades, and
        cores  in   the   Puebloan   tool
        assemblage.  Society of American
        Archaeology Memoir 19:19-29.

WINDES, THOMAS C.
  1980  A review of extramural greathouse
        middens in Chaco Canyon National
        Monument.  On file, Division of
        Cultural Research, National Park
        Service, Albuquerque.

  1981  A new look at population in Chaco
        Canyon.  Paper  presented at the
        47th  Annual  Meeting  of   the
        Society for American Archaeology,
        San Diego.

  1982  The prehistoric road network at
        Pueblo Alto, Chaco Canyon, New
        Mexico. Paper presented to the
        American Anthropological Associa-
        tion Annual Meeting, Washington,
        D.C.

WINDES, THOMAS C., and F. JOAN MATHIEN
  1984  Historic  Structure  Report  Kin
        Nahasbas  ruin,  Chaco  Culture
        National  Historical  Park,  New
        Mexico.  On file, Division of
        Cultural Research, National Park
        Service, Albuquerque.

WINDHAM, MICHAEL DENNIS
  1976  A  preliminary  analysis  of  the
        ceramics of Una Vida ruin, Chaco
        Canyon,  New  Mexico.   On  file,
        Division  of  Cultural  Research,
        National Park Service, Albuquer-
        que.

WINKLER, ERHARD M.
  1973  Stone:  Properties, durability in
        man's  environment.    Springer-
        Verlag, New York.

WOODS, JANET McC.
  1934  Excavation  of  the  Court  Kiva,
        Chetro Ketl.  On file, Division
        of  Cultural  Research,  National
        Park Service, Albuquerque.

ZUBROW, EZRA B.W.
  1974  Population, contact, and climate
        in  the  New  Mexican  Pueblos.
        Anthropological  Papers  of  the
        University of Arizona 24.

# Index

This index is applicable to the text, excluding the Preface and Appendixes.